Theories of Revelation

Theories of Revelation

AN HISTORICAL STUDY

1860–1960

———

H. D. McDONALD

B.A., B.D., PH.D. (LONDON)

Vice-Principal London Bible College
and
Lecturer in Historical Theology

London

GEORGE ALLEN & UNWIN LTD

RUSKIN HOUSE MUSEUM STREET

FIRST PUBLISHED IN 1963

PRINTED IN GREAT BRITAIN
in 11 point Bell type
BY UNWIN BROTHERS LIMITED
WOKING AND LONDON

THIS BOOK IS DEDICATED TO

ANNE

Who possesses in fullest measure the greatest
gift
and to that theological trio
Oonagh, Beryl and Neil
who together have made our household
a

THEOLOGICAL FORUM!

PREFACE

The Introduction will have made sufficiently clear our particular motive and method in presenting what follows. We have, on the one hand, endeavoured to be fair in our exposition of all the views with which we are concerned, and, on the other hand, we have not been hesitant in criticizing what we consider defective and commending what we regard as adequate. Whether we have been successful in these two intentions it must be left with the reader to judge. Our own position we have made no attempt to disguise.

In a passage quoted by Pascal from a book by the Jesuit Garasse, which calls forth his scorn in his *Provincial Letters*, there occurs the statement that 'God, who is perfectly just in all His proceedings, has capacitated even frogs to enjoy their own croaking'. In this assurance we may at least take some comfort.

It only remains to add a word of thanks where it is due. First to my elder daughter, Oonagh A. McDonald, A.L.B.C., B.D., M.TH., for checking the proofs and compiling the Indexes; and then to Messrs George Allen and Unwin for the consideration shown by the members of the Staff with whom we have had to deal.

INTRODUCTION

The problem of Revelation continues to be the central issue in the modern theological scene. And it promises to remain so for a long time to come. There can be no more momentous subject for theological thinking and no more important one for theological debate than that which is enshrined in the question: Can we be sure of a real self-disclosure of God?

We have endeavoured in a previous volume to give an account of the way this issue first forced itself upon the Church.[1] It was indicated how two broadly opposed emphases emerged. On the one hand, there was with some, such a strong emphasis upon the objective aspect that revelation came to be regarded as a body of Divinely communicated truths stated in strict propositional fashion to which all that was needed was to give the appropriate mental acknowledgement. Once the required assent had been given then the individual was designated as 'one of the Faith', since he had returned the desired 'I do' to the question, Do you believe in the body of sacred truths of the Christian faith which to doubt means anathema? Such an understanding of revelation left it soulless. It was something without heart and spirit; and especially did it appear to be very much without the Holy Spirit of God. In 'such a cheap and agreeable way, in a half-hour and with a turn of the hand, to get the whole thing about eternity settled, in order to be thoroughly able to enjoy life'.[2] On the other hand, there were those who with resentment and ridicule regarded the idea of revelation as existing *ab extra* as the worst of all follies and the wickedest of all fancies. To such revelation was essentially and entirely subjective. God was to be sought and found, neither in the starry skies above nor in the sacred Scripture without, but in the mystic depths of a man's own soul. It is something deeply inward. Such an understanding of revelation, however, left it without any truth-content: and tended to substitute individual feelings for historical facts.

[1] H. D. McDonald, *Ideas of Revelation*, 1959.
[2] Soren Kierkegaard, *Attack on Christendom* (E.T. 1946), p. 151.

As the study developed several clear-cut ideas of Revelation were noted. There were, for example, the opposite positions demonstrated by the Deistic emphasis upon the supremacy of reason and the stress given by the Friends to the adequacy of the inner light: and there were the no less extreme antitheses exemplified by the Orthodox theorists and the Coleridgeans. The exaggerations to which these views gave expression, it was shown, were corrected, in some measure, by the teaching of Charles Simeon, on the one side, who in contending for the objective Word saw also the need for the inner action of the Spirit, and, on the other side, by John Wesley, who, while emphasizing the Spirit's work, did not fail to insist upon the need for the Word without. But even their views brought no permanent settlement: they could not, for example, take into account the difficulties which came about only at a later time.

Yet the ideas which thus came into sharp relief in this earlier period, are precisely those which, after a short time of hesitancy occasioned by the publication of Darwin's *Origin of Species*, were taken up again later with varying degrees of clarity and confusion. As, however, we seek to follow the discussion of the subject of Revelation throughout the century beginning 1860, it will not meet the situation to continue the same procedure and merely to collect quotations from authors who group themselves behind one or other of the ideas which were thus earlier brought into prominence. The careful reader of the following pages will himself become aware of the preference of each writer to whom we must refer. Another method of procedure is demanded to understand the nature of the conflict in the new era.

The century with which we are to be occupied is characterized by the presence of other influences which had an important bearing on the subject of Revelation. The controversies initiated by Darwin's evolutionism and the coming of the Higher Criticism focused attention upon the Scriptures and raised the question of their place in the scheme of revelation. The Bible, in fact, became the storm centre and the main problem of the period was to give a convincing statement of its significance. The problem concerned the relation between Revelation and the Bible. And since an influential body of opinion came to the conviction that the Scriptures could be no longer regarded as an objective infallible authority, the whole question of religious authority was opened for discussion. In fact, as time went on these two subjects—Revelation and Authority—became merged so that a discussion of the problem of Revelation has become one and the same with a discussion of the subject of Authority. Our penultimate chapter will show the truth of this observation: while in the last chapter we have sought to give a summary statement of 'Revelation and Authority', in which the final section will indicate what we conceive to be the results for the present time.

It should be made clear that throughout an effort has been made to let writers on each side in the controversies, especially those concerned with the subjects of Biblical inerrancy, inspiration and authority, speak for themselves, as far as practical, in their own words. But we have not hesitated at various places to give our own criticisms; as we have also sought to give, as far as we conceive it, a positive statement.

In taking such an attitude we have not been unmindful of the subtitle which announces our investigation as 'an historical study'. We would, however, plead that it is quite impossible to approach a subject without any presuppositions. This is specially so in theology where a man's convictions should be deep and meaningful. Even those who approach theology purely from the historical point of view will betray on numerous occasions their own religious understandings. One has for example only to peruse Adolf Harnack's *History of Dogma* to be convinced of the justice of this remark. The truth is that the man who says he is altogether objective in this study knows not of what he speaks. Even in the realm of science it is no longer a tenable view to conceive of the scientist as, so to speak, one who stands over against his data having no postulates. Indeed the whole scientific endeavour would be a fruitless proceeding if this were so. In fact, as A. F. Smethurst and C. A. Coulson have shown, the postulates of the scientific enquiry when consciously thought out are essentially ethical, if not positively religious.[1]

It will be observed, however, that in our case we have not only criticized negatively where we have felt it to be needed, but we have, especially when dealing with the three related subjects

[1] Cf. A. F. Smethurst, *Modern Science and Christian Belief*, 1955. C. A. Coulson, *Science and Christian Belief*, 1955.

referred to above, given a positive account of our own convictions. In this way, we think, we have sought to avoid giving a mere dry catalogue of facts, like those 'stamp collector' type of scientists to whom Lord Rutherford used to refer. They are of the kind who lose themselves in their finds and admire their collection just as would any contented philatelist.

It remains to be added that we have sought to cover in an adequate manner the literature of the whole period. Doubtless some reviewer will have knowledge of some article or book to which reference, in his judgement, should have been made. We can only say that we have not ourselves made reference to every single source that was before us, because such a contribution did not seem to us to be of decisive significance in the development of the discussion. Or, of course, which is not impossible, it may have been because the work was unknown to us!

One result of our study, it is hoped, will be that there will be a clearer understanding by all of the ideas of revelation. An historical background will provide a truer perspective for discussion. The tendency in the past has been for each side to conduct a sort of private monologue and to proclaim its views in hostile disregard of what the other side was seeking to say. What is required today, and what is possible, is that which is involved in the expressive word of recent days, dialogue. And we have made some attempt to bring this about by seeking out the understanding of revelation and by stating as clearly as we are able our own position for the sake of those who would understand us.

LONDON BIBLE COLLEGE

CONTENTS

CHAPTER ONE

The Division of the Period

A. THE STARTING DATE OF THE PERIOD

History has been marked throughout by certain decisive events which have, as it were, become the occasion of marking off one era from another. Sometimes these events have appeared at the time to be almost accidental, and yet later ages have turned back to them as having been of radical significance. Other divisions in the history of human thought can be dated from the work and worth of some significant personality who has succeeded, for one reason or another, in stamping his signature upon the brow of the hurrying centuries. The presence of such a person has often been revealed in some special contribution or some shattering act which appears to the following generations to have altered the direction of history. It is in such periods that history can be read, in Walt Whitman's pregnant phrase, as the lengthened shadow of a man. But when some decisive event, which has in itself creative significance, and, the presence of some man who is believed to have made some important contribution, coincide, then that date can be marked off with more assurance as the start of a new era.

Writers have perceived, although they have not always made the reasons clear, that the year 1860 is one of those dates which can be taken as the commencement of another state and stage in the history of ideas. It will, of course, be understood that no division in history is clear-cut. It is a fact more clearly emphasized today than ever before that there are no breaks in history; that the past is not isolated from the present, and that the present is creative of the future. The realization of this fact will be sufficient to warn us against the tendency to make neat divisions of history. The views which in one period become

dominant are those very tendencies which stirred in the under-
growth of that which preceded. These are the creative under-
tones which indicated the pattern of the dawning era. Yet the
truth remains that each age does reveal its own special characteristics and these special features can be generally marked and
indicated.

The year 1860 is one of these significant dates which termi-
nated one era and commenced another. The contribution of event
and personality united to mark it out in this special way. L. E.
Elliott-Binns points out that the year 1860 witnessed two events
which were to have particular importance for religion and
theology. These were the repeal of the paper duty in that year
and the beginnings of a national system of education.[1] These
events, to be sure, were not immediately recognized as destined
to have such far-reaching consequences. The repeal of the paper
duty which lifted from the trade a crippling burden, made
possible an immediate increase in literature. One of the
immediate results of the relief was an astonishing development
in the production of newspapers and periodicals. Never before
in history was it so possible for ideas to be as widely dis-
seminated. Theological and religious subjects were eagerly
discussed and debated. Among the most influential of these new
media was the recently founded *Fortnightly Review* which took
up a hostile attitude to orthodox beliefs and secured for itself an
aura of authority on religious and theological questions. As a
result of these new publications the country was thrown into a
welter of conflicting ideas, in which, for a quarter of a century,
the religious interest was uppermost.

The press found a public ready to receive its comments for or
against established religious institutions and orthodox beliefs.
Indeed so evident was this interest that Aubrey Moore could
declare in 1889 that 'No periodical is complete without an
article in which Christianity is defended or attacked'.[2] Not only
was the interest there, but the effort to extend education meant
that there were more persons whose interest was to be aroused.
It was beginning to be seen that no one class had any monopoly
upon knowledge. It was the right of every individual to enter in
and to possess the land. This awareness, allying itself with the

---

[1] L. E. Elliott-Binns, *English Thought, 1860–1900*, 1956, p. 5.
[2] Aubrey Moore, *Science and the Faith*, 1889, p. 113.

growing democratic spirit of the times, was making it evident that every individual was significant, as such, and was entitled to have his say.

There were other events, too, which the year 1860 was to witness and which played their lesser part in making that date important. But the two just mentioned, when reinforced by the contribution made at that time to biological science, had the effect of initiating a crop of new ideas and problems of a nature different from any which had gone before.

Although it was in the preceding year that Darwin's *Origin of Species* appeared, its full meaning, as far as theological views were concerned, was to be more clearly seen in the following year. By 1860 it was evident that the book was to have a decisive influence in many realms. Ideas which had previously been generally accepted were turned upside down. The story of the reception given to Darwin's volume is generally known, and certain aspects of its influence will engage us later. But we may note, for the present, that it soon became evident that the new biological evolutionism would affect the historic Christian view of the uniqueness of man and the meaning of original sin. As the fuller implications of the thesis were understood, the whole question of revelation was given a new context. An apologetic of a type not previously conceivable was required. There was, to begin with, the serious question of the very possibility of any revelation at all. 'The doctrine of evolution practically began its reign with the theory of natural selection. It was crowned with shouts of "Down with Christianity! Long live Materialism!" No wonder if theologians were prejudiced against it.'[1] True enough, the Darwinian hypothesis, as such, did not appear to touch the fundamental question of Theism and the possibility of revelation. It is, indeed, a fact that Darwin, in the closing section of the first edition of his *Origin of Species* had given reverent acknowledgement to the idea of a Creator, and had, also, entered the claim that the conception of nature to which his book gave exposition involved a far loftier conception of God's wisdom and power than the orthodox doctrine of the appearance of separate species by distinct acts of God.

The first and immediate result of Darwin's own view was to

---

[1] D. Matheson in Review of A. Barry's *Some Lights of Science on the Faith*, being the Bampton Lectures for 1892, *Expository Times*, Vol. IV, 1892-3, p. 415.

raise the question of the validity of the early chapters of Genesis.
Prior to Darwin, apart from certain thinkers to whom the notion
of evolution was a mere philosophical presupposition without
any scientific evidence, the accepted Christian view was that
Genesis had recorded a factual account of the origin of organic
life. The record had to be read as a literal account more particularly of man's beginning. With such a reading of the story the
Darwinian hypothesis was in evident conflict. This impression
was given further emphasis by the subsequent publication of
Darwin's *Descent of Man*. The issue was clear-cut. If Darwin
were right then the Genesis account was wrong, and vice versa.
Either God was in at man's beginning or He was not.

But this narrower discussion was to be held up for some years
and to become one of the issues in the conflict between the
Higher Critics and their opponents. Beguiled, it appears, by
Darwin's rather accommodating reference to a Creator, a contemporary edition of the *Saturday Review* assured its readers
that the views set forth in the *Origin of Species* were not in the
least 'hostile to the truths of Revelation'. Yet this was not the
conviction which even Darwin himself was to retain for long.
Doubts were creeping over him: and any faith he had in the Old
Testament was being undermined. Having rejected the miracles
of the Old Testament he goes on to declare that those of the New
cannot be regarded as authentic. In a later period, as by a
natural transition, he does not hesitate to avow his disbelief in
any supernatural realm. 'For myself', he states uncompro-
misingly, 'I do not believe that there ever has been any
revelation.'

What influence Herbert Spencer had upon Darwin in bringing
about this result is not easy to estimate. But the fact is that the
association of Spencer's *Synthetic Philosophy*, of which the 'First
Principles' was the introduction, with the *Origin of Species*,
served to call in question the whole idea of a revelation. Spencer
took up the evolutionary principle and applied it in a thorough-
going fashion to the wider issues and problems of life. This
wider application of Darwin's distinctive principle of natural
selection is what is called, 'Ultra-Darwinianism'.

At the beginning Darwinianism as such was thought to be a
purely scientific view of a limited part of the cosmos—the
organic. But the extension of the principle of continuity was an

expression of the philosophical spirit as distinct from the specifically scientific. Darwin's principle, it came to be urged, was
necessarily included in the wider Spencerian system, which
sought to explain the universe in terms of an anti-Theistic
naturalism. The consequences appeared inescapable. There was
no supernatural; nothing, indeed, other than the natural. The
organic evolutionism of Darwin, boldly asserted as the scientific
view of the origin of species, was, then, declared to have made
the teaching of Genesis unacceptable: and, in so far as it
appeared to imply the universal action of natural causes, it cast
doubts upon any supernatural element in Christianity. The
cosmic evolution of Spencer completed the picture. It was in
open conflict with the idea of revelation. It was a definite and
hostile repudiation of a divinely-instituted religion. It was, in
fact, a complete rejection of Theism.

Throughout the period the fortunes of theological studies
were bound up, or connected either directly or indirectly with
the problems raised by Darwin. It would not, indeed, be very
wide of the mark to say that the whole era might be designated,
The Era of the Rise and Decline of Darwinianism. At its
appearance in 1859, the ideas contained in the *Origin of Species*,
were seen to be opposed to accepted biological and theological
views.

T. H. Huxley, looking back from a later period, was able to
declare concerning the position in 1860, 'The supporters of Mr
Darwin's views were numerically extremely insignificant. There
is not the slightest doubt that if a general council of the Church
scientific had been held at the time, we should have been condemned by an overwhelming majority'. But the situation was
soon to change. Reinforced by T. H. Huxley and Herbert
Spencer, the Darwinian thesis was not only to gain ground, but
its fundamental idea was to be extended to include every realm
of life and thought, and to be applied especially to religion and
ethics. The day was not far distant when its triumph seemed
overwhelming. As early, indeed, as the year 1863 Charles
Kingsley wrote to F. D. Maurice to the effect that 'Darwin is
conquering everywhere'.[1]

As is so often the case, however, the period of triumph began
the period of decline. This is the one certain truth that the

[1] F. E. Kingsley, *Charles Kingsley*, 1877, Vol. II, p. 155.

Hegelian dialectic of history has taught us. A dominant idea gives birth to its opposite and initiates tension and conflict. Or, as it is put in the Marxian philosophy, every triumphant system contains within it the seeds of its own destruction. Whilst the idealistic application of the principle as in the case of Hegel or the materialistic application of it as in the case of Marx can be rejected, the broad truth which Hegel and Marx took as the fundamental basis of their opposing dialectic remains. Nowhere is this more clearly illustrated than in the case of the triumph and decline of Darwinianism. That later years have seen a modification, and even a repudiation, of many of Darwin's ideas there is not the slightest doubt. Exactly when the tide began to turn against Darwinianism it is not easy to say. At any rate, a few years after the beginning of the century such a book as George Paulin's, in which he attacks the basic principle of Darwin's thesis, received favourable reviews.[1] Paulin had been for years a staunch advocate of Darwinianism. But fuller investigation had led him to the conclusion that there was no substantial evidence for it. He points out that Darwin himself took the idea of natural selection for granted. Paulin's book is not in itself specially important. But the very fact that it should have been published by T. & T. Clark, and that it should have been commended by some reviewers who showed no particular sympathy with a non-evolutionary approach, can be taken as showing that there was some willingness to question the finality of Darwinianism. There is no doubt that this readiness to re-examine the evidence for Darwin's fundamental idea, without the presupposition that it must be right, had grown with the years.

Twenty years later scientists themselves were expressing openly their uncertainty about the whole Darwinian thesis. In the year 1921, to take but one such example, there appeared the volume *The Advancement of Science*. This book contains a series of addresses by the President of the British Association for the Advancement of Science and the Presidents of its constituent sections. With one voice they spoke against the Darwinian conclusion. Reference need be made only to the remarks with which Dr D. H. Scott, the botanist, closed his discourse. After

[1] George Paulin, *No Struggle for Existence: No Natural Selection*. A Critical Examination of the Fundamental Principles of the Darwinian Theory, 1908.

giving due acknowledgement to the work of Darwin, and according to him credit for the illumination which his theory of natural selection has brought, he adds: 'For the moment, at all events, the Darwinian period is past; we can no longer enjoy the comfortable assurance, which once satisfied so many of us, that the problem has been solved—all again is in the melting-pot. But now, in fact, a new generation has grown up that knows not Darwin.'

In this regard it is of interest to note that in the year 1959 a commemorative edition of the *Origin of Species* was published. There are some astonishing remarks in the Introduction written by W. R. Thompson, FRS. Thompson openly confesses grave doubts about the beneficent effects of Darwin's theory on scientific and public thinking. He maintains that personal convictions and simple possibilities have been presented without real proof. He personally regards the whole thesis as inconclusive, and declares that 'the long-continued investigations on heredity and variation have undermined the Darwinian position'.[1] The 'mutations' of the modern evolutionists are not 'adaptive'. They are, in fact, he contends, 'useless, detrimental, or lethal'. In this Introduction to the *Origin of Species* the whole stately ediface is brought to collapse. Thompson sees the world of clear-cut entities separated by gaps which the evolutionary theory cannot bridge. Fossils show 'a remarkable absence of the intermediates required by the theory'. Damaging, too, is his statement that 'modern palæontologists are obliged, just like their predecessors and like Darwin, to water down facts with subsidiary hypotheses which, however plausible, are in the nature of things unverifiable'.[2] Thompson is quite certain that the success of Darwinism was accompanied by a decline in scientific integrity. The whole is built, he maintains, upon 'fragile towers of hypotheses based on hypotheses, where fact and fiction intermingle in an inextricable confusion'.[3] The result of which is to bring about a decline of Christian faith and a consequent abandonment of belief in the supernatural.

This Introduction by Thompson is a remarkable pronouncement. The question which arises is just this: Does it signify the fall of Darwinianism? This is, perhaps, something which it is

---

[1] *Origin of Species*, 1859 (Everyman's Edition, 1959), Introduction, p. xii.
[2] *Op. cit.*, p. xix.   [3] *Op. cit.*, p. xxiv.

not for us to answer. But it does, at least, serve to strengthen
the view which we have taken that the century which began with
the publication of the *Origin of Species*, and ends with the
appearance of this centenary edition, can be referred to as the
period of the rise and decline of Darwinianism.

B. THE CHANGING TEMPER OF THE PERIOD

Along with the rise and the decline of Darwinianism there went,
in keeping with its changing fortunes, what we may call, a
prevailing public temper. Whether this mood was a cause or an
effect of the changing estimations of the evolutionary theory is
not easy to say. At all events the fact of this parallel of temper
with theory is undoubted. So evident is this that the century
which began in the year 1860 can be divided broadly into two
periods following the rise and decline of Darwin's influence.
There is the period of confident optimism and the period of
disillusioning pessimism.

The overweening optimism arose out of a strange faith in the
ability of science to cure all ills. The age of religion, which had
been of service at a time when men were in the twilight, was
now to be superseded by the age of science. But science was the
final stage which would not only render religion impossible, but
would reveal its own inherent greatness by providing a world
fit for progressing man to live in. Hitherto science had been
regarded as the concern of a select class who enjoyed its pursuit
in isolation from the common people. It was now conceived to
be the only gospel giving promise of an endless progress and
assuring to men an earthly paradise.

This sort of optimistic evaluation of science can be seen, for
example, in the statements made by two writers who became
intoxicated with the new power which science had provided.
W. K. Clifford (1845–79), while pouring forth a torrent of
vehement indignation against Christianity, was compelled to
find a substitute for religious faith in a reverent awe and devout
worship of the marvellous world which had already come to such
perfection from so unpromising a beginning. He felt himself
animated by what he called a 'cosmic emotion'. Indeed, as
Rudolf Metz remarks, 'the temple of this religion was for
Clifford the proud edifice of science, and it was from science that

he hoped that all further progress of the spirit of man would come'.[1]

Karl Pearson (1857–1936), in his *Grammar of Science*, which first appeared in 1892 (cheap edition, 1937), took up the position that science is really divine; and whatever is not of science is not of truth. Pearson, indeed, carried his laudation of the scientific spirit to the point of apotheosis. The mission of modern science is to serve the human spirit: and the genuine scientist is the only true saint.

William James gives exposition to this optimistic result of evolution. He sees it as 'a new sort of religion of Nature, which has entirely displaced Christianity from the thought of a large part of our generation'.[2] He contends that the 'idea of a general evolution lends itself to a doctrine of general amelioration and progress which fits the religious needs of the healthy-minded so well that it seems almost as if it might have been created for its use'. He sees evolutionism 'interpreted thus optimistically and embraced as a substitute for the religion' of Christianity by those who have been scientifically trained and by those who have developed an interest in its popular exposition, and who have, as a consequence, become 'inwardly dissatisfied with what seemed to them the harshness and irrationality of the orthodox Christian scheme'.[3] Philip Leon contrasts the temper of the most modern science with that which prevailed some sixty years ago. 'Then "Science" was, except in details practically synonymous with "Omniscience", and the universe of possibilities, which is to lay the field open to speculation, was limited in the extreme, "Science" dogmatically laying it down before hand that only a very few things were possible.' Science was supposed to have liberated man from his mediaeval prison-house of dogmatic theology. 'Now, on the other hand', Leon states by way of contrast, 'the sciences are felt to be lucky guesses in a universe in which anything is possible, while a priori dogmatic pronouncements as to impossibility are regarded with less and less favour: the omniscience of "Science" has been replaced by the multi-possibility of the universe.'[4]

[1] Rudolf Metz, *A Hundred Years of British Philosophy*, 1938, second impression, 1950, p. 127.
[2] William James, *The Varieties of Religious Experience*, 1902, sixteenth edition, 1909, p. 91.   [3] *Ibid.*, pp. 91, 92.
[4] Philip Leon, *Body, Mind and Spirit*, 1948, p. 21.

The second half of the nineteenth century was, then, to witness the proclamation of another gospel—which a later period was to find out was not another—a gospel in which man was promised an earthly Utopia, a paradise regained by the magic of science. Endless progress was confidently assured. And in a few decades the earlier superstitions of basic social moralities and believed supernatural realities would be swept away by being revealed as the pathetic follies and fallacies of a past unenlightened age. The Religion of Nature was destined to take the place of the old notion of the existence of a supersensual realm. So optimism reached its height as it was reinforced by the glory of an expanding empire and the triumphant extension of the influence of the Mother Country which was regarded as the guardian of international morality and the conscience of the world.

In such a context Christian faith had no easy task to maintain itself. The thought of the people was, by the very method of science, the value of which was becoming every day more evident, directed to the present, the terrestrial and the human. And there was enough here to occupy the thoughts, to usurp the talents and to fill the time of every educated man. One could be a man of one world only. The notion of another world was too problematical for occupied lives. Besides, the whole idea of religion was attended by one big haunting question-mark.

It was in this spirit of optimism that the nineteenth century drew to its close. And it reached its crescendo in the early part of the twentieth century, by becoming wedded to the confident humanism of the times.

Gradually, however, the rosy picture was to become upset by the presence of harsh and ugly facts which could not be explained away. At first, of course, there appeared clouds only the size of a man's hand. Soon these were to thicken and darken into the grim night of the First World War. Then the whole optimistic spirit was dissipated and lost in the abyss of disillusionment and despair. The result of the great conflict was to leave us with a country which heroes did not find to be what was promised. Darkness still covered the face of the land in the form of unemployment, frustration and the loss of hope in man's ability to rise to new heights on the stepping stones of the dead of the recent past.

There were, to be sure, brave souls who sought to console

their fellows. There were insistent voices urging humanity to take up the task again and regain the far-off optimism of former years. But on the whole these voices were lost in the din of uncertainty. It was felt that they were pathetically unaware of the fresh evidence of human sinfulness which an earlier effete optimism had never seriously faced. There were, therefore, other teachers who were not prepared to accept the gay picture of man's growing perfectibility through the enlightening influences of an expanding education and political compromise.

C. E. M. Joad, who lived through the earlier period of optimism and on into the later period of pessimism recalls his own reactions. Like many others, he had been captivated by the glowing picture of the brave new world which was to be built by human endeavours. He, as they, abandoned what he believed was the out-worn superstition of orthodox Christianity. Joad grew up in a world which was intoxicated with the optimistic belief in 'man as infinitely perfectible'. Spencer had given the assurance that 'the ultimate development of the ideal man, is certain—as certain as any conclusion in which we place the most implicit faith, for instance that all men die'. Progress is, he urged, no accident. It is necessary and inevitable. And because it is so, 'man must become perfect'.

J. Addington Symonds, the Victorian poet, sang of this new religion.

> These things shall be! A loftier race
> Than ere the world hath known, shall rise
> With flame of freedom in their souls
> And light of science [*sic*] in their eyes.
>
> They shall be gentle, brave and strong,
> To spill no drop of blood, but dare
> All that may plant man's lordship firm
> On earth and fire and sea and air.
>
> Nation with nation, land with land,
> Unarmed shall live as comrades free;
> In every heart and brain shall throb
> The pulse of one fraternity.

New arts shall bloom of loftier mould,
And mightier music thrill the skies,
And every lift shall be a song,
When all of earth shall be a paradise.

These words found their way into many of the hymn books
and were sung with religious fervour and faith. The sentiment
which was here given poetic expression was for many a burning
conviction. And C. E. M. Joad, like the rest, passionately
believed it was all true. He was, however, to find out it was not
so easy and so confident. Speaking generally, he observes, 'the
era which came abruptly to an end in 1914 was one of the most
confident and successful in the history of mankind'.[1] With the
passing of the prophetic hope of Spencer during the years
following, Joad, from his own experience, recounts the sense of
disillusionment. He became aware that he had fallen 'a victim
to a shallow optimism in regard to human nature'. In the
presence of the burdening reality of the 'ineradicable nature of
human sinfulness' he confesses, 'that the rationalistic–optimist
philosophy, by the light of which I had hitherto done my best to
live, came to seem intolerably trivial and superficial—a shallow-
rooted plant which, growing to maturity amid the lush
and leisured optimism of the nineteenth century, was quite
unfitted to withstand the bleaker winds that blow through
ours'.[2]

The glowing picture of man's perfectibility and adequacy was
also to receive a blow from the findings of the psychoanalyst-
psychologists. Freud, Adler and Jung, each in his own way, had
uncovered the unconscious and maintained that the hidden
depths of human life were a veritable jungle of repressed desires
which, if they were to find an outlet in society without purification, would make human life a hell. Here within man's being
was a chamber of horrors, a charnel-house of every possible evil.
Every man was no longer to be thought of as a possible gentle-
man who needed only to be taught good manners. He was an
abyss containing the frightening possibilities of incalculable evil.

It was no wonder that such being the revised view of man
that the existentialist doctrine should make an appeal. It was

---

[1] C. E. M. Joad, *The Recovery of Belief*, 1952, p. 47.
[2] *Ibid.*, p. 82.

inevitable that Kierkegaard should come to his own. And then, as if to take away the last shreds of optimism, there came the Second World War with its Belsen and its Hiroshima.

In the context of this waxing and waning optimism, ideas of revelation can be seen to emerge in general harmony with it. The broad outline of these views can be indicated here.

The first shock of Darwinianism, it may be observed, was to give immediate birth to naturalism. Any idea of a revelation was thought to be ruled out as being incompatible with the new scientific understanding of the origin of life. But for one reason or another naturalism did not long appeal. It is simply not natural for a man to be a consistent naturalist.

Thus, before many years had passed, the teleological argument was rehabilitated. Hitherto, beginning from what was virtually a Deistic emphasis upon the divine transcendence the argument was from design to the idea of an existent designer. Now the stress was put upon the divine immanence and the argument was to design. All nature was regarded as instinct with divine life. It was to be thought of as the unfolding of the indwelling spiritual ζωή. Thus was all history to be understood as the general unveiling of immanent divinity, and revelation to be conceived of as the totality of human history, which, in greater or lesser measure, discloses the divine indwelling. In this way the clear-cut distinction between natural and revealed religion was broken down. There was no single people and no special history which could be claimed as the specific sphere of the divine activity. All religions developed from one common origin. There were cruder religious ideas suited to the under-developed state of the religious instinct. But, as the *sensus numinis* grew, so too did religion; from the natural to the spiritual, from the tribal to the universal. And through all the human spirit was showing its awareness of the divine working itself out within the movements of history and the events of experience. God was there as the immanent reality, energizing and unifying.

Such an idea, however boldly proclaimed as it was by its advocates, did not meet the need. It was too general, too indefinite, too vague. It attempted to be rid of any idea of a 'special' revelation by making all history revelational. But the effort to obliterate the distinction between general and special revelation could not be maintained.[1] It failed altogether to take account of the fact that Christianity is connected 'with a real event in time and space, which, so it affirms, is the unique, final revelation for time and for eternity, and for the whole world'.[2]

The view of all history as revelatory of the divine immanence only was seen to be further defective because it provided no 'clear standard of discrimination'. 'Where all is equally revelation, who shall determine what is being said, and what, of all that is being said, is most important?'[3]

There is need of something more precise, more particular. How, for example, could account be taken of the otherwise unaccountable existence of Israel? Thus was the idea of revelation narrowed down to read as the divine acts in history. It is in certain transforming events, like the Exodus of Israel from Egypt, the significance of which had been appreciated by men with a genius for religion or by men who had experienced a certain illumination, that we are to see the divine revelation. Reading these events as God's 'actuality' in the history, man is made aware of the living God, or as G. E. Wright puts it as the title of his book, *The God Who Acts*. Since God's divinest act is in the Incarnation, it is in such terms that His 'special' unveiling is to be sought at its highest.

Yet there is a difficulty. Human history, after all, is just *human* history: it cannot be other than that. And humans, especially in a period which has lost its optimistic view of man, are not little pieces of divinity. Thus human history is but the record of man's sinfulness; of man's varying and false estimate of himself. God who is distinct from man, who is the 'Wholly Other', cannot be brought into the record. He cannot be imprisoned within such a chronicle. God is, therefore, outside it all. We shall consequently 'need to think through the category of revelation again'[4] in such a context. Obviously, the story which tells of God's work for man's salvation cannot be read according to the usual understanding of human history. It is supra-historical— *Heilsgeschichte*. Revelation is, therefore, God's inbreaking into human lives in the grace of redemption. God is, after all, *actus*

[1] Cf. Emil Brunner, *The Mediator* (E.T. 1934), Chapters I and II.
[2] *Ibid.*, p. 30.
[3] Edwin Lewis, *A Philosophy of the Christian Revelation*, British edition, 1948, p. 4.
[4] Karl Barth, *The Word of God and the Word of Man*, 1928, p. 250.

purus.[1] Man has no natural 'point of contact' with Him. The idea
of revelation as having any propositional form is consequently
anathema. Man has sinned away his rationality and cannot be
appealed to as a creature of reason. It is in the Divine–Human
Encounter, an encounter in which God as the living God is the
sole actor, and, in which man, whose whole history is but the
chronicle of his sinning, can do nothing but wait to be awakened
to response by the very impact of the Divine revelation. In all
these views any idea of revelation as a communication of truth
is sternly repudiated. No less rejected is any conception of
Scripture as in itself revelational.

C. THE DISTINGUISHING VOLUMES OF THE PERIOD

Coming now to a more precise division of the period of our
investigation, we may note how certain volumes had the effect
of marking off new stages in the discussion of our subject by
initiating fresh conflicts and controversies. These distinguishing
works may be set out as follows.

(1) 1860—'*Essays and Reviews*'

This volume, it will be observed, appeared a year after Darwin's
Origin of Species and purported to be in some measure a
rapprochment with the new biological hypothesis. The outburst of hostility which greeted its coming astonished its contributors. None of them, we cannot but feel, was more surprised by
the blunt criticisms, than Frederick Temple. Temple who was at
the time headmaster of Rugby School was later to become
Archbishop of Canterbury. He took only ten hours to write the
essay and we are assured that he had no idea that he was sharing
in a sort of manifesto.[2] The fact is, the essay was only a rehash
of a sermon he had already preached at Oxford.

The seven essays which comprise the volume have really no
binding idea. They are a miscellaneous collection of varying
value. Stanley, who like Hort, had refused to contribute to the
symposium, is certainly right in his criticism of them as too
negative. Morley has observed that with the exception of Mark

---

[1] Karl Barth, *Church Dogmatics*, 1, i (E.T. 1936), p. 44.
[2] E. G. Stanford, *Frederick Temple*, An Appreciation, 1906, p. 205.

Pattison's 'Tendencies of Religious Thought in England, 1860–1750', the rest 'was neither learned nor weighty'. The 'tone was not absolutely uniform', he continues, 'but it was as a whole mildly rationalistic'.[1] Benjamin Jowett's essay 'On the Interpretation of Scripture', although modified we are given to understand at the instigation of Tennyson, was especially offensive at the time because of his apparently low view of the Bible.

Not all of the Essays have relevance to our topic. Temple took as his subject a title which Lessing had given earlier to his treatise, *The Education of the World*. He compared the human race to a colossal man which went through the stages of childhood, youth and manhood. God's progressive education of the race was suited to each stage, first according to laws, then by examples and finally by principles. In the Bible, he concludes, must be found these principles by which grown man is to live. And should 'careful criticism' he asserts 'prove that there have been occasional interpolations and forgeries in that Book'[2] the result need not be unwelcomed. The teaching of the Bible remains unaffected by any changes in the idea of inspiration which present knowledge necessitates. True enough, its hold upon the mind of believers and its power to stir the depths of the spirit of man may be weakened at first. But in the long run these shall be 'immeasurably strengthened' 'by the clearing away any blunders which may have been fastened on it by human interpretation'.[3]

In Rowland Williams's Essay entitled 'A Review of Bunsen's Biblical Researches' there is a clear acceptance of a rather advanced German liberal criticism. Bunsen virtually denies the supernatural outright and confines revelation within the sphere of the natural. Williams, indeed, accords Bunsen (should later generations be wise enough to follow his lead) 'a foremost place among the champions of light and right'.[4] A layman, C. W. Goodwin, writes on the 'Mosaic Cosmogony'. There are, he states, two accounts of the creation in Genesis. The first professing to be a scientific presentation has been demonstrated as clearly out of harmony with recent scientific findings. The

---

[1] J. Morley, *Life of Gladstone* (in three volumes), 1911, Vol. 2—1859–1880, p. 125.

[2] *Essays and Reviews*, 1860, tenth edition, 1861, p. 47.

[3] *Op. cit.*, p. 48.   [4] *Op. cit.*, p. 93.

second account may be regarded as poetical. Benjamin Jowett in his Essay 'On the Interpretation of Scripture' argues 'that any true doctrine of inspiration must conform to all well-ascertained facts of history or of science'.[1] He then goes on, after he has repudiated the orthodox view of inspiration, to deal with the question of interpretation. His main contention may be summed up in his own canon under which all else he has to say can be subsumed. It is simply this: 'Interpret the Scripture like any other book'.[2]

It might well have been that this volume would have caused little excitement but for the notice given to it by the Positivist, Frederic Harrison, in an article in the October 1860 issue of the *Westminster Review*. Harrison entitled his article, 'Neo-Christianity', and contended that the position reached by the essayists was that of his own. Here were denied miracles, inspiration and the Mosaic history: and gone with this denial was the whole idea of Biblical revelation.

This notice given to the volume by Harrison caused a stir. Hostility was at once shown to it by the two great parties of the Church. In January 1861, Wilberforce, Bishop of Oxford, in an article in the *Quarterly Review*, bluntly stated that the ultimate conclusion of the Essays must be infidelity, if not atheism. Two main replies soon appeared seeking to refute the position advanced in the *Essays and Reviews*. The first called *Aids to Faith*, edited by William Thomson, Bishop of Gloucester and Bristol and afterwards Archbishop of York, followed the same pattern as the essays it sought to correct. The second volume, *Replies to Essays and Reviews* was edited by the redoubtable Samuel Wilberforce.

(2) 1862—'*The Pentateuch and the Book of Joshua Critically Examined*' by J. W. Colenso

In the previous year Colenso who in 1853 had been consecrated Bishop of Natal, South Africa, had produced a *Commentary on Romans*. This book did not create the stir which he had apparently expected. But his critical analysis of the Pentateuch and Joshua occasioned alarm. He rejected the Mosaic authorship of the former and pronounced the Bible to be no infallible Book.

---

[1] *Essays and Reviews*, 1860, tenth edition, 1861, p. 348.
[2] *Op. cit.*, p. 377.

It is not to be identified with revelation. Following F. D.
Maurice, by whom he was strongly influenced, he maintained
that while the Bible is not itself the Word of God it can be said
to 'contain' His Word.

Colenso, a skilled mathematician, made much sport of the
figures in the early biblical books especially that of Numbers.
Wilberforce, with his usual ready wit, explained that the real
trouble was that the Mathematical Bishop was unable to forgive
Moses for writing a Book of Numbers!

Yet Colenso, although he proclaimed an advanced liberal view
of the Pentateuch insisted that these 'narratives by whomsoever
written' still imparted 'revelations of the divine will and
character'. None the less they 'cannot be regarded as historically
true'.[1]

This volume caused bitter antagonism. For the first time a
bishop's name was associated with what was regarded as open
infidelity. Demand was made by the English bishops, with the
famous Thirlwall dissenting, that Colenso should be excom-
municated. The result was a schism in the South African Church
which was not eventually healed until nearly another half
century had passed.

(3) 1881—'*The Old Testament in the Jewish Church*', *William
       Robertson Smith*

'The lectures entitled *The Old Testament in the Jewish Church*, by
W. Robertson Smith, may be taken as the sign of the beginning
of a new era.'[2] It was Smith who really popularized Old Testament German criticism. He followed Ritschl in repudiating any
supernatural character in the records of revelation as such.[3]
Robertson Smith had already made himself the centre of a stormy
controversy by his article 'Bible' in the first volume of the ninth
edition of the *Encyclopaedia Britannica*. He gave wholehearted
support to the Graf-Wellhausen critico-literary method and
conclusion. A gradual and natural evolutionary development of
Israel's religion was advanced.

The views expounded in the article 'Bible' resulted in
Robertson Smith's removal from his professorial chair in

---

[1] J. W. Colenso, *The Pentateuch and the Book of Joshua Critically Examined*, 1862,
p. 81.

[2] J. K. Mozley, *Some Tendencies in British Theology*, 1952, p. 14.

[3] L. E. Elliott-Binns, *English Thought, 1860–1900*, 1956, p. 73.

Aberdeen. But it has been contended that although he had to forfeit this position the result was that 'the Church was allowed to find room for methods of research and for views of inspiration more free from the errors of tradition, and more true to the facts of Scripture itself'.[1] It was in this way, it is claimed, that the Free Church of Scotland secured its freedom by the sacrifice of one man.[2] Upon his dismissal from the chair at Aberdeen, Smith became joint editor of the *Encyclopaedia Britannica*.

The volume entitled, *The Old Testament in the Jewish Church*, is, from one point of view, Robertson Smith's most influential work. Having lost his case before the Presbytery of Aberdeen, he made an appeal to the Scottish laity in the form of a series of popular lectures in which he introduced the idea of biblical criticism to large audiences in Edinburgh and Glasgow. These lectures were given a wider public in book form in 1881 and in the short space of fifteen months 6,500 were sold.

Smith constantly urged that the new criticism could be held consistently with the conception of Scripture expounded in the catechisms and confessions of his Church. This is a point he laboured especially in the first lecture.

The ideas which he advanced in his article 'Bible' were reiterated and elaborated in the lectures. The fundamental thesis is that the religious history of the Hebrew people is to be reconstituted and reinterpreted in terms of a gradual evolutionary development in which the prophets of Israel are to be seen as key figures marking the advance of theological understanding. The history itself may be conceived as a natural development involving no supernatural elements. Or it may be regarded as the method chosen by God for man's discovery of enlarging ideas of the character and conduct of Deity.

The utmost stress was placed upon the subjective idea of revelation. Revelation was to be understood as the direct witness of the Spirit to the individual soul. It was not to be identified with the words of the Bible. Revelation is God Himself coming forth in direct personal encounter with human lives. It is not the giving of objective truths about God. And least of all is it to be thought of as an inerrant catalogue of

---

[1] George Adam Smith, *The Life of Henry Drummond*, 1898, New York, p. 142.

[2] *Ibid.* Cf. 'Robertson Smith became "not only the protagonist, but the martyr of Biblical criticism." ' T. H. Darlow, *William Robertson Nicoll*, 1925, p. 39.

doctrinal propositions. At the same time note must be taken of the historical nature of revelation. The historical process is marked by certain purposeful interventions in which God has disclosed Himself. The Bible is the record of this historical revelation which has culminated in Christ. It is here we have the account of God's gracious self-disclosure. But being a record of men, especially illuminated though they may have been, the Bible cannot but betray evidences of verbal and historical errors. But these errors do not detract from its worth; for the Word of God is not the Scripture, but is that into which we are introduced by the Scripture and to which it is a witness.[1]

Although we are concerned at the present mainly with an account of Robertson Smith's views, it may be, none the less, relevant to point out that there were vast problems left unsolved and difficulties left untouched. It was not made clear, for example, how the historical nature of revelation could be upheld when it was maintained, at the same time, that the history was not itself reliable. Nor was it at all easy to see how an understanding of God's revelation could be gained by those who were unlearned. Even the broadest outline of the historical events as they were claimed to have taken place by the new criticism cannot be seen in the Bible as we have it. It is only those who have special techniques and specialized equipment who can discover, by a thorough reconstruction of its history, meaning and significance in the Bible. Further, Smith gave stress, on the one hand, to the subjective idea of revelation as the action of the Divine Spirit within, and, on the other hand, he did allow for an objective historical account, but he failed altogether to show the relation that may be supposed to exist between them. He was emphatic enough in his rejection of the so-called propositional and intellectualistic view of revelation, yet, when he desired to prove a point, he quoted the Scripture in propositional form which he seemed to regard as sufficient to silence objections. These are but a few of the serious weaknesses in Smith's idea of revelation.

It was inevitable that such a conception of the Bible should initiate a new outburst of controversy. In fact, T. K. Cheyne sees the 'modern period' begun with the name of W. Robertson

---

[1] Cf. T. M. Lindsay, 'Professor W. Robertson Smith's Doctrine of Scripture', *Expositor*, fourth series, 1894, pp. 241–64.

Smith 'who from the first gave promise of becoming the most brilliant critic of the Old Testament in the English-speaking countries'.[1] Into the details of the ensuing conflict we need not enter.[2] Robert Rainey was one of Smith's most formidable opponents, He addressed the students of the English Presbyterian College, London, and contended that since Christianity is an historical religion based upon an historical revelation it need not fear the most rigorous historical criticism. He stoutly maintained the inerrancy of Scripture and warned against the eagerness manifested by some to accept the conclusions of criticism which were in conflict with tradition. Rainey confesses that there are, and, indeed, must be, obscure passages in the Bible but he will not allow that there are any 'minor inaccuracies' in the sacred volume.[3]

Alfred Cave, a conservative Congregational scholar, made a strong attack upon Smith's position in *The British and Foreign Evangelical Review*.[4] The *London Quarterly Review* sees the critical view gaining its measure of success because of the temporary ignorance of many and the scientific scepticism of others. But, since truth must triumph in the end, it is assured that the Newer Criticism is destined to pass away.[5]

The fact, however, is that Robertson Smith's subjective understanding of revelation has remained and is specially influential at the present day.[6]

(4) '*The Lux Mundi*', edited by Charles Gore

'Few books in modern times', contends J. K. Mozley, 'have so clearly marked the presence of a new era and so deeply influenced its character as the volume of essays by a number of Oxford men

---

[1] T. K. Cheyne, *Founders of Old Testament Criticism*, 1893, p. 212.

[2] Cf. 'Smith, William Robertson', *Dictionary of National Biography*; also Sutherland Black and George W. Chrystal, *The Life of William Robertson Smith* 1912, pp. 179 ff.

[3] Robert Rainey, *The Bible and Criticism*, 1878, pp. 69–70.

[4] Cf. *op. cit.*, 'The Latest Phase of the Pentateuch Question', Vol. XXIX, 1880, pp. 248–67; also, *ibid.*, 'Professor Robertson Smith and the Pentateuch', pp. 593–621.

[5] Cf. *op. cit.*, 'The Newer Criticism on the Old Testament', 1882, p. 305.

[6] Cf., e.g. *Revelation, A Symposium*, (ed. John Baillie and H. Martin), 1937: esp. W. Temple, pp. 106–7, 114–15, 119–23; Gustaf Aulén, pp. 275–6; H. Richard Niebuhr, *The Meaning of Revelation*, 1941, pp. 143–54; Ernest A. Payne, H. Wheeler Robinson, 1946, 'The Principle of Authority in the Christian Religion', pp. 177–8.

B

which was published in the latter part of the year 1889 under the title of *Lux Mundi*.'[1] The aim of the work is clearly stated as an 'attempt to put the Catholic faith into its right relation to modern intellectual and moral problems'.[2] The writers, it is averred, are no 'guessers at truth', but interpreters of the faith they have received. Elliott-Binns contends that the '*Lux Mundi*, when compared with *Essays and Reviews*, is remarkable for its constructive spirit'.[3] This is, perhaps, a little generous. The subtitle states *Lux Mundi* to be 'A Series of Studies in the Religion of the Incarnation'. But some of the subjects have little relation to this topic, yet it would be incorrect to say, as A. M. Fairbairn does, that 'the Incarnation is the very thing the book does not, in any more than the most nominal sense, either discuss or construe'.[4]

There are three essays in the volume which are important for their influence upon the understanding of revelation. J. R. Illingworth and R. C. Moberly wrote on aspects of the Incarnation, while C. Gore, who edited the work, caused excitement by his essay on 'The Holy Spirit and Inspiration'.

Illingworth stressed the idea of the divine immanence and sees in the Higher Pantheism 'which is so common in the present day',[5] the feeling for this neglected emphasis. The 'physical immanence of God the Word in His creation can hardly be overstated' he says, 'as long as His moral transcendence of it is also kept in view'.[6] He regards the Incarnation as the climax of the evolutionary process; as the introduction of a 'new species into the world'.[7] The world is instinct with the Word, thus all truth is a disclosure of His life. Consequently 'all great teachers of whatever kind are vehicles of revelation'.[8] Yet 'the Word did not desert the rest of His creation to become incarnate',[9] therefore, 'the discoveries of science' may be welcomed 'as ultimately due to Divine revelation'.[10]

Moberley in his 'Incarnation as the Basis of Dogma' maintains that 'the claim of the Church to knowledge through the

[1] J. K. Mozley, *Some Tendencies in British Theology*, 1952, p. 17.

[2] *Lux Mundi*, 1889, third edition, 1890, Preface, p. vii.

[3] L. E. Elliott-Binns, *Religion in the Victorian Period*, 1936, p. 238.

[4] A. M. Fairbairn, *The Place of Christ in Modern Theology*, 1908, p. 451 (footnote).

[5] *Lux Mundi*, 1889, third edition, 1890, p. 191.

[6] *Op. cit.*, p. 192.   [7] *Op. cit.*, p. 207.

[8] *Op. cit.*, p. 198.   [9] *Op. cit.*, p. 212.   [10] *Op. cit.*, p. 213.

Incarnation can only be rationally met, and only really answered, when the claim itself, and its evidence, are seriously examined'.[1]

Gore, too, sees Christianity as 'the religion of the Incarnation'.[2] With reference to the understanding of revelation he quotes Lotze's remark that revelation is 'either contained in some divine act of historic occurrence, or continually repeated in men's hearts'.[3] Gore maintains that it is both. But the history as we have it is not the history which contains these divine acts. This history has undergone 'unconscious idealizing'.[4] True, 'Our Lord, in His use of the Old Testament, does indeed endorse with the utmost emphasis the Jewish view of their history',[5] but in such instances He speaks as a man subject to the limitations of human knowledge. Critical questions concerning the Old Testament cannot be foreclosed by quoting Christ as an authority in this sphere. The Davidic authorship of Psalm cx. cannot be maintained because He referred it to David. 'The Incarnation' states Gore with emphasis 'was a self-emptying of God to reveal Himself under conditions of human nature and from the human point of view'.[6] His knowledge was, therefore, a natural human knowledge. As Gore states elsewhere, 'He exhibits no miraculous knowledge of history or of nature, such as was not accessible to other men'.[7] The 'kenotic' doctrine which Gore alludes to here in his essay in the *Lux Mundi* he develops and defends in his later *Bampton Lectures* and his *Dissertations*. By means of his kenotic doctrine Gore feels himself able to maintain that our Lord, because of His limited human knowledge, accepted the revised and idealized history which He found in His Old Testament.

There is, however, a problem here that Gore, and for that matter others who have followed him, have failed to meet. The question which has to be seriously faced is just this: Is human knowledge limited because man is finite or because he is a sinner? The answer which seems to be too readily given is 'because he is a sinner'. But none of us does or can know what knowledge is open to even a perfect human being, much less to

---

[1] *Lux Mundi*, 1889, third edition, 1890, p. 218.
[2] *Op. cit.*, p. 329.　　　　　[3] *Op. cit.*, p. 338.
[4] *Op. cit.*, p. 353.　　　　　[5] *Op. cit.*, p. 358.
[6] *Lux Mundi*, p. 359.
[7] Charles Gore, *The Doctrine of an Infallible Book*, 1924, p. 25.

One who is God-man. At any rate, discussing this subject in another context, J. V. Langmead-Casserley has rightly observed that there are those who have taken 'copious draughts of the critical epistemology of Immanuel Kant and his successors' who really say 'that it is the finitude of man's being which restricts his rational powers' and 'that the trouble with human reasoning is not so much that man is a sinner as that he is finite'.[1]

Gore is emphatic that inspiration does not assure inerrancy. He seems to regard inspiration as illumination, differing in degree, perhaps, from that which is common to all believing men. But, he contends, this 'spiritual illumination, even in the highest degree' has no tendency 'to lift men out of their natural conditions of knowledge which belong to their time'.[2] He can admit that 'almost from the first inspiration was regarded as "verbal" ' and 'commonly identified with infallibility'. But this false and fatal view, he states, following Coleridge, the Christians learned from the Jews.[3]

The chief merit of the *Lux Mundi* essays, as they touch upon our subject, was the clarity with which they stated the position. It may have been true as Scott Holland, one of the contributors, later contended, that what they said was not new. They were just repeating what they had been saying for years and what everybody else was saying. They were taken aback by its being spoken of 'as a bomb'.[4] The volume was, however, vigorously attacked in Convocation by Archdeacon Denison and was dismissed with contempt by Canon Liddon. It was, however, because it was so well said, and said by men whose names were coming to the forefront, that the *Lux Mundi* became so influential. The ideas which were here being elaborated were in essential harmony with the prevailing tone and temper of Old Testament criticism.

(5)   1901—*Article on the 'Gospels' in the 'Encyclopaedia Biblica' by Paul W. Schmiedel*
        Translation into English of 'What is Christianity?' by Adolf Harnack

[1] J. V. Landmead-Casserley, *Graceful Reason*, 1955, p. 35.
[2] *Lux Mundi*, p. 254.
[3] Charles Gore, *The Doctrine of an Infallible Book*, 1924, p. 46.
[4] S. Paget, *Henry Scott Holland*, 1921, p. 281.

These two works may be taken as marking another stage in the development of ideas which were to react upon the understanding of revelation. As the century began to draw to its close the extreme critical theories of the Old Testament were being either abandoned or greatly modified. There was a toning down of certain exaggerated views. In some quarters averse to the critical procedure, it began almost to be felt that there was a return to the traditional position. It is, at any rate, a fact that the more outrageous theories were being repudiated by critics of a more conservative outlook.

But the publication of Schmiedel's article was to open another era of fresh conflict. Here radical criticism was applied to the New Testament, and a new type of 'liberal Christianity' made its appearance. There must be a getting back to the Jesus of history. And to find Him there must be a clear understanding of the relevance and value of the records which tell of Him. When we discover Him, the real Christ of the Galilean road, apart from any idealization of Him by the later Church, then we are at the heart of the Christian gospel. Then we will know what He, the Mightiest among the mighty, the Greatest religious genius, the Man among men, believed and felt and knew about the Father of all. This is indeed revelation. It is the discovery in the ideals and ideas of Christ that we are of infinite value to God whose love must at last enclose all in its embrace.

It is to such a view as this—to revelation as centred in the historic Jesus—that Harnack's, *What is Christianity?* gave vogue. The gospel records, even when stripped of their miraculous legends, are still 'weighty'. They are so because 'they give us information upon three important points: In the first place, they offer us a plain picture of Jesus' teaching, in regard both to its main features and to its individual application; in the second place, they tell us how his life issued in the service of his vocation; and in the third place, they describe to us the impression which he made upon his disciples, and which they transmitted'.[1]

Yet the gospel is no creed about Jesus. 'Jesus never spoke of any kind of "creed" ' except 'to do the will of God, in the certainty that He is the Father'.[2] Such a declaration, for example, as 'I am the Son of God', Harnack maintains, was not

---

[1] Adolf Harnack, *What is Christianity?* (E.T. 1901), p. 31. [2] *Ibid.*, p. 147.

a word of Jesus Himself.[1] In one clear statement found in italics, he states 'The Gospel, as Jesus proclaimed it, has to do with the Father only and not with the Son'.[2]

The influence of such ideas was, we believe, profound. It set scholars out on the Quest for the Historical Jesus, although it must be acknowledged that the Jesus who was discovered was not very much like the Christ of general Christian faith.

Into the obvious weaknesses and the glaring contradictions of *What is Christianity?* we need not enter. It is sufficient to observe that the 'boldness with which Harnack shifted the centre of Christianity from Christology to the Divine Fatherhood, certainly the most indefensible characteristic of the book from the point of view of historical criticism, caused a storm of protest in every theological and philosophical camp in Germany'.[3] Not less in England did its translation, coming at the same time as Schmiedel's article, have the effect of moving the locus of revelation from God's 'actuality' in history, to the 'historic' Jesus. But the tragic fact which emerged was that the Christ presented to men had no sure historical reality. It was a Figure constructed by men with an excessive confidence in their own reason and 'finding the sanction of truth in the mind of the individual and being in consequence arbitrary and subjective'.[4]

(6) 1933—*English Translation of Karl Barth's 'Commentary on the Epistle to the Romans'*

This is, we think, the next and last of the distinguishing volumes in our period to which we need to make special reference. There were, of course, many other works of major importance, but it is, we believe, true to say of them all that the ideas which they elaborated can be subsumed under one general view or other. The famous volumes, the *Cambridge Theological Essays* (1905) and the *Cambridge Biblical Essays* (1909), important as they are in themselves, do not seem to us to mark a new stage in the understanding of revelation. And the same is true of other writings which appeared.

But Barth's *Romans* does seem to indicate the introduction into theological thought of the Kierkegaardian idea of

---

[1] Adolf Harnack, *What is Christianity?* (E.T. 1901), p. 145.   [2] *Ibid.*, p. 144.
[3] E. Digges La Touche, *The Person of Christ in Modern Thought*, 1912, p. 100.
[4] E. Troeltsch, Art. 'Enlightenment', *The New Schaff-Herzog Religious Encyclopædia*, IV, p. 141.

'encounter'. In the Preface to the second German edition, he states: 'if I have a system, it is limited to a recognition of what Kierkegaard called the "infinite qualitative distinction" between time and eternity, and to my regarding this as possessing negative as well as positive significance: "God is in heaven, and thou art on earth". The relation between such a God and such a man, and the relation between such a man and such a God, is for me the theme of the Bible and the essence of philosophy'.[1]

It is well known that Barth has of recent years urged that he no longer occupies the position that he held when his *Romans* was first published. We are convinced in spite of this protest that what he has to say by way of exposition of the first chapter of the epistle is precisely that which he has expounded at great length in his *Church Dogmatics*.[2]

He writes, for example, of the 'incomprehensible' nature of grace. 'Grace', he observes, 'is the gift of Christ, who exposes the gulf which separates God and man, and, by exposing it, bridges it.'[3] He sees men standing so out of relation to God, that it is only in and through God's act that there can be reconciliation. 'Their union with God is shattered so completely that they cannot even conceive of its restoration.'[4] In such statements as these we have already in Barth the teaching of the complete obliteration of the divine image in man. Thus, he goes on to assert his characteristic repudiation of natural theology. There is no possibility, in the least, of knowing anything about God unless and until He Himself breaks into our darkness and night in the revelation of personal encounter. Yet it must be made clear that in the encounter the whole initiative is with God. 'To those who have abandoned direct communication, the communication is made. To those willing to venture with God, He speaks. Those who take upon them the divine "No" shall themselves be borne by the greater divine "Yes".'[5] The wisdom of the natural man issues in the Night of Folly. His so-called

[1] Karl Barth, *Epistle to the Romans*, (E.T. 1933), p. 10.

[2] Cf. 'In view of a controlling tendency at the present time to speak of two Barths, an earlier and a later Barth, it should perhaps be said at the outset that his position on this particular matter has not changed materially since the appearance of his epoch-making commentary on Paul's letter to the *Romans*.' R. C. Johnson, *Authority in the Protestant Church*, 1959, p. 162. What Johnson states here concerning Barth's understanding of authority is true also of other issues as well.

[3] *The Epistle to the Romans*, p. 31.   [4] *Op. cit.*, p. 37.   [5] *Op. cit.*, p. 41.

natural knowledge of God is an illusion. What he knows is
'No-God', since the true God is not a God to be known; He is a
God to make Himself known. He is 'other' than we are. 'We
press ourselves into proximity with Him: and so, all unthinking,
we make Him nigh unto ourselves.'[1] It is when we know that
we can never know Him, when we renounce our sophistication
and are in despair that there is the possibility of God disclosing
Himself to us. We have to learn that 'God is He whom we do
not know' and so discover that 'our ignorance is precisely the
problem and the source of our knowledge'.[2] It is here that faith
comes, faith not of ourselves, but a faith brought to birth in the
revelation of God's grace in His divine inbreaking. Such, indeed,
is revelation: while 'Faith is awe in the presence of the divine
incognito'.[3]

Looking back through the years of the century, then, it will be
clear that certain distinctive types of revelation can be seen
to emerge. While it would be inaccurate to attribute a separate
origin for each to the volumes which we have seen to mark new
stages in the development of religious ideas, it is, we believe,
correct to see in these works more than suggestions which were
bound to give rise to clearly stated positions. In a broad and
general sense, then, the ideas of revelation, which at least find
their germ, or were given impetus, by the books specified, can
be singled out as follows.

Beginning with *Essays and Reviews* we can see the idea of
revelation as historical process gaining ground. Colenso gave
vigour to the subjective emphasis which was earlier set forth
with such warmth and spirit by F. D. Maurice. Robertson Smith
gave effect to the notion of revelation as God's acts in history.
The *Lux Mundi* school emphasized the idea of revelation as
finalizing the evolutionary process in Divine incarnation.
Schmiedel and Harnack turn attention to the Jesus of history and
locate revelation in the Figure reconstructed from the records
after they had eliminated from them what they felt and fancied
were *post factum* idealizations of the Church. And, finally, Barth
seeks to make men aware of the living God as present and
active. There thus comes the idea of revelation as divine
encounter.

---

[1] *The Epistle to the Romans*, p. 44.   [2] *Op. cit.*, p. 45.   [3] *Op. cit.*, p. 39.

CHAPTER TWO

The Ideas within the Era

The changing climate of opinion throughout the century which began with the year 1860 is such that it is not easy to follow the weather chart. There were, in fact, times when contrary winds appeared to be blowing and many voyagers were caught in the place where two seas met. Sometimes, as far as it concerns the ship of the faith, it seemed that the wind 'blew softly', while at other times it was 'tempestuous'. There were those who deluded by the gentle breeze set forth with sails set optimistically only to find themselves caught in the storm and either stranded or shipwrecked. There were others who thought that they had discovered 'a bay with a beach' believing it to be 'commodious to winter in'. Others, however, still pressed on and at length reached the satisfying security of the shore.

It is possible, we think, to set forth the ideas which, throughout the century, brought changes to the winds of opinion. We must not suppose that these occurred in strict chronological order. There were, indeed, times when certain views existed as it were side by side and do not seem to have come into conflict. There were other times when there were clashes of opinions: times when the ideas which make for unbelief and the ideas which make for faith were in open war. But even in those periods when one opinion seemed to be dominant, others were not absent. It is these facts which must be kept in mind throughout this chapter.

A. THE CHALLENGE OF MATERIALISM

It was, it appeared, the first result of the theory of evolution to make men feel that the key to the riddle of existence had been discovered by natural science. The whole enigma of the universe was about to be solved. In earlier days the presence of mystery had created the superstition of religion. But now, it was confidently asserted, there was nothing which science could not explain.

Many of those who had come to treat the world as a machine came to believe that it was only such. What was legitimate as a scientific method was set forth as a body of doctrine claiming to be the only truth about the universe. While it is a fact that the greater minds among those who became absorbed in the study of physical nature did not lose completely the sense of the more than natural, it is clear that the idea was entertained by a large number that science had given the lie to the existence of a supernatural. At the same time, as we noted in the previous chapter, the omnipotence of science was unquestioned. What A. Wood calls 'the movement of self-criticism' which in more recent times 'has revolutionized the scientific outlook and completely changed the relation of natural science with theology and philosophy'[1] had not come about. Science had not yet learned its limitations: nor had scientists as yet admitted the fact that it too worked by faith no less than did religion. It was believed by not a few that religion could have no place in the new scientific world. Religion, it was proclaimed, was finished. Now that the age of science had begun it was 'something unverified and unverifiable by the only methods which were generally regarded as rational and scientific'.[2]

The more the scientific method yielded results, the more thoroughly many came to disbelieve in the existence of anything other than the material. It was, of course, not easy to be absolutely certain that there was really nothing beyond the things which could be seen and felt, measured and mastered. In the nature of the case the scientific method could not be used to test the reality of the non-material. Since, then, there was no possibility of scientifically demonstrating spiritual realities it was better to say that one was uncertain of their existence. Consequently it was thought to be more honest to admit that you did not know whether there was anything beyond or above the mundane. And for this attitude of ignorance T. H. Huxley coined the term 'agnosticism'.

[1] A. Wood, *The Pursuit of Truth*, n.d., p. 19.
[2] C. C. J. Webb, *A Study of Religious Thought in England from 1850*, 1933, p. 7.

It was, then, a chill wind which blew in the years immediately following 1860. And with the winds of doubt and dogmatism there went, as F. W. H. Myers saw it, a 'very flood-tide of materialism and Agnosticism, the mechanical theory of the universe, the reduction of all spiritual facts to physiological phenomena. It was a time when, not the intellect only, but the moral ideas of men seemed to have passed into the camp of negation. We were all in the first flush of triumphant Darwinianism, when terrene evolution had explained so much that men hardly cared to look beyond. Among my own group (at Cambridge), W. K. Clifford was putting forth his series of triumphant proclamations of the nothingness of God, and the divinity of man. Swinburne had given passionate voice to the same conception. Frederic Harrison was still glorifying Humanity as the only 'Divine'. George Eliot strenuously rejected all prospect save in the mere terrene performance of duty to our human kin. And others maintained a significant silence, or fed with vague philosophizings an uncertain hope'.[1]

Nor did the challenge of materialism with its attendent agnosticism quickly pass: perhaps, indeed, it can never quite do so, for all men have not faith. At any rate, in the year 1894, we find F. H. Woods of Oxford in an article entitled, 'Hebrew Prophecy and Modern Criticism', maintaining 'Now the spirit of the age is on the whole against the supernatural. This feeling sometimes takes a form definitely hostile to religion; but leaving this out of the question, there are many who feel the claim which Christianity makes to supernaturalism, so far from being the main ground for believing it to be true, is rather a hindrance to accepting it'.[2]

At the beginning the challenge of materialism was felt by many friends of religion to be formidable. There were some who resorted to the pathetic refuge of belittling science. Others took to reconciling what was regarded as the results of science with religious faith in a way which did credit to neither. Others seemed to fall back on the theory of double truth or to find consolation in the distinction between knowledge of facts and

---

[1] F. W. H. Myers, quoted in *The Life of Bishop Moule*, Hartford and Macdonald, 1922, p. 34.

[2] F. H. Woods, 'Hebrew Prophecy and Modern Criticism', *Expository Times*, Vol. V, 1893–4, p. 257.

knowledge of values. There were, however, those who were ready to eliminate the supernatural altogether from Christianity and to present it as little more than a system of naturalistic ethics. It was felt by those who yielded to this compromise that any idea of a divine activity within the world which operated according to unchanging natural laws, any idea of miracle and of answers to prayer, that is, was an unnecessary burden, and a hindrance to the defence of religion.

It was only gradually that the philosophy of materialism revealed itself as having no satisfactory solution for the deeper problems of man's unquenchable spirit. It was easy enough, at least for a time, to maintain the system by ignoring any facts which appeared to conflict with it. But gradually it began to be seen that to dismiss from consideration whole areas of experience as illusory or incompatible was itself unscientific. In spite of the vehemence with which materialism was maintained and in spite of the evident value and the good results of the application of the scientific method, it was soon realized that the mere multiplication of luxuries could provide only fleeting benefits. The human spirit began to reassert itself. Man needed the promise of another realm as well as possessions in this. Tyndall in 1874, in his wearying volume, *Eirenicon*, had, according to von Hügel 'offered to religion the shells of the oyster', and 'retained for mathematics and Natural Science and for Agnosticism' 'all the succulent food of truth and reality'.[1] But on the whole, people were not so easily satisfied. They were not convinced that the requisite diet for their lives was to be found there. They wanted eggs not shells, and certainly not oyster shells. The idea of the spiritual came creeping back, and, as William James asserts, 'spiritualistic faith in all its forms deals with a world of *promise*, while materialism's sun sets in a sea of disappointment'.[2]

But meanwhile the problem for Christian faith was a real one. It may be said, in this context, to centre around the question of miracles.

(1) *Miracles: Maintaining their Possibility*

In his lectures, *The Miraculous Element in the Gospels*, A. B.

---

[1] F. von Hügel, *The Reality of God*, 1931, p. 196.
[2] William James, *Pragmatism*, 1916, p. 108.

Bruce observed that 'The apologist of the present time has an interest in minimizing the miraculousness of miracles, and making them appear as natural as possible'.[1] This fashion had, indeed, been already set by Baden Powell, who, in his contribution to *Essays and Reviews*, had virtually denied their possibility. He maintained that Revelation is not established by these 'alleged external attestations', since their evidence could only be 'physical', and God's moral government does not need such 'proofs'.[2] Powell, in fact, goes so far in his essay as to assert his acceptance of materialistic determinism.[3]

It may be noted, too, that what Higher Criticism there was in England prior to Robertson Smith's appearance, who was able to unite his criticism with belief in miracles, was decidedly anti-supernaturalistic in its basic assumptions. Those who were earlier influenced by the continental schools of radical criticism seemed willing to reject any historical evidence in which a supernatural element was implied. Continental criticism was wedded to naturalism, and was not far removed from infidelity.

Even Robertson Smith's avowal of belief in miracles did not satisfy all. They could not see how a history which was to be interpreted as a natural process could be admitted to contain supernatural intrusions. There was consequently effort made by a variety of writers to naturalize, to minimize, or to eliminate the miraculous. Matthew Arnold, for example, made a bold attempt to preserve Christianity while denying miracles. They were explained, or, perhaps it would be better to say, explained away, as being the result of obscure physical activity of which we are but partially acquainted.[4] Without going into any details concerning Arnold's doctrine, it will be obvious that he has not dispensed with the divine working, he merely pushed it back to the origination of the system. Such a theory is certainly not compatible with atheism, but it most definitely is with deism. If Arnold sought to naturalize the miracles there were others who sought to minimize them.[5] A number of writers were ready to maintain that miracles have no necessary place in the Christian

---

[1] A. B. Bruce, *The Miraculous Element in the Gospels*, 1886, p. 43.

[2] *Essays and Reviews*, 1860, tenth edition, 1861, p. 133.

[3] Cf. *Cambridge History of England Literature*, XII, p. 327.

[4] Cf. M. Arnold, *Literature and Dogma*, popular edition, 1900, Chapter V.

[5] Cf. J. R. Illingworth, *Personality Human and Divine*, 1894, p. 203 f. H. Drummond, *The New Evangelism*, 1899, pp. 107 ff.

scheme. They may consequently be explained as either the relic of primitive beliefs, as the tendency of unenlightened man to attribute to God what he has been unable to explain by natural laws, or to the equally human desire for following generations to associate mighty deeds with the great figures of the past. Others seemed to have no inhibitions in the slightest, and resolutely eliminated miracles altogether. In 1902, for example, there appeared the work entitled *Contentio Veritatis*, in which it was roundly stated that miracles 'are unmeaning'.[1] This book professes to be a philosophical defence of the Christian Faith, yet it is declared, concerning miracles, that to admit the possibility of such events 'is to destroy the canons upon which not only our ordinary reasoning about matters of science, but in particular our ordinary canons of historical criticism, are based'.[2]

Not all, by any means, were prepared to take this line. It seemed to others obvious that miracles were somehow associated with the Christian message, and the very fact of them was an essential demonstration of a supernatural realm. An explanation of them must therefore be sought. In the period there were three main apologetic works on miracles, three series of Bampton Lectures, in which the subject received special attention. While it is a fact that the position taken by each one of these lecturers was not acceptable to the others, yet a reference to the volumes themselves will reveal how the idea of miracles was regarded as in some way essential for Christianity. The apologetic for miracles can be subsumed under the point of view taken by these Bampton lecturers.

We must begin with J. B. Mozley. In 1865 he focused attention on the miracles, the reality of which he had no doubt. His method was to reject the idea of a universal law as conceived by those who would have a world enclosed in iron and the Diety in adamantine fetters.[3] Mozley defends miracles by accepting Hume's theory of causation. Law is not, so to speak, something embedded in the constitution of the universe: it is really 'the perception of harmony and relation in nature'. The order of nature, to which the term law is given, is the observation only

[1] *Contentio Veritatis*, 1902, p. 88.

[2] *Contentio Veritatis*, p. 53. Cf. Aubrey Moore's statement to Reading Church Congress of 1883: a miraculous intervention is 'as fatal to theology as to science'. Cf. also his *Science and the Faith*, 1889, p. 225.

[3] J. B. Mozley, *Eight Lectures on Miracles*, Bampton Lectures, 1865, 1865, p. 59.

of sequence which begets the expectation of its continuance in the future. Mozley sees philosophy as having 'loosened the connection of the order of nature with the ground of reason, befriending, in exact proportion as it has done this, the principle of miracles'.[1] The argument against miracles on the score of law is, then, he says, 'answered by saying that we know nothing in nature of law in the sense in which it prevents miracles'.[2] Not only are the miracles not made impossible because incompatible with law, but, no less, are they not to be thought of as 'against experience; because we expect facts *like* to those of our experience; and miracles are *unlike* ones'.[3] Mozley contends that the general order of nature is not really disrupted by these miraculous interventions. The sense of sequence and harmony is not lost by these occasional intrusions. He concludes that 'it is not in the sense of harmony and system that the order of nature is opposed to the miraculous at all'.[4] The perfectly designed machine does not lose its perfection by being 'interrupted designedly for some purpose'. Indeed an injurious interruption of the relations of the human body does not make less wonderful our bodily structure. 'What', he therefore asserts, '*is* disturbed by a miracle is the mechanical expectation of recurrence, from which, and not from the *system* and arrangement in nature, the notion of immutability proceeds.'[5]

This defence of miracles is certainly a bold one. Mozley has taken up the weapons which Hume had used against their reality and used them instead to assure their certainty. It was, at the time, an original approach; although, at the present we are more familiar with the notion of science as an observation of the behaviour of phenomena, than, as it was mainly conceived to be then, a reading of the inner necessities of noumena. Huxley was impressed by Mozley's arguments and admitted the abstract possibility of miracles. Mozley was not, however, able clearly to establish that these unusual occurrences have necessarily a divine origin. Mozley's onslaught on the order of nature met with strenuous opposition from the author of *Supernatural Religion*.[6] A. B. Bruce rejects the validity of Mozley's thesis and while he

---

[1] J. B. Mozley, *Eight Lectures on Miracles*, Bampton Lectures, 1865, 1865, p. 49.
[2] *Ibid.*, p. 49.   [3] *Ibid.*, p. 50.
[4] *Ibid.*, p. 55.   [5] *Ibid.*, p. 56.
[6] Cf. *Supernatural Religion*, 1874, p. 59 f.

admits it to be 'as ingenious as it is bold' contends that 'it belongs to that class of arguments which silence rather than convince'.[1] He describes it as an 'eccentric attempt to confound unbelief by an assault on the natural order of which it makes an idol'.[2]

R. W. Church in a review of Mozley's lectures, however, took the opportunity of stating that 'The way in which the subject of Miracles has been treated, and the place which they have in our discussions, will remain a characteristic feature of both the religious and philosophical tendencies of thought amongst us'.[3]

While Mozley defended miracles, then, by an attack upon the idea of natural law, C. A. Row rejected Mozley's method and sought justification for the miraculous in man's freedom to act in an ordered universe. This is the presupposition of his Bampton Lectures of 1877. It is right to point out that Row had already given an intimation of his idea in his earlier work, *The Supernatural in the New Testament, Possible, Credible, and Historical* (1875). In this volume Row argued that man's freedom to act in a world ruled by law is a genuine fact. In this we have evidence for, as well as an illustration of, God's right and ability to act within His own world: and to act in special ways for special purposes. Man's freedom is not annulled by order, neither is order nullified by man's freedom. So, too, is it with God.

This is the idea which comes out in his lectures of 1877 whenever he touches upon the subject of miracles. Quite evidently, 'The conception of a miracle involves neither a suspension of the forces, nor the violation of the laws of nature'.[4] Man of his own free agency, he argues again, can modify the order of nature by imparting to its forces.[5] 'If man can change the direction of the forces of the universe, combine them, and neutralize one by the superior energy of another in such a way as to effectuate the results of purpose, without suspending them, much more must God be able to do the same for the effectuation of His purposes;

---

[1] A. B. Bruce, *The Miraculous Element in the Gospel*, 1886, p. 46.
[2] *Ibid.*, p. 48.
[3] Cf. R. W. Church, *Occasional Papers*, 1897, Vol. 2, p. 82 f. (Reprinted from *The Times*, June 5th, 1866.)
[4] C. A. Row, *Christian Evidences Viewed in Relation to Modern Thought*, being the Bampton Lectures for 1877, 1877, pp. 54–5.
[5] *Ibid.*, p. 61 f.

since His ability to effectuate the results of purpose without
suspending the action of existing force, or introducing a new
one, must be so much the greater as He is mightier and wiser'.[1]

This refusal of Row to define a miracle as in any way a
violation of the laws of nature was an important emphasis.
Christian apologists had too often needlessly embarrassed their
arguments by accepting Hume's definition.[2] It was far wiser to
insist that since man can bring about results which would not
otherwise have come about except by his interference, so was it
possible for God. A miracle is not, then, as Newman Smyth had
correctly insisted, 'a sudden blow struck in the face of nature,
but a use of nature, according to its inner capacities, by higher
powers'.[3] Row's stress upon man's free agency in an ordered
universe has been given much attention in recent years as having
an important bearing upon the whole argument for the possibility of miracles. Earlier H. L. Mansel, in his essay on miracles
in *Aids to Faith*, had shown awareness of its relevancy. Recent
writers such as C. S. Lewis in his *Miracles, A Preliminary Study*
and H. H. Farmer, in his discussion of the subject in his *World
and God*, make effective use of the same idea of man's ability to
initiate new results by his free activity without either suspending
or destroying the order of nature.

Frederick Temple, in his Bampton Lectures of 1884, makes
much of the concept of religious development as he had done in
his contribution to *Essays and Reviews*. He maintains that there
is really no final contradiction between the idea of evolution and
that of revelation. He deals in one lecture with the 'Apparent
Conflict between Religion and the Doctrine of Evolution',[4] and
in another with the 'Apparent Collision between Religion and
the Doctrine of Evolution'.[5] He concludes that 'we cannot find
that Science, in teaching Evolution, has yet asserted anything
that is inconsistent with Revelation, unless we assume that
Revelation was intended not to teach spiritual truth only, but

---

[1] C. A. Row, *Christian Evidences Viewed in Relation to Modern Thought*, being
the Bampton Lectures for 1877, 1877, p. 63.
[2] Cf. *Hume's Enquiries* (ed. L. A. Selbie-Bigge), 1951, pp. 105 ff.
[3] Cf. Newman Smyth, *Old Faiths in a New Light*, 1879, revised edition, 1891,
Chapter 1; J. Wendland, *Miracles and Christianity* (trans. H. R. Mackintosh, 1910),
Chapter 1; H. H. Farmer, *The World and God*, 1935, pp. 148 ff.
[4] Frederick Temple, *The Relations between Religion and Science*, being the
Bampton Lectures for 1884, 1884, Chapter IV.   [5] *Ibid.*, Chapter VI.

physical truth also'.[1] Temple finds religion to be a deep
necessity of the human soul and says that 'it is in knowledge of
God that man finds himself divine'.[2]

It is, however, on the subject of revelation and miracles that
the discussion is centred. And it is just here that we find the
lecturer, from one point of view apparently looking back to an
older apologetic, and, from another point of view, making
statements which are characteristically modern. In his defence
of miracles Temple falls back upon the hypothesis that they are
an effect due to the action of some higher law. This idea seems
to have had a wide appeal. It was used earlier by C. Babbage in
the *Ninth Bridgewater Treatise*. It was also the position
maintained by C. H. Curteis in the Boyle Lectures of the same
year as Temple's Bampton Lectures. Curteis contended that a
miracle is to be explained 'as a point of intersection between
some vast outer circle of God's ways and the smaller inner circle
to which we ourselves are better accustomed'.[3] Almoni Peloni,
likewise, sees miracles as due to the operation of a higher law.
He asks how some scientists can pronounce miracles to be impossible 'when even they themselves possess and wield a power
by which the ordinary course of nature is constantly modified'?[4]

Temple, however, was not ready to maintain that in every
case the higher law was itself an unknown physical one. He does,
indeed, say that certain miracles of healing, for example, can be
so explained. He regards a miracle as in some sense a 'break of
uniformity', and, he declares that 'Revelation has no interest in
denying' that 'the intervention which has apparently disturbed
the sequence of phenomena is, after all, that of a higher physical
law as yet unknown'.[5] Applying this canon, Temple can state
that such events as, for example, the Resurrection of our Lord
and the general resurrection, need not be considered miracles in
the scientific sense. At the moment the higher law, so to speak,
is not made active. At the time of the resurrection of Christ this

[1] Frederick Temple, *The Relations between Religion and Science*, being the
Bampton Lectures for 1884, 1884, Chapter IV, p. 188; cf. pp. 123, 220.

[2] *Ibid.*, p. 65.

[3] C. H. Curteis, *The Scientific Obstacles to Christian Belief*, Boyle Lectures, 1884,
1885, p. 76.

[4] Almoni Peloni, 'Miracles: The Problem Stated', *The Expositor*, second series,
Vol. IV, 1882, p. 240. Cf. 'Miracles: The Problem Solved', *The Expositor*, second
series, Vol. VI, 1883, p. 161 f.

[5] Frederick Temple, *The Relations between Religion and Science*, 1884, p. 195.

higher natural physical law operated, and at the time of the general resurrection it will operate again. Meanwhile the Divine will, we must suppose, acts to counteract these laws and to render them dormant. On this hypothesis much of what we have been in the habit of calling miracles are but 'the natural issue of physical laws always at work'.[1] The impression that one receives from some of Temple's arguments is that the miracles appear to be the natural results of the permitted operations of natural law.[2] If this is so, then a comment of Delitzsch can be understood: 'it is a most disheartening sign of the times' he once observed, 'that even such as in theory acknowledge the miracles, in practice really reckon on naturalistic assumptions'.[3]

At the same time Temple does give supremacy to the Moral Law and finds for some of the miracles an instance of the assertion of that law in human affairs. In this way he is able to put stress on the spiritual value of the miracles. He seems to draw a sharp distinction between the moral and the scientific understanding of a miracle. This point is constantly made. He says, to quote but one reference, that 'it must therefore be always remembered that Revelation is not bound by the scientific definition of a miracle, and that if all the miraculous events recorded in the Bible happened exactly as they were told, and if Science were one day able to show that they could be accounted for by natural causes working at the time in each case, this would not in any way effect their character, as regards the Revelation which they were worked to prove or of which they form a part. Revelation uses these events for its own purposes'.[4]

It would seem from these words that Temple could regard a miracle as the religious reading of a natural event. It is certainly a correct thing to emphasize that miracles were performed for a religious purpose. This, indeed, is one of the points which has been given special stress today. Thus Wendland, for example, contends that the Scriptures make clear 'that no miracles are ever experienced by unbelievers'.[5] He goes on to urge that it is in the context of religious experience that their independent, unique

---

[1] Frederick Temple, *The Relations between Religion and Science*, 1884, p. 197.

[2] Cf. A. B. Bruce, *The Miraculous Element in the Gospels*, 1886, p. 51.

[3] F. Delitzsch, 'The Deep Gulf between the Old Theology and the New. A Last Confession', *The Expositor*, third series, Vol. IX, 1889, p. 54.

[4] *The Relations between Religion and Science*, 1884, pp. 195-6.

[5] J. Wendland (E.T. 1910), p. 3.

and real significance is to be found. This point is made with
particular effectiveness by H. H. Farmer. He premises that
'Miracles being fundamentally a religious category and not a
scientific or philosophical one, the proper place to begin is within
the sphere of living religion itself'.[1] The very first thing to be
considered, he maintains, is 'what is the significance of miracle
for religion'. Justification for this way of regarding a miracle he
finds in the etymology of the word 'miracle' itself which fixes
attention upon the profound feeling response, akin to wonder
and awe, which the event evokes. The 'mirabile' in the
'miraculum' has significance for the religious life as such. It is
for this reason that Farmer can contend that 'a miraculous event
always enters the religious man's experience as a *revelation* of
God'.[2] The awareness of God as living is the decisive fact in the
miraculous event.

Farmer argues with cogency in favour of the assimilation of
the idea of a miracle with the idea of revelation.[3] He makes the
point that 'a miracle for the religious mind is pre-eminently an
event in which God is apprehended as entering succouringly
into the situation'.[4] This insistence on the religious understanding of a miracle will mean, as, indeed, Farmer declares,
that what is a miracle for one, is not for another. He is in agreement with Hunzinger that 'Only those who believe through the
miracle can believe in the miracle'.

That there is valuable truth in this subjective emphasis there
need be no doubt. The New Testament gives us warrant for
stressing the religious significance of the event designated a
miracle. The miracle is no arbitrary act of God, no stunning and
silencing wonder. A miracle is a sign, a wonder wrought to
express some spiritual reality. In a sense as Erasmus once
remarked, 'the doings of Jesus are parables'.

Yet it must be made clear that it is not enough to regard a
miracle as an event from which we simply gain the impression
that God is working. There must be, in addition, the cognitive
assurance of the metaphysical actuality of the event. A mere
emotional impression is no satisfactory understanding of a
miracle. There must be objective reality of the power displayed
as well as subjective valuation of a spiritual disclosure.

[1] H. H. Farmer, *The World and God*, 1935, p. 108.
[2] *Ibid.*, p. 109.   [3] *Ibid.*, p.111 f.   [4] *Ibid.*, p. 116.

It is the error of the Ritschlian theology that miracles are given a completely subjective significance. A miracle is nothing more than a subjective impression.

Ritschl himself left the question of miracles in obscurity. His whole theology, it seems, begins with the Kantian stress upon the authority for religion of the moral proof and the impossibility of our knowing anything about noumena. Ritschl draws a sharp distinction between the practical and the religious view of the world. He desired to exempt religion altogether from the criticism of science by insisting that religion relates only to the category of value. Theology is altogether divorced from metaphysics. In the first edition of his *Justification and Reconciliation* he went so far as to set religious and theoretical knowledge in opposition. Although the antagonism is smoothed over in the third edition of the same work it is still asserted that the two are distinct functions which, even when applied to the same object, do not even partially coincide, but go wholly asunder.

It is this clear-cut distinction which lies behind his treatment of miracles. The idea of a metaphysical miracle is looked upon with disfavour as being incompatible with the modern scientific view of the world. But the religious idea of a miracle is still allowed since any event or experience which gives an immediate impression of God's presence and power is so designated. A miracle is therefore, not a scientific concept, but altogether a religious one. Ritschl states in the first sketch of his *Dogmatic* (1853) that a 'miracle has its truth, not for science, but for religious experience'. Later modifications and expositions do not alter this essential position.

How far Temple was influenced by this view is hard to say. But it is certain that some of his period were. There are, for example, a couple of articles entitled, 'God in Nature and History, Contributions towards a true Theory of Revelation' in which P. Thomson makes, what we cannot but call, this Ritschlian distinction. 'The physical or scientific interpretation of natural phenomena' he declares, 'is quite independent of their religious interpretation; they are of different spheres, and their propositions therefore can never come into collision'.[1]

[1] P. Thomson, 'God in Nature and History, Contributions towards a true Theory of Revelation', *The Expositor*, second series, Vol. I, 1885, p. 179; cf. also p. 250.

Ritschl's followers certainly saw that amid the ambiguity of their master's scheme it was clear that he regarded a miracle as the religious name for any event which might evoke a kindling impression of God's help, but, as an event which, none the less, did not require to be brought into relation with the scientific doctrine of the unbroken connection of natural law. It became a dictum, therefore, with those who took their cue from Ritschl, that faith was not concerned with the acceptance of special miraculous incidents. Harnack and Herrmann, for example, carried through the Ritschlian presuppositions. Harnack is emphatic that the 'historian cannot regard a miracle as a sure given historical event'. He goes on to assert that 'Every individual miracle remains historically quite doubtful, and a summation of things doubtful never leads to certainty'. He will grant that a historian may be convinced that Jesus did extraordinary things, which may be referred to, as in the strict sense miraculous. Such a conviction, however, derives from the unique impression he has obtained of His person which leads him to credit to Him supernatural power. Harnack is emphatic that 'This conclusion itself belongs to the province of religious faith'.[1]

Herrmann declares that the question of the trustworthiness of the miracle narratives of the gospels is, for the present-day theology, a matter of indifference. As the most thorough exponent of the Ritschlian theology, he defines a miracle as 'Any event in which we clearly perceive the impinging of God upon our lives'.[2] Such miracles cannot be made 'intelligible' to others, and they need no 'defence'. They lie in the realm of faith and have no real connection with the natural order, the province of scientific knowledge. In no sense can it be said that God breaks through the natural order. 'Our faith can only recognize miracle when in an event within our experience we recognize the impact upon our life of a power not ourselves'.[3]

Such statements as these could be paralleled in the thought of Sabatier. He, too, insists upon the religious understanding of a miracle; but he does not seem to regard it as metaphysically factual. He certainly divorces it from the world of scientific

---

[1] Adolf Harnack, *History of Dogma* (in seven volumes, E.T. 1902), Vol. I, p. 65 note.

[2] W. Herrmann, *Systematic Theology* (E.T. 1927), p. 83.   [3] *Ibid.*, p. 85.

knowledge. 'The affirmation of piety is essentially different from scientific explanation,' he says, 'it places us in the subjective and moral order of life, which no more depends on the order of science than the scientific order depends on piety. There cannot be conflict between the two orders, because they move on different planes and never meet. Science, which knows its limits, cannot forbid the act of confidence and adoration of piety. Piety, in its turn, conscious of its proper nature, will not encroach on science; its affirmations can neither enrich, impoverish, nor embarrass science, for they bear on different points and answer different ends'.[1]

It is in the context of this understanding of the separate and distinct realms of science and religion that Sabatier treats of the idea of miracle. It is for Sabatier, as it is for all who take the exclusively subjective point of view, the religious reading of any event. The event may, of course, be in itself extraordinary but it still belongs to the realm of nature. It is piety which sees in the event some revelation of God. This is the conception which was given persuasive exposition by Schleiermacher. He sees 'Nature as the Vestibule of the Living Temple' as he puts it in his second *Discourse*, and religion produced 'chiefly where the living contact of man with the world fashions itself as feeling'. The prophet is the one who is the most sensitive to the actings of the Divine Force and the one who is able to make a living communication of its presence to others. Such a man needs no mediator for himself, he is rather a mediator for many. In the events which others pass by, he, seer that he is, stops, and feels the upsurgings of divine life.

The ideas of all these writers had become familiar to British readers and their views had a profound influence. With the passing of the years there was a growing tendency to press and stress the subjective understanding of miracles. But by so doing there was an evident danger that miracles would lose their sense of uniqueness. It is, of course, perfectly true, as W. N. Whitehead has said, that 'Every event on its finer side introduces God into the world'.[2] The Christian believer will have no doubt about that. He cannot think otherwise since he believes in

---

[1] A. Sabatier, *Outlines of a Philosophy of Religion*, third edition, 1906, p. 79.
[2] W. N. Whitehead, *Religion in the Making*, Lowell Lectures, 1926, 1926, pp. 155–6.

the immanence of God. But a miracle is not, however, a mere religious reading of every event. It is a religious reading of an event which is itself unique, and which would still be so however read. In other words, the objective reality of the event as resulting from God's act must be maintained. A miraculous event is not just an awareness of that general providential regard of God for His creation. There will be occasions, no doubt, when the man of faith will become strangely stirred as he contemplates the beauty of the natural order and the bounty of the divine provision. 'Yet the religious man would not spontaneously call such a revelation of God to him at such a moment a miracle; nor would he use the term of those orderly processes of nature which he apprehends as wonderful manifestations of the bounty and steadfastness and creative power of God. Reference is, indeed, sometimes made to the "miracles of nature", and we are bidden wonderingly to discern the miracles of God in the most humdrum familiarities of life, the growth of a plant, the pattern of a snowflake. We are far from suggesting that such phrases are improper, still less the sentiments they express; yet such a usage of the term miracle can hardly be taken as spontaneous and typical. There is an element of philosophic theorizing, perhaps even at times of self-conscious attitudinizing, in it. That this is so, is shown by the fact that if such a line of thought be consistently carried through, it ends in the view that everything is a miracle, and the term is evacuated of any distinctive meaning at all, except the quite jejune one that there is, despite all our knowledge, a residuum of the mysterious in every event. If there is one thing quite certain in this connection it is that the word miracle on the religious man's lips indicates something distinctive which is *not* applicable, even after reflection, to all events indiscriminately. In other words, the more generalized the awareness of God's goodness and succour, the less the word miracle is applicable.'[1]

(2) *Miracles: Indicating their Purpose*

It is impossible to mark the precise time when the transition was made from regarding miracles as compelling evidences for Christianity to the idea of them as having an intimate association with it. The usual line taken by the older apologists was to argue

[1] H. H. Farmer, *The World and God*, 1935, pp. 118–9.

that miracles (and prophecy) were to be taken as evidential adjuncts to revealed doctrines. It was in this way that the cause of Christianity was maintained against the deists.[1] And the method was continued into the first part of the second half of the nineteenth century. Bishop Butler had given the most polished exposition of the thesis that miracles and prophecy were the 'two direct and fundamental proofs' of the Christian revelation. All other evidences were to be viewed in the light of these two. Such, too, was the position urged by Paley. But the emphasis was to be changed.

W. E. Gladstone, in his edition of Butler's *Works*, expressed his awareness of the revised understanding of miracles in relation to revelation. He adds a footnote to the words just quoted: 'After the discussion of the last century and a half, Butler would perhaps have somewhat altered what he has written respecting the twin office of miracle and prophecy as evidences of revealed religion'.[2] Another writer a few years later contends that Paley's view of miracles gives them a sort of mechanical efficacy. 'Every divine revelation must be replete with miracles and with wisdom. A revelation without miracles cannot be proved to be divine; without consummate wisdom it is proved not to be divine. But we must advance further. The wisdom and the miracle are both of the very essence of revelation. In regarding miracles as only external buttresses of faith, Paley falls into the same mistake as to rest in the *opus operatum* of a sacrament.'[3]

In his characteristic manner P. T. Forsyth, writing in the *London Quarterly Review* for July 1909 on the subject 'Evidential Value of Miracles', contends that as evidences they can have little appeal. He quotes the saying 'Miracles, which were once the foundation of Apologetic, became in time its crutch; and now they have become its crux'. He even goes so far as to evince some sympathy with a remark of Rousseau who declared, 'Get rid of your miracles, and the world will fall at Christ's feet'. Yet Forsyth, who argues elsewhere against the tendency which some reveal to proclaim an undogmatic and toned-down

---

[1] Cf. H. D. McDonald, *Ideas of Revelation*, 1959, p. 98 f.
[2] Joseph Butler, *The Works of Joseph Butler* (ed. W. E. Gladstone), Oxford, 1896, pp. 302–3.
[3] *Expository Times*, Vols. I and II, 1889–91, I, p. 9.

Christianity, has no intention of getting rid of miracles. He is acutely aware of their difficulty for the modern mind. He thinks that the day has passed when they can be adduced as proofs of revelation. It is his conviction that now they embarrass faith, they do not support it, if used as external evidences.

Such statements as these could be continued but enough has been recorded to show how definite was the change in the understanding of the purpose of miracles.

It is certainly a question of fundamental importance to ask how miracles are related to revelation. Are they evidences or media? It was agreed by all theists that miracles, in some way, make God better known. 'They may communicate to men a knowledge of God's character and purposes higher in degree, if not different in kind from, that derived from the ordinary course of nature.'[1]

The so-called Evidential School of apologists had all along maintained that revelation was the communication to men of doctrinal truths which were authenticated by miraculous proofs. This was the view, general in the previous century and a half, which was brilliantly maintained by Mozley in his Bampton Lectures. Even to the present day writers of repute may be found who maintain this evidential regard for miracles. Christianity, contends a recent apologist, 'is under a special obligation to produce miraculous evidence of the truth of its claims. The Founder of Christianity, wiser than some of His modern followers, clearly recognized this obligation.'[2]

At the same time, we may not be far wrong in contending that J. B. Mozley was the last great exponent of the evidential idea of miracles. The first of his famous lectures is entitled, 'Miracles Necessary for a Revelation'. He regards revelation as the communication of truths otherwise undiscoverable by the human reason. This 'supernatural scheme for man's salvation' is not established 'without the evidence of miracle'. After what he calls a 'prefatory note', he states that 'There is one great necessary purpose, then, which divines assign to miracles, viz. the proof of a revelation. And certainly, if it is the will of God to give a revelation, there are plain and obvious reasons for asserting that miracles are necessary as the guarantee and

[1] A. B. Bruce, *The Miraculous Element in the Gospels*, 1886, p. 284.
[2] Charles Harris, *Pro Fide*, fourth edition, 1930, pp. 417–18.

voucher for that revelation. A revelation is, properly speaking, such only by virtue of telling us something which we could not know without it. But how do we know that that communication of what is undiscoverable by human reason is true? Our reason cannot prove of it, for it is by the very supposition beyond our reason. There must be, then, some note or sign to certify to it and distinguish it as a true communication from God, which note can be nothing else than a miracle'.[1]

Neither commendation nor criticism of this evidential regard for miracles needs to be made here. There is, without doubt, something to be said for and against the procedure. It may well be that the reaction has been too violent and that there is real need to reconsider the question.

But the evidential understanding of miracles could not be well maintained in the climate of opinion which prevailed in the last half of the nineteenth century. For one thing, the early apologetic view had begun from the standpoint of the divine transcendence. God was conceived of as standing outside and intruding, on occasional times and in special ways, to direct men's attention to the truths He had seemed fit to reveal. This emphasis upon the divine transcendence has been replaced by one upon the divine immanence with the result that a new appreciation of miracles was inescapable. For another reason, it was a period of stirring individualism, in which men were jealously aware of their liberty as single individuals, consequently anything in the nature of coercion of belief was resented. It was considered by believers and unbelievers alike that to adduce miracles as evidences of revelation is to seek to tyrannize men into faith. Emerson had given blunt repudiation of the idea of a faith resting upon the external attestation of miracles. To seek to convert a man by an appeal to such evidence is, he says, a profanation of the soul.

In a chapter entitled 'Signs as a Vehicle of Revelation', Wescott argued that faith is not born of the inescapable proof of compelling signs. It comes through the warm eagerness of the responding heart and does not really require such evidential appendages.[2] There was also a tendency to reject the apologetic

---

[1] J. B. Mozley, *op. cit.*, pp. 6–7.
[2] B. F. Wescott, *The Gospel of Life*, 1892, Chapter VII. Cf. '. . . absolute loyalty of God as recognized and known in the individual conscience must prevail **over**

view of miracles because of the apparent difficulty felt in giving any clear and convincing account of them in the light of the scientific understanding of the universe then prevailing. There could be no miracle possible, it was supposed, in a world controlled by unbreakable laws. There was consequently, in some quarters, a readiness to disparage the physical and natural and to emphasize the moral miracles of Christianity.

This emphasis on the moral miracles was a complete reaction from the supreme place given to the natural miracles by the Evidential writers. 'Even in the case of apologists of too well-balanced judgement to be guilty of totally neglecting the argument from miracles, the influence of reaction is apparent in a marked preference for other lines of argument. Thus the favourite theme for some time past has been the *moral* miracles of Christianity, the very title implying a disparaging reference to the physical miracles which form the basis of so much elaborate reasoning in older apologetic treatises.'[1]

C. A. Row, for example, in his Bampton Lectures of 1877 appears to take this position. He gives little significance to the evidential value of miracles. 'The proof of Christianity', he says, 'has been hitherto based on what is called its miraculous attestation. Miracles have been placed in the forefront of the Christian argument, and other evidences have occupied in it a very subordinate position.'[2] But it is the moral evidences, he contends, which should occupy the first place. It is these which decisively attest Christianity to be a divine revelation. The difficulties which have recently been brought to light concerning miracles make it clear that they 'should no longer occupy the van of our evidential position'.[3] The earlier apologists, he points out, were content to recommend Christianity on the strength of its attestation by miracles. This method is no longer either possible or valid. 'One feels a difficulty in believing', he urges, 'that if Paley's argument had been placed before a Father of the second or third century, it would have commended itself

every external sign . . . and no array of external "miracles" can justify us in referring to Him, as authoritative for our direction, any act or word which our moral constitution made in His image forces us to regard as immoral'. *Op. cit.*, pp. 215–16.

[1] A. B. Bruce, *The Miraculous Element in the Gospels*, 1886, p. 294.

[2] C. A. Row, *Christian Evidences Viewed in Relation to Modern Thought*, 1877, p. 25.　　　　　　　　　　　　　　　　　[3] *Ibid.*, p. 36.

to him as an efficient mode of persuading an unbeliever to embrace the Christian faith.'[1]

This repudiation of miracles, as having any real value for faith, was taken up by many succeeding writers. One more recent illustration of the desire to set Christian faith free from what is held to be the burden of miracles comes in the *Contentio Veritatis*. This work was hailed by one reviewer as 'a new *Lux Mundi*', which, it was declared 'will do for the beginning of the Twentieth Century what *Lux Mundi* did for the end of the Nineteenth'.[2] The volume is composed of seven essays contributed by six Oxford tutors. Among the names are Rashdall and Inge, whose scholastic stature grew with the years. The whole work from beginning to end is really concerned with the miraculous. The possibility of miracles is allowed by all the writers. But each one is acutely aware of the strength of scientific criticism. Yet for all the desire to admit the reality of the miraculous there is hesitancy. Rashdall, for example, contends that, while certain miracles may be due to the introduction of some unsuspected law, our knowledge of the ways of nature make it quite impossible to admit others as genuine. He instances the reference in Joshua to the 'stopping of the sun', and adds that 'The raising of the saints out of the tomb in their bodies, and some of what are called the "nature-miracles", may surely, with tolerable confidence, be placed in this class'.

There are two passages which may be quoted from this volume which give the viewpoint of all the contributors, 'The time is past', it is declared, 'when Christianity could be presented as a revelation attested by miracles, depending on these for the main evidence of its truth'.[3] In another passage illustration is made of the thesis with reference to the Incarnation. 'We should not now expect, a priori,' it is affirmed, 'that the Incarnate *Logos* would be born without a human father, that He would suspend His own laws during His sojourn on earth, or that He would resuscitate His earthly body, and remove it to the sky, nor do we see that those events, however well proved, are of any value as evidences of His divinity.'[4]

[1] C. A. Row, *Christian Evidences Viewed in Relation to Modern Thought*, 1877, p. 32.

[2] *Expository Times*, Vol. XIII, 1901–2, p. 343; cf. J. B. Mozley, *Some Tendencies in British Theology*, 1952, p. 27.

[3] *Contentio Veritatis*, 1902, p. 144.   [4] *Op. cit.*, p. 88.

It would seem that writers who follow this method, while allowing for the possibility of miracles, were prepared to divorce them altogether from the essential Christian message. There were others, however, who were not committed to this conclusion. They preferred to see the miracles as having their place in the whole context of Christ's life and work, and as taking their part as media of revelation. Frederick Temple, for example, argued against the possibility of separating or eliminating the miraculous element from the history. In the Old Testament, indeed, 'the miraculous element in it occupied comparatively so small a place, and was so rarely, if ever, contemporaneous, that it might be left out'. In the New Testament, it is, he contends, otherwise. Here the 'miracles are embedded in, are indeed intertwined with, the narrative. Many of our Lord's most characteristic sayings are so associated with narratives of miracles that the two cannot be torn apart'.[1] Later, rejecting the evidential value of miracles, he states, 'to us they are, if accepted at all, accepted as a part of the revelation itself'.[2]

This idea of miracles as an integral part of the whole Christian story was given strong emphasis throughout the following years. They were more and more connected with God's redemptive purpose for the world and were regarded as occasioned by man's sin and disorder. They were held to be worked, as Leibniz had urged long before, not 'in order to supply the wants of Nature, but those of grace'. Thus what we may call a redemptive explanation was given to them.

One of the most sensitive and suggestive expositions of this idea will be found in a volume by Theodore Christlieb translated into English in 1874. Christlieb, the professor of theology at Bonn, accepted the Biblical miracles with conviction. Having urged, first of all, that miracles are not to be thought of as suspending the laws of nature, he goes on to argue that the internal aim of miracles is a redemptive one. They are not 'an unnatural breach of Nature, but a supernatural interruption of the unnatural'. They are needed for the redemption and consummation of the world. 'We can now recognize in the condition of the world as vitiated by sin, not only the possibility, but also

[1] Frederick Temple, *The Relations between Religion and Science*, 1884, p. 153.
[2] *Ibid.*, p. 203.

the *necessity of miracles*,[1] he asserts. It is in the moral condition
of the world after the entrance of sin that the reason for miracles
is to be found. 'We, too, are well aware of a rent in the world
and a disturbance of its original laws, not caused, however, by
God, but by man; not *provoked* by miracles, but rather *remedied*
by them. Our opponents say that the world would go to ruin if
God through His interference were to violate the order of
nature. To this we reply, that, on the contrary, since sin has
entered the world, it would immediately go to ruin if left to
itself, and therefore it only exists to this day because God in
every age has graciously interfered in its self-inflicted disorder.'[2]

This point is much stressed. Again and again Christlieb
argues that 'sin has made a "rent" in the world; but miracles
only enter in for the removal of the already existing disturbance'.[3] He notes that in the Bible the miracles are often called
signs, but he insists that they 'are always signs of the divine
intention which aims at the salvation of the world'.[4] They can be
understood only in this connection with the history of redemption. Christlieb sees the whole life of Christ as the supreme
miracle. 'The entire *history of miracles*', he adds, 'is grouped
around this central miracle, and stands in internal connection with
it, either as a prophecy or as an echo of that which is begun in Him.'[5]

A. B. Bruce likewise relates the miracles of the gospel to the
redemptive purpose of Christ. 'The simplest and most satisfactory view to take of these miracles,' he states, 'is to regard
them as the forthflowing of that love which, according to
prophetic oracles, was the chief Messianic charism.'[6] This view
may not indeed be obviously applicable to all the miracles. Bruce
specifies the nature-miracles in this connection, but he is
emphatic that the healing-miracles must be so understood. The
healing-miracles certainly indicate our Lord's concern for human
ills. But Christianity is more than a religion of Humanity: it is

[1] Theodore Christlieb, *Modern Doubt and Christian Belief*, 1874, p. 312.
[2] *Ibid.*, p. 312.　　　　　　　　[3] *Ibid.*, p. 314.
[4] *Ibid.*, p. 315.　　　　　　　　[5] *Ibid.*, p. 320.
[6] A. B. Bruce, *The Miraculous Element in the Gospels*, 1886, p. 258. Cf. 'Christ's
miraculous deeds were all useful, morally significant, beneficent works, rising
naturally out of His vocation as Saviour, performed in the course of His ministry
in the pursuit of His high calling, and just as naturally lying in His way, as
unmiraculous healings lie in the way of the ordinary physician'. A. B. Bruce, *The
Chief End of Revelation*, fifth edition, 1896, pp. 168–9. The whole chapter entitled,
'The Function of Miracle in Revelation' is important.

essentially a religion of Redemption. In this context the miracles are to be seen as 'parables' of Christ as the great spiritual Healer of man's sin-shattered and morally defeated lives. 'He healed their diseases that they might think of their sins and seek deliverance from them. In this point of view the whole healing ministry was one grand parable of Redemption. Jesus dealt with the physical effect, the evil of which all could appreciate, to advertise Himself as one prepared to deal with the spiritual cause, to the evil of which many were insensible. He healed disease with an unsparing hand that the presence of the Spiritual Physician might be the better known, and to proclaim a plenteous redemption.'[1]

In contrast, then, with those who had no useful place for miracles, this view brings them into the very heart of the divine purpose of God's revelation. Following writers, more aware perhaps of the difficulty which Hort saw in such an emphasis as early as 1859, continued to stress the connection between the miracles and redemption, but, at the same time, they seemed to be more ready to recognize their evidential value.[2] Thus, to take one later example, Marcus Dods insists that above all else miracles give expression to the mercy of God. 'What, then, was our Lord's purpose in performing miracles?' he asks. 'The answer is', he replies, 'He performed them not to convince people that He was the Messiah, the messenger and representative of God, but because He had that understanding of God's love and that perfect fellowship with God which made Him the Messiah. . . . But just because the primary purpose of the miracles was to give expression of God's mercy and not to prove our Lord's Messiahship, on this very account they can be appealed to as evidence that Jesus was the Messiah. The poet writes because he is a poet, and not for the purpose of convincing the world that he is a poet. And yet this writing does convince the world that he is a poet.'[3]

---

[1] A. B. Bruce, *The Miraculous Element in the Gospels*, 1886, p. 309.

[2] Cf. L. E. Elliott-Binns, *English Thought, 1860–1900*, 1956, p. 57.

[3] Marcus Dods, *The Bible: Its Origin and Nature*, 1905, pp. 225–7. Cf. 'There is no claim that Jesus Christ made, there is no truth that Jesus Christ taught that is not bound up with His signs. If we leave His signs out of sight, we must leave Him out of sight. . . . In short, we find not that miracles prove doctrine, but that *miracles are doctrine*'. A. A. Brockington, 'Miracles as Signs', *The Expository Times*, Vol. XVII, 1905–6, p. 495.

In reaction, then, from the earlier readiness to discard miracles, the later period was to see them as an integral part of the Christian revelation. The day when men professing allegiance to the Christian faith and saying at the same time in the blunt words of Matthew Arnold, 'miracles do not happen', had passed. Strauss had 'explained' miracles (away) as the legendary creations of a later generation. Renan in his *Life of Jesus* had maintained that they were thaumaturgical activities of Jesus into which He was occasionally forced by circumstances, but which He performed only after prayer, and with a sort of bad humour, and with a rebuke to those who demanded them on account of their carnal desires. The newer emphasis made much of the Redeemer and the miracles were related to His redemptive purpose.

There was one other question which arose in connection with our Lord's miracles which had interest and importance for Christology. The discussion centred on the way by which Christ performed His miracles. Had He resident within Himself a natural faculty of miracle-working power or was He by reason of His nearness to God the vehicle of a divine ἐξουσια και δυναμις? Many able writers took the view that the former position harmonizes best with a right understanding of Christ's Person. In this context the supreme miracle is Christ Himself; all His words and works are divine wonders. And what are termed miracles are outflashings of His divine Person. The whole of Christianity rests upon a supernatural basis and the gospel story unveils a supernatural Person, not only when what are called miracles are being wrought, but all the record through. Christianity is itself supernatural, it was urged. The question is, then, 'not about isolated "miracles", but about the whole conception of Christianity—what it is, and whether the supernatural does not enter into the very essence of it? It is the general question of a supernatural or non-supernatural conception of the universe. Is there a supernatural Being—God? Is there a supernatural government of the world? Is there a supernatural relation of God to man, so that God and man may have communion with one another? Is there a supernatural Revelation? Has that Revelation culminated in a supernatural Person—Christ? Is there a supernatural work in the souls of men? Is there a supernatural Reedmption? Is there a supernatural hereafter?

c

It is these larger questions that have to be settled first, and then the question of particular miracles will fall into its proper place'.[1]

Others, wishing to give due regard to the human conditions of our Lord's life on earth, maintained that life in its divine aspect was depotentiated by subjection to 'kenosis', and in its human aspect it was a life lived in dependence on and faith in God His Father. He, too, like those He is not ashamed to call His brethren, had to walk by faith. And the more assurance He received that He was the Father's Elect One, the more did His confidence of success in His beneficent ministry of love increase.

This kenosis view was given impetus by Charles Gore. Gore quite unhesitatingly asserted that Christ's knowledge was limited by its human conditions.[2] Consonant with this he maintained that 'His powerful works, no less than His humiliations, are in the Gospels attributed to His manhood'.[3] He is able to quote Wescott in support of his view. 'His greatest works' Wescott comments 'during His earthly life were wrought by the help of the Father through the energy of a humanity enabled to do all things in fellowship with God.'[4]

The human character of our Lord's miracles is one of special emphasis of recent years. Whether it is 'one particularly fruitful insight that has been gained in the modern world in the interpretation of the Gospel story', as D. M. Baillie suggests,[5] is something about which opinions will necessarily differ.

It is certainly true that the idea has come into special vogue in later years. Leonard Hodgson in a chapter on 'Miracles' has stated quite categorically that Christ performed His miracle-signs, not through any exercise of inherent divine energy, but by virtue of His perfect manhood. 'The miracles of Christ are worked through "faith". That "faith" was born of knowledge that certain things were necessary for Him to fulfil His mission.'[6]

---

[1] J. Orr, *The Christian View of God and the World*, Kerr Lectures, 1890–1, pp. 10–11.

[2] Cf. C. Gore, 'The Consciousness of Our Lord in His Moral Life' in *Dissertations on Subjects connected with the Incarnation*, 1895; cf. H. R. Mackintosh, *The Person of Christ*, second edition, reprint, 1937, p. 397 f.

[3] C. Gore, *Dissertations*, etc., p. 140 f.

[4] B. F. Wescott, *Epistle to the Hebrews*, 1889, 'Additional Notes on ii.10: The τελέωσις of Christ', p. 66.

[5] D. M. Baillie, *God Was In Christ*, 1947, p. 13.

[6] Leonard Hodgson, *And Was Made Man*, 1928, p. 140.

In an earlier passage he put his position with uncompromising clarity. We are to think, he says, 'of the powers exercised by Christ as being powers open to manhood where manhood is found in its perfection'.[1]

The same idea is advocated in challenging form by D. S. Cairns in his persuasive volume, *The Faith that Rebels*, which appeared in the same year—1928—as Hodgson's work. Cairns can accept neither the Modernist notion of miracles as 'anomalies' in a world subject to absolute uniformity,[2] nor the 'portent theory'[3] of the traditionalists. He cannot regard our Lord's miracles as signs of 'some inherent and unconditional Divine energy'. Having examined the miracles of Christ, he concludes, 'The Gospel theory of the "miracles" of Jesus is that they are the answers of God to the prayers of the Ideal Son, the Man who is the supreme instance, in history, of Faith, Hope, and Love; and they say with unambiguous plainness that the ideal Man invited His disciples to similar enterprises of faith, encouraging them to believe that in proportion to their faith would be the manifestation of God's order, the revelation of man's life as God meant it to be'.[4] That this is a suggestive and inspiring view none can doubt. And it will come as a rebuke to us men of little faith. Some will, however, feel that all has not been said here. To refer the miracles to Christ's humanity, perfect though it was, seems to admit to a Nestorian view of Christ's Person. What He did, He surely did as the One Christ; as the God-Man.

The point which can be emphasized following the discussions of the past years is that 'Christ and His works are all of a piece, and he who has apprehended Christ, or rather been apprehended by Him, will not seek to reduce the self-manifestation of the Saviour to the measure of humanity. . . . To prove the miracles one by one is as impossible as to disprove them in the same way, but they unite with the Person and the words of Jesus into one divine whole through which God reveals His very heart to man'.[5]

[1] Leonard Hodgson, *And Was Made Man*, 1928, p. 133.
[2] D. S. Cairns, *The Faith that Rebels*, 1928, p. 34.
[3] *Ibid.*, p. 73; cf. Chapter I, 'The Rival Theories of Miracles—Traditional and Modernist'.
[4] *Ibid.*, p. 85.
[5] James Denney, *Studies in Theology*, 1894, p. 208.

The ultimate fact, as far as we can see it, seems to be, that it is the one who has experienced a miracle who will be the more ready to believe in miracles.[1] What Hamann says is certainly cogent, 'Miracles cannot even be believed without a miracle'. He who has experienced in his own heart the power of Christ to forgive and redeem will have no doubt that miraculous power is the most certain of all things possessed by Him who was God manifested in the flesh.

B. THE REACTION OF IDEALISM

The history of ideas, whether religious or philosophical, it has been noted, is characterized by reaction. This fact, and the results which flow from it for the understanding of revelation in the previous period, have been investigated and illustrated in an earlier volume.[2] There the main oscillation was seen to be between what was termed the rational and the mystical. First there was emphasis upon reason with the consequence that the theology of the era was abstract. God was viewed as a mere transcendental Object whose existence had to be proved by discursive reasoning. But soon reaction set in[3] and a type of philosophical mysticism developed. God was sought, not above but below, not without but within. He was not detached from the human consciousness. God is the Eternal Spirit, occupying the innermost shrine of man's spirit to be discovered by an intuitive awareness. Emphasis is placed here upon the 'kinship' between God and man; upon the divinity of man and upon the humanity of God.[4]

The new era, in a broad sense, followed the same pattern, except that the rationalism with which it started tended towards agnosticism, whereas the rationalism of the old tended towards deism. The middle of the nineteenth century initiated the modern world view which at the beginning was essentially antisupernaturalistic. The religious reading of the world had given place to the scientific. A. M. Fairbairn points out the main feature of the new Weltanschauung. 'Its characteristic is Naturalism, the expulsion from thought, not merely of the supernatural, but of

[1] Cf. P. T. Forsyth, *The Principle of Authority*, 1913, second edition, 1952, p. 153.
[2] H. D. McDonald, *Ideas of Revelation*, 1959.
[3] Cf. C. C. J. Webb, *Problems in the Relation of God and Man*, 1911, pp. 69, 73.
[4] H. D. McDonald, *op. cit.*, pp. 14–15.

the ideal, of the transcendental and spiritual, and a return to a nature sensuously interpreted. This Naturalism is so marked as to constitute the differentiating element of our intellectual movement. The thought of the Christian centuries, even when it has been least Christian, has still been penetrated by the ideal and theistic elements. Theism has been, as it were, its common basis.'[1] Deism, it may be observed, although it moved away from Christ, did not discard God. By relieving Him of the care of the universe it doubtlessly gave Him little to do. Still God was necessary for thought, and the fact of His being an essential postulate to account for the beginning of the world.

Darwin's theory altered all this. The new account of the origins of human life and thought to which his researches had appeared to give scientific justification made naturalism seem to be the only apparent logical conclusion. It therefore became the fashion to declare, not simply as the deists had done, that there was no special revelation, but to assert doubt about any existing God and the possibility of any revelation at all. The progress of science, it was confidently asserted, had rendered all such belief invalid. Thus T. H. Huxley in his 'Lecture on the Physical Basis of Life' maintained that 'the extension of the province of what is called matter and causation' means 'the concomitant gradual banishment from the region of human thought of what is called spirit and spontaneity'.

As, however, the years of the second half of the nineteenth century passed, a change can be discerned in the theological and philosophical atmosphere. In the earlier period the reaction was broadly from naturalism to idealism in philosophy. And Philosophical idealism always tends towards mysticism in religion. 'The challenge of Darwinism', says Spinks, 'drove the churches into various theological camps. The High Churchman retired to a castle of transcendence-and-mysticism. The Broad Church party set out to rationalize the records of the Old Testament; and educated lay men, while not ceasing to regard themselves as Christian, ceased to regard themselves as members of organized churches. All this was in keeping with the general change in theology which went by the name of immanentism.'[2]

[1] A. M. Fairbairn, *Studies in Theology and Religion*, 1910, p. 80.
[2] G. S. Spinks with E. L. Allen and James Parkes, *Religion in Britain since 1900*, 1952, p. 20; cf. C. C. J. Webb, *Religion and the Thought of Today*, 1926, pp. 36 ff.

It is certainly clear that with the passing of the years the trend
towards naturalism which is usually connected with the laws of
physical evolution became less pronounced. It was becoming
evident to thoughtful and religiously inclined men that the moral
history of man could not be resolved into a natural history. In the
sphere of theology there was a new stress given to the idea of
the divine immanence. The half truth in Pantheism which the
orthodox apologists of the former period in their combat with
deism overlooked, was being given serious recognition. The
deistic habit of thought which made man's relation to the
universe external and artificial was being supplemented by a
more intimate connection of God with the world. It was this
change, as we have seen, which brought about the altered
attitude to the question of miracles in the scheme of divine
revelation. 'Darwinianism', declared Aubrey Moore, writing on
'The Christian Doctrine of God', 'under the guise of a foe, did
the work of a friend. It has conferred upon philosophy and
religion an inestimable benefit, by showing us that we choose
between two alternatives. Either God is everywhere present
in nature or He is nowhere. He cannot be here and not
here.'

Religious mysticism and philosophical idealism—the emotional and the rational side of the one approach to reality—are,
then, the characteristic features of the reaction to the earlier
naturalism. Mysticism, it is true, during the greater part of the
century had been suspect. The excesses of the Enthusiasts of the
previous period had not been forgotten.[1] Mysticism was, too,
regarded as hazy and dangerous. Indeed, as late as 1888, Aubrey
Moore is able to awaken caution by writing of 'the dangerous
haze of mysticism'.[2] The revived interest in mysticism owes
something to a renewed appreciation of the sense of wonder
which became evident in general literature which was itself a
part of the reaction from the naturalistic estimation of the world
in which all was explicable. It is of interest therefore to observe
that Watts-Dunton's novel, *Aylwin*, which did much to stimulate interest in mysticism generally, appeared in 1898 just a
year before Dean Inge delivered his famous Bampton Lectures
entitled *Christian Mysticism*.

[1] H. D. McDonald, *Ideas of Revelation*, 1959, Chapter IV.
[2] Aubrey Moore, *Science and the Faith*, 1888, p. 56.

The mysticism, however, which emerged at this period was characterized by a certain depth of understanding which brings it into favourable contrast with that of the previous age. 'A measure of reasonableness', observed G. P. Fisher, 'is conceded to the Mysticism which, in the past ages, in varied forms, has made much of the inward, living presence of God in the devout soul.'[1] Some evidence of this intelligent appreciation of mysticism may be seen in a number of volumes of permanent value which appeared around the same time. At the turn of the century George Tyrrell made an important contribution to the subject. In 1898 came his *Hard Sayings*, and in 1901 the two volumes entitled, *The Faith of the Millions*, which, according to von Hügel are 'full of insight into mysticism'.[2] Inge's *Studies in English Mystics* appeared in 1906 and Rufus Jones produced his suggestive *Studies in Mystical Religion* in 1909. In the same year von Hügel's profound work, *The Mystical Element of Religion*, was added to the list. In 1917–18 Inge gave the Gifford Lectures on *The Philosophy of Plotinus*. And in 1924 Franz Pfeiffer's edition of the works of Meister Eckhart were translated into English 'with some omissions and additions' by C. de B. Evans; a second edition of these two volumes was called for in 1947. Note, too, must be taken of Evelyn Underhill's several contributions, of which, *The Mystic Way* (1913), is, we consider, the most important.

There are two volumes, however, in which philosophic idealism, which is the other side of mysticism, is the more obviously exhibited. There is Robert Flint's work, *On Theological, Biblical and Other Subjects* (1905). Flint is opposed to Ritschl's expulsion of metaphysics from theology and of his criticism of mysticism. He insists upon the necessity of metaphysics and on the value for mysticism in religion. Flint acknowledges that mysticism has had its shortcomings, but he contends that 'it has often been of great service, and carries with it a large fund of truth, which the theologian of no period can afford to neglect'. Dean Inge, likewise, in his *Personal Idealism and Mysticism* (1907), speaks out against the Ritschlian school, especially as represented by Herrmann and Harnack. Flint had remarked that he was 'inclined to think that there has been too

[1] G. P. Fisher, *History of Christian Doctrine*, 1902, p. 545.
[2] F. von Hügel, *The Mystical Element in Religion*, 1909, Vol. I, Pref. p. xv.

much mysticism in the Catholic and too little in the Protestant Church' and with this verdict, however much some might be ready to question it, Inge was in the fullest sympathy.

Just a cursory reference needs to be made to the philosophic idealism of the period which expressed in rational form the mystical reaction from naturalism. The view derives from Hegel and may with equal propriety be called neo-Hegelianism. While J. H. Stirling's book, *The Secret of Hegel* may be taken as the starting point of the new Idealistic movement in British thought, John Caird may be singled out as giving the most effective emphasis to the idealistic view. 'The religious aspect of neo-Hegelianism is nowhere presented with more lucidity and more attractively than in the pages of the eminent theologian John Caird.'[1] It is a question whether Caird's doctrine is essentially pantheistic. W. Preston Warren in his *Pantheism in Neo-Hegelian Thought* (1933) quotes extensively from his works and concludes that he is correctly to be described as a pantheist. At any rate, there is, we think, no doubt about John Caird's idealism. His brother Edward states that 'Christianity and Idealism were the two poles of my brother's thinking, and the latter seemed to him the necessary means for interpreting the former'. In his Memoir prefixed to John's Gifford Lectures, Edward, however, notes that there are respects in which certain of Hegel's ideas are repudiated. He observes that Hegel is seldom quoted, but he still grants that his brother was profoundly influenced by him. Passing beyond, what appeared to him to be the limitation of Kant's epistemology, Edward Caird goes on to remark that his brother's 'thought turned more and more to the Hegelian development of this principle and its application to theology. He was interested in Hegel mainly for two reasons: first, by the thoroughness with which he carries out the idealistic principle, and, secondly, by the strong grasp of ethical and religious experience which is perhaps Hegel's greatest characteristic'.[2] He adds later, 'He was drawn to Hegel, therefore, most of all, because he seemed to find at the basis of all Hegel's speculation a close and living perception of the facts of the moral and religious life'.[3] John Caird was then one of the

---

[1] Hiralal Halder, *Neo-Hegelianism*, 1927, p. 135.
[2] John Caird, *The Fundamental Ideas of Christianity*, 1899, Vol. I, p. lxxiv.
[3] *Ibid.*, p. lxxv.

most eloquent advocates of a sort of spiritual idealism which was characteristic of the period and which regarded revelation in terms of the apprehension of the divine immanence. His brother Edward in his own Gifford Lectures on *The Evolution of Religion* (1893) gives weighty exposition to the same fundamental view: 'the unity of God and man' and 'the self-revelation of God in humanity'. Yet while it is true that there is no simple identification of God with the world in this type of idealism—the stress was upon immanence and manifestation—there were others like Bradley in his *Appearance and Reality* (1893) who has a world of ideas without God.

Without continuing further we may note something of the strength of the movement by a remark of Quiller-Couch concerning its chief centre, Oxford. 'The young tenants of the Home of Movements, turning from Mill and Mansel to Kant and Hegel, pursued the evasive Absolute far into the night.' On the other hand something of the popular preaching of the pantheistic outcome of the idea can be seen in R. J. Campbell's *New Theology*, in which we have, as has been stated, immanentism 'run mad'.

C. THE PROTEST FROM PLURALISM

Pluralism is a distinctive philosophical doctrine which stands in opposition to every 'block-universe' theory whether materialistic or idealistic. In pluralism the claims of the Many are upheld against that of the One. 'Pluralism', says William James, 'lets things exist in the each-form or distributively. Monism thinks that the all-form or collective-unity form is the only form that is rational.'[1] The idea is, of course, not an altogether new one. Throughout the history of philosophy there have been occasions, when under one label or another, the reality of the particular has been maintained against the tyranny of the One. This may be seen in the case of the mediaeval nominalists such as Duns Scotus and William of Occam, who against the realistic philosophy of the scholastic Churchmen generally, sought to emphasize that particular things are real.

The classical type, as well as the fountain-head of modern pluralism is, however, Leibniz, whose *Monadology* is a vigorous

[1] William James, *A Pluralistic Universe*, edition, 1916, p. 324.

repudiation of Spinoza's monism. Leibniz, it is worth noting, did not regard particulars as having independent existences. All simple existing substances are ultimately derived from the one supreme and necessary substance, the ultimate Monad. Unlike the modern advocates of pluralism, Leibniz does not regard God as merely *primus inter pares*. It is characteristic of the pluralism of more recent times that in stressing the autonomy and freedom of finite centres of existence it has found it necessary to limit God by the existence of such beings. There have therefore been a number of writers, who in their effort to safeguard the existence of particulars, have advocated the idea of a finite God. God is regarded, in William James's famous phrase as 'one of the eaches'. A popular statement of the idea of a finite God can be found in H. G. Wells's *God the Invisible King*;[1] while a more religious exposition of the view, if the term 'religious' is not too narrowly defined, is that found in Henry Jones's *A Faith that Enquires*.

More to the point of our study is the fact that pluralism came into vogue towards the end of the nineteenth century in conscious opposition to the prevailing idealism of F. H. Bradley, Bernard Bosanquet and especially that of T. H. Green.[2] The most consistent exponent of the doctrine was the American philosopher G. H. Howison (1834–1916). He was 'impressed by the danger which monism threatens to the integrity of ethical freedom, and it is to save these that he sets out to develop, on a Kantian basis, an idealistic pluralism'.[3] He sees a 'universal world of Spirits, every one of whom is free—that is, independently self-active, self-moved from within and none operated either directly or indirectly from without by any other'. He speaks of an 'Eternal Republic', and declares that God is One among the Many. 'He is if they are, they are if He is; but the relation is freely mutual, and He only exists as *primus inter pares*, in a circle eternal and indissoluble.'[4]

William James gained a public for the pluralistic philosophy in his Hibbert Lectures of 1909. He rejects the 'all-form' of

[1] Cf. 'The Doctrine of a Finite God in War-time', R. H. Dotterer, *Hibbert Journal*, Vol. XVI, No. 3, April 1918, p. 428; also *Pluralism and the Problems of Religion*, New York, 1915.

[2] Cf. William James, *op. cit.*, p. 6 f.

[3] A. K. Rogers, *British and American Philosophy since 1800*, 1923, p. 303.

[4] G. H. Howison, *The Limits of Evolution*, 1901, pp. 328–9.

absolutism and contends for the 'each-form', a distributive form of reality, as 'logically as acceptable and empirically as probable'.[1]

The influence of pluralism was many-sided. In politics it manifested itself in the form of a sturdy individualism. In the field of practical ethics it tended to humanism. The human individual, the reality of which was assured by pluralism, became the centre of the picture. Thus W. K. Clifford, influenced by the conclusion to be drawn from evolution that man had made a great move forward and was, indeed, being made the measure of all things, writes in the closing section of his work, *Cosmic Emotion:* 'Those who can read the signs of the times read in them that the kingdom of Man has come.'

One important aspect of pluralism was the regard it created for the real individual. It is interesting to observe how in this period what is known as Personalism came to the fore. Personalism may be defined as the psychological counterpart of pluralism. More particularly, personalism gave focus to the single individual as a moral and spiritual entity. The beginning of this emphasis can be seen already in a work by John Grote who held the chair of moral philosophy at Cambridge from 1855 to 1866. Personalism is anticipated in his volume, *A Treatise on the Moral Ideals* (1876).

It is, however, to Hermann Lotze that we can trace the first of the creative influences in the direction of a spiritual personalism. He began a reaction from the prevailing Hegelian idealism in which man's personality was lost in a devouring Whole. T. H. Green, in fact, testifies to the influence of Lotze, who, he says, made him dissatisfied with Hegel. The important place he gave to the idea of the Divine Personality rescued Haldane from the materialism to which he had turned after the abandonment of his early faith.[2]

It is through his huge work, *Microcosmos,* which was translated into English in 1887, that his ideas became known. As far as we are concerned, his teaching can be best summed up in a few words from his work on the *Philosophy of Religion.* His message is that ' "self-consciousness" is a spiritual phenomenon'.[3]

---

[1] William James, *op. cit.,* p. 34.

[2] Cf. L. E. Elliott-Binns, *English Thought, 1860–1900,* 1956, p. 69; see Hastings Rashdall's remark on Lotze, in *Contentio Veritatis,* 1902, p. 43.

[3] Hermann Lotze, *Philosophy of Religion,* trans. G. T. Ladd, 1887, p. 55 f.

Lotze has, of course, much to say about the ultimate unity of all in God, but he insists upon the reality of the individual. It is true that throughout his works 'there is an opposition to idealism, yet a rejection of materialism; the reality of the individual is asserted, yet the unity of all in the universal spirit is maintained'.[1] A. E. Garvie notes the inconsistency in his teaching concerning the basic unity and adds, 'To very many he will seem rather to emphasize individuality at the expense of unity. He does not care at all for the immanent development of the Absolute Idea; his enthusiasm he reserves for the beatitude of finite spirits. To him the world-aim is not the progressive realization of an ideal rational or ethical, but the self-realization of personal existences'.[2]

This was the point to be emphasized in different ways by a number of personal idealists, such as the brothers, Andrew Seth Pringle-Pattison and John Seth, W. R. Sorley and Hastings Rashdall, and by Theistic philosophers of religion such as James Ward, C. C. J. Webb, A. E. Taylor and William Temple.

All these writers, it may be said, reserved their enthusiasm 'for the beatitude of finite spirits'. A. S. Pringle-Pattison's successive works show a gradual movement away from Hegel. In his *Hegelianism and Personality* (1887) and his later *Man's Place in the Cosmos and Other Essays* (1887), this growing dissatisfaction may be noted. W. R. Sorley, especially in his Gifford Lectures of 1914–15, stresses the factuality of the individual whom he regards supremely as a bearer of value. It is in this way, indeed, that he argues for the objectivity of value. 'It is therefore in the existent, the individual, that value is found, not in the general or universal. Now the individual is always unique. . . . As value belongs to the existent or individual, and as the individual is unique, we tend to think of uniqueness as essential to value.'[3]

James Ward refuses the term pluralism as descriptive of his position because he was emphatic upon the need for an ultimate One as the ground of the Many. Pluralism, he observes, 'assumes that the whole world is made up of individuals, each

---

[1] A. E. Garvie, 'Hermann Lotze', *The Expository Times*, Vol. IV, 1892–3, p. 540.
[2] *Ibid.*, p. 541.
[3] W. R. Sorley, *Moral Value and the Idea of God*, 1918, third edition, 1935, p. 113.

distinguished by its characteristic behaviour'.[1] And it further assumes, he states later, 'that there exists an indefinite variety of selves, some indefinitely higher, some indefinitely lower than ourselves. But even the highest, if there be a highest, will, it is assumed, be only *primus inter pares*, one among the many, and not an absolute reality including them all'.[2] It may be said to be Ward's purpose to retain the first characteristic of pluralism, that the world is made up of separate individuals, and to deny the second, that there is no absolute unity to include them all. He maintains that there is need of the One as the ultimate source and the ultimate end of the Many. His final position is, then, a pluralism supplemented by Theism. But Ward does not rob the individual of having independent worth.

Another effort to do justice to the free, moral and independent reality of personality from several points of view can be found in the volume, *Personal Idealism* (1902) to which a number of Oxford men contributed. Here is to be found, brought together in one work all pointing to the same conclusion, the voluntaristic psychology of G. F. Stout, the Berkeleian theism of Hastings Rashdall, the Pragmatism of F. C. S. Schiller, and H. Sturt, and the spiritualistic idealism of Boyce Gibson, who translated and made popular the ideas of Rudolf Euchen.[3]

The question may be asked, What bearing had these ideas on the understanding of revelation? In all its forms and phases it gave emphasis to the inward aspect. It accentuated the subjective appreciation of revelation. More particularly in personalism, in which man is seen as a spiritual entity, it was to give point to the idea of man's religious development, to the growth of his religious consciousness and its advancing discovery of divine truths. As a consequence there was a tendency to regard the great prophets as supremely outstanding examples of religious geniuses, pioneers in the realm of the spiritual. While, in regard to the subject of Biblical inspiration, place was given to the human bearers of revelation. The human, it was argued, was not to be overridden in the interests of the divine. The emphasis upon the freedom of the human spirit was thought by some indeed to reinforce the growing denial of Biblical inerrancy, since, it was urged, to preserve the writers from all error would

---

[1] James Ward, *The Realm of Ends*, 1911, third edition, 1920, p. 51.   [2] *Ibid.*, p. 52.
[3] Cf. C. A. Richardson, *Spiritual Pluralism and Recent Philosophy*, 1919.

be inconsistent with man's true nature as a free being. The human errors in the Bible, of course, it was allowed, were no rejection of its essential message, which, too, was often regarded from man's point of view, as teaching the intrinsic value of every individual.

Along with pluralism there went empiricism. And in the realm of religion this was to turn attention to religious experience. The psychological approach to religion became, therefore, a olive issue. Important, in this context, are the Gifford Lectures of 1901–2 by William James, *The Varieties of Religious Experience.* 'His arguments reinforced the current tendency to look for guidance in religion less to authority and more to experience. . . . Increasingly the Bible was read as the record of a growing religious experience and Christian doctrine was assessed, as by Schleiermacher, in accordance with its reflection in the "religious consciousness".'[1]

The result of all this was clearly seen in the state of affairs which could be observed in the religious situation. The foundation of faith was changed from that of dogmatic inspiration to that of current experience. Theology was placed at the mercy of psychology with rather precarious consequences. Belief was, in fact, put under the authority of the laws of thought and incurred the bane of an alarming subjectivism: or, more tragic still, it was sometimes debased by an unhealthy preoccupation with inner states and sympathies, processes and problems, and lost vital contact with that reality behind and beyond these and the authority over them.

D. THE INFLUENCE OF HISTORICISM

The opening years of the nineteenth century witnessed a remarkable revival of the historical spirit. It is, indeed, in its appreciation of historicism that we have its distinctive feature. Looking back over the years of the nineteenth century, V. F. Storr contends that it is in its feeling for history that we have 'the most marked characteristic of the intellectual development of the last hundred years'.[2] The previous age, by contrast, had no real

---

[1] G. S. Spinks with E. L. Allen and James Parkes, *Religion in Britain since 1900*, 1952, pp. 52–3.

[2] H. V. Storr, *Development of English Theology in the Nineteenth Century*, 1913, p. 1; cf. his *Development and Divine Purpose*, 1906, pp. 210 ff.

or clear understanding of history. Continuing the Enlightenment's repudiation of the historical in the interests of the rational
the writers of the eighteenth century showed a complete
indifference to its significance. 'The ideas then prevalent of an
ideal primitive society and of a social contract which was the
result of deliberate action, were "the negation of history".'[1]
History was conceived of as static. That age, according to Leslie
Stephen, failed through lack of historical imagination.[2] And its
apologists were able to keep apart in their thought a natural and
a supernatural view of the world by simply separating them in
time. 'They combined, that is', Stephen says, 'Hume's view of
the eighteenth century with Wesley's view of the first.'[3]

Attention has been given elsewhere to some of the influences
which shaped the direction of historicism in the period prior to
1860. A reference was made to the importance of Leibniz who
expounded the idea of continuity in his doctrine of the gradua-
tion of the monads, as well as stressing, at the same time, the
conception of connection and union, albeit in an artificial manner,
in his principle of pre-existing harmony. Lessing, taking these
fundamental principles, saw in them the key to the understanding of history. In this way, it is said, he brought about 'a
deeper sense of the meaning of the historical'.[4]

After the middle of the nineteenth century the revived
historical spirit wedded itself to the idea of evolution. As a result
it became the fashion to seek an explanation of all things in
heaven and on earth, in theology no less than in biology, by the
application of the historical method. Historicism, in fact,
became a sort of magic wand by which, at last, the riddle of the
universe was about to be solved.

History and development were conceived to be synonymous
terms, and, it was supposed, to trace out development was to
state history. In this way mystery was expunged and the truth
laid bare. So it was thought; but it was wrongly thought. L. E.
Elliott-Binns points out that 'The new scientific influence,
however, was not without its drawbacks, for it led to the

---

[1] L. E. Elliott-Binns, *Religion in the Victorian Era*, 1936, second edition, 1946,
p. 172.

[2] Leslie Stephen, *History of English Thought in the Eighteenth Century*, second
edition, 1881, Vol. I, p. 192; cf. p. 378.

[3] *Op. cit.*, Vol. II, pp. 414–5.

[4] A. K. Rogers, *A Students' History of Philosophy*, new revised edition, p. 410.

extension of the idea of "evolution" to departments of knowledge
to which strictly speaking it did not apply. The crude transference
of the hypothesis to the conduct of human affairs, for example,
did much harm, for "evolution" in history is a very different thing
from "evolution" in Nature, since the human element takes a
conscious part, exhibiting will and purpose. Furthermore, the
notion began to prevail that to have traced out the development
of an idea or an institution was fully to have accounted for it'.[1]

For the first part of the story, it may be noted that
immediately after Darwin, historicism, uniting with the doctrine
of biological evolutionism, gave the notion of a mechanical
development of all life and thought. Haeckel regarded the
'scientific' right to account for life by a purely mechanical process
as 'the inestimable value' of Darwin's contribution. Historical
occurrences, it was urged, were to be explained as the product of
natural laws. The creative causes of all such events must be
sought in man's physical environment. As a consequence history
was said to be based on anthropogeography. Several writers
looked to the social environment as providing the answer to the
riddle of existence. While Spencer, Comte and writers of like
mind, developed the notion of society as itself a sort of higher
organism, which, like other living things, is subject to biological
laws and will eventually come to perfection in the struggle for
existence by natural selection and heredity.

Not for long, however, did the view that all existences are the
result of the operation of natural laws survive. There was too
much missing from the account. 'Evolution in its Darwinian
form—the only form ever heard of by many—has been used as
the foundation of a materialism which does not, like the old law
of gravitation, require even the Great Mathematician. It
manages everything by the ingenious process of spreading
sufficiently small changes over sufficiently long time. This way
of begging the cause piecemeal of so vast and wonderful a
phenomenon as the world grows less and less convincing,
especially as it cannot move a step without admitting a goal
regarding every detail as directed towards it.'[2]

Under the pitiless assaults of James Ward, *Naturalism and
Agnosticism*, Frazer, *Philosophy of Theism* and Kennedy, *Natural*

[1] L. E. Elliott-Binns, *English Thought, 1860–1900*, 1956, p. 93.
[2] John Oman, *The Problems of Faith and Freedom*, 1906, pp. 199–200.

Theology and Modern Thought, the materialistic tendency of historicism, in the immediate post-Darwinian period, was vastly weakened.

The fact is that it was not from the notion of biological evolution 'but from the less ostentatious advances in the field of history that faith received its greatest blow'.[1] It was, indeed, the strong historical sense which developed throughout the earlier period which formed the climate of opinion in which the idea of biological evolution was but a natural result.

As time went on, historicism was wooed by idealism. Materialism weakened by the attacks made upon it was compelled to accept the divorce. This marriage of the historic spirit with idealism was given philosophical dress by Hegel. History was exalted by the union. It was no longer conceived to be a mere chronicle of successive events, but as C. C. J. Webb puts it, as 'the actual unfolding of the nature of mind or spirit'.[2] In such a context, revelation ceased to be regarded as something coming from without, but as the progressive unfolding of the immanent principle of divine life.

But apart from the results deriving from historicism in its union, first with materialism, and then with idealism, it had significant consequences on its own account. It gave strength to a tendency and vogue to a method.

The idea of evolution produced an interest in the study of comparative religion which was to become a characteristic feature of the second half of the nineteenth century.[3] The new awareness of history inspired a desire to trace the growth and development of religion from its early beginnings in animism, or magic, or ancestor worship, or whatever idea appeared the most reasonable to the individual writer. This tracing out of the gradual evolution of religion is considered by F. S. Marvin to be 'among the greatest of the conquests of the nineteenth century'.[4] Hastings Rashdall insists that 'To underestimate the importance of the great historical Religions and their creators has been the besetting sin of technical religious Philosophy'.[5]

[1] W. B. Glover, *Evangelical Nonconformity and the Higher Criticism in the Nineteenth Century*, 1954, p. 13.
[2] C. C. J. Webb, *History of Philosophy*, 1915, p. 224 f.
[3] Cf. S. A. Cook in the *Encylopædia of Religion and Ethics*, Vol. X, pp. 664 ff.
[4] Quoted in *The Century of Progress*, F. S. Marvin, 1919, p. 217.
[5] Hastings Rashdall, *Philosophy and Religion*, 1909, p. 149.

By this study of comparative religion, it was claimed, a clearer conception was to be gained of the phenomenon of religion. It was seen to be a necessity of human life; whether instinctive or acquired, was not, however, quite clear. In a variety of forms it manifested itself, but shows throughout a gradual, and virtually a straight-line development from its early beginnings.

The particular interest was in the study of origins. A vast literature dealing with such titles as the Origin, the Growth, the Evolution of Religion appeared. But besides this interest in religion generally there was particular account given of special religions. Direction was given to this phase of the study by Robertson Smith in his work, *The Religion of the Semites*, and it was he, we are told, who 'opened out a new field of research or rather he opened it out in a new manner'.[1]

This attention to the study of comparative religion caused much disquiet. Rashdall might assure that 'because we recognize a measure of truth in all the historical Religions, it does not follow that we can recognize an equal amount of truth in them all'.[2] Elliott-Binns contends that had the 'ultra-orthodox souls' as he calls them, 'been better acquainted with the Logos theology they might have been saved from much needless heart-burning'.[3] But there were those who were acquainted with the Logos doctrine, and with the use made of it by F. D. Maurice in his Boyle Lectures of 1846 in his discourses on *The Religions of the World*, who felt that there was something suspicious about the result brought about by the application of the historical method to religion.

Questions began to arise in the hearts of not a few who were concerned with Christian faith and the mission of the Church. Was Christianity to be regarded, after all, merely as a special expression of man's religious spirit? Was it the latest phase in the evolutionary process and perhaps not therefore the last and the best? Point was given to these doubts by the outspoken scepticism of a number of critical writers on comparative religion. Advocates might protest that by such study a clearer view of the element of divine revelation in these other religions

[1] W. Robertson Smith, *The Religion of the Semites*, 1907, third edition, Pref. p. xxix.
[2] Hastings Rashdall, *Philosophy and Religion*, 1909, p. 149.
[3] L. E. Elliott-Binns, *English Thought, 1860–1900*, 1956, p. 208.

can be discovered, and thereby the superior revelation in Christianity could be seen. But so long as the study was continued in the context of the historical method with its essentially critical and apparently destructive spirit doubts could not but persist. Fears could not be allayed so easily since historicists seemed to be attempting to 'gather apologetic figs from sceptical thistles' as Harnack once charged Friedrich Loofs about the latter's somewhat analogous endeavours in theology.[1]

Time revealed that it had to be made clear and certain that the unique in Christianity is not the mere greater clarity of ideas obscure in other religions. Christianity is not just the best of a class. It is what it is, not by its *continuum* with other religions, but by its *peculium.* It confronts other creeds; it does not prolong them. Its distinctiveness lies not in what it shares with other beliefs but in how it separates from them. 'It is not under the control of natural religion, of general spiritual truths enacted in some parliament of religions. Such rationalism is the worst Erastianism. Christianity is not the dominant partner in the world's religion, the *doyen* of equal faiths.'[2] The fact is as R. E. Speer has remarked, 'Calvary closes the issue of comparative religion'.[3]

Not only did the feeling for history give strength to a tendency but it also gave vogue to a method. The historical method became one of the major factors in the theological reconstructions of the period.

The feeling for history was a very real thing during the later years of the nineteenth century. Interest was taken in the subject for its own sake and a serious attempt was made to discover the actual happenings of the past. Impetus was given to the movement by the establishment in 1866 of *The English Historical Review* with Creighton as editor. Some years later Lord Acton, who in 1895 succeeded Seeley as Regius Professor of Modern

[1] Quoted D. M. Baillie, *God Was In Christ*, 1947, p. 23; cf. F. Loofs, *What is the Truth about Jesus Christ?* 1913, p. 122.

[2] P. T. Forsyth, *The Principle of Authority*, 1913, second edition, 1952, p. 77.

[3] Cf. 'Christianity holds no brief whatever for false gods. The modern vague idea, which has even infected a good deal of our missionary work, that there is much truth in all religions and that the task is to bring out and strengthen this indigenous approach to God rather than preach the gospel of Jesus Christ, is no part of the authentic Christian tradition'. L. W. Grensted, *Psychology and God*, 1930, p. 60.

History at Cambridge, was responsible for planning the *Cambridge Modern History* series.

It was characteristic of the new school of historians to pay attention to facts. And in thus following the dictum of Ranke there was a tendency to concentrate on the study of details. The older school of historians were considered to have been deficient in critical ability and consequently permitted to pass for facts what an enlightened scrutiny would have shown to have been fancy. They were unable to distinguish what was genuine from what was fiction: and they could not observe the later accretions which like rust on iron had gathered round the original event. The new school, by contrast, set out to expose all that was fictitious. They thus subjected past statements, stories and statistics to a serious scrutiny. Much that was hitherto accepted without question was, as a result, cast aside as worthless. In the eyes of those who regarded such a method as an iconoclastic excess the whole procedure appeared to be destructive.

Criticism which expressed itself in minute analysis and showed itself ready to cast aside much which the earlier age had taken as fact may, then, be regarded as the chief characteristic of the historical method. Storr who lived through some of this period of changing outlook well remarked, 'The Spirit of the age is pre-eminently historical; and because it is that, it is also critical'.[1]

The application of the historical method to the Old Testament was immediate and was, at first, used as a synonym for the 'Higher Criticism'. The conflict which ensued will concern us in the following chapters, but, as was inevitable, it was not possible for the method to be restricted to the Old Testament. By the turn of the century the New Testament was also set in the context of historical development. Quest was made for 'the Jesus of History'. The result was the 'Liberal Protestant' reconstruction in which the Gospel Figure was said to have been rescued from the debris of dogma under which the later Church had submerged Him. The Jesus, coloured and characterized by an excess of enthusiasm, was set forth, recaptured from the traditions of Church and creed. We need not refer here to the many 'reconstructions' which were presented for acceptance, some dull, some daring, and some dangerous, as they were.

[1] V. F. Storr, *Development and Divine Purpose*, 1906, p. 211.

A general account of the result of the application of the historical method, however, is required since it will be helpful in understanding the more recent position. To begin with, emphasis was put upon the teaching of Jesus and the impression He made upon His first disciples. He is to be seen supremely as One who rose out of humanity and who is Himself a great and good human. It was Paul who inserted into the story the leaven of the Pharisee, and became the arch-corruptor of the Gospel of Jesus. Then, too, confusion was worse confounded, when the Gnostic poison, which seduced even St John, got wedded to the story of the Peasant of Galilee. Historicism was recovering the truth and presenting us with the significance of Jesus by providing us with the 'clue' to the history. It has rescued from the confusion and misfortune His real message which can be found amidst the rudiments of St Mark's Gospel, and which has its formal statement in the Epistle of James. The rest of the New Testament can be written off as a speculative excrescent and a blind-alley for the true purpose of Christ. In such a reconstruction Harnack was to take the lead. But, as George Tyrrell remarks, 'The Christ that Harnack sees looking back through nineteen centuries of Catholic darkness, is only the reflection of a Liberal Protestant face, seen at the bottom of a deep well'.[1]

It was not, however, so easy to scrap the rest of the New Testament. The less the historical method was vitiated by presuppositions the more difficult it became to write off what remained outside a 'reduced' gospel, as of no account.

So a compromise must be found, which it was hoped would satisfy all who have a regard for Jesus. Two types of Christianity are then stated to exist side by side in the primitive Church. Some there are who followed Christ and others who worshipped Him. Those who have a care for the facts of history, it was maintained, will consider Jesus as the first Christian, and will seek to imitate Him. Others there were, and these for the most part those who were healed and helped by Him, who worshipped Him. This is an understandable extravagance, to which later the great-hearted Paul sought to give theological justification. Those who belong to the imitation school claim to stand so close to the sound realism of the simple truth that they can afford to be tolerant of those who worship Christ as God. The hope was

[1] George Tyrrell, *Christianity at the Cross-roads*, 1909, p. 44.

expressed that both sides should live together in the same Church, with equal rights, common charity and mutual respect. Although the historical method has made the Christ of the Epistles a mere creation of the Church's faith there is no reason to rob the simple believer of the consolation and comfort which the creation gives. After all, if it has value to him and if it works, what more need be said?

This tendency to admit such a value in the Christ of faith was important. It reinforced the growing suspicion concerning the validity of the results of the application of the historical method which was producing so many conflicting and competing Figures all claiming to be the real 'Jesus of History'. Besides, the whole idea of 'history' was itself under review. There began to appear a crop of volumes claiming to present its 'meaning', or to give its 'clue', or to indicate its 'significance', and so forth. There was, in fact, a repudiation of historicism. That the movement did give full justice to the essential humanity of Jesus is to be granted as its permanent good result. But its total rejection of the Christ of faith as essential to the authentic gospel was both false and fatal. It was bound not to survive. 'Theological thought', rightly observes D. M. Baillie, 'has largely left behind the movement which we symbolize by the phrase "the Jesus of history".'[1] The modern reconstruction which can say *with* it, 'No more docetism', can say *against* it, 'No more historicism'.

E. THE CATEGORY OF GESCHICHTE

'No more historicism', such has become the modern cry for many. Herein lies the contrast between the older liberalism and the new modernism, or, as some would prefer to call it, the 'neo-orthodox' position.[2] 'Neo-orthodoxy', contends W. M. Morton, 'differs from scholastic and fundamentalistic conservatism in its free and symbolic use of the Bible, and its impressionistic interpretation of orthodox doctrines; from radical Protestantism in its profound distrust of natural science and natural theology as possible paths to deliverance; from liberal Protestantism, in

[1] D. M. Baillie, *God Was In Christ*, 1947, p. 9.
[2] Cf. E. J. Carnell, *The Theology of Reinhold Niebuhr*, revised edition, 1960, Chapter I.

its sharp opposition to every theology based on human experience, even if the experience be "religious" and "Christian".[1]

The main emphasis of this new theological reconstruction is the place it gives to the Christ of Faith and its disregard for the Jesus of History. The Jesus of history has little or no significance, it is claimed, since Christian faith does not rise out of any appreciation of the historic Jesus. The Jesus of history has, indeed, relatively no importance: what really matters is the interpreted Jesus, the Christ of faith. It will be seen, then, how opposed and opposite, are the two views, the Jesus-of-History cult and what we may call the newer 'Geschichte' cult.

With the Dialectical theologians, for the most part Continentals, and, therefore, less compromising than the British, the pendulum swing has gone its full length. The repudiation of the 'historical Jesus' is complete.

In this country, years before the appearance of Barth and Brunner, one of its greatest theological thinkers, said many of the corrective things that they have been saying of recent years, but, at the same time avoiding the exaggerations which weaken their position. Barth has given us to understand that he knew nothing of P. T. Forsyth's work before he had developed his own ideas. But Forsyth had made many of the points which are now stated to be characteristic of the Dialectical theology.

Those acquainted with the special stresses of the Crisis theologians will recognize at once the parallels in the thought. Forsyth insists upon the 'otherness' of God in a manner characteristic of Barth. 'God is God by His difference, even more than by His unity with us', he says.[2] Forsyth's whole theology is built upon this fact: and it was a position more difficult for Forsyth to defend, living in the period when there was emphasis put upon the idea of monistic continuity and affinity, than for Barth. Forsyth's world was not congenial to such a doctrine. Forsyth, too, makes much of the point that faith is not natural to the natural man. In the divine–human encounter it is created. 'The Gospel must *create* the power to believe it' he says in almost 'Barthian' language. 'Revelation here is so radical that in the

[1] W. M. Horton, *Christian Theology: An Ecumenical Approach*, 1955, first British edition, 1956, p. 32.

[2] P. T. Forsyth, *The Principle of Authority*, 1913, second edition, 1952, p. 151.

same act there must be Regeneration. The calling voice of a holy
God to us sinners is such a judging, crushing voice that it
becomes effectual only as a new-creating word.'[1] Such parallels
and echoes as these could be multiplied, but it is not our
particular interest to find them.

With reference to our special subject we are to note that in
contrast with the earlier view which repudiates the Christ of
faith in the interests of the Jesus of history, and the recent view
which repudiates the Jesus of history in the interests of the
Christ of faith, can be placed Forsyth who seeks to do justice to
both.

(a) Forsyth's 'Geschichte' view a necessity for the full reality of
revelation in Christ. In an important passage Forsyth discusses
(as indeed Barth does later) the meaning of Lessing's famous
dictum: 'The accidental truths of history can never become proof
for the necessary truths of reason.' To get at Lessing's 'real
meaning', Forsyth draws a distinction 'between history in the
great sense and history in the small, between history as a tissue
of great ideas and powers and history as a mass of empirical
events, between history as divined and history as proved'.[2] To
designate these two types of history, Forsyth uses two German
words which Wobbermin had already applied with the same
effect. There is Geschichte and there is Historie. 'Historie is
history as it may be settled by the methods of historical science,
where our results, like those of all science, are but relative, and
either highly or poorly probable. Geschichte on the other hand
is a larger thing, out of which Historie has to sift, but which may
embody or convey ideas greater than the critical residuum
retains power to express.'[3]

How Forsyth applies this distinction to Lessing's dictum we
need not pause to indicate. But what it is important to observe
is that Forsyth will not discard Historie for the sake of
Geschichte nor will he allow that Geschichte can be ultimately
divorced from Historie. The revelation was not complete in the
historical Jesus. It had to be continued and completed in the
apostolic word. 'The apostolic interpretation is an integral part
of the revelationary fact, process, and purpose, a real, though

---

[1] P. T. Forsyth, The Principle of Authority, 1913, second edition, 1952, p. 119.
[2] Ibid., p. 112; cf. K. Barth, Church Dogmatics, I, i, p. 166, iii, pp. 112–13.
[3] Ibid., pp. 112–13.

posthumous, part of Christ's own continued teaching.'[1] It is in the Jesus of *Historie* and the Christ of *Geschichte* that we have the full disclosure of God; not in the one as against the other, but in the one as permeated by and as necessary to the other. Revelation 'is not simply the critical residue of the Synoptics, but their totality—the whole apostolic burthen of the New Testament, pervading the Synoptics themselves. The only fact ever offered by the Church is the total New Testament fact, where the synoptic figure of the Lord is self-interpreted by the same Lord acting as the Spirit. The New Testament revelation is the person of Christ in its whole and universal action, and not the character of Christ in its biographical aspect'.[2] Forsyth points out that the criticism which has abolished the apostolic interpretation has gone on to abolish Christ's historic reality.[3] Evidence of this fact was abundant all around him in the variety of contemporary 'Lives of Jesus', all claiming to portray the Jesus of History. But Forsyth will not permit the synoptic facts to be torn away nor the apostolic interpretation to be discarded. 'We have no access to the fact but through them. If they are final for the historic fact, they are no less final for its central interpretation.'[4]

Forsyth's final position can, then, best be put in one significant sentence: 'The great fact' he urges 'is the historic phenomenon, Jesus, *plus* its "meta-historic" Word'.[5] Forsyth, therefore, so to speak, puts *Historie* and *Geschichte* side by side, and maintains that they belong together in the totality of revelation. With the 'Barthians' it is otherwise.

(b) With the Crisis theologians the category Geschichte is used for the repudiation of the historical Jesus. In contrast with Forsyth their position might be stated as seeking the locale of revelation in the 'meta-historical' Word *minus* the historical phenomenon, Jesus. They do not merely subject the Jesus of history to the Christ of faith, but actually glory in the repudiation of the historical—in the sense of *Historie*—altogether. The recorded events of the gospels are not history in the sense of actual historical happenings. The gospel 'events' fall within the realm of Geschichte, to denote that which is above history. Thus is

---

[1] P. T. Forsyth, *The Principle of Authority*, 1913, second edition, 1952, p. 133.
[2] *Ibid.*, p. 130.   [3] *Ibid.*, p. 135.
[5] *Ibid.*, p. 115.   [4] *Ibid.*

repudiated any literal reading of, for example, the 'Fall'. The account of which is to be understood as a type, a parable, a myth. It is essentially *Urgeschichte*, supra-temporal and supra-historical. It belongs to the realm of *Heilsgeschichte*.

Something of the application of this idea to the understanding of the gospel can be seen in Brunner's *Mediator*. Brunner shows no particular interest in the 'historic' figure of the Synoptics. Forsyth made the point, following Kierkegaard, that the current interest in the 'personality' of Jesus was a decidedly wrong beginning. It focused attention upon the human history, the human Figure, and the human circumstances. But the locale of revelation was in the divine drama, in the supernatural happenings, and not in the reconstructed human personality of Jesus. Brunner presses this point. The Jesus of history has no significance for faith. 'Faith presupposes, as a matter of course, *a priori*, that the Jesus of history is not the same as the Christ of faith.'[1] Faith is not the least concerned with the Jesus presented by critical investigation. In fact the most radical biblical criticism, of which Brunner is an ardent adherent, does not affect the issue in the slightest. It may well be, indeed, that the Synoptic gospels do less than justice to the stark literal humanness of Jesus. The fact, not for Brunner in any way disturbing, is that any genuine picture of the historical Jesus cannot be salvaged from the records. But this is a matter of no great moment since 'Christian faith does not arise out of the picture of the historical Jesus, but out of the testimony to Jesus'.

Barth is even more emphatic in his rejection of the 'Jesus-cult'. He vigorously repudiates any attempt to reconstruct a picture of the 'personality' of Jesus. He takes delight in stressing that the historic Figure is not revelation but a hiding of the Divine. Herein God is veiled rather than revealed. His human personality, he declares, was not very attractive, nothing convincing or winning. The Word became 'flesh'; but the 'flesh' assumed, Barth declares, well knowing that he is not taking the orthodox position, was 'fallen' human nature.[2] As such it cannot be the sphere of revelation. Revelation belongs rather to the realm of *Heilsgeschichte* which hovers over and acts within the otherwise unknowable and undiscoverable 'historical' Jesus. The

[1] Emil Brunner, *The Mediator* (E.T. 1934), p. 184.
[2] Karl Barth, *Church Dogmatics* (E.T. 1956), I, ii, p. 151 f.

resurrection can be taken as an example which will make clear
the significance of Barth's idea. The resurrection is 'true', not in
the sense of recoverable history, but as *Geschichte*. It need not
be thought of as following chronologically Christ's death.[1] It belongs to the realm of the supra-temporal and the supra-historical.[2]

The neo-orthodox, then, sharply oppose the liberal attempt to
build theology on human experience, even if designated as
'religious' and 'Christian' experience. Emphasis is placed, in
contrast, upon the transcendence of God and His difference from
man. He is the 'Wholly Other' and there is no natural unity—so
especially Barth—between God and man. Special revelation is
located in the Word of God, God the Son. But it is not 'Christ
after the flesh, the Christ who is tractable to historical and
critical enquiry, but the Christ after the Spirit is the subject of
revelation'.[3]

Into the implications of all this we need not enter here. It
could be shown that for all their emphasis upon objective
revelation, Brunner and Barth have really returned to the
Kierkegaardian subjectivity—a subjectivity which in their
respective criticisms of Schleiermacher they have professed to
renounce.[4] And, further, by eliminating the historical Jesus from
account they can entertain the most radical critical conclusions
regarding the records, but they appear to be left with a Christ
who remains, only because He has the value of God for man,
since He is who He is by the Church's valuation and interpretation of Him. In the end it appears that we have a Christ who has
the 'value' of God for us. It is when I am 'convinced in my

---

[1] Cf. Karl Barth, *Church Dogmatics*, I, ii, p. 147 f.; IV, i, pp. 331 ff.; IV, ii,
pp. 118–22.

[2] Cf. E. J. Young, *The Study of Old Testament Theology Today*, 1958, pp. 13–31.

[3] F. W. Camfield, *Revelation and the Holy Spirit*, 1934, p. 64. The whole passage
could have been quoted as it gives the essential position of the Dialectical theology.
'. . . historical criticism of the records (of the New Testament) for the purpose of
discovering the actual human Jesus and reconstructing the events of his life, do not
touch the nerve of revelation. For the New Testament witness is that not in him
treated from the historical point of view does revelation lie. Not the Christ after the
flesh, the Christ who is tractable to historical and critical enquiry, but the Christ
after the Spirit is the subject of revelation'. F. W. Camfield, *Revelation and the
Holy Spirit*, 1934, p. 64. Cf. 'The new doctrine seems to say "Jesus of Nazareth was
truly a human historical person; but his history and personality do not matter in the
revelation of the Word of God".' D. D. Williams, *What Present Day Theologians
are Saying*, New York, 1959, p. 129.

[4] Cf. H. D. McDonald, *Ideas of Revelation*, 1959, p. 269.

conscience' of 'Christ as the truth' that I can believe in the
Scripture testimony to Christ.[1] Here Ritschl has come back to
his own, edged himself in at the back door having been rather
violently flung out at the front. This riddance from reckoning of
the Jesus of history does injustice, not only to the facts, but much
more to the necessities of the faith. It is the whole Christ of the
New Testament, as Forsyth had so clearly insisted, who is the
source and the object of faith. Faith presupposes, as a matter of
course, *a priori*, that the Jesus of history *is* the same as the Christ
of faith. The position of the neo-orthodox is all very one-sided
and is the result of a reaction from the Jesus-of-History cult. It
is right in its emphasis upon the necessity of the New Testament
interpretation of the Christ Figure, but it is false in its repudiation of the historical Jesus. 'It is not the mere picture of the
Jesus of history, constructed by historical science, that lays hold
of us for our salvation, but the whole Christian story, with both
its historical and its supra-historical elements, which is the
substance of the original *kerygma*'.[2]

(c) The lack of interest in the historical Figure of the
gospels finds its completest expression in the 'Form-Geschichte'
school which blends in an extraordinary way theological
dogmatism and historical scepticism.

The chief advocates of this view take their stand against
'liberalism' in theology. Here we have a radicalism which
professes to be both 'confessional' and 'biblicist'; but it is a
radicalism, nevertheless, which has no place for the Synoptic
account of Jesus. Modern radical Protestantism, it seems to us,
sets out from the neo-orthodox conclusion and develops a
'reconstructionist' theory which is reactionary indeed. Its
advocates seem to be agreed that their position is an 'advance'
on that of Barth and Brunner. But agreement among themselves
is more difficult to come by. Not only is it insistently denied that
finality can be claimed for their constructions, but special delight
is expressed by exponents over disagreements among themselves. Paul Tillich writes of the 'many theological disputes' he
has had with his 'great friend' Niebuhr.[3] Niebuhr maintains that

[1] E. Brunner, *Christian Doctrine of God, Dogmatics*, I, 1950, p. 110.
[2] D. M. Baillie, *God Was In Christ*, 1948, pp. 51–2.
[3] Paul Tillich, 'Reinhold Niebuhr's Doctrine of Knowledge', *Reinhold Niebuhr,
His Religious, Social, and Political Thought* (ed. Charles W. Kegley and Robert W.
Bretall), 1956, p. 43.

an indebtedness to Greek intellectualism was necessary so that Christianity might convincingly adapt itself to prevailing views. This was a missionary requisite. Tillich denies the legitimacy of this type of intellectualism and insists, in opposition, that Greek thought was not in fact rationalistic but 'mystical', a claim which would put Greek thought in harmony with his own 'mystical' position. Brunner states that the label 'neo-orthodox' is unfortunate and really inapplicable to Niebuhr 'since in all the world there is nothing more unorthodox than the spiritual volcano Reinhold Niebuhr'.[1]

Bultmann, the new monarch in the theological arena, seems to be viewed with a little suspicion by the Dialectical theologians. Brunner, at all events, charges that he 'thins out the Gospel too much'.[2] Bultmann, certainly the most thorough exponent of the 'Formgeschichte' theory, openly rejects the factuality of the gospel records. They are legend-tinted and altogether fragmentary. This 'Strauss of the twentieth century', as he has been called, declares that his is convinced 'that we can know almost nothing concerning the life and personality of Jesus, since the early Christian sources show no interest in either, are, moreover fragmentary and often legendary; and other sources about Jesus do not exist'.[3] This lack of possible knowledge concerning the life and personality of Jesus is not a matter for regret. The earlier Jesus-of-history cult focused attention on the records and gave too much authority to the 'reconstructionist' critic.

Bultmann, then, dogmatically excludes any interest in the personality of Jesus. But the reason, he adds, is not merely because of the absence of any sure information which would compel him to make virtue out of necessity. For him the truth is that Christian faith is not concerned with an historical Figure at all, but with the Christ of dogma, the interpreted Jesus. Those whose interest is in the personality of Jesus are told that 'the

[1] Emil Brunner, 'Some Remarks on Reinhold Niebuhr's Work as a Christian Thinker', *op. cit.* above, pp. 28–9.
[2] H. D. McDonald, 'The Conflict Over Special Revelation', *Christianity Today*, Vol. V, No. 8, January 16, 1961; cf. the remark of Tillich '. . . R. Bultmann's bold programme of a "demythologization of the New Testament" aroused a storm in all theological camps and the slumber of Barthianism . . .' Paul Tillich, *Systematic Theology*, Vol. II, 1957, p. 102.
[3] Rudolf Bultmann, *Jesus and the Word* (E.T. New York, 1958), p. 8; cf. p. 13.

situation is depressing or destructive'. For Bultmann the Jesus of history in so far as the account can be stripped from its later colouring by the Church's faith and dogma, is of no account. As far, indeed, as we are allowed any glimpse of the real Jesus we see a none-too-compelling Figure; virtually, in fact, an ignorant Gallilean peasant. But we are hastily assured that this need not be a cause for alarm: what matters is the Jesus of faith.

The task of theology today, for the newer school of radical Protestants, is not to be content with the neo-orthodox, super-historical Christ but to reconstruct the whole by 'demytholo-gizing' the 'myths'. It is consequently urged, for example by Niebuhr, that such ideas as the Trinity are mere symbolic expressions, quite meaningless if read literally. Since it would be absurd to assert that the finite can be infinite, we are told that Jesus was not really, literally divine. Only in a 'gnostic, symbolic' sense can it be said that He died and rose again.

The upshot of this line of thought is that we are left with a new humanism in which revelation seems to be nothing other than the unveiling to man of the ultimate divinity of his own being. We are back again to Schleiermacher's subjectivism and to Ritschl's value-judgement epistemology.

In Paul Tillich this strange combination of Schleiermacher and Ritschl meets. Tillich contends that the 'biblical picture of Christ' is not an historical presentation.[1] 'The search for the historical Jesus was an attempt to discover a minimum of reliable facts about the man Jesus of Nazareth, in order to provide a safe foundation for the Christian faith. This attempt' Tillich adds, 'was a failure.'[2] The character reconstructed is no certain historical reality. The picture possesses, at most, a faint possibility.[3]

It is in this context of ideas that the concept revelation is to be understood. 'Revelation is the manifestation of what concerns us ultimately'[4] it is declared. Everything is a bearer to man of such a revelation when it seizes him as a 'miracle' and as 'ecstasy', thereby inducing an 'elevation of heart'. Of this reality Christianity is the profoundest 'symbol'. 'A Christianity which

---

[1] Cf. Paul Tillich, *Systematic Theology*, Vol. II, 1957, pp. 101 ff.
[2] *Ibid.*, Vol. II, p. 105.
[3] Cf. Paul Tillich, *The Interpretation of History*, 1936, p. 260; cf. p. 165.
[4] *Systematic Theology*, Vol. I, 1951, p. 110.

does not assert that Jesus of Nazareth is sacrificed to Jesus as the Christ is just one more religion among many religions', he says. But this too is 'symbol'; indeed, 'tis 'symbol' all. The 'symbol' Son of Man is to be regarded as the symbol of the original unity between God and man. In fact 'The whole picture given by Tillich of Jesus becoming "the Christ" is one of the gradual divination of a man. A divination which occurred fully in him and which must occur to some extent in all if they are to have what Tillich calls "eternal life", that is to enjoy a union with the Ground of their being or God'.[1] Jesus, it seems, was the first who just happened to unite the estranged conditions of existence, He is thus the picture of that 'new being' which all can attain. The development of the 'divinity' in Christ is what, in its measure, the process should be in ours if we are to be united with that Ground of our being which is for us a matter of 'ultimate concern'. Man must become 'grasped by the ultimate power' which is the Ground of his being, Tillich asserts; and when this happens there is a 'miracle'.[2] But a 'miracle' however is not quite what we might suppose; it must be defined in the context of Tillich's ontology. There is no supra-natural interference by Being-Itself in nature. Such an idea would mean that 'God would be split within himself' and as a house divided against itself it would result in collapse of the very concept of God. God, as the Ground of being, would be at odds with the structure of being, therefore this 'bad connotation of a supra-natural interference' must be abandoned. A miracle is not supernatural in the sense of a Divine intrusion, it is rather the result of a group of elements in reality itself being brought into relationship with a group of elements in the mind of man, in such a way that the rational elements in the mind are neither destroyed nor removed.[3] Ultimately, as in Schleiermacher, miracles are limited to personal subjective experiences.

It seems to us that the whole strange thesis which Tillich elaborates in the two volumes of his *Systematic Theology* as well as in his other several writings is best summarized in a sermon which he preached on the 'Holy Spirit' at the Rockefeller Chapel

[1] R. Allan Killen, *The Ontological Theology of Paul Tillich*, 1956, p. 167.
[2] Cf. Paul Tillich, *The Protestant Era*, 1948, p. 88.
[3] Cf. R. Allan Killen, *op. cit.*, p. 69; cf. also *The Theology of Paul Tillich* (ed. Charles W. Kegley and Robert W. Bretall), 1956.

at the University of Chicago. Referring to his topic as a 'neglected subject' Tillich proceeds to advance ideas about the Holy Spirit which have little resemblance to the orthodox Christian doctrine. He maintains that the Spirit of God is virtually another way of asserting the immanence of God. True, God is always near and far, but He becomes the 'absent God' to us if our awareness of Him should become shallow, or habitual or familiar. But the divine Spirit is really God everywhere, not bound to Christianity or any one of its Churches; he works 'in every human situation'. This means for Tillich that 'spiritual experience' is a reality for everyone, it is 'as real as the air we breathe'. 'For this is what Divine Spirit means; God present in our spirit', he says. 'Spirit is not a mysterious substance, it is not a part of God. It is God Himself . . . present in communities and personalities, grasping them, inspiring them, transforming them.'[1] In such an account Tillich reveals how much he has reacted from the Barthian emphasis on transcendence and has returned to the Schleiermacherian immanence and mysticism.

Tillich is as insistent as any follower of Schleiermacher or Coleridge or Maurice could be that revelation is something inward. And he is as scathing in his repudiation of a 'book religion' and a 'verbal revelation'. 'Probably nothing has contributed more to the misrepresentation of the Biblical doctrine of the Word than the identification of the Word with the Bible', he says.[2] When once the Bible is called the Word of God theological confusion results; a dictation theory of inspiration, dishonesty in dealing with the biblical text and a 'monophysitic' dogma of infallibility of a book.[3]

Basic to all these ideas which have reacted against the Jesus-of-history cults is the assertion that faith has nothing to do with the historical Figure which, as a matter of fact, cannot be drawn from the gospel records. The 'Christ-event' is the creation of the Church.[4] British writers, not, it must be admitted, with the same devastating thoroughness as in Bultmann or Dibelius, have also contended for the Christ of faith as the true locale of revelation. 'It seems, then', says R. H. Lightfoot at the

[1] Cf. Report of Sermon, by Dave Meade, *The Chicago Daily News*, Monday, January 16, 1961.

[2] Paul Tillich, *Systematic Theology*, Vol. I, 1951, pp. 158-9.

[3] *Ibid.*, p. 158.

[4] John Knox, *Jesus, Lord and Christ*, 1958, pp. 63 ff., 145 f.

conclusion of his Bampton Lectures, 'that the form of the earthly no less than the heavenly Christ is for the most part hidden from us. For all the inestimable value of the Gospels, they yield us little more than a whisper of his voice; we trace in them but the outskirts of his ways. Only when we see him hereafter in his fulness shall we know him also as he was on earth. And perhaps the more we ponder the matter, the more clearly we shall understand the reason for it, and therefore shall not wish it otherwise. For probably we are as little prepared for the one as for the other.'[1]

This, as we should expect from R. H. Lightfoot, is a spiritually sensitive statement of the case. Yet the strange fact is that even he seems to give more credit to the records and more appreciation of the 'historical Figure' than his fundamental thesis would seem to permit. John Knox, in like manner, talks of the 'importance of the "Quest" for the historical Jesus' as an 'indispensable theological task', yet how it can be important and why it should be undertaken we just cannot make out.[2]

Bultmann, Tillich and Niebuhr, having renounced the thesis that divine revelation contains truths, are left without any rational basis for theology. This in a lesser way is also true of their more moderate supporters. It is not very evident to us why Tillich especially, whose position is a sort of Christianized Neoplatonism, speculative after the fashion of Johannes Scotus Erigena[3] and mystical after the style of Dionysius, can be so dogmatic about the Christian faith when its central Figure is no historical reality.

Revelation it seems to us must come as truth as well as act. And most certainly the knowledge of God which is discovered by experience is not a knowledge which could have arisen in experience. Man's encounter with God comes by way of the truth communicated to God's chosen prophets and apostles. The acts of God and the word of God are not two separable realities.

[1] R. H. Lightfoot, *History and Interpretation in the Gospels*, Bampton Lectures 1934, 1935, p. 225. Cf. 'As a figure calculated to inspire men to heroic acts of self-sacrifice, it may be doubted whether the figure of Jesus, if detached from what Christians have believed about Him, is adequate'. Edwyn Bevan, quoted by D. M. Baillie, *God Was In Christ*, 1948, p. 38; cf. Edwyn Bevan, *Christianity*, 1932, p. 239 f.

[2] John Knox, *Jesus, Lord and Christ*, 1958, p. 240.

[3] Cf. Richard Kroner, *Speculation and Revelation in the Age of Christian Philosophy*, 1959, p. 146 (footnote).

D

God's acts are known only as they are interpreted by His word, and by His word we are brought into saving contact with His acts. With the neo-orthodox, and more particularly with the modern school of radical Protestantism, the pendulum swing, as Donald Baillie points out, has gone too far. There is an essential place for the Jesus of history in the creation, as well as in the upbuilding of faith. It is altogether impossible to dispense with the Jesus of history completely, needful as it was to insist that we do not really know Christ if that knowledge is limited to the synoptic picture. It is a fact that 'The Jesus of history Himself can tell us that the Jesus of history is not enough'.[1] But it is also true as Nathan Söderbloom says, that 'If you wish to have Christ, you must take history with him'.[2]

Radical Protestantism, it seems to us, has no objective Word of God, with the result that it flounders in the abyss of irrationalism and subjectivism.

[1] D. M. Baillie, *God Was In Christ*, 1948, p. 42; cf. H. R. Mackintosh, 'Christ and Historical Research', *The Doctrine of the Person of Christ*, 1912, pp. 310 ff.
[2] Nathan Söderbloom, *The Nature of Revelation*, E.T. 1933, p. 171.

CHAPTER THREE

The Battle of the Standpoints

One of the most distinctive features of the last quarter of the nineteenth century as it concerns the subject of revelation was the conflict over what became so well known as the 'Higher Criticism'. It was regarded by its opponents as a novel brand of scepticism, and by its advocates as the truly scientific approach to an understanding of the Bible. Higher Criticism became at the time the centre of discussion and the focus of debate. It was the one vital topic which drew forth a flood of letters, pamphlets, articles and books. The press was inundated with calls upon its space for expressions of opinions for and against this new method of dealing with the Scriptures, and the new verdict which was being passed upon its contents.

'It is a paper war', it was declared in a contemporary issue of the *Expository Times*, 'As no theological controversy ever before, it is being fought out in the periodical press'.[1] An examination of such periodicals as, for example, *The British Quarterly Review*, *The British Weekly*, *The British and Foreign Evangelical Review*, and *The Contemporary Review*, will give some impression of the seriousness of the debate.

The Church was in a state of turmoil; forces were arrayed in opposition. It was indeed 'a paper war', a battle was being waged for the Bible. The issues at stake concerned an understanding of its historicity, its inspiration, its accuracy, its authority, and its interpretation. That these were considered the real problems may be gathered from the debate between Alfred Cave, on the one side, and, on the other side, T. K. Cheyne and S. R. Driver. In an issue of the *Contemporary Review*, Cave wrote an article entitled, 'The Old Testament and its Critics'[2] and he

---

[1] *Expository Times*, Vol. III, 1891–2, p. 292.
[2] Cf. *op. cit.*, No. lvii, 1890, pp. 537–51.

followed this in the next year with another on, 'Canon Driver on the Book of the Law',[1] in which a severe attack was made on Driver's, *Introduction to the Literature of the Old Testament*. Driver replied in the February issue of 1892, under the caption, 'Principal Cave on the Hexateuch'.[2] Already in 1890 Cave had shown his hostility to the higher criticism in an address on 'The Old Testament and the Higher Criticism', given to the Manchester Conference of the Evangelical Alliance. This address appeared in print in the December issue of *Evangelical Christendom*,[3] and was later expanded and produced in a pamphlet form with the title, *The Battle of the Standpoints*, which has been taken as the heading of the present chapter.[4] That this may be regarded as a fairly accurate account of the conflict the later part of this chapter and the one following will make evident. Each side certainly had its presuppositions, the critics no less than their opponents, although it must be confessed that the critics of the time believed themselves to be without any. Each side from its own standpoint attacked the other, and it is this conflict which demands our attention. Meanwhile, however, we must note how the issue of the higher criticism took the first place in this particular period.

In the first year of the appearance of the *Expository Times*, it is observed in one issue that 'In some circles in England the discussion of the Higher (or Historical) Criticism of the Old Testament has, since the publication of *Lux Mundi*, and Canon Liddon's St Paul's sermon on the other side, reached a tolerably acute stage'.[5] A little later F. H. Woods in an article entitled, 'A Critical Examination of Genesis i to vi' begins with the observation that 'One of the most remarkable features of Biblical study is the attention which is being increasingly paid to what is called "the higher criticism" '.[6] In a long review of Driver's *An Introduction to the Literature of the Old Testament*, A. K. S. Kennedy noted the 'daily increasing attention which is being paid by all sections of the Church to the questions of Old Testament criticism'. The higher criticism was, then, the big

---

[1] Cf. *Expository Times*, Vol. III, No. lx, 1891, pp. 892–910.
[2] Cf. *op. cit.*, No. lxi, 1892, pp. 262–78.
[3] Cf. *Evangelical Christendom*, Vol. XXXI, 1890, pp. 370–7.
[4] Alfred Cave, *The Battle of the Standpoints*, 1890.
[5] *Expository Times*, Vols. I and II, 1889–91, i, p. 146.
[6] *Op. cit.*, 1889–91, ii, p. 102.

issue of the closing years of the nineteenth century. The main storm-centre was, of course, the Old Testament. It was not, as we have already noted, until the beginning of the new century that critical opinions concerning the New Testament were given any serious place in the Church.

In the present chapter the main problem remains of bringing some sort of order into the bewildering amount of literature which is before us in periodicals and pamphlets, in letters and books. We are not intending a full scale history of the conflict over higher criticism—that would take a volume on its own account—but we must give some attention to it as it was finally concerned with the question of the way God has revealed Himself and how this revelation is known to us.

A. THE ADVENT OF CRITICISM

Our summary can best begin with a reference to the contention of C. J. Ellicott, Bishop of Gloucester and Bristol. He dates the beginning of criticism in the English Church with the publication of the *Lux Mundi*. Before then it stood outside the main stream of 'the Catholic faith', and was generally associated with German scepticism in which the tendency was more and more to disintegrate the inspired records. 'The pedigree is certainly not satisfactory', he remarks.[1] Ellicott's pin-pointing of the publication of the *Lux Mundi* as the start of the higher criticism conflict is broadly true. It may, however, be more properly stated that the period began with the appearance of Robertson Smith's lectures, *The Old Testament in the Jewish Church*. The truth in Ellicott's remark is that before the date of the *Lux Mundi* anyone advocating a critical position was soon made to feel, by the strength of the opposition to it, that it had no general support either of the scholar or the ordinary Christian.

Taking, then, the date 1880 as marking out a new stage in the controversy, the period prior to that may be called, as in our title to this section, the advent of criticism.

At the beginning the term 'higher criticism' was used as a synonym for historical criticism, but, as time went on, as we shall see, higher criticism was stated to be other than historical

[1] C. J. Ellicott, 'The Teaching of Our Lord as to the Authority of the Old Testament', *Expository Times*, Vol. III, 1891–2, p. 158.

criticism and was identified more particularly with literary criticism. The first occurrence of the designation 'the historical method' seems to come in Joseph Priestley's *History of the Corruptions of Christianity*, 1782, in the Preface of which Priestley maintains that the historical method 'will be found to be one of the most satisfactory modes of argumentation'. The term 'higher criticism' was used as early as 1787 in the Preface of J. G. Eichhorn's *Einleitung in das Alte Testament*. Eichhorn is referred to by T. K. Cheyne as 'the founder of the modern Old Testament Criticism'.[1]

In England, the higher criticism did not make any significant headway prior to 1880. Alfred Cave, writing in this very year in *The British and Foreign Evangelical Review*, was certainly correct in stating that the overwhelming weight of current Biblical scholarship, both in the British Isles and America, supported the traditional Mosaic authorship of the Pentateuch.[2] Yet even before this date there were those who afterwards were to attain positions of authority in the Church who did express critical opinions. There was, for example, Edmund Law (1703–87), who became Bishop of Carlisle in 1768. In his *Considerations on the State of the World with Regard to the Theory of Religion*, Law argued that the Scriptures must be approached 'with the same freedom that we do, and find we must do, every other book we desire to understand'.[3]

In 1825 there appeared an English edition by an anonymous translator of Schleiermacher's *Essay on the Gospel of St Luke*. It was subsequently revealed that Connop Thirlwall (1791–1875), later to become Bishop of St David's, was responsible for the work. Bishop Perowne, making special reference to this production, contends that the volume marks 'an epoch in the history of English theology'. An attack, he notes, is made upon verbal inspiration, and the 'historical method' is used to establish 'critical' conclusions. Account has already been given of the critical presuppositions of *Essays and Reviews* and of the reception given to Colenso's work. Concerning the latter it was estimated by William Boyce, a Wesleyan minister who wrote

[1] T. K. Cheyne, *Founders of Old Testament Criticism*, 1893, p. 13.
[2] Alfred Cave, 'Professor Robertson Smith on the Pentateuch', Vol. xxix, 1880, p. 597.
[3] Edmund Law, *Considerations on the State of the World with Regard to the Theory of Religion*, 1745, sixth edition, 1774, p. 71, cf. p. 264.

decades later, that 300 replies were forthcoming, although, he adds, 'few of them dealt with the critical bearings of the questions at stake'.[1] Boyce urges preference for Colenso's work to that of the Germans because he at least wrote in 'plain English!' The verdict given in Colenso's favour by the Lord Chancellor, Lord Westbury, February 4, 1864, declared among other items that it was not penal for a clergyman of the Established Church to assert that the Bible is not inspired in all its parts. This judgement was claimed by later critics to constitute the charter of free enquiry into the origin and composition of the Scriptures in the Church of England and to secure for it the liberty of biblical criticism.[2]

Two other names, both Congregationalists, need to be mentioned. First chronologically comes Samuel Davidson, who became lecturer in Manchester Independent College in 1842. For the opinions he expressed in the revised tenth edition of *Horne's Introduction to the Critical Study and Knowledge of the Holy Scriptures* (1856) Davidson lost his position at the College in 1857.[3] Not only had Davidson denied the Mosaic authorship of the Pentateuch but he had compromised the traditional view of inspiration by admitting a strong element of German naturalistic criticism.[4] He had propounded a 'lower' view of inspiration than that held by the Church at large. A review of *Horne's Introduction* was given in the *Wesleyan Methodist Magazine* for 1856. The theory of inspiration which Davidson had suggested could not be permitted since it admitted the 'perilous experiment' of 'distinguishing the human and the Divine' 'in the Record which is "given by inspiration of God"'. The 'whole speculation', it was declared, was 'quite modern' and had no justification whatever in the Scripture itself.[5] The action of the College committee in dismissing Davidson was generally approved and strongly supported.[6] Indeed, Watkins in his Bampton Lectures goes so far as to suggest that the more

[1] William Boyce, *The Higher Criticism and the Bible*, 1881, p. 129 f.

[2] Cf. J. Estlin Carpenter, *The Bible in the Nineteenth Century*, 1903, pp. 38 ff.

[3] Cf. *The Autobiography and Diary of Samuel Davidson*, edited by his daughter, 1899, pp. 35–70.

[4] Cf. *British and Foreign Evangelical Review*, Vol. VII, 1858, pp. 470–1.

[5] Cf. *Wesleyan Methodist Magazine*, Vol. LXXXIX, 1856, p. 116.

[6] Cf. John Kelly, *An Examination of the Facts, Statements, and Explanations of Rev Dr S. Davidson*, relative to the second volume of the tenth edition of *Horne's Introduction*, etc., Liverpool, 1857.

extreme critical opinions which Davidson expressed in his later work, *An Introduction to the Old Testament, Critical, Historical, and Theological* (three volumes, 1862–63), were due to his resentment at his expulsion from his professorship. Davidson certainly advanced further towards a more and more liberal attitude towards the great central message of the faith. As time went on he drew away from its essential truths. He came to regard Christianity as little more than an ethical code although he retained a vague belief in God as a sort of good-natured Father.[1]

The other name is that of Archibald Duff, who became lecturer in the Airdale College, Bradford, in 1878. Duff, who had received part of his education in Germany, had evidently imbibed a fair measure of its critical views. This is clear from his inaugral address in 1878 in which he suggested his belief that the earlier parts of the Old Testament could not have been prior to 800 BC. He also doubted whether even the prophets had arrived at the conception of pure monotheism.[2]

It has been stated that the famous trio of the Cambridge school—Lightfoot, Hort and Wescott—are to be reckoned amongst the critics. Their interest was, of course, in the New Testament, but they were by no means critics of the radical type. Their whole approach was conservative. Indeed Wescott declared his own position, which was broadly that of the other two, in a paper entitled 'Critical Scepticism' read before the Church Congress at Brighton in October 1874. He maintained that the claim of those who pursue criticism that they are merely being impartial is to be gravely doubted. Concerning the records of our Lord's life, he says, 'fantastic scepticism is not consistent with their truth'.[3] Sceptical criticism, he states, fails to recognize the nature of the problems discussed. He adds several further charges against the 'sceptical' position implicit in 'criticism' which may be best put in his own words: '(1) Sceptical critics fail to take account of the culminative and total

---

[1] Cf. *British Quarterly Review*, Vol. LXXXV, 1882, pp. 521–6. Cf. *Autobiography and Diary of Samuel Davidson*, 1899, pp. 334–5. Cf. H. W. Watkins, *Modern Criticism and the Fourth Gospel*, Bampton Lectures, 1890, 1890, pp. 284 ff.; also *Dr Davidson, his Heresies, Contradictions, and Plagerisms*, by Two Graduates, 1857.

[2] Archibald Duff, *The Use of the Old Testament in the Study of the Rise of our Doctrines*, 1878, p. 12 f.

[3] Cf. *Expositor*, first series, Vol. I, 1875, p. 215.

force of the direct evidence in favour of the facts alleged. (2) They criticize special documents without regard to the general belief which the documents express. (3) Of these documents they criticize special parts without regard to the relation in which the parts stand to the entire book. (4) They isolate the documentary evidence from the testimony of the living body'.[1]

The period, then, prior to 1880 we may regard as one of the preparation of the stage for the appearance of the real protagonists of criticism.

B. THE ADVANCE OF CRITICISM

The 'modern period' of biblical criticism has been dated from the year 1880, the year of Robertson Smith's lectures on the *Old Testament in the Jewish Church*. Two names already prominent were to take the lead in establishing it in these isles. They were T. K. Cheyne in England and A. B. Davidson in Scotland. O. C. Whitehouse in a review of Cheyne's *Founders of Old Testament Criticism* associates Davidson with Cheyne as having 'the honour of being the real "Bahnbrecher" of our modern British Old Testament research by the work contributed by each during the eventful decades 1870–1880'.[2]

Back in the year 1867 Cheyne, then but twenty-eight years old, was given charge of the Biblical department of the newly created *Academy*. At that period he was the acknowledged disciple of the leading German rationalistic critics. And as such he had little influence in this country; indeed, in the earlier period there was very little serious attention paid to the Old Testament.[3] In the year 1880 Cheyne underwent some sort of spiritual experience, which affected, at least for a time, his attitude to the Scriptures. He came to see that certain of the radical views of the German sceptics if carried to their conclusion would be destructive of real religious faith. He did not abandon, by any means, his main critical ideas, but his change in spiritual orientation was noted, and as a consequence his works were more readily received. In fact the impression was given in some over zealous reviews of his *Isaiah* (1880–1) that he had altered

---

[1] *Expositor, ibid.*, pp. 215–16.

[2] *The Thinker*, Vol. IV, 1893, p. 280.

[3] Cf. W. Robertson Nicoll, 'Professor Cheyne', *Expositor*, third series, Vol. IX, 1889, pp. 61–2.

his critical views. This is evident, for example, in two issues of
the *British Quarterly Review*, as well as two of the *Expositor*.[1]
The truth is, however, that Cheyne reverted to his earlier radical
tendencies and in his later criticism put forth ideas which were
fruitless as well as fanciful.

Yet Cheyne has been given the reputation of being the chief
initiator of higher criticism in England. 'Though he had
predecessors', says A. S. Peake, 'it is to Cheyne that the
distinction belongs of initiating with adequate scholarship the
critical movement in his native country'.[2] Up to 1880, Peake
notes elsewhere, Cheyne was dominated by rationalism. And he
makes reference to his confession 'that his too exclusive devotion
to criticism was injurious to his spiritual life'.[3] By the influence
of 'one obscure student' at Oxford 'Johannine religion' asserted
'its supremacy over criticism and speculation'.[4] This changed
tone and temper which began to appear in his works has been
noted. Yet it is certain that he soon became fascinated again by
criticism and speculation and showed a readiness to accept the
most audacious views of the Old Testament books. Peake,
indeed, remarks with commendable mildness that 'Perhaps he
has a tendency in criticism to lay stress on minute indications
of date, and to give too much play to imagination'.[5]

A. B. Davidson has been hailed by this same Cheyne as the
chief advocate of criticism beyond the border. Cheyne, in fact, is
emphatic that 'no one has done more to "found" criticism, at
least in Scotland, than this eminent teacher'.[6] Robertson Smith
had been one of Davidson's students, and it was not until after
the storm caused by Smith's views that Davidson came out in
the open defence of criticism. Earlier, indeed, Davidson had
given very definite hints of his sympathy with it; and because
of his avowed allegiance to the main evangelical doctrines he
was able to express this sympathy in the pages of the *British and
Foreign Evangelical Review*.[7]

[1] Cf. *British Quarterly Review*, No. lxxii, 1880, p. 544; lxxiii, 1881, pp. 518–20.
Expositor, first series, Vol. XI, 1880, pp. 399–400; second series, Vol. I, 1885,
p. 237.
[2] 'Cheyne, Thomas Kelly', *Dictionary of National Biography*, ad. loc.
[3] A. S. Peake, 'Thomas Kelly Cheyne', *Expository Times*, Vol. VI, 1894–5,
p. 441.   [4] *Ibid.*   [5] *Ibid.*, p. 443.
[6] T. K. Cheyne, *Founders of Old Testament Criticism*, 1893, p. 225.
[7] Cf. *British and Foreign Evangelical Review*, No. xxi, 1872, pp. 618–19; No.
xxviii, 1879, pp. 337–67.

At the same time, S. D. F. Salmond, while he acknowledges
that Davidson 'was the first to teach in any proper and continuous way in Scotland the methods of Higher Criticism'[1] also
stresses that 'The self-restraint which is natural to him has been
one of the best notes of his criticism'.[2] 'He had a better appreciation than is often possessed by critics', Salmond continues, 'of
the limits which are imposed upon Old Testament science, by
the comparative scantiness of the Old Testament literature'.[3]
Davidson's hesitancy in giving strong statement to the critical
ideas disappointed those who wished for this emphasis. Thus
A. B. Bruce in an article in the October 1896 issue of the *Biblical
World* says, 'Dr Davidson has rather disappointed his admirers
even in the region of criticism. He has not kept his place in the
van of the movement which he created. He has rather lagged
behind or stood on one side, while the company of the prophets
marched on, wondering what had possessed them'. The
Expository Times makes reference to Bruce's remarks and asks,
'*Are* they prophets that march past?' True Bruce fortifies his
judgement with the opinion of Cheyne. 'But is it not possible
that there are those whom Professor Cheyne would call prophets
of Old Testament criticism, while Professor Davidson would
not; and is it not possible that Professor Davidson would be
right? . . . Is it possible that both Professor Bruce and Professor
Cheyne have placed him (i.e. Arndt from whose tract, *The Place
of Ezekiel in Old Testament Prophecy*, Davidson dissents)
among the prophets? Is their judgement better than his? For is it
not, after all, a matter of position? Again and again Dr Cheyne
publicly declared himself in advance of his colleague Dr
Driver. He may be also in advance of Dr Davidson, and
Professor Bruce may be forward at his side. Whereupon it were
just as easy and just as reasonable for Dr Davidson and Dr
Driver to say that *they* were in the midst of the prophets, and
that their distinguished colleagues had moved somewhere out
of line'.[4]

There is no doubt but that in the eyes of some critics Davidson
had failed to keep pace. The fact is, however, that he was not

---

[1] S. D. F. Salmond, 'A. B. Davidson, D.D., LLD,' *Expository Times*, Vol. VIII
1896–7, p. 445.
[2] *Ibid.*   [3] *Ibid.*
[4] *Expository Times*, Vol. VIII, 1896–7, pp. 102–3.

happy about the growing tendency to excessive analysis which certain of them displayed. He apparently came to feel that such criticism in the hands of some uninhibited critics would issue in lamentable absurdities. He is to be found, as a consequence, protesting against the minute dissection of the Old Testament books. In a notice in the *Critical Review* (Vol. II, p. 31), concerning Cornhill's *Einleitung* he observes: 'The criticism of the Pentateuch is a great historical drama, which needs to be put upon the stage with appropriate scenery and circumstances. When performed by a company of puppets called J.E.D.P., with all their little ones down to J^1 and P_P, it loses its impressiveness. It will not be strange if some spectactors mistake the nature of the performance and go home with the impression that they have been witnessing a farce'.

(1) *Hindrances to Advance*

For the first half-dozen years or so after 1880, higher criticism did not make any rapid progress in this country. The reasons, were, on the one hand, its pedigree, and, on the other hand, the object of the critical investigation.

(i) The Source of the Critical View.

Higher criticism, it is well known, was born in Germany and came to maturity amongst a company in which rather outspoken sceptical pronouncements were being made concerning the Bible and even the Lord of whom it spoke. The pedigree certainly was not considered satisfactory. The term 'Germanism' was in vogue at the time to designate the rationalistic Hegelianism of much German theology.[1] And it was used at the beginning of the conflict as a synonym for higher criticism as such. Thus in a review of William L. Alexander's *Christ and Christianity* (1854), the *British and Foreign Evangelical Review* refers to the invasion of Christian evidences 'by transcendental modes of thinking, and by a destructive criticism imported from Germany'.[2] The same journal, fifteen years later, reviewed Samuel Davidson's *An Introduction to the Study of the New Testament* (1868) and makes mention of German intellectualism which 'soars away through thin air'.[3] The truth is that for long,

---

[1] Cf. Ernest A. Payne, *Studies in History and Religion*, 1942, pp. 239–40.

[2] *British and Foreign Evangelical Review*, Vol. III, 1854, p. 683.

[3] *Op. cit.*, Vol. XVII, 1869, pp. 502–15.

and it must be admitted not without reason, higher criticism and 'German rationalism' were regarded as one and the same.[1]

A. H. Sayce, then Professor of Assyriology at Oxford, did not feel it was an injustice to speak of 'the exaggerated scepticism of the so-called "Higher Criticism" ', although by so characterizing it he irritated S. R. Driver.[2] In a passage in his book, *The Higher Criticism and the Monuments*, he remarks that 'a good deal of historical criticism which has been passed on the Old Testament is criticism which seems to imagine the compiler of the Book of Judges or the Books of Kings was a German scholar surrounded by volumes of his library, and writing in awe of his reviewers'.[3] Once again Driver did not like the insinuation. Thus in a review of Sayce's book in the *Contemporary Review* of March 1895 he took exception to Sayce's use of the designation 'higher criticism'. Driver was however ready to accept some of Sayce's conclusions but he contended that what Sayce credited to the 'higher critic' should rather be spoken of the 'hypercritic'.

Not only professors but preachers felt bound to associate criticism and German scepticism. J. D. Jones refers to his famous predecessor, Ossian Davies, at Richmond Hill, Bournemouth, who often 'spoke rather scornfully of the men who cut up the Bible with "German scissors" '.[4] The renowned Baptist preacher, C. H. Spurgeon, who cannot be brushed aside as an obscurantist, also comments upon the 'German poison'.[5]

Born, then, in an atmosphere of German rationalism and scepticism, it is not difficult to understand how the higher criticism came to be regarded as its product. How, it could be asked, can a fountain bring forth at the same time sweet water and bitter? Thirlwall had, indeed, earlier rebuked a Bampton lecturer for denouncing the theology of a people whose language he did not know. And it is said that two persons only knew German at Oxford at the time Pusey began his study of the language there between the years 1880–2. But what had been

---

[1] Cf. Leslie B. Peake, *Arthur Samuel Peake, A Memoir*, 1930, p. 113.

[2] A. H. Sayce, 'The Fourteenth Chapter of Genesis', *Expository Times*, Vol. IV, 1892–3, p. 14. See S. R. Driver's reply, *ibid*, p. 95, and Sayce's answer, p. 118.

[3] A. H. Sayce, *The Higher Criticism and the Monuments*, 1895, fifth edition, p. 15; cf. 'The arrogancy of tone adopted at times by the "higher criticism" has been productive of nothing but mischief', *op. cit.*, p. 5.

[4] J. D. Jones, *Three Score Years and Ten*, 1940, p. 71.

[5] Cf. *The Sword and the Trowel*, 1891, p. 87.

imported in English dress, however, did not inspire general confidence: there was enough to hand to make it appear that higher criticism and unbelief went together.

(ii) The Object of the Critical Enquiry.

'The real battle is over the Old Testament', wrote W. R. Nicoll in 1887.[1] And so it was. Yet the Old Testament was an integral part of the Christian Bible. And it was this which was being subjected to the critics' analysis. Throughout the history of the Church, the Old Testament, no less than the New, had been accepted as a divine revelation. In fact successive confessions and creeds had stated that Book to be an unerring and inspired record. It was the conviction of Christians through the ages that the Holy Spirit's inspiration, of which all the Scripture is a product, was not limited to the men who wrote. It was held that the sacred volumes themselves contained the words of God.

It was, then, this Book which was the object of the critical enquiry. And there was the allied question of Christ's authority. The very Old Testament which some critics gave the impression of handling lightly and dissecting freely was the Old Testament which He read and quoted. In and through its pages He found His Messiahship authenticated and His Mission vindicated. What was to be said about our Lord's authority in relation to the Old Testament? This was the issue which was to become central in the discussion.

In a comment in the *Expository Times* concerning the 'great controversy raised by the *Lux Mundi*' it was remarked, 'the real subject of dispute has been the limitation of Christ's human knowledge—a subject with which it is doubtful' the writer himself thinks, 'if the criticism of the Old Testament has anything to do'.[2] But there was no reason for this doubt. How indeed could it be otherwise? George Adam Smith, in a work in which he made a strong plea for the recognition of the higher criticism, states in the same breath the high regard our Lord had for the Old Testament. 'Above all, He fed His own soul with its contents, and in the great crises of His own life sustained Himself upon it as upon the living and sovereign Word

[1] W. Robertson Nicoll, 'The Coming Battle', *The British Weekly*, Vol. II, 1887, p. 225.

[2] *Expository Times*, Vols. I and II, 1889–90, i, p. 242.

of God.'[1] If He so accepted the Old Testament Scriptures, and
there was no doubt that He did, then the question pressed, Was
He altogether ignorant of the 'true' nature of their history and
compilation? And, further, How far is that acceptance of the Old
Testament, as He found it, a warrant for those who follow Him
to receive it in the same way? These and other questions, as we
shall see, and as later editions of the *Expository Times* came to
recognize, had to be faced. Cheyne in fact openly asserted that
it was the idea of our Lord's absolute authority in the whole
domain of Old Testament studies which stood in the way of
'critical progress'. The real issue, he notes, is a theological one
and concerns the amount of knowledge that Christ in the days
of His flesh may be said to possess.[2]

(2) *Reorientation for Advance*

It will be clear from what has been observed that if the higher
criticism were to advance it must needs be toned down in
certain important respects. The British critic must rid himself,
and openly profess that he has done so, of the taint of German
scepticism. Only thus will the critical reconstruction of the Old
Testament gain any wide acceptance.

(i) To begin with, a more acceptable colouring, so to say, had
to be given to the historical method.

At the first, we noted earlier, historical criticism and higher
criticism were virtually regarded as one and the same. And by
their application of the method German critics were constantly
found making statements concerning the Old Testament of a
radical and revolutionary nature. The impression was given, not
without reason, that the Old Testament was the result of the
stringing together of stories which in themselves were rather
fanciful and fabulous, but which religious men of genius and
insight were to take up and use to teach certain great spiritual
truths which they had discovered. Historical criticism had
consequently appeared to be in the hands of such investigators

[1] G. A. Smith, *Modern Criticism and the Preaching of the Old Testament*, Layman
Beecher Lectures, Yale, 1899 (New York, 1901), p. 11. Cf. '. . . the Old Testament
Canon is credited in addition by an authority of which the New Testament is devoid.
This is the authority of Jesus Christ Himself. . . . What was indispensable for the
Redeemer must always be indispensable for the redeemed', *op. cit.*, pp. 10–11.

[2] T. K. Cheyne, *Aids to the Devout Study of Criticism*, 1892, p. 392. Cf. S. R.
Driver, *Introduction to the Literature of the Old Testament*, 1891, seventh edition,
1898, Preface, p. xii f.

the very destruction of history. The very term seemed to be a misnomer. Higher criticism, thus identified with historical criticism, was considered to have torn from the pages of the Old Testament the historical reality of men whose presence was found and felt in subsequent periods.

In this country, too, there was at the beginning a tendency to give rigorous application to the historical method. George Adam Smith is therefore able to state that the criticism of the Old Testament is mainly 'historical'.[1] And as a result of the 'unsparing criticism' and the 'industrious research' of recent years many of the figures which appear in the early records were virtually eliminated from history. Allowing, for example, to the patriarchs the smallest 'substratum of actual personal history', G. A. Smith asks us, 'But who wants to be sure of more? Who needs to be sure of more?' The fact is many did: They wondered, if being left with so little, were they really assured of even this 'substratum'. If so much were gone, why was anything left? George Adam Smith was able to console his readers with the information that there was a reaction of late in favour of admitting the historical personality of Abraham. While A. M. Fairbairn, no friend it may be admitted of the critics, pronounced with emphasis his own belief in the 'real historical personality of Moses', and maintained that 'everything distinctive' in the history of Israel, 'runs back into him'. This historical significance of Moses, he insisted, can be accepted 'in face of the most recent criticism'.[2]

We will not, then, be surprised to read A. H. Sayce charging the critic with treating the biblical history 'unfairly'.[3] He begins, Sayce argued, 'with certain fixed ideas and presuppositions, which have made him deny the historical character or early date of all statements and documents which run counter to them'.[4]

There was no doubt much justification for the strong opposition to the higher criticism for its pronouncements upon the historicity of the Old Testament. History was being read as a natural development, and into that picture the Old Testament was made to fit. No catena of quotations are needed to show how

---

[1] Cf. G. A. Smith, *Modern Criticism and the Preaching of the Old Testament*, New York, 1901, p. 46 f.

[2] A. M. Fairbairn, *The City of God*, 1897, p. 110.

[3] A. H. Sayce, 'Biblical Archaeology and the Higher Criticism', *Expository Times*, Vol. III, 1891–2, p. 15.   [4] *Ibid.*

this 'naturalistic' view was a fundamental one in much earlier criticism. 'The Old Testament as now interpreted', observed J. Estlin Carpenter, 'tells the story of the rise and growth of a religion.'[1] And the tendency was to explain this rise and growth very much in naturalistic terms. Critics, with a certain 'naturalistic' bias, have continued this stress. Thus as late as 1932, S. A. Cook declares, 'In the Old Testament some fundamental religious ideas not unique in themselves, were uniquely shaped by Israel'.[2]

But it was not long before the radical denials of historical criticism were repudiated, and the admission of a more than natural element was being allowed.

Historical criticism tended more and more to be understood in terms which granted a larger area of historical facts which were later interpreted for the nation of Israel in a religious sense. Importance was attached to this 'tendency' view of the Old Testament accounts; the regard, that is, more for the religious valuation than the historical actuality of an event. H. Wheeler Robinson, in his most influential book, observed, 'the ancient writer felt free to mould the traditions of the past into an illustration of the convictions of the present'.[3] A. F. Kirkpatrick had earlier remarked that 'The prophets were the historians of Israel (a footnote reminds us that the Books of Joshua, Judges, Samuel and Kings are classed in the Jewish Canon as "the former prophets"). They regarded the history of the nation from a religious standpoint. They traced the direct control of Jehovah over the fortunes of His people, in mercy and judgement. It was their function to record and interpret the lessons of the past for the warning and encouragement of the present and future'.[4] Driver had laid down as a dictum that 'None of the historians of the Bible claim supernatural enlightenment for the *materials* of their narrative'.[5] In a paper entitled 'The Claims of Criticism upon the Clergy and Laity', read at the

---

[1] J. Estlin Carpenter, *The Bible in the Nineteenth Century*, 1903, p. 463.

[2] S. A. Cook, *The Place of the Old Testament in Modern Research*, 1932, p. 28.

[3] H. Wheeler Robinson, *The Religious Ideas of the Old Testament*, 1913, seventh impression, 1947, p. 4.

[4] A. F. Kirkpatrick, *The Doctrine of the Prophets*, the Warburtonian Lectures, 1886–90, third edition, 1901, p. 14.

[5] S. R. Driver, *Introduction to the Literature of the Old Testament*, 1891, seventh edition, 1898, Preface, p. x.

Church Congress at Northampton in October 1902, Kirkpatrick emphasized this natural aspect of Israel's story. God's revelation, he declared, was a gradual one 'affected to a large extent by the action of ordinary forces, developed in ways which we should call natural rather than supernatural'.[1]

This rather forbidding statement was somewhat modified by Wheeler Robinson. He appears to stress the importance of historical criticism and tells us that the religious ideas of the Old Testament are in a sense a product of its evolving history. 'Underneath the conventional form of the Old Testament literature', he states, 'critical scholarship has taught us to recognize successive strata that have built up the mountain peaks of faith and vision, each with its own fossil survivals from the past.'[2] He admits that the 'critical view of the Old Testament seems to many to exclude the reality of revelation by surrendering the history to purely naturalistic, or, at any rate, purely human factors'.[3] But he will not allow that this is so, for he claims the critical arrangement 'yields a view of the history of Israel which is natural without being naturalistic'.[4] 'The issue is not', he affirms, 'as to the presence here or there of a "supernatural" element amid "natural" conditions. The distinction, so used, is a legacy from the categories of the eighteenth century. We gain a much deeper insight into the divine activity, when we conceive the evolution of the nation's life as both natural and supernatural throughout, and not a mosaic of both.'[5] It is to Wheeler Robinson's merit to give greater emphasis to the supernatural aspect, even if, as we believe, it is not adequately related to the Old Testament account, for he tends to equate the supernatural with the prophets' religious reading of 'natural' happenings. In a later essay, he stresses the intimate connection between the natural and the supernatural within events in a more suggestive way, although, even here, we would like to have seen a greater emphasis put upon the result of God's impact upon the 'prophet's own consciousness and outlook' as yielding a permanent divine self-disclosure.[6]

[1] S. R. Driver and A. F. Kirkpatrick, *The Higher Criticism*, 1911, p. 11.
[2] H. Wheeler Robinson, *The Religious Ideas of the Old Testament*, 1913, seventh impression, 1947, p. 2.   [3] *Ibid.*, p. 216.   [4] *Ibid.*, p. 6.   [5] *Ibid.*, p. 25.
[6] H. Wheeler Robinson, 'The Philosophy of Revelation', in *Record and Revelation*, 1938. *Essays on the Old Testament* by members of the Society for Old Testament Studies (ed. H. Wheeler Robinson), pp. 315–16.

There was, however, a certain measure of dissatisfaction expressed by one and another, concerning the historical method. This can be seen in a remark of Driver's: 'I readily allow', he says, 'that there are some critics who combine with their literary criticism of the Old Testament an *historical* criticism which appears to me to be unreasonable and extreme'.[1] He, therefore, seeks to distinguish between the two.[2]

In a chapter entitled 'The Methods of Higher Criticism', T. H. Robinson draws the distinction, upon which Peake had so much insisted, between 'higher' and 'historical' criticism. Higher criticism is described as the study of the structure of any particular book or collection of books. Historical criticism deals with 'the historicity or otherwise of any narrative that may be involved'.[3] It is an 'attempt to reconstruct the history from the conflicting material at our disposal'.[4] The whole purpose, then, of all genuine Old Testament study, it is declared, 'is to discover the process by which God led Israel to higher truth'.[5] More and more, in this way, some of the outrageous statements of certain historical critics, to whom the Old Testament was merely 'idealized' history, could be discounted as not the necessary results of higher criticism. Much which the historical critic brushed aside as folk lore and legend was treated in a more factual way by the higher critic and in this respect it appeared to be less 'destructive'.

(ii) There was indeed a growing willingness to assert the *religious* value of the Old Testament, and to insist, at the same time, that the purpose of criticism was not to rob the Church of the Old Testament but to gain for it an enriched understanding. There was an evident disarming flavour about the very title T. K. Cheyne chose for his book which he entitled, *Aids to the Devout Study of Criticism*. And at the beginning of it he urges that 'true criticism must be constructive'.[6] This theme was reiterated by writer after writer. Carpenter, although he maintains that the Bible must be interpreted 'in the light of historical

---

[1] S. R. Driver, *Introduction to the Literature of the Old Testament*, 1891, Preface, p. xviii.

[2] Cf. S. R. Driver and A. F. Kirkpatrick, *The Higher Criticism*, 1911, Preface.

[3] T. H. Robinson, 'The Methods of Higher Criticism', *The People and the Book* by members of the Society for Old Testament Studies (ed. A. S. Peake), 1925, p. 154.

[4] *Ibid.*, p. 174.   [5] *Ibid.*, p. 175.

[6] T. K. Cheyne, *Aids to the Devout Study of Criticism*, 1892, p. 15.

imagination' (although some could not help feeling that the emphasis might be put on the word 'imagination' rather than 'historical'),[1] still insists that 'the true value of the Bible has been enhanced'.[2] It 'supplies the noblest witness which we have to the reality of divine things'.[3] Driver, also, in a lecture on 'The Old Testament in the Light of Today', given at the Jubilee of New College, Hampstead, Wednesday, November 7, 1900, spoke much of the 'new light' criticism has brought. Beyond the 'idealized' history, he says, there may be realized those abiding truths which lie beyond the range of criticism.[4] And H. E. Ryle, speaking at the Church Congress at Folkestone in 1892 on the 'Holy Scripture and Criticism' made the point that there can be no real quarrel between criticism and the Bible. The real conflict is between the 'progress of truth' and the sluggish inability of some minds to keep pace with it.

With assurances of this nature the higher criticism made rapid advance. George Adam Smith, before the turn of the century, contended that the battle was won. Peake's, *A Guide to Biblical Study*, and a popular and unscientific account of the higher criticism by an American, I. Gibson entitled, *Reasons for the Higher Criticism of the Hexateuch*, did much to accelerate the progress. Thus before the century ended it was declared that the Churches had 'passed from opposition to acquiescence'.[5] While a comment on W. H. Green the author of *The Higher Criticism and the Pentateuch*, refers to him 'as the one scholar who rejects the results of criticism'.[6] Although this remark is certainly exaggerated it serves to indicate its spread. The influence of the higher criticism, says a reviewer of H. T. Knight's *Criticism and the Old Testament*, had already penetrated to 'the country clergyman'. 'Now', he continues, 'however, he (i.e. the country clergyman) seems to be awake all over the country. One evidence of this is the meetings of the Church Congress, another the letters in the newspapers, a third the books on Higher Criticism that are written and read so numerously.'[7]

---

[1] J. Estlin Carpenter, *The Bible in the Nineteenth Century*, 1903, p. 511.
[2] *Ibid.*, p. 453.   [3] *Ibid.*, p. 512.
[4] Cf. S. R. Driver, 'Essay in The Higher Criticism', 1911, reprinted from the *Expositor*, January 1901, p. 27 f.
[5] *Expository Times*, Vol. VIII, 1896–7, p. 196.
[6] *Op. cit.*, Vol. VII, 1895–6, p. 227.
[7] *Op. cit.*, Vol. XVIII, 1906–7, p. 279.

Higher criticism seemed to be so well established that it was possible for Peake to talk of its 'assured results'. As time went on, however, these began to appear less secure. Thus in the volume *The People and the Book*, J. E. McFadyen has things to say to those who had supposed that all was settled. Allowing that there is a certain agreement on the broad outline, he adds, that on details 'there is at the moment practically no unanimity anywhere'.[1] No sooner is a position 'established' than it is challenged and critics professing to use the same methods arrive at widely different conclusions. McFadyen does not admit that this 'kaleidoscopic confusion' discredits the use of the method,[2] but he does quote Herrmann to the effect that today the Pentateuchal problem is more open than ever and that the era of purely literary criticism, which was believed to be as good as closed, is far from anything of the kind.

More recently the same point is made with sharpness by H. H. Rowley. 'Many of the conclusions that seemed most sure', he writes, 'have been challenged, and there is now a greater variety of view on many questions than has been known for a long time.'[3] This statement needs to be well pondered by those parsons and school-teachers who are teaching with an assured dogmatism theories they learned in their training colleges years ago. Rowley maintains that 'In general, it may be said, that there is a tendency towards more conservative views on many questions than were common at the opening of our period'.[4] This conservatism, he agrees, is the fruit of the critical method. And he believes it to be, therefore, 'both other and firmer than the old conservatism, just because it is critically, not dogmatically based'.[5]

It was, perhaps, inevitable that criticism should find itself in this position. Many of the ideas from which it sprang seem to be no longer tenable. The whole environment of thought has changed, and gone with it are the optimism and confidence displayed by the earlier advocates of the critical method. Besides, the claim that criticism was giving a Bible more readily under-

---

[1] J. E. McFadyen, 'The Present Position of Old Testament Criticism', *The People and the Book* by members of the Society for Old Testament Studies (ed. A. S. Peake), 1925, p. 183.   [2] *Ibid.*, p. 184. Cf. p. 194 f.

[3] H. H. Rowley, *The Old Testament and Modern Study* by members of the Society for Old Testament Studies, 1951, Preface, p. xvi.

[4] *Ibid.*, p. xvii.   [5] *Ibid.*, p. xviii.

stood has not been fulfilled. The reconstructions suggested have been so many and so intricate that the ordinary person has not been able to follow. Indeed, it was boldly stated by J. Estlin Carpenter that the Bible which must be interpreted in the light of historical imagination means that 'modern study has not made it an easy book for the casual reader'.[1] Herbert Danby has observed that 'There has been a lessening of interest in the Old Testament since the beginning of the present century. Old controversies have died down, and indifference has taken their place. A defensive, almost a diffident, attitude is considered fitting to him who today would put forward the Old Testament's claim to be a usable and even a useful item in the Christian's spiritual armoury'.[2] How much this indifferent attitude derives from the uncertainty concerning the Old Testament due to the higher criticism is not easy to assess. But it is without doubt that the influence in this direction is not small.[3]

C. THE ATTACK ON CRITICISM

There has always been a readiness among critics to dismiss as obscurantists those who refuse to credit their views. They could not believe it possible for any to be thoroughly acquainted with and aware of their arguments in favour of the critical position and honestly to reject their validity. But the sheer fact is that some did, and more do. It was too confidently claimed that scholarship was always on the critics' side. Emil Reich, who for many years, he tells us, 'fully believed in the "scientific character" of Higher Criticism' recalls something of its ' "scientific" spell'.[4] He observed with some justification that 'By far the majority of the public bow to Higher Criticism out of a vague yet strong

[1] J. Estlin Carpenter, *The Bible in the Nineteenth Century*, 1903, p. 511.

[2] Herbert Danby, 'The Old Testament', *The Study of Theology* (ed. H. E. Kirk), 1939, p. 189.

[3] Cf. 'Foremost among the influences causing unbelief was that of modern Biblical Criticism', W. B. Selbie, paper on 'Difficulties of Belief' read at the Congregational Union, Glasgow, 1902.
Referring to A. J. Balfour's address at the Centenary of the British and Foreign Bible Society in the Mansion House, London, March 6, 1903, in which Balfour speaks of the critical view of Scripture which chills enthusiasm and damps ardour, the *British Weekly*, March 13, 1903, adds: 'Mr Balfour must surely know that many of the Higher Critics have ceased to be believers'.

[4] Emil Reich, *The Failure of the Higher Criticism*, 1905, Preface, p. v.

feeling of awe caused by the alleged character of that Criticism. People really do think that Higher Criticism is part of the undoubted scientific progress in which we moderns glory'.[1]

The attack on criticism was long and sustained. It will be already realized how vehemently opposed to higher criticism was A. H. Sayce. He was, of course, not chiefly an Old Testament scholar, but an Assyriologist. In his book, *The Early History of the Hebrews*, however, he gives a fairly competent summary of the critical reconstruction. He then contends, on the basis of archaeology and other data, that the correct reading of the history of the Hebrews is in conflict with that reconstruction. To choose the one, he argues, is to reject the other. The critical method of writing, or, as he thinks, of rewriting Israel's history, is, he declares, 'worthless'. In an article in the *Expository Times*, he asserts that 'the term "higher criticism" is an unfortunate one. It has the appearance of pretentiousness, and it is to be feared that in some cases it has led to the unconscious assumption of a tone of superiority on the part of its confessors and their followers'.[2] Sayce argues that 'The conclusions of the "higher criticism" were supported by an assumption and a tendency'. The assumption was that writing was unknown at the time of the Exodus; and the tendency 'was the extreme scepticism with which the earlier periods of secular history were regarded'.[3] Ellicott, too, from the point of view of our Lord's authority took exception to the critical methods and conclusions.[4] Under the title, 'Is the Old Testament Authentic?', J. Elder Cumming of Glasgow contributed a series of articles to the *Expository Times* in which he sought to meet certain stated results of criticism. The 'authors of the New Criticism' he says, 'have claimed to have invalidated the entire historical accuracy of the earlier portions of the history of Israel, as well as the still earlier history which the Old Testament embodies'.[5] This claim Cumming will not grant. He cannot admit an opposition between the priestly and the prophetic elements in Israel, and

[1] Emil Reich, *The Failure of the Higher Criticism*, 1905, pp. 72–3.
[2] *Expository Times*, Vol. III, 1891–2, p. 15.
[3] *Op. cit.*, p. 17.
[4] *Op. cit.*, Vol. III, 1891–2, pp. 157 f., 235 f., 359 f., 457 f., 538 f.; Vol. IV, 1893–4, pp. 169 f., 362 f., 450 f.
[5] *Op.cit.*, Vol. VI, 1894–5, p. 61; cf. pp. 166, 308 f., 421 f. Vol. VII, 1895–6, p. 38 f.

consequently duplicate documents reflecting these separate outlooks. He cogently repudiates the idea that the discovery of the book in the Temple in the reign of Josiah in 620 BC was, as Cheyne and a number of other critics maintained, its first appearance. It was, he insists, not the original authorship of Deuteronomy that is here recounted, but the discovery of that lost book.

These references are taken from substantial articles attacking criticism. But there were besides, on platform and in pamphlet, much more of a popular kind most of which was ranting rather than relevant. Many, not understanding criticism, fell upon the critic. As a consequence action was often substituted for argument: zeal was mistaken for knowledge. What was lacking in information was made up for in perspiration. The loud voice, the thumped pulpit, the poorly written booklet were thought by many a sufficient answer to the patient and scholarly work of the Old Testament critic. Some imagined it to be enough to surround the term 'critic' with a distasteful odour. It can therefore be understood why the careful critic impatiently dismissed some of his opponents as obscurantists.

But this was not the whole story. There were critics of criticism as painstaking as those who took the other view. Some of these works can still be examined with profit; and they must be by anyone who seeks to give any sort of true account of the battle of the standpoints.

We will refer first in chronological order to some major works. One of the most scholarly opponents of criticism was Professor James Robertson of Glasgow. In his Baird Lectures he sought to establish that the prophets are not earlier than the law. Then in his later Croall Lectures of 1893–4 on *The Poetry and Religion of the Psalms*, he rejected the position of those who sought a later date for the Psalms. Robertson, therefore, endeavoured to restore the traditional order of Law, Psalms and Prophets. He was convinced that we do possess pre-exilic psalms and he sees no valid arguments which hinder David from being a psalmist. Driver takes Robertson to task in a contemporary issue of the *Critical Review* and urged that his conclusions are out of touch with even those of 'moderate criticism'. Commenting on Driver's notice of Robertson's work the *Expository Times* remarked that the Glasgow professor 'seems to be the only opponent of the Higher Criticism whom the critics now consider worthy of reply'.[1]

In 1894 the formidable volume entitled, *Lex Mosaica, or The Law of Moses and the Higher Criticism* appeared. This is a work by a number of scholars well acquainted with the critical arguments. The Introduction was written by the Bishop of Bath and Wells: and among the contributors are men of such reputation as George Rawlinson, who was at one time Camden Professor of Ancient History at Oxford; F. Watson, Lecturer of Theology and Fellow of St John's College, Cambridge; Henry Wace, Principal of King's College, London; Stanley Leathes, Professor of Hebrew in the same place. The Preface of this considerable tome refers to the 'Sporadic efforts' that 'have been already made by responsible writers to show that the new position is either untenable or fraught with greater difficulties than the traditional view'. The writers show thorough competence in dealing with their subject. In every case the critical view is given fair statement. It is noted in one place that the concern is not for those critics who deny the supernatural. It is for 'those who admit a revelation from God in the sense in which the term is ordinarily understood'.[2] Lias in his essay on 'The Times of Samuel and Saul' urges that no one need repudiate criticism as such. There is a good and a bad criticism. Much criticism, however, is destructive. Lias comes out strongly against the historical criticism of Robertson Smith. 'The history, we are told, has been re-written at a later period, and these details have been introduced, some say with a purpose, and others under a mistaken impression. Anyhow, the history, in the opinion of the critics, has been falsified, or at the least revised, under the influence of a dominating idea. But this is not to study documents "in the light of history", it is to study them in the light of historical speculation.'[3] It is not, of course, possible, nor is it quite to our purpose, to summarize in any detail this massive volume. Throughout its pages all the works then available of the leading critics, German, British and American, come into review. There are abundant references to Wellhausen, Keil, Briggs, Robertson Smith, Driver, Cheyne, and so on. The writers are convinced about the importance of their task. They

[1] *Expository Times*, Vol. X, 1898–9, p. 242.
[2] *Lex Mosaica*, 1894, p. 77.   [3] *Op. cit.*, p. 207.

feel that the critical ideas are inconsistent with a true understanding of Scripture; it is declared 'that the view put forward
by the new school of criticism is inconsistent alike with the
language of the prophets and the facts of history'.[1] The critical
theory, it is stated, 'has already involved grave questions
respecting the limits of our Lord's authority and knowledge, and
it must entail not less grave questions respecting the authority
and the inspiration of the Apostles and Evangelists'.[2] The
writers claim to have subjected the issue of criticism 'to a fresh
and thorough historical investigation'. And they conclude that
as a result the critical theory is unacceptable. They find nothing
to compel the conclusion that this ancient book, any more than
any other ancient historical record, was 'composed like a
tessellated pavement, in which several unknown sources are
dovetailed into one another, sometimes in the most minute
pieces'.[3] Any other nation would have found the process difficult,
'but it would be tenfold more difficult in the case of the Jews,
one of whose chief characteristics, at once their strength and
their danger, is their intense tenacity, and who were always, for
good or for harm, "a stiff-necked people" '.[4]

Her Majesty's Printers, Eyre and Spottiswoode, in 1894,
published a book by W. L. Baxter called *Sanctuary and Sacrifice,
A Reply to Wellhausen*. The first of the two parts into which the
book is divided consists of a series of four contributions to *The
Thinker* magazine for November and December 1893, and for
March and April 1894. Baxter really limits himself to an
examination of Wellhausen's *Prolegomena to the History of
Israel* in this volume of his of over 500 pages. 'We have not
sought', Baxter declares, 'to weigh the *theological value* of
Wellhausen's conclusions; our exclusive occupation has been in
*assailing the truth, and the warrantableness of the definite positions,
which he successively propounds.*'[5] He believed that the errors
which he has revealed in the pages of the 'most admired
champion' of the Higher Criticism will show how fragile the
whole critical thesis is.

Baxter's book cannot honestly be said to have had any great
effect. It was limited to one individual whom the British critic

[1] *Lex Mosaica*, p. 612.
[2] *Op. cit.*, p. 611.   [3] *Op. cit.*, p. 617.   [4] *Op. cit.*, p. 618.
[5] W. L. Baxter, *Sanctuary and Sacrifice*, 1896, p. 505 (italics in original).

could plead did not represent their more believing approach. At any rate Wellhausen was not stirred to reply: this may, of course, have been because a much more formidable attack was about to be issued against him by Hommel, Professor of Assyriology at Munich, and he, we are told, was 'a foeman worthy of any critic's steel'. It is, however, much more likely that Wellhausen did not deem it necessary to reply to Baxter. Yet A. S. Peake does rally to Wellhausen's defence. In a long and detailed review of *Sanctuary and Sacrifice*, he asserts that 'Wellhausen's contribution is relevant to the state of criticism at the time'.[1] It seems that Baxter was assailing a position which was already out of date. Yet there is a remark made by Baxter which hints that he was expecting some such 'defence'. Baxter refers to 'A recent volume, with a notable affectation of "Lux", was fain, on this topic, to execute a somewhat helpless retreat into "Flux". But there may be times', he adds, 'when "Flux" is treason'.[2] Peake maintains that Baxter's arguments will make no difference to others, as, is to be expected, they have made no difference to him. Baxter comes back to the attack upon Peake's criticisms in a later issue of the *Expository Times*.[3]

John Smith calls his book in which he attacks criticism, *The Integrity of Scripture*. There is a subtitle describing it as 'Plain Reasons for Rejecting the Critical Hypothesis'. Smith had been for a year a class-fellow of Robertson Smith at Aberdeen. The book is really a series of discourses given to the congregation of Broughton Place Church, Edinburgh, and the Preface states that 'They are not to be considered as a discussion from a purely critical standpoint, though it is believed that they expose the fundamental logical fallacies pervading the critical method'. The titles of the chapters show that Smith knew how to make his points. He was well aware of the issues involved in the 'new construction'. He is also convinced that 'The standpoint of the prophets is the reverse of what modern criticism avers'.[4] They do not speak, he argues, to a people slowly emerging from polytheism to monotheism. He objects to the reduction of the authentic history of the Old Testament to the barest minimum

---

[1] *Expository Times*, Vol. VII, 1895–6, p. 401; cf. pp. 400–5.

[2] W. L. Baxter, *Sanctuary and Sacrifice*, 1896, p. 505.

[3] *Expository Times*, Vol. VII, 1895–6, p. 505 f. But the battle of words continued, cf., e.g. Peake's reply, *ibid.*, pp. 559 ff.

[4] John Smith, *The Integrity of Scripture*, 1902, p. 57.

as evidenced by his namesake, Robertson Smith and George
Adam Smith. He shows the difficulties in the disintegrating
process and the embarrassing results.

There are, he contends, 'no external standards outside the
sacred writings by which to judge of their date and authorship'.[1]
He will not allow that it was the imagination working on 'the
tabula rasa of the wilderness', quoting Wellhausen's phrase,
which reared the hierarchical system pictured in Exodus. 'Where
the Higher Critics, in our judgement', he says, 'have gone astray
is, in supposing, against tradition and the strongest internal
evidences, that, with whatever differences, Jewish sacred history
followed the same course of natural development; and in
applying methods, suitable enough in dealing with common
human fact and growth of legend, to a totally different situation,
the incoming of a true revelation of God, and its creative
influence on the life and institutions of the people.'[2] The critical
reconstruction of Scripture he regards as inadequate and
improbable. The result is an hypothesis built upon hypotheses.
'Thus pulled down and built up, the Old Testament is a book out
of which the very soul of revelation has gone.'[3] Smith's book
breathes the very atmosphere of devotion. He was, as one
reviewer states, 'absorbed in the religion of the Bible'. 'The
critics have their minds on its science, Dr Smith has his on its
religion.' 'And in these days', the same writer adds, 'when so
many preachers of the religion of the Bible are spending their
time on its science, we rejoice exceedingly in the whole-hearted
devotion to what is first and last in Bible study.'[4]

A year after Smith's work came Thomas Whitelaw's *Old
Testament Critics, An Enquiry into the Character, Effect, and
Validity of their Teaching*. This volume is marked by an adequate
scholarship. The author was well acquainted with the main
teachers and theories of criticism. It is, however, not his
intention 'to vindicate the traditional theory of the origin and
structure of the Old Testament or to undertake the removal of
such difficulties in connection therewith as are usually felt by
honest doubters or anxious seekers after truth'.[5] It will be his

---

[1] John Smith, *The Integrity of Scripture*, 1902, p. 117.   [2] *Ibid.*, pp. 131-2.
[3] *Ibid.*, p. 163.
[4] *Expository Times*, Vol. XIII, 1901-2, p. 472.
[5] Thomas Whitelaw, *Old Testament Critics*, 1903, Introduction, p. xiii.

endeavour to present the doctrines of the critics 'in as colourless a light as possible, with no exaggeration in either one direction or other'.[1] Whitelaw restricts his enquiry to four main topics: The Manufacture of the Hexateuch, The Colouring of the History Books, The Extrusion of David from the Psalter, and The Disintegration of the Prophets. In part two of the volume he deals with 'The Indemnity of the Critics, or The Cost of the Higher Criticism (to be paid by the Christian People)'. He notes what the 'advanced' German critics have surrendered and what the 'believing critic' questions. In the third part of the book, Whitelaw institutes a 'criticism of the critics'. He quotes the words of Dr Mead: 'The right to criticize a critic's theories, is as sacred as the right of the critic to propound them'.[2]

Whitelaw questions what he regards as certain critical presuppositions. It is maintained that the Bible was subject to the usual processes of composition and should be approached as any other book. Having said that and done that then the critic goes on to insist that the Bible is no ordinary book. Sanday remarks, 'Let us by all means study the Bible, if we will, like any other book, but do not let us beg the question that it is wholly like any other book'.[3] It is to be approached critically like any other volume, but as John Ker asks, 'Is this possible?'[4] There is a spiritual and moral element in the Bible which are absent from all other books. It is indeed itself the critic, judging our thoughts and uncovering our need.

Certain 'improbabilities of criticism' as Whitelaw calls them[5], are considered, as, for example, the complete disappearance from the world's and the Church's knowledge of all the great men the critics have discovered to have been authors and redactors of the principal parts of the Hebrew Scriptures. Cornhill has identified twenty-six hands at work in the production of the Hexateuch. But 'the alphabetical gentlemen who have been ticketed J,E,D,P,R,&c', have passed into oblivion.[6] The pros and cons of the documentary hypothesis are intelligently discussed.[7] Whitelaw cannot accept the contention that

[1] Thomas Whitelaw, *Old Testament Critics*, 1903, p. 1.
[2] *Ibid.*, p. 169.
[3] W. Sanday, *Inspiration*, Bampton Lectures, 1893, third edition, 1908, p. 2.
[4] John Ker, *Thoughts for Life and Heart*, n.d., p. 89.
[5] Thomas Whitelaw, *Old Testament Critics*, 1903, pp. 192 ff.
[6] *Ibid.*, p. 205.   [7] *Ibid.*, pp. 212 ff.

there are no Davidic psalms.[1] Concluding with the three criteria of 'immediate luminousness, philosophic reasonableness, and moral helpfulness', which William James has set forth in his recent Gifford Lectures,[2] Whitelaw maintains that the critical theory examined in the light of these tests is found wanting.

It will be expected that a reference should be made to James Orr's Bross Prize volume, *The Problem of the Old Testament*, which was published in 1906. No justice can possibly be done to its contents here. It is a work of accurate scholarship and profound knowledge of the subject.[3] Orr gives due respect to those critics who are 'convinced upholders of supernatural revelation'.[4] He understands that there is a right higher criticism which is 'simply the careful scrutiny, on the principles which are customary to apply to all literature, of the actual phenomena of the Bible, with a view to deduce from these such conclusions as may be warranted regarding age, authorship, mode of composition, sources, etc., of the different books'.[5] But he then goes on to bring weighty arguments against the critical presuppositions. These he regards in general as the ideas of the natural development of Israel's religion and the equation of revelation with a mere providential guidance of history. Having attacked these necessary assumptions, Orr then deals with the superstructure which has been reared upon such foundations. He concludes his book with a reference to the culmination of the progressive revelation of the Old Testament in the Christ of the New. It is He who clasps the two into one: and in His light the Old Testament finds its significance. He calls for, what is now seen to have been needed, a deeper understanding of the connection of the Old Testament with the New. It is this connection, he declares, which gives to the critical problems their keenest interest. 'The tendency of late', he maintains, writing at the beginning of the century, 'has been to make too light of this connection. The storm of criticism which, in the last decades, assailed the Old Testament, was fondly thought by

---

[1] Thomas Whitelaw, *Old Testament Critics*, 1903, p. 307.

[2] Cf. William James, *Varieties of Religious Experience*, 1902, sixteenth edition, p. 18.

[3] Cf. 'Dr Orr's work is of a very different quality from the screaming invective of an Emil Reich', *Expository Times*, Vol. XVII, 1905–6, p. 320.

[4] James Orr, *The Problem of the Old Testament*, 1906, seventh impression, 1909, p. 8.   [5] *Ibid.*, p. 9.

many to leave intact the New Testament. What mattered it about Abraham and Moses, so long as Jesus and His Gospel remained? This delusion is passing away. The fact is becoming apparent to the dullest which has long been evident to unbiased observers, that much of the radical criticism of the Old Testament proceeded on principles, and was conducted by methods, which had only to be applied with like thoroughness to the New Testament to work like havoc. The fundamental ideas of God and His revelation which underlay that criticism could not, as we set out by affirming, lead up to a doctrine of the Incarnation, but only to a negation of it.'[1]

In addition to these larger works there were others of lesser proportions emanating from the learned which attacked criticism. Of the more important of these volumes of slender dimensions a passing reference need only be made here.

The volumes of the Bible Students' Library were designed to meet the critical challenge. R. B. Girdlestone in the first book in the series set forth the results of his own 'studies in Old Testament criticism'. He assures his readers that neither the increasing knowledge of Old Testament Hebrew, nor the discoveries of some old manuscripts have tended to shake men's faith in the trustworthiness of the Sacred Books, but rather is it because 'the critics have been influenced by a growing disinclination to regard the Bible as *unique*'.[2] He believes that the traditional view of the Old Testament 'fits fairly with the facts all round'. He has sought throughout his discussion to be 'rational and reverential'.[3] Critics, he claims, do not pay enough attention to what the author of an Old Testament book 'says of himself'. He admits that both sides in the controversy have not been blameless. 'We have been afraid', he says, 'of allowing textual corruption, late editorial work, the use of ordinary materials, and human ways of putting things. We have confused inspiration with omnipotence, and have forgotten that the Sacred Truth is committed to earthen vessels. We have minimized inconsistencies and refused to face difficulties. We have imported modern science into ancient books, and have sought to shut up those questions of age and authorship which

---

[1] James Orr, *The Problem of the Old Testament*, 1906, 1909, p. 477.
[2] R. B. Girdlestone, *The Foundations of the Bible*, 1890, fourth edition, revised, 1892, Preface, p. v.   [3] *Ibid.*, p. 193.

God in His providence has left open.'[1] Yet the Bible is falsely regarded if it is thought of as an ordinary book. It is not an ordinary Book, since it is the result of the action of the Spirit of God, who restrained and impelled its writers. It was produced by inspired men: and this reality no critic can dare to neglect. Things human and divine are woven throughout. We have natural phenomena and national polity and history from a Divine point of view, and we must throw all the side-lights we can on the physics and metaphysics, on the history and biography, of Scripture.[2] These books of Scripture are evidently on the side of truth and righteousness. They bear the marks of fidelity and reveal themselves to be of God.

Leathes, who had already given the Bampton Lectures on the subject 'The Religion of Christ', dealt with *The Law and the Prophets* in the second volume and refused the critical conclusions. Lias, who with the other two contributed to the *Lex Mosaica*, wrote in the third book in the series on *Principles of Criticism*. The *Church Times* describes this work, though small of compass, to be an 'admirable . . . exposition of the ingenious puzzles which German criticism has been weaving under the guise of truth'. Lias, who had been a Hulsean lecturer, in this work enforced some of the points he makes in the *Lex Mosaica*.

In 1900, at the invitation of W. Robertson Nicoll, D. S. Margoliouth produced in a book a series of articles he had contributed to the *Expositor* for the same year. Margoliouth was at the time the Laudian Professor of Arabic in Oxford, and this work is punctuated with discussions of Arabic and Hebrew words and passages. His purpose is to show the genuineness of the Christian revelation in the Bible and exhibit its superiority and supremacy. In Chapter VII, the only one which did not appear in the *Expositor*, he deals with 'The Principles of Criticism'. A 'sound argument' he urges, 'is one in which the major premise claims assent on all occasions, whether the particular consequence deduced gives pain or pleasure to him who deduces it'.[3] It is his idea that certain facts have thrown the

---

[1] R. B. Girdlestone, *The Foundations of the Bible*, 1890, fourth edition, revised, 1892, p. 196.

[2] *Ibid.*, pp. 196–7.

[3] D. S. Margoliouth, *Lines of Defence of the Biblical Revelation*, 1900, p. 277.

major premise of criticism into confusion. To face these facts would be to discredit 'the *whole* of the Higher Criticism'. He charges the critic with evading these disconcerting facts rather than acknowledge that they have made the colossal error which they have.

A passing reference was made earlier to Emil Reich's *The Failure of the 'Higher Criticism' of the Bible*.[1] Of the five chapters in it the first two appeared in the *Contemporary Review* for February and April 1905. Reich was an historian of some repute. It is, however, impossible to credit him with having fulfilled his intention in this volume. 'It is intended', he declared, 'not only to destroy the "scientific" spell of "Higher Criticism", but also to construct the right method of comprehending the Bible.'[2] The most enthusiastic supporter of his position must allow that he has not carried out his promise. A reading of the book will reveal, however, that he was in touch with an extensive literature in French and German as well as English. Reich maintained that it was impossible to separate between historical and literary criticism. And as a consequence he insists that to 'deny or question the received authorship, text, and dates of the books of the Bible, i.e. the Higher Critics, do thereby declare that the Bible is a forgery'.[3] To deny Abraham is, he contends, to deny Jesus. His conclusion is: 'Higher Criticism stands condemned by history fully as much as by true religion. It is neither true nor helpful. It is the distortion of historical truth as well as the desecration of true religion'.[4]

In his *Bible Under Trial: Apologetic Papers in View of Present-Day Assaults on Holy Scripture*, James Orr gives a popular exposition of critical conclusions and his attack upon them. The volume is marked by Orr's usual accurate scholarship. He shows, and he has Cheyne for his support, how indebted criticism is to Deism.[5] He feels that criticism 'is for the present so settled on its lees in its confidence in its immoveable results that little anyone can say will make any impression on it'.[6] Orr, however,

[1] Cf. p. 118 and see p. 126 (footnote).
[2] Emil Riech, *The Failure of the Higher Criticism*, 1905, Preface, p. vi.
[3] *Ibid.*, p. 82. [4] *Ibid.*, p. 193.
[5] Cf. James Orr, *The Bible Under Trial*, 1907, p. 16; see T. K. Cheyne, *The Founders of Criticism*, 1893, pp. 1–2 and H. D. McDonald, *Ideas of Revelation*, 1959, Ch. iii.
[6] James Orr, *The Bible Under Trial*, p. 54.

E

is quite convinced that neither is the confidence justified nor are the results secure. 'No argument', he observes, 'is more frequently employed to silence objection to modern critical theories than the alleged agreement of competent scholars as to the main results of their criticism.'[1] Orr, however, contends that these 'settled results' are advertised rather than actual. He is certain that the new view which reconstructs the Old Testament record 'not only inverts the Bible's own account of Israel's history and institutions; it cancels that history in large part altogether, and proposes for acceptance another'.[2] It 'lifts off its hinges the history of worship and literature in Israel as hitherto accepted' as Delitzsch remarked concerning Wellhausen's theory. Orr will not grant that the Old Testament history can be resolved into myths.

He points out how naturally the ideas undergirding Old Testament criticism are passed on into the New Testament. He can quote N. Schmidt's *The Prophet of Nazareth* in this connection. Schmidt boldly affirmed that 'The movement could not stop at the Old Testament'.[3] Applying the so-called 'historical–religious' method to the gospels, What view of Jesus results? We are left with a sketchy Picture of a Humanitarian Jesus who, by reason of His good deeds, was supplied with supernatural qualities by His enthusiastic followers. Against such a naturalistic conception, the natural result of the critical doctrine continued into the New Testament, Christian faith and experience are in flat contradiction. Dealing with the 'Opposition of Science', Orr declares 'that neither Christianity nor the Bible are in the slightest danger from the results that genuine science has succeeded in establishing'.[4] He warns, however, against trying to read the Bible as a textbook on modern science. It was not within its purpose to anticipate recent astronomical discoveries.

In two of his volumes, Robert Anderson dealt with Higher Criticism from the point of view of a legal expert. His *The Bible and Modern Criticism* carries a Preface by Bishop Moule of Durham, and was noted in *The Times* as 'A vigorous criticism of the methods of the "Higher Critics" '. His *Pseudo-Criticism*,

---

[1] James Orr, *The Bible Under Trial*, p. 73.   [2] *Ibid.*, p. 97.
[3] *Ibid.*, p. 150; cf. N. Schmidt, *The Prophet of Nazareth*, 1905, p. 29.
[4] *Ibid.*, p. 200.

or The Higher Criticism and its Counterfeit, was, according to *The English Churchman*, 'a masterpiece of apologetics'.

In his *Daniel in the Critics' Den*, Anderson makes a spirited attack on Farrar and Driver. He had earlier made a 'Reply to Dean Farrar's *Book of Daniel*' in the *Blackwood Magazine* and this volume contains that 'Reply' as well as an examination of Driver's *Book of Daniel* in the Cambridge Bible series. Anderson cogently argues for the historicity of Daniel and he cannot justify in any degree Farrar's statement regarding it as an 'avowed fiction'.[1] It is not as the Dean openly contended an 'idle legend abounding in "violent errors" of the grossest kind'.[2] The higher criticism is, according to Anderson, 'a rationalistic "crusade" ' which seeks 'to account for the Bible on naturalistic principles'.[3]

If Robert Anderson seeks to rehabilitate Daniel as an historical reality in Israel's story, the same desire is shown for Jonah by L. T. Townsend. In his book, *The Story of Jonah in the Light of Modern Criticism* (1897), he writes with conviction regarding the literal truthfulness of the account. There is a compelling logic in his approach.

In 1896 J. Cynddlyan Jones delivered the Davies Lectures on 'The Mosaic Theology'. These were published under the title *Primeval Revelation*. They are really a consideration of the first eight chapters of Genesis. Jones tells us that he examined the critical hypothesis and also the traditional view and having 'once and again wavered in my decision', he says, 'he dipped finally on the traditional side'. It must be confessed, however, that Jones introduced certain 'liberal' views into his allegiance to the traditional idea. He maintained for example, that Moses wrote the fragments which have gone into the composition of the Pentateuch during the period of the wilderness wanderings and that these were later cemented into a whole.

Henry Harris in 1890 produced his book, *The Old Testament Scriptures*—a work of a sound scholar and a clear thinker. He endeavoured to allay the rising fears over the outcome of the critical procedure. He maintained that there was much in the Old Testament beyond the ability of criticism to touch.

[1] Robert Anderson, *Daniel in the Critics' Den*, n.d., fourth edition, p. 7; cf. F. W. Farrar, *The Book of Daniel*, 1901, p. 43.
[2] *Ibid.*; cf. F. W. Farrar, *The Book of Daniel*, p. 119.   [3] *Ibid.*, p. 11.

The following year Clement Clemance wrote on *How to Treat the Bible*. He had no desire either to bless or to ban higher criticism, but he sought to guide puzzled readers to find a meaning in the Scriptures for themselves. James Lindsay about the same time, writing on *The Significance of the Old Testament for Modern Theology*, after a summary account of the criticism of the previous fifty years, concludes with the assurance that the Bible still possesses a spiritual significance for 'the wise reader'.

Other writers were even more anxious to stress the continual usefulness and value of the Bible even allowing for the acceptance of certain critical ideas. J. B. Snell in his *Gain or Loss?*—a series of five lectures given at Brixton Independent Chapel on the topic 'Recent Biblical Criticism' concludes that, in spite of all that has been said about the Bible it is still with us and still speaks to us: and if it is not God's word, it is very like it! R. L. Ottley in his Bampton Lectures of 1897 on *Aspects of the Old Testament* entered the field of Old Testament study, not as an authority himself but, he says, as one who has made himself acquainted with what was going on in this sphere. His intention in these lectures is to relieve the stress on faith which recent criticism has introduced, and to make people, especially teachers and students, appreciate the religious significance and value of the Bible itself.

We shall conclude this account of the battle of the standpoints with a reference to two volumes, one at the end of the last century and one of recent date, in which it will be noted how from different approaches the same conclusion is reached.

The first volume is that of Adolph Saphir, *The Divine Unity of Scripture*. Saphir originated in Germany and had a thorough training in German philosophy and literature. As a youth he had been attracted by Hegelianism as well as the prevalent materialism. He had also been a Jew but was converted to Christianity, so that here too he had an advantage. Saphir had a thorough grasp of the critical thesis.[1] The book to which we refer comprises a series of lectures delivered in Kensington at the close of the year 1888 and the beginning of 1889. The date

---

[1] Cf. 'He (Saphir) goes to the facts himself with as much knowledge and discernment as the ablest, and he fairly states the things he has himself honestly come by. If there are any persons who have been shaken through the incredible answers of hurried orthodoxy, let him seek this book. It is clear, considerate, and convincing', *The Expository Times*, Vol. V, 1893–4, p. 46.

is important since it was right in the midst of an era when all the stress was on the diversity of the Bible, and it was viewed, for the most part, as a collection of heterogeneous fragments.

Saphir's approach is that of a strictly conservative evangelical. He saw, as few in his day saw, the need to pay attention to the unity of the Bible. He says, 'notwithstanding all the complex and manifold character of the Old Testament revelation, which was unfolded very slowly "at sundry times, and in diverse manners", and in which there were a great many elements combined, that appear to us at first sight not to be spiritual but rather ephemeral—notwithstanding all this, there was great simplicity and great unity'.[1] He refers, for example, to the idea of the divine 'election' into God's 'covenant' mercy as consti-tuting a fundamental principle of that divine unity.[2]

Saphir stresses also that the history of Israel is 'theological' history.[3] It is history written in the prophetic spirit, the object of which is to show God's will to us and His purposes concerning the human race, what man is to think of God, and what life it is that God requires of man.[4] He will, however, insist that it is genuine history which is being recorded. The Greeks and Romans as they advanced sought to discard their early history. It was otherwise with Israel. Old Testament history, unlike ancient history generally, is as Niebuhr remarked, free from all 'national patriotic falsehood'. It is unadorned, sober and severe. In the Bible ideas and facts unite to make it the history of redemption. 'Ideas without facts make up a philosophy. Facts without ideas make up a history.' But 'all Scripture facts are full of ideas'.[5] The history of the Bible cannot however be under-stood in any 'natural' way. The difficulty in accepting its history is not due to lack of evidence for its historical and geographical accuracy. 'The difficulty lies in this, that the things which are spiritual—and, above all, God Himself—can only be the object of faith; and this whole Bible history is a history in which God is the great agent, and Israel only responding to His agency, and afterwards the Church only responding to His agency.'[6]

Saphir contends, without any reserve, for the human element in the Bible. It is 'the Word of God', he says, 'and yet an

---

[1] Adolph Saphir, *The Divine Unity of Scripture*, 1892, p. 244.
[2] *Ibid.*, cf. pp. 250 ff.   [3] *Ibid.*, p. 303.
[4] *Ibid.*, p. 241.   [5] *Ibid.*, p. 201.   [6] *Ibid.*, p. 210.

intensely human book, written by men and for men, and breath-
ing everywhere the atmosphere of human life and human
emotions'.[1] He notes nevertheless that Christ never spoke 'of the
ideas of Scripture, of the teaching of Scripture, of the promises of
Scripture, of this or that in Scripture, of "the divine element" in
the Scripture, as our moderns would say, or of the Word of God
contained in the Scripture'.[2] He simply spoke of 'the Scripture'.
He therefore rejects the need for and the possibility of any
verifying faculty for judging of the disclosures within the Bible.
Saphir is however concerned throughout to maintain the unity
of the Scripture. Its truths are not put before us 'in a systematic
and methodical form, so that doctrine succeeds doctrine, and
that the facts and the promises are arranged for our learning'.[3]
The 'harmonious irregularities' found in nature are seen
likewise in the Bible. Yet it is 'the golden history of election
and grace'. It has its divine unity which brings it into organic
union with the New Testament so that the Old Testament must
be in some measure Christologically interpreted.

No one has done more within recent years to give the fullest
recognition to the history and theology of the Old Testament
than H. H. Rowley. His later books seem to show a greater
tendency to stress the deep spiritual realities of Israel's story.
This is seen, for example, in his suggestive volume, *The Faith
of Israel*. Our reference here, for the second volume to which we
desired to draw attention to conclude this chapter, is to his *Unity
of the Bible*. Rowley begins by remarking that when he started
his own theological studies such a topic as the unity of the Bible
would have been viewed with suspicion, as evidence of 'an out-
of-date obscurantist'. It was a day when the antithesis between
the legal and the prophetic books was over-emphasized and
when the predictive element in prophecy was minimized and
Messianic prophecy largely explained away. The prophets were
for the most part regarded as preachers of righteousness and
moral reformers rather than as men who in any sense pointed
onward to our Lord.

The New Testament robbed of its essential message was
severed from the Old, and exclusive emphasis was placed upon
the diversity of the Bible. This was, as we have seen, the actual

---

[1] Adolph Saphir, *The Divine Unity of Scripture*, pp. 1–2.
[2] *Ibid.*, p. 48.   [3] *Ibid.*, p. 34.

situation in which Saphir found himself and which makes his book all the more significant and suggestive. It is the purpose of Rowley, while urging that due recognition should be given to the diversity in the Bible, to stress the fact of its fundamental unity: 'the diversity of the Bible must be recognized fully and clearly', he says, 'even though we see a more profoundly significant unity running through it all'.[1] This regard for the unity of the Bible is, he notes, a recent thing. But it is, he urges, a real fact.[2] Rowley sees the unity not as 'static' but as 'dynamic'.[3] Israel's history is 'no automatic spiritual growth': God is active within its history. 'To study the Bible simply as a human story, and to treat men's beliefs about God without asking what validity they have, is sometimes thought to be the scientific study of the Bible. This tacitly assumes that there was no validity in their beliefs, since if there was validity, and if men were genuinely moved by God, the story cannot be fully understood while ignoring the supremely important factors in it. . . . But it is just as dogmatic to suppose that God is not a vital factor in human affairs as to suppose that He is.'[4]

The human element in the Bible is to be recognized because 'Divine inspiration came through the organ of men's personality'.[5] Yet for all that it possesses a divine authority. Rowley, too, like Saphir, lays hold of the ideas of the divine election of Israel into covenant relationship with God as the fact which gives to the Old Testament its fundamental unity. Here is the 'thread that runs all through the Old Testament at least from the time of Moses, and that gives unity to its thought. The principle of election is carried back, indeed, far beyond Moses in the Bible. But here it takes a new, and richly significant, form. God chooses Israel in unmerited grace, and not because of her worth; and having chosen her, He claims her for Himself by what He does for her'.[6] Rowley concludes with the observation that 'A historical sense is essential for all satisfying study of this Book, but along with that sense there must go a perception of the continuing thread that runs through all, and that makes this library also a Book'.[7]

---

[1] H. H. Rowley, *The Unity of the Bible*, 1953, second impression, 1955, p. 3.
[2] *Ibid.*; cf. references quoted by Rowley on p. 29.   [3] *Ibid.*, p. 7.
[4] *Ibid.*, p. 9.   [5] *Ibid.*, p. 15.
[6] *Ibid.*, pp. 26–7; cf. H. H. Rowley, *The Biblical Doctrine of Election*, 1950.
[7] *Ibid.*, p. 29.

Here, then, we have two books separated by over half a century both stressing the need to see the unity in the Bible. But the standpoint from which each writer begins differs. Saphir's position is traditionally conservative having no compromise with higher criticism. Rowley, on the other hand, begins from the critical position, although many of the more recent conclusions of the critics are much more moderate than those claimed as assured results at the end of the last century. Yet both Saphir and Rowley come out with the same emphasis upon the need to recognize a fundamental unity in the diversity of Scripture: and they both see that unity in the same basic facts. The future outlook may therefore be regarded as promising.

CHAPTER FOUR

The Focus of the Conflict

The Battle of the Standpoints, it will be clear from the last chapter, brought the Bible, in a new way, into the storm centre of controversy. Questions at once arose regarding its origin, its purpose, its authority and the like. But, perhaps, the most fundamental issue brought to the fore concerned the relationship of our Lord to the subject of Old Testament criticism. As we have noted, the new theory had played havoc with many traditional views. Yet the one undoubted fact stood out clearly: the same Old Testament which appeared to many to be roughly handled by many moderns, was the same Book from which Christ quoted with a certain ring of authority and in the spirit of which He lived, and moved and had His being. What, therefore, was to be thought of His relationship to those Scriptures? This was the most urgent question which had emerged from the heated discussions concerning Biblical criticism. In this connection, as we shall see in more particular detail later, one of the 'much discussed references', as it was alluded to by one writer of the period, was the authorship of Psalm cx.[1] This aspect of the controversy flared up as a result of an article by W. E. Gladstone in *The Record* of January 8, 1892. The controversy centred around the subject: 'Has modern criticism the right to question whether Psalm cx was written by David or not?' This problem, however, soon opened out into the larger one, or, perhaps, it might be more correct to say, that it was an instance of a wider issue—an issue which involved the whole question of the extent of our Lord's knowledge.

This is a point made in a notice of H. C. Powell's book, *The Principle of the Incarnation*. 'It was the discovery', the observer

[1] Buchanan Blake, *Expository Times*, Vol. III, 1891–2, p. 519.

states, 'that the 110th Psalm was *not* written by David' which 'opened the whole question of our Lord's personality, producing the great theological controversy of our generation'.[1] Thus had the problem been raised, but soon it became evident that even if it were conclusively proved that David *did* write the psalm the controversy would not have been settled. The issue concerning our Lord's knowledge would have remained.

Although it is a fact that the question came to prominence in connection with criticism, it is probable that it could not have been evaded in view of the emphasis which Gore had given to the doctrine of 'Kenosis' in his *Lux Mundi* essay. By the year 1891 it was observed, 'The controversy raised by the *Lux Mundi* has nearly spent itself'. The question was asked, 'What has it brought us?' Our writer answers his own query with the assurance, 'no real gain to the cause either of the science of theology or the cause of true religion'. Yet there was something which did remain to become the point of theological debate for some years as the letters in contemporary issues of *The Spectator* (Nos. 3222–5) and *The Record* (Nos. 7556–64) show. 'The real subject of dispute' the writer just quoted adds, 'has been the limitation of Christ's human knowledge.'[2] Although doubt is expressed by him as to whether the criticism of the Old Testament has anything to do with such a subject, it is quite evident that numbers on both sides were satisfied that it had. While those who thought it had not were compelled, at any rate, to show why it had not, and in so doing they committed themselves to a positive statement concerning our Lord's knowledge.

A. CHRIST AND THE SCRIPTURES

Looking back at the host of letters and articles which appeared in the general and religious press over the period of the last ten years of the century, one becomes aware of how important were the subjects of Christ's attitude to the Old Testament and the wider question of the area of His knowledge. It is not easy to convey to the modern reader, unfamiliar with this literature, in addition to the larger works which have remained as general

[1] *Expository Times*, Vol. VIII, 1896–7, p. 174.
[2] *Op. cit.*, Vols. I and II, 1889–91, i, p. 242.

reading, how vast and vital the subject was. The issue was deeply felt. Those who sought to accord to Christ the high place He had occupied in orthodox faith could not but believe that His deity and uniqueness were being jeopardized and compromised. Those who believed in an infallible Bible regarded such statements of Christ as 'And Moses wrote', and, 'And David said', as sufficient attestation and warrant of the truth. They were able to point out that it was only in the interests of a preconceived theory that the critic had to set about weakening the force of Christ's authority. It was out of regard for their acclaimed scientific method that the critic had in some way to restrict the sphere of our Lord's knowledge. It was, they felt, a case of special pleading.

The 'devout' critics, on the other hand, while at pains to state their belief in the deity of Christ, yet maintained that the authority of Christ could not be adduced to foreclose the right of criticism. It did not belong to His purpose either to validate or to correct current ideas of Old Testament authorship and dates. Some argued that He could not do so even if He had desired since such knowledge lay outside the religious purpose for which He came. Others preferred to urge that He did not really bother Himself about such general notions on these matters, but rather accepted them, and without involving Himself in irrelevancies sought to get men to face the deeper issues of faith and destiny.

Seeking now to reduce the material of the conflict to some sort of order we shall bring quotations to show that it resolved itself, in the main, into two clear-cut oppositions. There were those, the critics generally, who maintained that Christ's knowledge, in the days of His flesh, was relative, whereas their opponents were emphatic that it was absolute.

(1) Christ's Knowledge as Relative

We are concerned here, it should be stated, with what Cheyne would call the 'devout' critic. There were radical theorists like T. H. Green, J. Warschauer, P. Gardner, whose views lie outside our particular interest.

Leaving then out of account these rationalist constructions, we are to see how the moderate critic sought to explain our Lord's quotation of certain Old Testament passages and the wider question of His knowledge.

A beginning may be made with a reference to W. Sanday's volume, *The Oracles of God* (1891). Sanday recognized what he calls 'the change of front as to the nature of God's revelation of Himself in the Bible respectively in the Old Testament, or more accurately, as to the nature of the methods by which the revelation has been conveyed'. Sanday cannot be regarded either as a vigorous opponent of criticism or as an ardent advocate of the traditional view. Actually his interest lay elsewhere than in the sphere of biblical criticism. But he sought to assess the position as he saw it in his day. He draws attention to the way that Christ's authority has been used in the controversy. Sanday regarded reference to that authority as authenticating the Mosaic authorship of the Pentateuch or the Davidic authorship of the Psalms to be a mistake. He regrets that the controversy respecting criticism of the Old Testament should have taken this 'unfortunate turn'. The question which has to be faced, however—the question which is now inescapable is, he sees, that of our Lord's knowledge and authority. Of the enormous correspondence which in recent months has appeared on the subject—he is writing in 1891—two different solutions only are, he thinks, possible. The one is that Christ accommodated His language to the current opinions of the Jews of His day regarding the Old Testament Scriptures. The second suggestion, which Sanday in this volume favours, is that His knowledge was limited by His incarnation experience on such subjects.

It is the first view, however, the 'Accommodationist'[1] which seems to have been followed by Gore in his Bampton Lectures of 1891 on *The Incarnation of the Son of God*. Gore, it is right to point out, defends our Lord's infallibility as a teacher as well as

---

[1] The accommodationist theory was not, of course, specially devised at this time to meet the needs of critical conclusions. The Fathers had spoken of a certain 'economy' (*δικνομια*), or 'condescension' (*συγκαταβασις*), or 'accommodation' (*συμπεριφορά*) as characteristic of God's revelations, but they were careful to distinguish it from all forms of 'hypocrisy' (*υπόκρισις*) in which, for one reason or another, truth was concealed; and from 'dissimulation' (dissimulatio) which to attain its ends stoops to tolerate error (cf. ,e.g. Cyril of Alex., Thesaur., Assert. xxxiv, t. 5; Theodoret, Dial. 11, t. iv; Tertullian, Avd. Marcion, Book IV, c. 36). Spinoza seems to have been the first to use the 'accommodationist' idea in a manner characteristic of later biblical critical scholars (cf. Tractatus Theol. Polit., cap. ii, circ. fin.). See also the discussion by William Lee, *Inspiration of Holy Scripture*, 1854, fourth edition, 1865, pp. 63 ff.

the impeccability of His character.[1] At the same time he emphatically maintains the limitation of His knowledge in His incarnated life.[2] He elaborates in this way the kenosis theory which he had advocated earlier in his *Lux Mundi* essay, and applies it to the realm of Biblical theory. Whatever our Lord teaches He did with 'plenary authority'; although, speaking continually under the limitations of a properly human consciousness He never yielded Himself up to fallible human reasonings.[3] Gore pays special attention to what he calls 'the argument from Psalm cx'. He has already contended that it was not part of Christ's purpose to bind us 'to the acceptance of the Jewish tradition in regard to the Old Testament'.[4] The declaration 'Moses wrote of me' does not tie us to the Mosaic authorship as a whole; nor does the reference to Jonah's three days' sojourn in the belly of the great fish authenticate the story 'as simple history'. About the psalm itself, he is sure, that by referring it to David our Lord never intended to support Jewish tradition with an infallible guarantee. He will allow that our Lord's argument does in some way depend upon David's personal authorship of the psalm, but 'there are reasons which draw us back from accepting the conclusion that He in fact meant to teach us the authorship of a psalm'.[5] Gore believed that there is evidence of 'accommodation' in our Lord's teaching. He accepted ordinary assumptions in order to cross-examine His critics or to check His seekers. In this way He desires them to face the real questions which on their own assumptions should have been faced. He was not, therefore, either proving or disproving, affirming or denying, these ordinary assumptions; He was merely using them for a higher and diviner end.

Somewhat akin to this statement of Gore's is that of S. R. Driver's. Driver was apparently upset by the suggestion that the authority of Christ forbade the full application to the Old Testament of critical methods. In the Preface of his *Introduction to the Literature of the Old Testament* (1891), he says: 'It is objected, however, that some of the conclusions of critics respecting the Old Testament are incompatible with the authority of our blessed Lord, and that in loyalty to Him we are

---

[1] C. Gore, *The Incarnation of the Son of God*, 1891, p. 154.
[2] *Ibid.*, pp. 147 ff.   [3] *Ibid.*, p. 199.
[4] *Ibid.*, p. 195.   [5] *Ibid.*, p. 197.

precluded from accepting them'.[1] Driver was himself convinced that it is not so. It was not Christ's purpose to pronounce upon critical conclusions, he declares. Questions of authorship and date of this or that writing were never, it appears, submitted to Him, or, if they were, there is no record of what His views were. He accepted the prophetic significance of the Old Testament and its spiritual lessons. Judging from a footnote reference to Psalm cx, it seems that Driver was satisfied with Gore's explanation of the limitation of our Lord's knowledge. And he finds support for this elsewhere.[2] Driver insists that since Christ's aim was a religious one it was no part of that aim to give a verdict upon the authorship and date of the different parts of the Old Testament. He accepted, as the basis of His teaching, the opinions current at the time. 'In no single instance' says Driver, 'so far as we are aware, did He anticipate the results of scientific inquiry or historical research.'[3] Driver's neat expression of the position backed by the authority of his own name tended to silence those who might otherwise have sought to raise a protest. Many were overawed, and succumbed to the suggestion that to think other was to fail to keep abreast of the modern advancing scientific study of the Old Testament.

T. K. Cheyne openly acknowledged that the principle which stands in the way of 'critical progress' is a theological one. 'Jesus Christ, being the "teacher come from God" and even "the Son of God", cannot be liable to error.'[4] He asks whether it was necessary that the Messiah should at that period have a clear intuition as to the date and authorship of the Psalms. Cheyne dated Psalm cx as 'post-Exilic', but he allows that this conclusion is still exposed to much criticism from those who claim Christ's authority for its Davidic authorship. Cheyne argues that in the discourse of Matt. xxii. 41–3, Christ's purpose was merely to get the Pharisees to see that no mere son of David or King of Israel could fulfil the highest prophecies respecting the bringing in of Divine salvation. The question of the

[1] S. R. Driver, *Introduction to the Literature of the Old Testament*, 1891, seventh edition, 1898, Preface, p. xii.

[2] Cf. Bishop Moorhouse, *The Teaching of Christ*, 1891, Sermons I and II; A. Plummer, 'The Advance of Christ in σοφιά', *The Expositor*, p. 891; W. S. Swayne, 'An Enquiry into the Nature of our Lord's Knowledge as Man', *op. cit.*

[3] S. R. Driver, *Introduction to the Literature of the Old Testament*, Preface, p. xii.

[4] T. K. Cheyne, *Aids to the Devout Study of Criticism*, 1892, p. 392.

authorship of the psalm was beside the point. 'Our Lord made no declaration of His own belief or knowledge.'[1] He may, indeed, have accepted 'the current ideas of the schools'. At any rate so ignorant are we of the 'inner life of Jesus Christ' that we cannot pronounce with certainty concerning His attitude on questions of criticism.

Cheyne joins issue with an able writer in the *Church Times* (December 11, 1891) who in a review of Gore's lectures expressed the doubt whether critical scholars 'have done justice to the difficulty which now exists of verifying traditions about the original authorship of poems handed down through successive generations amongst the members of musical guilds, and liable from time to time to such modifications as we see exemplified in Psalms xiv and liii'. Cheyne weakly replies that if such psalms did exist in pre-exilic days they would have had to be modified or 'even recast' to adapt them to post-exilic use. Psalm cx he cannot conceive to have existed in any form 'either as Davidic or even pre-exilic'.[2]

What may be regarded as a less question-begging statement of the accommodationist theory is that advanced by Buchanan Blake. Blake argued that 'The Law', 'The Prophets' and 'The Psalms' were the three recognized divisions of the Old Testament. By referring the 'Law' to Moses, and the 'Psalms' to David, Christ was merely using a recognized and familiar formula. The question of authorship, or, indeed, of the substantial truth of a particular passage was not in mind. 'In an *argumentum ad hominen* He used a recognized book in a recognized interpretation. He asks men, who were putting captious questions to Him, to reconcile their own beliefs.'[3]

Here and there among the abundant correspondence it is evident that there were those who found no difficulty in accepting the accommodationist solution. A typical statement occurs in an issue of the *Expository Times* for the year 1900. It comes in the form of a short article by Herbert W. Horwill.

[1] T. K. Cheyne, *Aids to the Devout Study of Criticism*, 1892, p. 393.

[2] *Ibid.*, p. 394. G. H. Rouse in his *Old Testament Criticism in New Testament Light*, 1905, upholds against Driver the Davidic authorship of Psalm cx on the basis of Christ's authority. The words of Mark xii. 35–7 he suggests settles the matter, since, he argues, the pronoun 'himself' appears twice in the passage and should be emphasized.

[3] *Expository Times*, Vol. III, 1891–2, p. 519.

Horwill begins with the observation that 'There are many biblical students who would accept the newer views respecting the date and authorship of the books of the Old Testament but for one difficulty—the apparent sanction given by our Lord to the older position'. They refuse, out of a high regard for His person, to accept either His ignorance due to limitation or that He accommodated His teaching to current views. The writer himself takes the accommodationist position. He supports his argument by reference to the narrative of Luke xi. 19, and the story of the man born blind in John ix. Horwill contends that the latter passage proves that the disciples believed in transmigration but that our Lord did not correct their mistaken view. In fact, His reply, he says, 'must be understood as sanctioning the doctrine of metapsychosis' if it be contended that He did not accommodate His views to current belief. He concludes that 'those who refuse to allow the possibility of our Lord's reference to Old Testament authorship being accommodation to the critical position of the time must be prepared to accept, on the same authority, the contemporary belief in *exorcism and transmigration*'.[1]

It need hardly be pointed out that the evidences here for the accommodationist theory are very insecurely based. There is little convincing proof that the Jews held to a belief in transmigration and there is not the slightest evidence that the disciples, even at this early period of their association with Christ, accepted such a notion.

In spite of the care with which the theory was propounded and the apparent eagerness with which the use of the word 'accommodate' was avoided, there was still, in many minds, something suspect about the whole procedure. It did not seem right somehow to credit Him who came as the Truth, with unreadiness, on any pretence, to correct a known error. It was, of course, clearly stated by some that in accommodating His language to current ideas our Lord was not sanctioning any error which would have had any real religious significance or repercussions.

But if it is a harmless thing to accept the Mosaic authorship of the Pentateuch or the Davidic authorship of Psalm cx, then, the question must have arisen in many minds, Why all the fuss about

[1] Herbert W. Horwill, 'Christ and the Old Testament', *Expository Times*, Vol. XI, 1899–1900, p. 477.

the results of criticism? Were not the critics telling their readers that at last the key to the true understanding of the Scriptures had been discovered? How then could it be supposed that our Lord interpreted them rightly if He did not openly interpret them as the new analysis and the historical method demanded? These are but a few of the thoughts which must have arisen in many hearts. And the fact is that the accommodationist view, however important were the names attached to it, did not appear to capture general consent.

There seemed to many minds more reason in the 'limitationist' view. 'I should be loath to believe', Sanday acknowledged, 'that our Lord accommodated His language to current notions, knowing them to be false. I prefer to think, as it has been happily worded, that "He condescended not to know".'[1]

It appeared therefore to many that the idea of a limited knowledge in the incarnate Lord, which restricted the area of His knowledge, was more reverent and a truer induction from the facts. 'If our Lord had not Himself declared', states one, 'that there was one subject of which He was ignorant, few of us would have found it difficult to ascribe to Him omniscience. That declaration being there, one subject being unmistakable beyond His ken, other items may be found to go along with it.'[2] The one subject upon which our Lord was said to be ignorant regarded the time of His second coming. On the basis of this many were ready to argue that this lack of knowledge was to be extended to include such items as the authorship and dates of the Old Testament. In the eighth of his articles on 'Hebrew Prophecy and Modern Criticism', F. H. Woods of Oxford rejected the accommodationist view and concluded, 'The most natural alternative is to suppose that our Lord's knowledge on these points was really limited by the conditions of the times in which He lived'. The supposition of ignorance, he thinks, cannot be rejected on the grounds of Christian doctrine or reverence. He contends, however, that a devout agnosticism is the only wise conclusion: 'to confess honestly that the union of an omniscient Godhead and a limited humanity in one Person absolutely transcends our human faculties; and that we therefore cannot say *a priori* what limitations to the one nature or the other, from

[1] W. Sanday, *The Oracles of God*, etc., 1891, fourth edition, 1892, p. 111.
[2] Cf. *Expository Times*, Vol. VIII, 1896–7, p. 148.

one point of view, that union necessarily involved'.[1] Attention
need not be focused upon the Apollinarian flavour of this
conclusion of Woods, but the theologically minded will look
askance at the thought of a limitation of either the one nature or
the other.

Two series of Bampton Lectures of the period show concern
for the subject of our Lord's knowledge and its relation to
biblical criticism. We have referred to Sanday's volume, *The
Oracles of God*. In his later lectures on *Inspiration*, Sanday seeks
to explain the nature of the restriction of that knowledge to
which his earlier work had made reference. He asserts that it is
not inconsistent with Christian belief to suppose that our Lord
with the assumption of human flesh and a human mind should
also have assumed the natural workings of such a mind, even in
its limitations.[2] In order to make his position clear, Sanday now
speaks of what he calls 'a neutral zone' in our Lord's knowledge.
'Is there not', he asks, 'what we may call a *neutral zone* among
our Lord's sayings? Sayings, I mean, in which He takes up ideas
and expressions current at the time and uses them without
endorsing them.'[3] It is in this way that he seeks to explain the
reference by Christ to Psalm cx (Matt. xxii. 45). 'It is not
criticism or exegesis that were at issue', he says.[4] The true
method of these might well be left to later discovery. In the
quotation, 'the Pharisees were taken on their own ground:
and the fallacy of their conclusion was shown on their own
premises. All that we need say is that our Lord refrained from
correcting these premises. They fell within His "neutral
zone" '.[5]

There appears to be a change of view here. A reading over the
passage just quoted from his *Inspiration* seems to link him with
the accommodationist view. The suggestion of a change of view
was early noted; but Sanday denies it. In a letter discounting the
idea he states that the word 'refraining' which he had used must
not be wrongly pressed. We are not to 'regard this refraining as
merely the suppression *at the moment* of something which it was
(so to speak) on His lips to say, but did not say. Imagine that it
goes much further back, and was implied in the limitations which

---

[1] *Expository Times*, Vol. VI, 1894–5, p. 371.
[2] W. Sanday, *Inspiration*, 1893, seventh impression, 1911, p. 415.
[3] *Ibid.*, p. 419.   [4] *Ibid.*, p. 420.   [5] *Ibid.*

He assumed when He became man. The one great *condescension* included all other smaller condescensions'.[1]

Three years later R. L. Ottley gave his Bampton Lectures on *The Doctrine of the Incarnation* (1896). In the closing section of this scholarly tome Ottley concerns himself with the problem of our Lord's knowledge. He has a number of references to the early Fathers, drawn mainly from A. B. Bruce's *Humiliation of Christ*. A typical quotation is one from Athanasius: 'In the Godhead there cannot be ignorance; but ignorance is proper to the flesh'.[2] Ottley states his own belief that 'Our Lord in His human nature possessed an *infallible knowledge*, so far as was required by the conditions and purpose of His incarnation'.[3] Outside of this necessity, however, Ottley seems to admit a certain area of which He could not pronounce because He did not know. He adopts an 'altruistic' view, to borrow a word earlier used by J. A. Clapperton,[4] and states that the limitation of our Lord's knowledge, whatever was its degree, was a fact resulting from *love*. Yet while he insists that Christ's knowledge was limited, He was Himself neither deceived nor could He mislead others. Our Lord, he states, though Divine, did not teach positively on all subjects which He incidently touched. 'It is admitted that He never teaches positively on points of science; analogy makes it equally probable that He never taught as to the authorship of different books of Scripture or their mode of composition.'[5] There is, he says, nothing to suggest that He possessed 'modern critical knowledge', or, indeed, 'that He intended to finally endorse the traditional views of His country-men in regard to the nature of their Scriptures'.[6] In a footnote Ottley draws attention to Sanday's 'law of parsimony'[7] which according to the earlier Bampton lecturer underlies revelation. Having assured so much and set out to explain so much Ottley falls back upon the limitation of our own knowledge concerning the Person of Christ. The reality of our own ignorance should make us hesitate to form clear-cut theories about Him who is so beyond us all. 'We may well shrink from constructing any

[1] Cf. *Expository Times*, Vol. V, 1893–4, p. 229.

[2] R. L. Ottley, *The Doctrine of the Incarnation*, 1896, third edition, 1904, p. 622; cf. Athanasius, Orat. c. Arian, iii, 27–8.   [3] *Ibid.*, p. 623.

[4] Cf. *Expository Times*, Vol. V, 1893–4, p. 277.

[5] R. L. Ottley, *The Doctrine of the Incarnation*, p. 625.   [6] *Ibid.*

[7] Cf. W. Sanday, *Inspiration*, p. 417 f.

general theory as to our Lord's human knowledge. We are too apt to discuss and dispute where we should wonder and adore.'[1] It is not very clear, however, how this last observation is to be related to his own general theory of our Lord's knowledge.

Despite his association with Driver, A. F. Kirkpatrick, too, seems to prefer the limitationist theory. He states, 'In condescending to become incarnate as a Jew at a particular epoch in a particular country, our Lord necessarily accepted the conditions and limitations of time and place'.[2]

Among a vast literature it will be found that those who took the critics' side were either accommodationists or limitationists. But there were others who sought to develop their own original line. H. C. Powell, for example, in his book *The Principle of the Incarnation*—a work which in its way is as able as either Gore's or Ottley's—sought to explain the position by what we may think of as two non-communicating centres of activity in Christ. The thesis worked out by Powell was suggested by an article which another writer had supplied to an earlier edition of *The Church Quarterly Review*. Powell claims that as far as he was concerned the idea was entirely his own and that he had not borrowed the *Review* article. For Powell divine knowledge or omniscience differs radically and structurally from that which arises out of the human consciousness. The difference is not simply one of degree, but fundamentally one of character. The knowledge which Christ has as a man, a knowledge, so to speak, derived from the structure of human consciousness, was necessarily limited. Thus, as man, Jesus could be ignorant of that which He knew most intimately as God. As he persuasively develops his theory, Powell takes account of the other prevailing views and shows them to be less tenable than they seemed.

Under the caption 'Christ's Knowledge, Was it Limited or Unlimited? A Solution in Altruism', J. A. Clapperton, to whom we made reference in our comments on Ottley, maintains that any limitation of our Lord's knowledge was due to His voluntary act. He illustrates his thesis by drawing attention to the distinction known to us all between knowledge present in the

---

[1] R. L. Ottley, *The Doctrine of the Incarnation*, p. 625.
[2] A. F. Kirkpatrick, 'The Inevitability and Legitimacy of Criticism' in *The Higher Criticism*, S. R. Driver and A. F. Kirkpatrick, 1911, p. 27; cf. A. B. Davidson, *Biblical and Literary Essays*, 1903, Chapter VII.

memory and knowledge at the moment in use. Christ, he states then, 'knew all things as we may be said to know everything that we can recall at a moment's notice. But . . . *He voluntarily* declined to take advantage of the power and joy that the facing of every truth would naturally bring Him. In His personal trials He *chose to be* ignorant'.[1] In reference to His own affairs He employed 'limited knowledge'. But for the sake of others He drew 'upon His omniscience'. For our sakes He would see to it that divine truth and fulness stamped His utterance, but for His own life and His own sake, He, like us, had to learn to 'cope with difficulty and darkness'. Clapperton applies this to Christ's use and knowledge of the Old Testament. When He used the Old Testament for the sake of its spiritual truth for others 'we cannot understand Him to speak with merely human wisdom as far as the lessons taught are concerned'. But as far as authorship and readings are concerned these were questions of no great moment in comparison with the messages He had to convey. Such ideas were 'so utterly out of touch with the moral and spiritual interest of those around Him, that He could scarcely concern Himself with the accuracy or inaccuracy of the traditions involved'.[2]

An interesting comment is made by W. C. Shearer of the United College, Bradford, on Mark xiii. 31–2, which was the passage adduced by the kenoticists as evidence of the limitation of our Lord's knowledge. Shearer points out that the verses are often taken as proof of Christ's ignorance. 'And the inference is drawn', he continues, 'If ignorant *then*, how much more in regard to the authorship and dates of the books of the Old Testament!'[3] Shearer contends that in interpreting the passage in this way the premise is wrong and the conclusion consequently false. After analysing the verses he states that it 'was not intended to be an acknowledgement of ignorance, in a special instance, on the part of our Lord; but was simply a devout ascription to His Father of an omniscience which transcended the conditions of time. What was known to the Son, in His temporal and relative condition, as an event occupying a considerable space of time, can be viewed by the Father as a day, an hour, a moment, an instant of time. It was a prompting of the same devout and

---

[1] *Expository Times*, Vol. V, 1893–4, p. 277.   [2] *Op. cit.*, p. 278.
[3] *Op. cit.*, Vol. IV, 1892–3, p. 554.

reverential feeling in the Lord's mind, as that to which He gave expression when He said, "Why callest thou me good? One is good, God". Our Lord no more denied His own goodness in the latter, than He asserted His ignorance in the former'.[1]

Before we turn to deal with the other position it is worthwhile to note that as time went on the discussion concerning our Lord's knowledge became divorced from the more immediate issue of His relation to critical questions about the Old Testament Scriptures. The problem became abstracted from its historical origins and was developed along the lines of a Christological interest as such. In this way kenotic doctrines of Christ's Person came into vogue, each with its own peculiarity, such as that of A. M. Fairbairn's, H. R. Mackintosh's, P. T. Forsyth's and others. At the present day kenoticism finds support in the writings of Vincent Taylor.

(2) Christ's Knowledge as Absolute

As was to be expected the idea that Christ accommodated Himself to popular notions or that He was ignorant about biblical facts came in for a lot of criticism. An immense amount of discussion took place, and, in many cases, it must be acknowledged, those who felt that they were upholding the honour of Christ and the Bible, plunged into the controversy with little reason and less result. Many of the letters and pamphlets and articles which are to hand were both furious and feeble. Too often the character of the individual critic was made the object of attack, and the impression was created, that those claiming to defend orthodoxy fulfilled the logical fallacy which in popular parlance has been put, when you cannot kick the ball, kick the man. But it would be altogether wrong, however, to conclude from the multiplicity of attempted replies which turned out to be hopeless irrelevancies, that this was the whole story. Some apologists for criticism, understandably impatient as they were with what was produced by way of answer, sought to win their case by dubbing all who could not readily accept their latest views as obscurantists. But all were not so. There were men, no less concerned for truth, who genuinely felt that the absoluteness of Christ was being undermined if His complete knowledge were denied. And they made a better showing of their cases than is sometimes known or allowed.

C. C. J. Ellicott was no obscurantist, but a careful student of Scripture. A series of articles from his pen appeared in the *Expository Times* between the years 1891–3 under the title 'The Teaching of our Lord as to the Authority of the Old Testament'. He shows in these contributions that he had a grasp of the recent critical theories and his exposition of them is clear. For what he calls the 'traditional view' he asserts that, in contrast with the new theories, it 'can with every appearance of probability, claim the authority of our Lord and Master Jesus Christ'.[1] He deals also with the question, Was the kenosis 'of such a kind that His knowledge in regard to the authorship and composition of the Books of the Old Testament . . . (was) no greater than that of the masters of Israel at His own time?'[2] He makes an extended reply and concludes with reasons that Christ's knowledge was not so restricted. It is impossible, he insists, to draw inferences from our human nature and transfer them to Him.[3] Allowance must be made in His case for the supernatural endowment of the Holy Ghost which fitted Him for His Messianic office. As a consequence of the union of the two natures in the one Person, it is impossible that He who quoted the Scriptures so frequently should know less about their composition than the critics of our times. In this connection the *Lux Mundi* comes in for Ellicott's severest treatment.

In reference to Psalm cx, Ellicott maintained that by the evidence David was necessarily the author. He asks, Could such a 'metrical fabrication claiming to be a psalm of David and an oracle of God, and challenging attention by setting forth a doctrine so unfamiliar as the Messiah's everlasting priesthood have crept into the jealously guarded Scripture, three or four centuries after the date of Ezra's Bible, and remained there undetected?'[4] Ellicott quotes Liddon's statement 'If it be obvious that certain theories of the Old Testament must ultimately conflict with our Lord's unerring authority, a Christian will pause before he commits himself to these theories'.[5] He realizes that 'those who have deliberately crossed the Rubicon' will be

---

[1] *Expository Times*, Vol. III, 1891–2, p. 458.
[2] *Op. cit.*, p. 539.   [3] *Op. cit.*, p. 544.
[4] *Op. cit.*, Vol. IV, 1892–3, p. 368.   [5] *Op. cit.*, p. 456.

unmoved by these considerations. But he thinks that the critical
views are at one with the growing minimizing of the supernatural, but whether as a cause or an effect he does not say. He
sees the loss of spiritual authority and the increase of spiritual
paralysis to be the result. 'This downward drift and ultimate
issue may easily be traced out . . . the temptation to believe in a
possible ignorance on the part of our Lord, becomes in many
minds irresistible, and the way is paved for a belief in the
possibility, not only of this ignorance, but even of our hope in
Him, here and hereafter, being found to be vain and illusory.'[1]
The final question to be faced is 'With whom have we to do, here
and hereafter; a fallible or the infallible Christ?'

In a series of articles in the same journal between the years
1894 and 1896, J. Elder Cumming asks, 'Is the Old Testament
Authentic?' In a section of one of these articles Cumming discusses
the relation of Christ to the Old Testament. He is emphatic that
Christ could and did teach with absolute authority. He was not
lacking in the knowledge concerning the authorship of the Old
Testament or its several parts. 'He, in His divine person, knew
what the truth was about these holy writings.'[2] We can be
absolutely assured that whatever He taught was true, whether
that truth was about the resurrection from the dead or about the
Scriptures. As a teacher He can be relied upon implicitly. True
He 'emptied Himself', and in this sense the words of Mark xiii.
32, are to be understood. 'But there is a whole hemisphere surely
between such a statement and the idea that what He *did* teach on
any subject, He taught without knowing!'[3] 'We, therefore, have
no doubt' he says again, 'that it lay in the power of Jesus Christ
to settle all disputed questions regarding the authority or the
meaning, or the truthfulness of the Old Testament Scriptures.'
He quotes Cheyne's comment on our Lord's reference to Jonah.
'Jesus interpreted the story as an instructive parable' declared
Cheyne. 'And then he adds' continues Cumming, 'Even if He
did, with His wonderful spiritual tact, so interpret it, we cannot
be sure' (*Expositor*, March 1892). 'Has it come to this' retorts
Cumming, 'that our Lord relied, in interpreting the Scriptures,
on "His TACT"? "His spiritual tact!" "His wonderful spiritual
tact"!'[4]

---

[1] *Expository Times*, Vol. IV, 1892–3, p. 458.
[2] *Op. cit.*, Vol. VII, 1895–6, p. 39.   [3] *Op. cit.*   [4] *Op. cit.*

The *Expository Times* gave hospitality also to Thomas Whitelaw to deal with the same subject in a further series of articles under the title 'Could Jesus Err?' Whitelaw took the opportunity to answer Paul Schwartzkopff of Wernigerode, whose brochure, *The Prophecies of Jesus Christ relating to the Death, Resurrection, and Second Coming, and their Fulfilment*, had, he states, just been translated into English.[1] Schwartzkopff had credited Jesus with a good deal of error, especially concerning the Second Coming. Whitelaw, in opposition, maintains that Jesus could not have been guilty of intellectual error and that this being so, His ascription to Moses of the Pentateuch and Psalm cx to David must authenticate these. The 'higher critics of today claim to have reversed the judgement of those who stood more than 2,000 years closer to the Psalms of David than we do'.[2] Schwartzkopff had rejected Kenoticism maintaining that it inevitably leads to a denial either of the true humanity or the Godhead of our Lord. A God depotentiated of omnipotence, omniscience and omnipresence, if such were conceived possible would, as Beidermann says, be a mythological and gnostical god —no real god at all. Schwartzkopff, however, denies outright the ascription to Christ of Godhead (Gottheit), and allows to Him merely godlikeness (Gottlichkeit). He is a God-filled man, and as such the possibility of error remains as an inseparable part of His teaching. Whitelaw attacks the view and shows the disastrous theological and soteriological consequences which must follow.

The writers to whom we have referred showed in their articles that they found it impossible to let go their belief in the absolute infallibility of Christ's knowledge. To do so would have been tantamount to denying His uniqueness even on the plane of the human. But apart from such articles there were several books which sought to establish the same conclusion.

In a massive volume of over 700 pages published by T. & T. Clark entitled *Is Christ Infallible and the Bible True?* Hugh McIntosh covers the whole field of contemporary thought and deals trenchantly with any theory which would limit the infallibility of either Christ or the Scriptures. McIntosh's book, into the bargain, is an elaborate exposition of numerous

[1] *Expository Times*, Vol. VIII, 1896–7, p. 299; but cf. p. 524.
[2] *Op. cit.*, p. 301; cf. p. 365.

Christological doctrines which, to borrow a word from T. P. Forsyth, had the effect of merely 'Boswellizing' the Figure of the Gospel.

It is impossible to convey any idea of the fulness of the treatment of the subject in this detailed work. McIntosh raises the serious issue whether Christ is to be regarded as an infallible teacher.[1] And if not so considered, then, What ground have we for certainty? May He not, indeed, be mistaken concerning the very possibility and method of salvation? He poses the question 'If not infallible, can He be Divine?' On the other hand, should His infallibility be admitted, then, according to McIntosh, it must be taken seriously. He is ready to admit to the reality of 'kenosis', as a Bible revelation and a profound fact,[2] but he denies that this provides any ground for questioning Christ's infallibility as a teacher. 'While holding as fully as any, and more fully than most, the veritable humanity, and the mental and moral development of Christ, and the reality of the Kenosis revealed in the Scriptures, we utterly repudiate the dangerous and anti-scriptural inferences drawn therefrom, limitative, and ultimately subversive of the Divine authority and infallibility of His teaching.'[3] McIntosh believes that Mark xiii, 32 gives no basis for the idea of our Lord's nescience, but boldly argues that the reverse is the case.[4] Having, then, in books i and ii concluded that there is nothing to tell against Christ's infallibility but rather that His infallibility is overwhelmingly established, McIntosh goes on to relate this conclusion to the Scriptures. He has stated in the concluding section of book ii that if Christ erred as the Word of God He may have erred as to His being the Son of God.[5] It is this conclusion that he has now to apply to the Scriptures. They are substantiated and authenticated by Christ's authority.

McIntosh does not, it ought to be pointed out, contend for 'absolute inerrancy in every trivial detail and possible aspect', but he does argue that 'there is no possibility of making it appear that Christ did not teach at least the truthfulness, trustworthiness, and the Divine authority of Scripture'.[6] He ends this long discussion with the answer to the question of the title, Is Christ

---

[1] Hugh McIntosh, *Is Christ Infallible and the Bible True?*, third edition, 1902, pp. 277 ff.   [2] *Ibid.*, pp. 238 ff.   [3] *Ibid.*, p. 238.
[4] *Ibid.*, p. 232.   [5] *Ibid.*, p. 261.   [7] *Ibid.*, p. 550.

infallible and the Bible true? with these words: 'the Bible, is true, because Christ is infallible: and He who is "The Truth" and the faithful and true Witness declares it to be true. The Bible, then, is the Word of God—true, trustworthy, and of Divine authority, and the Divine rule of faith and life; or the Bible is the Word of God, of infallible truth and Divine authority, *in all it teaches*, and the Divine rule of faith and life'.[1]

Another volume along the same lines is John Urquhart's *The Inspiration and Accuracy of the Holy Scriptures*. In the second of the books which comprise this composite work, Urquhart shows that he is thoroughly acquainted with the whole field of German rational criticism. The views of Eichhorn, Paulus, Astruc, Strauss, Vatke, Kayser, Kuenen have all been mastered as well as those of English critics. Urquhart deals with the doctrine of kenosis and examined the usage of the word κενοω and maintains that it does not mean the emptying of nature (cf. Jer. xiv. 2; September).[2] He is certain that our Lord was not reduced to a state of ignorance by His becoming flesh. And, he argues, therefore in His use and reference to the Old Testament He has given them their endorsement.[3]

In 1903 there appeared, condensed into one volume, *The Divine Rule of Faith and Practice*, three books by William Goode, which were first published in 1841. Goode was a Cambridge Scholar and has been Dean of Ripon. The work did not, of course, touch the special problems of the new period, but it was apparently felt that its appearance at such a time of unrest would give confidence to those who were through criticism losing faith in the Bible as the Word of God. Goode showed the place of the Bible in the early Church and maintained that it was the sole and sufficient rule of faith and practice. He concluded with a chapter in which it is asserted that the Church of England recognizes the Bible only as its authority and acclaims it as the Word of God without equivocation. A typical statement is a quotation from Dean Mowell's *Catechism*; 'the Christian religion is to be learnt from no other source than from the heavenly word of God Himself, which He hath delivered to us in the Holy Scriptures'. And another comes from Jewell's

---

[1] Hugh McIntosh, *Is Christ Infallible and the Bible True?* 1902, p. 664.
[2] John Urquhart, *The Inspiration and Accuracy of the Holy Scriptures*, 1895, p. 74.
[3] *Ibid.*, pp. 73 ff.

Apology: 'the very sure and infallible rule whereby may be tried whether the Church do swerve or err and whereunto all ecclesiatical doctrine ought to be called to account'.[1]

A work by H. D. Brown, at one time a barrister, and no mean scholar, who became pastor of the Harcourt Street Baptist Church, Dublin, should be given a passing reference. The substance of the book published under the title *Christ or Critics?* or, *God's Witness to His Word*, was a series of articles contributed to *The Sword and the Trowel*. Brown speaks of Christ's 'subservience' to the Scriptures. He raises the question, 'Was our Divine Lord's Knowledge Limited?'[2] He marshals the evidence of New Testament passages to prove that He knew Himself and showed Himself to be possessed of a unique understanding. The accommodationist theory he finds specially distasteful. 'Jesus', he retorts, was 'no Jesuit'. He did not simply accommodate Himself 'to the generally-accepted traditional and popular, albeit somewhat legendary and historically-false, views of the Jews, in order to evade unnecessary discussion and to avoid awakening continual hostility and prejudice'.[3] The idea of a limitation of our Lord's knowledge is also unacceptable. Thus, he says, 'while "Accommodationists" rob us of Christ's integrity, "Limitationists" would unintentionally but surely undermine His Godhead'.[4]

Our Lord's Use of His Bible by H. E. Fox, the honorary secretary of the Church Missionary Society, may be a slender volume, but it is closely reasoned. While acknowledging the 'reverent tone of many of the leaders' of criticism in England, Fox refuses their conclusion that the Bible is a 'literary patchwork'. In the case of the neo-criticism, the disciple is above his Master, and there are those 'to whom the Great Master seems to be a person less well informed about His own sacred literature, and the religious history of His own nation, than any callow divinity student of these days'.[5]

Fox cannot believe that if the story of His nation as given in the Bible had been only the legendary lore of an illiterate race, He would have failed to drop some hint to that effect. Parts of

[1] William Goode, *The Divine Rule of Faith and Practice*, edited by his daughter, Anne E. Metcalf, 1903, p. 314.
[2] H. D. Brown, *God's Witness to His Word*, 1905, second edition, p. 127.
[3] *Ibid.*, p. 133.   [4] *Ibid.*, p. 143.
[5] H. E. Fox, *Our Lord's Use of His Bible*, 1905, p. 23.

the Old Testament, for example, the Book of Deuteronomy, most roughly handled by the critics, were the parts to which He appealed the most. On Psalm cx he says, 'If the new criticism is right in saying that David had nothing to do with this Psalm, and that the Psalm had nothing to do with the Messiah, then the whole of our Lord's argument falls to the ground'.[1] Fox has a well written chapter on the kenosis theory. He believes, however, that it does not support the idea of a limitation of our Lord's knowledge. The whole passage is hortatory. He quotes from Dr Stubbs's recent *Visitation Charges* (p. 151) to the effect that kenosis should not be used as the keynote of a theory with which it has so little to do; or as the decisive proof of a doctrine which if it were intended to be taught, could not safely be left to an isolated text.[2] Christ, he says, did not accommodate Himself to other men's mistakes. It is essential for faith that He be absolutely trustworthy. 'The Saviour who cannot be trusted absolutely cannot be trusted at all.'[3] Fox shows some fatal consequences of accepting the kenosis doctrine: and he is emphatic that in emptying Himself Christ did not become void of 'the knowledge that He once possessed', which would mean His teaching 'His disciples to receive as genuine and authoritative Scriptures which in fact were neither'.[4] Neo-criticism fosters doubt, and, concludes Fox, 'to foster doubt is a strange way to preserve faith'.[5]

Beginning, then, with the conviction that Christ's knowledge is absolute, these writers felt themselves bound to the highest view of Scripture, which, they believed, He has validated. Their attitude was well stated by Bishop Moule: 'the Christian student sees the most impressive characteristic of the Holy Scriptures in the fact of the attitude towards them taken by Jesus Christ'.[6]

As time went on the discussion concerning our Lord's relation to the Old Testament seemed to be less bound up with the attempt to justify or to repudiate criticism as such. It became more concerned with wider issues as, for example, the way the Old Testament entered into the development of our Lord's Messianic consciousness, and how far the term, Son of Man,

---

[1] H. E. Fox, *Our Lord's Use of His Bible*, 1905, p. 47.
[2] *Ibid.*, pp. 73–4.   [3] *Ibid.*, pp. 79–80.
[4] *Ibid.*, p. 78.   [5] *Ibid.*, p. 92.
[6] H. C. G. Moule, *Christian Doctrine*, 1889, p. 5.

which He took as His own special designation for Himself, was to be understood against its Old Testament usages. At the same time there is evidence here and there, more particularly in the earlier part of the present century before the complete divorce between Christ's attitude to the Scriptures and the right of criticism came about, of allegiance being given by one and another to either the accommodationist or the limitationist view.

An illustration of the first comes in an essay by V. Storr. Storr writes of 'the grave problem of the authority of our Lord in regard to His references to the Old Testament'.[1] He notes the hostility to Biblical criticism springing from belief in our Lord's authority and he allows that 'He clearly regarded the Scripture as being of Divine origin'. Storr confesses the dilemma to be a serious one. But for him Christ's authority is essentially 'moral and spiritual'. He then asks, 'Does that authority suffer if we think of Him as sharing the current Jewish opinion about the Old Testament?'[2] The Jews, he maintains, believed in the Davidic authorship of Psalm cx: scholars say the psalm was much later. Jesus accepted the popular notion. 'Is His spiritual authority really lessened if we hold that David did not write the Psalm?'[3] Storr then goes on to answer these questions with the 'No' already implied in their formation.

While Storr favours the accommodationist hypothesis as the explanation of our Lord's references to the Old Testament, A. H. McNeile, in an essay of his on 'Our Lord's Use of the Old Testament' seems to accept the limitationist alternative. In 'emptying Himself' Christ became truly man, truly human. The 'one thing that was not at all essential', he states, 'was a super-human omniscience, and that we believe He continuously and consciously held in abeyance. It was part of the divine self-sacrifice to refuse to know, as man, anything which He could learn by human methods'.[4] His 'precocity' exhibited when speaking with the doctors in the temple was not, like ours, clouded by sin. Facts however relating to the literature and history of the Old Testament '*He could not because He would* not

[1] V. F. Storr, 'The Bible and Its Value', *Liberal Evangelicalism: An Interpretation*, by members of the Church of England, p. 96.

[2] *Ibid.*, p. 97.   [3] *Ibid.*

[4] A. H. McNeile, 'Our Lord's Use of the Old Testament' in *Cambridge Critical Essays*, Essays on Some Biblical Questions of the Day (ed. H. B. Swete), 1909, p. 249.

know'.[1] Traditional ideas about the Scriptures which were the 'intellectual standpoint of His day and country' He accepted because it would not become Him to be otherwise than really human for our sakes. '*And He could not because He would not know otherwise, for us men and for our salvation.*'[2]

The stress on the absoluteness of our Lord's knowledge, on the other hand, was also stated and applied with equal seriousness. This can be seen, for example, to permeate such a book as James Orr's *The Bible Under Trial*, which concludes with the declaration, 'But so long as Christ, in His self-attesting power, commands the allegiance of believing hearts, the Bible, which contains the priceless treasure of God's Word regarding Him, will remain in undiminished honour'.[3]

To balance the words of Storr from his essay in *Liberal Evangelicalism*, it seems proper to refer also to *Evangelicalism*. In a lengthy essay in this volume, T. C. Hammond writes of 'The Fiat of Authority'. Christ, he argues, taught with authority which 'could not have been of any external character, because our Lord never received an ecclesiastical imprimatur'.[4] His was the authority of truth, of God. Hammond maintains that 'Our Lord establishes once and for all the possibility of a perfectly human thought exhibiting absolute harmony with the Divine purpose: He set His seal to that sacred code which ages treasured as presenting the mind of God to man. Therefore alike the Sacred Scripture and He Who is the Subject of its eternal message are called the Word of God'.[5]

Of more recent days Evangelical scholars can be found referring to our Lord's ascription of Psalm cx as a sufficient authentication of its Davidic authorship.[6] Exception to the procedure continues to follow the line now axiomatic to those convinced of the validity of the critical position. Gabriel Hebert,

[1] A. H. McNeile, 'Our Lord's Use of the Old Testament' in *Cambridge Critical Essays*, Essays on Some Biblical Questions of the Day (ed. H. B. Swete), 1909, p. 250 (italics in original).   [2] *Ibid.* (italics in original).

[3] James Orr, *The Bible Under Trial*, 1907, second edition, p. 307. But see his observations on this point in his *Revelation and Inspiration*, 1910, p. 150 f.

[4] T. C. Hammond, 'The Fiat of Authority' in *Evangelicalism*, essays by members of the Fellowship of Evangelical Churchmen (ed. J. Russell Howden), 1925, p. 195.

[5] *Ibid.*, pp. 185–6.

[6] Cf. *The New Bible Commentary* (ed. Davidson, E. F. Kevan, A. Stibbs), notes on Psalms, Matt., Mark, Lk., *ad. loc.* Cf. R. V. G. Tasker, *Our Lord's Use of the Old Testament*, 1953, pp. 17 ff.

to take a typical example, asserts that 'we must not invoke our Lord's authority to decide a question He was not answering'.[1] This statement is a clear case of *petitio principii*, and leaves the question where it was. The fact is that the subject of our Lord's attitude to the Old Testament is for all Christians a vital one. For evangelicals it is decisive. It is maintained, for example, by J. I. Packer, with no uncertain emphasis, that Christ 'never opposed His personal authority to that of the Old Testament'.[2] He accepted its authority without question and submitted to it without demure.[3]

---

[1] Gabriel Hebert, *Fundamentalism and the Church of God*, 1957, p. 69.

[2] J. I. Packer, '*Fundamentalism*' *and the Word of God*, 1958, p. 55.

[3] Cf. R. V. G. Tasker, *The Old Testament in the New Testament*, 1953, Chapters 1 and 2; cf. 'The testimony of our Lord to the Old Testament and His claims to divinity are, it would seem, more closely associated than many in our day are prepared to acknowledge. I would therefore urge in conclusion that, while we should welcome all the light archaeological, linguistic and textual studies can throw upon the Old Testament, nevertheless, as Christians, we are bound to look at that unique literature primarily through the eyes of Him who claimed to be the light of the world, our Lord and Saviour' (*ibid.*, p. 19). See also J. W. Wenham, *Our Lord's View of the Old Testament*, 1953: 'To Him (i.e. Jesus), what the Scripture said, God said' (*ibid.*, p. 8). 'The total impression is that the mind of Christ is saturated with the Old Testament and that, as He speaks, there flows out perfectly naturally a complete range of uses varying from direct verbal quotation to an unconscious utilization of scraps of Old Testament phraseology. There is no trace of artificial quotation of Scripture as a matter of pious habit, but His mind is so steeped in both the words and principles of Scripture that quotation and allusion spring to His lips naturally and appositely in all sorts of different circumstances' (*ibid.*, p. 27). Cf. also F. F. Bruce, *The Christian Approach to the Old Testament*, 1955: 'To approach the Old Testament in the light of Christ's fulfilment of all its parts is to approach it aright; *this* is the Christian approach to the Old Testament' (*ibid.*, p. 20).

CHAPTER FIVE

The Scriptures and the Word

The discussion concerning Christ's relation to the Scriptures leads on to a review of the allied problem, which came to light, of how revelation was to be brought into connection with the Scriptures. It had been the prevailing view that revelation and the Bible were for all practical purposes to be equated. Deriving from the great Reformers, Protestant theology had stated a complete identification of Scripture with the Word of God.[1] The truth of God had been given and that truth was conserved and preserved in the Bible. But with the inerrancy and the infallibility of Scripture believed to be undermined, it was necessary to raise the question of the 'locus' of revelation.

A. REVELATION AND THE SCRIPTURES

There was, to begin, a sharpening of the divorce between revelation and Scripture, and, as we shall see more particularly later, revelation came to be identified with, for example, the spiritual experience or insight of the prophets or with the recognition by them of God's redeeming acts in history, and so forth. It is, however, the idea of revelation as divine activity which is the characteristic note of the modern era. The view that revelation was given in propositions, that it was in any sense a communication of supernatural knowledge, was vehemently repudiated. So, too, of course, was, in a measure, the earlier reactionist idea which interpreted revelation in terms of the subjective appreciation of the religious genius. Revelation was not to be understood as the mere stimulation of the numinous

[1] Cf. R. Preus, *The Interpretation of Scripture*, A Study in the Theology of the Seventeenth Century Dogmaticians, 1955, Chapter 2.

F

feelings.[1] Emphasis came to be placed upon what H. Wheeler Robinson called the 'actuality' of God in history.[2] John Baillie in his American series of Bampton Lectures, contends that the 'recovery of this fundamental insight', as he regards it, 'is the first thing we notice as running broadly through all the recent discussions, marking them off from the formulations of earlier periods'.[3]

The tendency has been of late to urge that revelation is an entirely personal, subject to subject, affair. This view has been given vogue by a number of writers who in other respects greatly differ. William Temple, it is well known, laid special stress upon the notion of revelation as a divine self-disclosure. A typical quotation can be taken from his rightly famous Bampton Lectures. 'What is offered to man's apprehension', he says, 'in any specific revelation is not truth concerning God but the living God Himself'.[4] This view elaborated in Chapter XII of his *Nature, Man and God*, is given emphasis in his earlier essay in the symposium *Revelation*. Here he makes the point that Personality is the nature of ultimate reality. Revelation must, therefore, be understood as a divine self-disclosure. 'The belief in Divine Personality and the belief in specific revelation go together: each necessitates the other.'[5] Such statements as these could be multiplied and others of similar import could be added from a host of other writers. But Temple, we think, did not limit revelation to the divine activity of God in history, to the meeting of event and interpretation, as other, and especially earlier writers seemed to do. The more recent tendency is to state revelation in terms entirely personal. The watchword of the modern era might then be put like this: revelation is personal encounter not propositional disclosure. An illustration of this shift of emphasis can be seen, for example, in William Nicholls's book, *Revelation in Christ*. Nicholls allows that the writers of the more immediate past have succeeded 'in the shifting of the locus of revelation from literature to history and from the

---

[1] Cf. Kitell's, *Theological Dictionary of the New Testament*, word, καλύπτω, *ad. loc.*
[2] H. Wheeler Robinson, *Redemption and Revelation*, 1942, Chapters IX and X; cf. 'The actuality of the Biblical history is vital to the process of revelation'. C. H. Dodd, *The Authority of the Bible*, 1928, Preface, p. xi.
[3] John Baillie, *The Idea of Revelation in Recent Thought*, 1956, p. 29.
[4] William Temple, *Nature, Man and God*, 1947, p. 322.
[5] William Temple in *Revelation* (ed. J. Baillie and Hugh Martin), 1937, p. 95.

propositional to the personal'.[1] But a firmer declaration that Christ is the proper 'locus' of revelation is called for at the present time. This is, of course, a very proper and needful insistence.

It is doubtful, however, if there is anything specifically original in the idea. It might, indeed, be convincingly demonstrated that this was the fundamental faith of the Church from the first. Brunner has some justification for his remark that the idea early arose in the Church under the influence of Greek philosophy that revelation was a communication of doctrinal truths which were otherwise inaccessible to human reason.[2] Although Brunner may be a little too confident about the earliness of the influence, it remains a fact that whenever the Church lost touch with the essential Biblical view of God in His gracious self-disclosure and trusted in mere philosophical wisdom and institutional authority, the true idea of revelation became obscured. It may be ungrudgingly acknowledged as one of the gains of the recent many-sided discussion of the subject of revelation that the essential personal note has been brought into its rightful place. In this sense point may be given to the claim that in emphasizing revelation as personal in Christ the modern era has made great gains. Perhaps it would be more correct to say it has recaptured an essential element which had been virtually lost during the period of controversy between the deists and their opponents. Yet as early as 1881, A. B. Bruce gives stress to the personal nature of revelation in words which could well have been written by some influential modern writer on the same subject. Bruce asks what the idea of revelation connotes. He is emphatic that it does not mean causing a sacred book to be written for the religious instruction of mankind. The term, he declares, 'signifies God manifesting Himself in the history of the world in a supernatural manner and for a special purpose. Manifesting *Himself*; for the proper subject of revelation is God. The Revealer is also the Revealed. This is the recognition in the words of the Westminster Confession: 'It pleased the Lord to reveal Himself . . ." '.[1]

---

[1] William Nicholls, *Revelation in Christ*, 1957, p. 9.

[2] Cf. Emil Brunner, *The Divine–Human Encounter* (E.T. 1944), p. 12.

[3] A. B. Bruce, *The Chief End of Revelation*, 1881, pp. 57–8; cf. Emil Brunner, *Revelation and Reason* (E.T. 1944), p. 8. The essays by Karl Barth, William Temple and A. Aulen in *Revelation* (ed. J. Baillie and H. Martin), 1937. H. Richard Niebuhr, *The Meaning of Revelation*, New York, 1941, pp. 143–54.

Three broad views of revelation affecting the subject of this section can, we think, be discerned in the period. Revelation is first stated to be located in man's growing enlightenment, then in the divine events of history, and finally in the living personality of Christ. The question then arises: What is the relation of revelation so conceived to the Bible?

(a) The Bible gives an account of man's developing religious experience. This was, of course, an extreme and radical view which failed altogether to commend itself in any general way to those who desired to remain within the sphere of acceptable Christian faith. It had, however, its enthusiastic advocates— Unitarians for the most part—who took delight in pointing out the 'humanness' of the biblical record. Yet in spite of its manifold 'imperfections' it was granted that the Bible 'supplies the noblest continuous witness which we know to the reality of divine things'.[1]

The most elaborate exponent of the idea was that of Martineau whose book *The Seat of Authority in Religion* was hailed at the time as 'for the present the most notable contribution to recent literature'.[2] Martineau rejected outright both Church and Bible as possessing external authority. His 'Messianic mythology', as S. D. F. Salmond called it, is 'an elaborate assault upon historical Christianity', on both the Christian doctrine of our Lord's Person and the Protestant basis of faith.[3] Martineau is at pains to show his disregard for the idea of Scripture as being either the vessel or the vehicle of revelation. Whatever revelation there is must be sought within; there it must be 'given'. It is not something discovered by man who of himself labours to peep behind the folds of the invisible world to seek God who coldly awaits there for the seeking man to arrive and find out the secret. The 'one condition that the desired Revelation must fulfil is plainly this', says Martineau, 'it must be *immediate*, living God and living man, Spirit present with spirit; knowing Him, indeed, but rather "being known of Him" '.[4] But the Spirit is everywhere and in all. The centre of man's personal

---

[1] J. Estlin Carpenter, *The Bible in the Nineteenth Century*, 1903, p. 512.

[2] *Expository Times*, Vols. I and II, 1889–91, i, p. 192.

[3] S. D. F. Salmond, 'Dr Martineau's "Messianic Mythology" ', *Expository Times*, Vols. I and II, 1889–91, ii, p. 125.

[4] James Martineau, *The Seat of Authority in Religion*, third edition, revised, 1891, p. 305.

life is enfolded by it, and 'though it ever speaks it cannot be spoken of; though it shines everywhere it can be looked at nowhere; and because presupposed as reality it evades criticism as a phenomenon'.[1] Revelation is essentially personal. Like the modern Tillich, whose views have a strange similarity to those of Martineau, he sees revelation as a sort of 'ecstasy' and he quotes Philo in this connection. In the nature of the case it cannot therefore be communicated from mind to mind for it is not a 'datum'.

It is no wonder that Martineau's volume called forth hostility from all quarters. William Sanday records how he felt compelled to yield to the request of the editor of the *Expository Times* and give his impressions of *The Seat of Authority in Religion*. He focused his attention upon Martineau's critical assumptions which were vulnerable because so many of them were fatuous. His exegesis, too, left much to be desired. Sanday may be thought a little unkind in his statement regarding the volume as a whole: 'I honestly do not think it an important book. It is not a book which needs to be read. To speak quite frankly, it is in my opinion a book which would be better left unread'. Sanday, indeed, calls it 'a dangerous book'.[2] It was regarded as having a 'greater success than it deserves'.[3] The volume appeared to many capable observers to suffer from wrong assumptions. It is not true, it was urged against its assertion, that Protestantism points conclusively 'to a field of divine revelation, discoverable only by the telescope, halfway towards the horizon of history'.[4]

The very radicalness of such a view of the relation between revelation and the Bible was its defeat. Its critical presuppositions were proved false and its tone and temper out of harmony with even the most 'advanced' of the 'devout' critics.

(b) A much more acceptable position was therefore sought by others who either felt the impact or accepted the conclusions of criticism. It was desired to accord to the Bible a more vital place in the process of revelation. It would be, we think, a fairly accurate generalization to say that during the early part of the period the Bible was regarded as having the sole power of

---

[1] James Martineau, *The Seat of Authority in Religion*, third edition, revised, 1891, pp. 305–6.

[2] *Expository Times*, Vols. I and II, 1889–91, i, p. 284.

[3] *Op. cit.*, ii, p. 2. [4] Cf. *op. cit.*, i, p. 193.

conveying revelation to man by awakening him to his need through the stimulation of his religious consciousness. Later, under the impact of criticism, when the doctrine of the Bible's inerrancy was in a large measure abandoned, the Scriptures came to be regarded as containing the record of God's revelatory acts in history.

As early as 1854, William Lee, Archdeacon of Dublin, in his weighty volume, *The Inspiration of Holy Scripture*, noted the difference between the new view, of which he considers Schleiermacher the fountain-head, and what he believes to be the historic doctrine of the Church.[1] The teaching of Schleiermacher, we have shown elsewhere, is the background of what Coleridge and Maurice had to say about the relation between revelation and the Bible.[2] It is their views which provide the clue for the modern understanding of revelation and its connection with Scripture. Maurice especially, whom A. C. Hebert speaks of as 'that seer and prophet of the future whose importance has never yet been recognized',[3] has been, in this context, specially influenced. It is of interest, therefore, in this connection, taking but one example, to observe the use made of Maurice by John Baillie in his own positive statements on the subject in his book, *The Idea of Revelation in Recent Thought*.

The view as it was developed by later writers is that revelation consists of a series of divine acts in which God enters into redeeming contact with human lives. Of these encounters the Bible is the record. The position was given precise statement by W. Robertson Smith. S. D. F. Salmond, giving an account of Smith's teaching on the death of the latter, declares, 'Revelation was to him not a communication of so much truth, but the entrance of God Himself into history and into man's life, the direct personal message of God's love to men. The Bible he held to be the record of this personal revelation of God'.[4]

Such a statement of the position has found vogue and favour. Writer after writer desires us to understand that the Bible is not

---

[1] William Lee, *The Inspiration of Holy Scripture*, 1854, fourth edition, 1865, p. 21; cf. J. D. Morrell, *The Philosophy of Religion*, pp. 143–4.

[2] Cf. H. D. McDonald, *Ideas of Revelation*, 1959, pp. 166 ff.

[3] A. C. Hebert, *The Function of the Church in the Modern World*, 1936, p. 108.

[4] S. D. F. Salmond, 'Professor William Robertson Smith', *Expository Times*, Vol. V, 1893–4, p. 361; cf. H. Wheeler Robinson, *Inspiration and Revelation in the Old Testament*, 1953, p. 281.

itself the revelation. However ideas about the Bible as such may have fluctuated, the one point of agreement amongst all those who reject inerrancy and infallibility is that the Scriptures are not to be equated with God's self-disclosure. Revelation is essentially personal whereas the Bible is a form of words and as such can only tell of revelation. Thus, to give a few illustrations of this insistence, A. B. Bruce writes, 'The Bible contains the record, the interpretation and the literary reflection of His (God's) grace in history'.[1] A. S. Peake argued that we have so identified revelation with its record that it is now possible only with great difficulty to recognize that in the strict sense of the term, revelation lies behind the Bible.[2] He argues further for the necessity to keep a clear distinction between the Bible as a record and the revelation to which it witnesses. He is prepared to grant that without the record we would be in a 'bad way'. 'The facts themselves and their interpretation are presented to us with far greater certainty and fulness in Scripture than they can be in institutions. Moreover, as experience abundantly proves, Scripture is among the most valuable means of grace... We must accordingly hold fast to the conclusion that it would have been an irreparable loss if the revelation had not been fixed in a written form.'[3]

The very title of the volume edited by H. Wheeler Robinson in 1938, *Record and Revelation* is indicative of the same outlook.[4]

[1] A. B. Bruce, *The Chief End of Revelation*, 1881, p. 280.

[2] A. S. Peake, *The Bible, Its Origin, Its Meaning, Its Abiding Value*, 1913, fifth edition, p. 290.   [3] *Ibid.*, p. 295.

[4] The position had been given popular and rather exaggerated emphasis by R. F. Horton in his volume *Revelation and the Bible*, 1892. Horton, it may be noted, however, had not come to regard revelation as personal and activist. He defines revelation as 'a truth or truths received from God into the minds of men, not by the ordinary methods of enquiry, such as observation and reasoning, but by a direct operation of the Holy Spirit' (second edition, p. 4). Not all in the Bible is, however, apparently revealed truth or truths. It is that which commends itself by 'direct manifestations of the Spirit to the Christian consciousness' which may be declared as revealed truth, as the word of God. The idea therefore 'of a revelation confined to the Sacred Writings cannot be said to be the idea of those Sacred Writings themselves' (p. 16). He opens his volume however with the remark 'It is proof of the revelation contained in the Bible that large numbers of Christian men cannot divest themselves of the idea that everything in the Bible is revelation' (p. 2). Cf. This idea of Horton's with a remark of Brunner's: 'We are not required to believe the Scriptures because they are Scriptures; but because Christ, whom I am convinced in my *conscience* (italics ours) is the Truth, meets me in the Scriptures—therefore I believe' (Emil Brunner, *The Christian Doctrine of God, Dogmatics*, Vol. I, p. 110, (E.T. 1950)).

A recent emphatic declaration, which could be paralleled from a hundred volumes, reiterates the same view: 'the Bible is not revelation, but the record of it'.[1] According to E. P. Dickie, it is the modern recognition of the Bible as 'the *record* of the most profound religious experiences leading up to and culminating in Jesus Christ' that we see its 'true nature'.[2]

(c) Those who have sought to lay stress upon the personal nature of revelation and especially those who have been influenced by Barth and Brunner, in regarding Christ as the 'Word of God' and the locus of revelation, have been eager to accentuate the distinction between revelation and the Scripture. These writers have been at pains to make two things clear. First, to deny, as Barth repeatedly does, that revelation is 'a static sum of revealed propositions'. Any such notion is declared anathema. Brunner in his *Revelation and Reason* reiterates the thesis that 'Divine revelation is not a book or a doctrine'.[3] Here we have what G. S. Hendry regards as 'a commonplace of modern theology' namely, 'that the Biblical revelation is not a system of abstract propositional truths, but, both in form and substance, a history of the acts of God'.[4] The second point these writers are anxious to guard against, to quote Barth again, is 'the freezing of the connection between Scripture and revelation'. The idea that revelation has to do with a communication of truth is usually attributed to the intellectualization of the Reformers' doctrine and as an illustration of the ever-recurring tendency to scholasticism.

Having then the idea of revelation as a divine self-disclosure of the 'Word of God' it remains to be noted that in this context the Bible is usually spoken of as a 'witness' to the actuality and the possibility of revelation. John Baillie, for example, sees the position of the Bible as that of John the Baptist: it, like him, is

---

[1] C. B. Moss, *The Christian Faith*, 1943, p. 211.

[2] E. P. Dickie, *Revelation and Response*, 1938, p. 129.

[3] E. Brunner, *Revelation and Reason* (E.T. 1946), 8; cf. p. 53. Cf. E. Brunner, *Dogmatics*, Vol. I (E.T. 1950), p. 53. K. Barth, *Church Dogmatic*, 1, i (E.T. 1936), p. 162 f. Nathaniel Micklem, *Ultimate Questions*, 1955, p. 55. F. W. Camfield, *Revelation and the Holy Spirit*, 1934, pp. 27 ff. and Chapter 2. H. Cunliffe Jones, *The Authority of Biblical Revelation*, 1946, Chapter II, etc. W. H. Morton, *Christian Theology*, An Ecumenical Approach, 1955, p. 46. *Liberal Theology* (ed. Roberts and Vandusen), 1942, p. 231.

[4] G. S. Hendry, 'The Dogmatic Form of Barth's Theology', *Theology Today*, Vol. XIII, 1956, 3, pp. 312 ff.

not the Light, but is to bear witness to the Light. Brunner[1] regards the Scripture as human testimony to revelation. True, he does not consider every part of the record as having the same witness value. Some parts of it do not 'point' to the inbreaking of God into human experience in the same decisive way. Some parts but 'stammer' out His name. Other passages, such as II Peter ii. 4, fall outside the 'rim' and have no witness value.[2]

The constantly reiterated statement that revelation is always communion and that it is never communication has, it should be noted, come in for increasing questioning of late. The Barthian activist view, of course, is an understandable repudiation of the exclusive emphasis upon the propositional notion which dominated a certain type of theological thinking of an earlier period. Many, however, have gone to an extreme position and deny that there is any doctrinal element at all in revelation. Some permit statements of biblical truths as inferences made by Christians under the influence of the Spirit; inferences which are based upon the knowledge of God's saving acts in history. William Temple, argued that 'there is no such thing as revealed truth'.[3] There are, he will allow, 'truths of revelation' which are 'propositions which express the results of correct thinking concerning revelation'.

A. E. Wright, in like manner, denies that the Bible contains, what he refers to as 'static, propositional' statements of doctrine. 'Does the Bible contain a *system* of doctrine?' he asks. His answer is: 'Certainly none of its writers was primarily concerned with the presentation of such a scheme. Consequently, we must say that static, propositional systems are those which the Church itself erects by inference from the Biblical writings'.[4] Emphatic declarations of this nature are constantly being made. But it is of interest to observe that those who are the most insistent that revelation is always in acts, never in propositions, find themselves unable to maintain their own thesis with any consistency. This is true even of Brunner and Barth. Brunner, to take him as an example, urges that 'A Church . . . can do

---

[1] John Baillie, *The Idea of Revelation in Recent Thought*, 1956, p. 125.

[2] E. Brunner, *Revelation and Reason* (E.T. 1938), pp. 15–17, 48, etc. E. Brunner, *The Philosophy of Religion*, 1937, p. 153 f; cf. H. D. McDonald, *Ideas of Revelation*, 1959, p. 191.

[3] William Temple, *Nature, Man and God*, 1947, p. 317.

[4] A. Ernest Wright, *The God Who Acts*, 1952, p. 35.

justice to her commission only when she recovers the unity of
the *Logos* and the *Dynamis*, of the word and the act of God,
which is the distinctive element in Biblical revelation'.[1] A. G.
Hebert in a chapter on 'The Biblical Idea of Revelation', makes
the significant observation that in the Scriptures there is
throughout a 'double conception of Revelation, as the revelation
of God Himself, and of truths concerning Him'.[2] We have
ourselves argued elsewhere that since man is a 'spiritual' and
'rational' being revelation must come to meet the whole man.
Because man is 'spiritual' it must come to him as 'Spirit', and
because he is 'rational' it must come to him as 'truth'.[3] It has
been our contention that the divorce between the activist and the
propositionalist ideas of revelation is ultimately invalid.
'Whether the Christian revelation is only personal and not to
some extent propositional is another question', states E. G.
Homrighausen in a review of Brunner's *Divine–Human
Encounter*, 'for if God reveals Himself adequately, man's mind
must be satisfied'.[4] Undoubtedly, as Louis Berkhof readily
admits, 'The view, once prevalent, that revelation consists
exclusively in a communication of doctrine, was clearly one-
sided. At present, however', he continues, 'some go to the other
extreme, equally one-sided, that revelation consists in communication of power and life'.[5]

It seems to becoming clearer as the subject becomes more and
more discussed that 'The modern view makes an unnecessary
cleavage between the personal and the propositional in revelation'.[6] The two are complementary, not contradictory. True,

---

[1] Emil Brunner, *Revelation and Reason* (E.T. 1946), p. 164; cf. 'Revelation is
a concept that both *relates* religious knowledge to the more ordinary forms of
knowledge and *distinguishes* it *from* them' (W. H. Morton, *Christian Theology*,
An Ecumenical Approach, 1955, p. 41).

[2] A. G. Hebert, *The Authority of the Old Testament*, 1947, p. 80.

[3] H. D. McDonald, *Ideas of Revelation*, 1959, p. 274.

[4] E. G. Homrighausen, *Theology Today*, Vol. I, No. i, April 1944, pp. 153 ff. Cf.
E. J. Carnell, *A Philosophy of the Christian Religion*, 1952, p. 29.

[5] Louis Berkhof, *Reformed Dogmatics*, Introductory Volume, 1932, p. 144. Cf.
'The Bible does contain much objective propositional truth. The central truths of
the Bible are literally correct; for example, God is love and was in Christ reconciling
the world unto Himself. Therefore Barth's contention that the Bible becomes the
Word of God *only* for faith is too deeply tinged with subjectivism to speak the full
truth'. Nels F. S. Ferré, *Christ and the Christian*, 1958, p. 37.

[6] Francis I. Andersen, *The Westminster Theological Journal*, Vol. XXII, No. 2,
May 1960, p. 127.

information is not God: but it seems certainly impossible to know God personally apart from the information. 'To belittle propositions because they are impersonal is to destroy human relations by despising their normal medium. The bliss of being loved is different from the words of love-making, but the "proposition", "I love you", is a welcome, nay, an indispensable means of the consummation of love in actuality. . . . But in modern theology we have a Lover-God who makes no declarations!'[1]

The idea that God can be known 'personally' apart from ideas, or at any rate apart from 'images' is given a specific and unique denial by Austin Farrer. Farrer agrees, to be sure, that the modern view of revelation in and by divine events alone is more satisfying than the theory of dictated propositions.[2] He is quite ready to admit, what, we suppose, all Christians do really maintain, that the primary revelation is Jesus Christ Himself. Farrer, however, is insistent that 'the events by themselves are not revelation'.[3] He therefore concludes that it is in the interplay of image and event where we have the locus of revelation. His thesis is, then, that 'the events without the images would be no revelation at all, and the images without the events would remain shadows on the clouds'.[4] Farrer opens Lecture IV with a statement of the conclusion to which his enquiry has so far led. It is a significant declaration; 'We have concluded', he says, 'that divine truth is supernaturally communicated to men in an act of inspired thinking which falls into the shape of certain images'.[5]

Farrer raises the question consequent upon his teaching: 'Does God feed His saints with nothing but figures of speech?'

[1] Francis I. Andersen, *The Westminster Theological Journal*, Vol. XXII, No. 2, May 1960, p. 127. Cf. 'For love is self-affirmation as well as self-impartation; it must be first self-affirmation in order that it may become self-imparting love'. Newman Smyth, *Christian Ethics*, 1896, p. 328.

[2] Austin Farrer, *The Glass of Vision*, 1948, pp. 36 ff.; cf. also his chapter 'Revelation' in *Faith and Logic* (ed. Basil Mitchell).

[3] *Ibid.*, p. 43.   [4] *Ibid.*

[5] *Ibid.*, p. 57. An interesting comparison could be drawn between Farrer and the teaching of Dionysius the Areopagite. Dionysius has the same idea of 'images', but perhaps he fails to stress the need for 'event' as does Farrer. 'Revelation' according to Dionysius, 'itself does not convey any knowledge of God that could be expressed in speculative terms. Revelation veils as well as reveals. It is for this reason that figurative speech, metaphor, image, and parable abound throughout the Bible'. Richard Kroner, *Speculation and Revelation in the Age of Christian Philosophy*, 1959, p. 134.

He insists that the 'images' will not be understood without the prior action of, what he calls 'supernatural life' in the soul.[1] Without this 'revealed truth is dumb to us'. He adds, however, that it is absurd to suggest that the supernatural action we exercise is the adequate real counterpart of the divine truth we believe. At this point, we believe John Baillie has misinterpreted Farrer.[2] As far as we can see, all that Farrer is saying in his own way is what orthodox faith has always stressed, namely, there must be for the subjective realization of saving truth, the inner witness of the Holy Spirit. It might, in fact, although Farrer might not concur, be contended that Farrer is using the term 'image' for what others refer to as 'proposition'. And if the term were substituted for Farrar's 'image' in the quotation at the end of the paragraph above then we have a clear enough statement of what conservative theology demands. God does not feed His saints on propositions and yet it is through propositions, in some sense, that they are fed.

In order to complete the story it remains to be pointed out that conservative evangelicals, as will be expected, maintain what they regard to be two important facts in their statement on the subject of revelation.

They insist that God's revelation consists of revealed truths. There must be a propositional, that is, a verbal aspect to it. It is regarded as a fallacy to reserve the idea of revelation for divine acts and to deny the reality of divine words. The position is clearly and unequivocally argued by J. I. Packer in his closely reasoned defence of the conservative evangelical case. 'God reveals Himself to men', he declares, 'both by exercising power for them and by teaching truth to them. The two activities are not antithetical, but complementary. Indeed, the Biblical position is that the mighty acts of God are not revelation to man at all, except in so far as they are accompanied by words to explain them.'[3] The same insistence is found to underlie the various essays to which a number of British conservative evangelical scholars have contributed to the volume *Revelation and the Bible*. In his essay on 'Contemporary Ideas of Revelation', R. A. Finlayson rejects the antithesis created by the modern school of

---

[1] Austin Farrer, *The Glass of Vision*, p. 59.
[2] John Baillie, *The Idea of Revelation in Recent Thought*, 1956, p. 39 f.
[3] J. I. Packer, *'Fundamentalism' and the Word of God*, 1958, p. 92.

theology, both neo-liberal and neo-orthodox, between revelation as encounter and revelation as communication. He urges
that 'our encounter with God rests upon the mediation of His
truth to chosen prophets and apostles. In virtue of the divine
inspiration that communication is for us completely trustworthy,
introducing us to the living and true God'.[1]

The other major antithesis, namely that between revelation
and Scripture, is also being strongly challenged. Brunner,
Barth, Baillie and numerous others, as we have indicated,
sharpened the divorce between them. Yet these very writers
themselves, it will be discovered, have found it hard to avoid the
identification which they so strenuously deny. One cannot read
very far in the writings of any one of them before one comes
upon a passage in which the identity of revelation with the
record is unwittingly made. Brunner who has been so strong in
his denial of the legitimacy of equating revelation with Scripture
can say: 'Holy Scripture therefore does not only speak of
revelation; it is itself the revelation'.[2] C. H. Dodd, in the same
manner, urges on one page that the Church offers the Bible 'as
the authoritative record of the divine revelation',[3] yet on
another page states in categorical fashion, 'The Church offers
this book as a revelation of God'.[4]

---

[1] *Revelation and the Bible* (ed. Carl F. H. Henry), 1958, p. 228. Carl Henry,
himself, argues in his massive volume, *Christian Personal Ethics*, 1957, that the
dialectical existential ethics by rejecting propositional revelation altogether has
denied a rational basis for theology and ethics. The message of the Bible, he insists,
'centres in the disclosure to mankind of a transcendent supernatural reality. Jesus,
in the tradition of the Hebrew prophets, upholds unconditional imperatives which
are transcendent to individual experience, objectively confronting man as divinely
authoritative. He asserts principles which have not arisen *in* human experience but
which are to be received as universally trustworthy and dependable guides for life.
They reflect ethical realities external to human experience' (p. 138). George F.
Thomas is quoted as urging that abandonment of ethical propositions discloses a
'nominalistic tendency to stress the particular at the expense of the universal aspect
or moral situations', and the result 'leads . . . perilously close to the abyss of
irrationalism'. *Ibid.*; cf. George F. Thomas, *Christian Ethics and Moral Philosophy*,
p. 386. The position from a Christian point of view might be simply put like this:
revelation is essentially redemptive and redemption is essentially ethical. The
ethical can only come in terms of ethical imperatives so that revelation must involve
essential ethical propositions. The same argument can be used to insist upon the
truth-content of revelation. '*Intellectual* evaluation and assent are indispensable
elements in significant moral decision. Moral decision which is wrenched from man
in the absence of rational criteria is deficient' (p. 139).

[2] Emil Brunner, *Revelation and Reason* (E.T. 1946), p. 21.

[3] C. H. Dodd, *The Bible Today*, 1946, p. 15.   [4] *Ibid.*, p. 12.

There is an apparent growing sensitiveness to the rightness of
the modern cleavage between revelation and its record. This is
seen, for example, in Lionel Thornton's important book,
Revelation and the Modern World. Thornton's thesis seems to be
that God's self-manifestation is bound up with the minutiae of
contemporary life. It is virtually impossible to abstract the
essence of revelation from the sacred literature in which it is
enshrined.[1] They stand together. Thornton declares that the
writers of the Bible 'wove the garments in which the theophany
is clothed, apart from which it cannot be manifested'.[2] Without
this dress it would disappear as surely as in the modern scientific
romance 'the invisible man' was no longer seen when he took off
his clothes. Thornton, therefore, stresses that 'Scripture as a
whole is the Whole with which Revelation is to be identified'.[3]
As the onion which cannot be peeled it must be accepted as it is.
It must not be supposed, however, that Thornton in rejecting
what he calls the Liberal Experiment, is committed to what he
refers to as 'the opposite error of bibliolatry or "fundamentalism" '.[4] Revelation has identity with the vessel, but there
is a real distinction at the same time between the two. He will
admit that there are 'imperfections of the earthen vessel in which
the divine treasure is conveyed', but even so, these 'are themselves integral to the very nature of revelation itself'.[5] Although
there is much in Thornton's thesis commendable and much
which is questionable, its significance in our present context lies
in its expression of obvious dissatisfaction with the neo-
orthodox complete separation between revelation and the record.

The necessity for a more intimate relationship between God's
self-disclosure and the Scriptures we ourselves have argued in
the closing section of our *Ideas of Revelation*.[6] Acknowledgement
was there given to the truth which the distinction seeks to
maintain. There is a real and objective revelation in divine works
and words, prior to and independent of, any written record. The

---

[1] L. E. Thornton, *Revelation and the Modern World*, 1950, p. 16.
[2] *Ibid.*, p. 53.   [3] *Ibid.*, p. 130.   [4] *Ibid.*
[5] *Ibid.*, p. 132. Cf. 'While we must accept the Bible as an earthen vessel with
flaws and limitations which are part of the living manifestation of God's word in
and through men, we must beware of magnifying these flaws so as to obscure the
great supernatural fact to which the Bible testifies.' H. Cunliffe-Jones, *The Authority
of the Biblical Revelation*, 1946, second impression, 1948, p. 117.
[6] H. D. McDonald, *Ideas of Revelation*, 1959, p. 282.

central aspect of revelation, so to say, is God's saving deeds in history, but these divine acts come necessarily in an historical context and, as C. R. North remarks, 'the historical occasion is an essential element in the revelation'.[1] It is, however, only as the 'historical occasion' of the divine act is recorded that it can be known to us. Revelation, to be sure, may be thought of as God's acts in history, but these 'actualities' of God in history would remain in the limbo of forgotten things if they were not preserved in record. In the last analysis, then, revelation must be taken to include, not merely the acts of God in history, but the history of these acts, and their interpretation and application to the concrete realities of human experience.[2] It is beyond question that as 'soon as we try to abstract the values from their concrete embodiment, we evacuate them of all reality and become sentimentalists. The spiritual must always be embodied to be known and faithfully served; the eternal must clothe itself in temporal form to enter effectually within our horizon'.[3]

James Orr, defending the evangelical assimilation of revelation with the record—and this is the second important fact conservative scholars desire to maintain—postulates that 'if a revelation has been given by God, it is reasonable to expect that provision will be made for the *preservation* of the knowledge of the revelation *in some permanent and authoritative form*'.[4] He argues that the recorders of revelation must be men who stand in a special intimate connection with the original act of self-disclosure and that they must be men who possess in an eminent degree the Spirit of the revelation. The revelation, he then urges, includes, 'not only direct acts and communications, but *the whole divinely-guided history* of the people of Israel, and in the New Testament, *the apostolic action* in the founding of the Church'.[5] As for the recorders themselves they must be given a special inspiration for the right use of their materials and a special illumination to see into the meaning of history. All must

---

[1] C. R. North, *The Old Testament Interpretation of History*, 1946, p. 153.

[2] Cf. 'Christianity in an historical religion is a particularly technical sense that the term possesses—it presents us with religious doctrines which are at the same time historical events or historical interpretations.' H. Butterfield, *Christianity and History*, 1950, p. 3.

[3] H. Wheeler Robinson, *Redemption and Revelation*, 1942, p. xlv; cf. p. 186.

[4] James Orr, *Revelation and Inspiration*, 1910, reprint, 1952, p. 155.

[5] *Ibid.*, p. 157.

be taken into account, not the divine side merely, but no less the human reception of the revelation and the actings of the human spirit under its influence, and in response to it. What is ultimately required in a book which is to be an adequate record of divine revelation is 'not only the record of what may be called its *external* historical course, but the record of its *internal* history in the life and experience of souls that have grasped their meaning, and felt their power'.[1]

Having in the Bible, Orr concludes, a record which fulfills all the required criteria, it becomes God's complete word. Beyond it there is no need to travel to discover God's whole will for our salvation. Consequently, he contends, this being the position and the purpose of the Scripture, 'the line between revelation and record is becoming very thin, and that, in another true sense, *the record*, in the fulness of its contents, *is itself for us the revelation*'.[2]

B. THE WORD OF GOD AND THE SCRIPTURES

From what has gone before, the reader will not be surprised to discover that a sharp antithesis was also set up throughout our period between what was regarded as the Word of God and the Scriptures. The distinction was already to hand, it should be noted, popularized more especially by S. T. Coleridge and F. D. Maurice who reacted vigorously against the orthodox apologists who, in their polemic against the Deists, had maintained revelation to be a body of divinely communicated truths unerringly given in the Bible. Attention had been focused, by way of opposition, on the inward and the subjective. Protest was raised against what was regarded as 'book worship' in Protestantism; and the important dictum was laid down by Coleridge that it is when the Bible 'finds me' that it authenticates its authority as a witness to the Word of God. This principle of Coleridge has been used with effect by many in the present period who have continued to distinguish between the Word of God and the Scripture in which it is contained or through which it is discovered.[3]

[1] James Orr, *Revelation and Inspiration*, p. 158.

[2] *Ibid.*, p. 159 (italics in original in each case).

[3] Coleridge's phrase is constantly quoted as a statement of the position of many modern writers: cf., e.g. the two writers, Alfred Peel and R. H. Lightfoot in *The Interpretation of the Bible* (ed. C. W. Dugmore), 1944, pp. 60 and 90.

Before the full effect of criticism had been felt, a large body of religious opinion was committed to the cleavage between the Word of God and the Bible. The number was greatly increased with the coming of the higher criticism. The vital and intended result of criticism was to give attention to the 'humanness' of the Bible. It was to be treated as any other book would be. So constantly reiterated was this point that some came to regard the Scripture as a very imperfect vessel whatever might be the treasure it was claimed to contain. It was false, it was declared, to speak of such a collection of books, compiled over a vast period from a multiplicity of documents of varying degrees of reliability, as the Word of God.

In the immediate post-Darwinian period, the Bible was thought of by many as giving a highly interesting account of man's progressive discovery of God. In the early days of criticism the tendency was, at first, to take the same line and to see the Bible as more or less a valuable record of vital religious experience. 'Thus the view of the Bible having the term "religious experience" for its key-word came to be widely accepted'.[1] Here, also, the historic identification of the Word of God with the Scriptures was rejected. The Word of God, the claim went, was a term to be reserved for the creative religious experience of all prophetic men in general and of the great men of the Bible in particular.

As more and more Christ was specified as the locus of revelation, it was maintained that He and He alone was properly to be designated the Word of God. In this the theologians of crisis have come to insist upon the idea for which the earlier Coleridgean school had contended.[2] The title belongs to

[1] A. G. Hebert, *The Authority of the Old Testament*, 1947, p. 33; cf. J. M. Graham, ' "After Fifty Years" Revelation and the Bible', *Expository Times*, Vol. I, 1938–9, pp. 537–40.

[2] B. E. Meland makes the interesting observation that whereas the feeling–experience derives from Schleiermacher the attention focused upon the Person of Christ is due to Ritschl. It was, he states, the reaction against rationalism which led theologians like Schleiermacher and philosophers like Coleridge to extend the appeal to religious experience. 'Ritschlian theology, while it continued the emphasis upon feeling and experience which had characterized the thought of Schleiermacher, narrowed the appeal to a specific object within the Christian tradition. The object was the *person* of the historic Jesus. Accordingly the appeal to Christ, or more particularly, the appeal to the immediate experience of the person of Christ, replaced the appeal to experience, based upon the "sense of dependence".' N. H. Wieman and B. E. Meland, *American Philosophies of Religion*, 1936, p. 42.

Christ alone.[1] Barth, it is well known, has put great emphasis upon this point. Revelation, he argues, is the *'Deus dixit'*, the 'one Word of God within which there can be neither a more or less'.[2] He maintained the two-way equation; 'God's Word is God's Son' and 'God's Son is God's Word'.[3] The constant note of much writing on the subject of revelation is that we must beware of imprisoning the Word of God within the covers of a book.[4] And fearful warnings are issued against 'bibliolatory', and against making, as the seventeenth century teachers are said to have done, 'absolute surrender' to a 'paper pope'. Brunner charges those whom he designates 'fundamentalists' with being 'in bondage to the Biblical text' and thereby making 'the Bible an idol and me its slave'. More recently Nels F. S. Ferré in America has been eloquent in repudiating the identification of God's Word in revelation with the Bible. He regards the desire to make such an equation as an illustration of Vaihinger's law of the tendency to substitute the means for the end. Thus the book comes to be considered perfect and its words inerrant. 'Fearful human beings, claiming a liberating Gospel, barricade themselves behind a book. God's good means is thus defiled through perversion. The false use becomes demoniac and destructive, and faith flees. Relaxed love and spontaneous creativity cease.'[5] Many would, of course, be ready to join issue with Ferré about the rightness of his charge and they would certainly wish to question the correctness of his conclusion regarding the dire consequences of regarding the Bible as 'perfect' and the complete container of the Word of God. But,

[1] Cf. 'The word of God which saveth and redeemeth the soul is not the word printed on paper, but is the . . . ever-speaking Word, which is the Son of God.' W. Law, *The Way of Divine Knowledge*, p. 137. 'More and more he (F. D. Maurice) had come to look upon all expressions implying that the letter of the Bible is the word of God as denials of the living "Word of God" of Whom the Bible speaks.' *Life of F. D. Maurice*, by his son, Vol. 2, p. 452.

[2] Karl Barth, *Church Dogmatics* (E.T. 1936), 1, i, p. 164.

[3] *Ibid.*, p. 156; cf. William Nicholls, *Revelation in Christ*, 1957, Chapter II.

[4] Cf. 'But if the Bible is called the Word of God, theological confusion is almost unavoidable. Such consequences as the dictation theory of inspiration, dishonesty in dealing with the biblical text, a "monophysitic" dogma of the infallibility of a book, etc., follow from such an identification. Probably nothing has contributed more to the misinterpretation of all biblical doctrine of the Word than the identification of the Word with the Bible.' Paul Tillich, *Systematic Theology*, Vol. I, 1951, pp. 158–9.

[5] Nels F. S. Ferré, *The Christian Understanding of God*, 1951, p. 179. See Chapter VII in that volume entitled, 'The Work of God in Revelation'.

be this as it may, it is a fact that the statement of an antithesis between the Word of God and the Bible became characteristic of the period. The result of this divorce has been a certain amount of hesitancy and doubt about the way the Bible itself is to be conceived. And as a consequence, as H. Cunliffe-Jones justly observes, 'for many reasons, the Christian Church is uncertain at the present time, how to treat the Bible as the Word of God'.[1]

In the main, however, it has become usual for those who, for whatever their reasons, accept the antithesis, to refer to the Bible as 'containing' or as 'speaking of', or as 'witnessing to', or as 'becoming' the Word of God. There is general agreement that it is not to be identified with the Word of God. Some of those who have adopted this understanding of the relation of the Word of God to the Scriptures have claimed the Reformers as their Fathers. But such a claim is unquestionably biased. Albert Peel asserts that the Reformers would have some criticisms to offer to those who speak today of the Bible as the Word of God.[2] He suggests that they drew a distinction between the Word of God and the Scriptures which convey or becomes it. It is not easy, we think, taking an objective view of the data, to get support for such a contention in the teaching of the Fathers of the Reformation. That Calvin equated the Word of God with the Bible is a certain fact. In the case of Luther, pre-eminently a preacher and little of a systematic theologian, there is less exactness and consistency of statement in this connection. Yet he opens his *Table Talks* with the words 'That the Bible is God's word and book I prove thus . . .'. G. B. Fisher correctly assesses the situation when he declares that 'the identity of the Holy Scriptures with the Word of God is generally assumed by Luther and occasionally expressed in explicit language'.[3] Recently the same position has been confidently maintained by Robert Preus who contends that the Lutheran reformers

---

[1] H. Cunliffe-Jones, *The Authority of the Biblical Revelation*, 1946, second impression, 1948, p. 132.

[2] Albert Peel, 'The Bible and the Book', *The Interpretation of the Bible* (ed. C. W. Dugmore), 1944, p. 67; cf. pp. 52, 66 and 68. Cf. E. P. Dickie, *Revelation and Response*, 1938, p. 130.

[3] G. B. Fisher, *History of Christian Doctrine*, 1896, edition, 1922, p. 280. Cf. W. P. Paterson, *The Rule of Faith*, 1932, p. 405. M. Reu, *Luther and the Scriptures*, 1944, pp. 17, 24, 35, 55, 63, 92, etc.

accepted the complete identity of Scripture with the Word of God.[1] While at an earlier date K. R. Hagenbach affirmed that 'During the preceding period', he is referring to the time prior to 1700, 'Protestant theology had been accustomed to call the Sacred Scriptures themselves the Word of God; in the course of the present a distinction was made between the *word of God contained in Holy Writ* and the Sacred Scriptures'.[2]

Whether, however, the Reformers are called upon to justify the distinction between the Word of God and the Scriptures, or not, the fact remains that many in our period have preferred to regard the Bible as 'containing' that Word. To think of Scripture itself as the Word of God, it has been argued of late by J. K. S. Reid, is to compromise the sovereignty of God and the result must be that 'God's word is petrified in a dead record'.[3] It is not very clear from Reid, it may be remarked in passing, why God's sovereignty is not rather revealed in His use of the Scripture as the source of His life-giving power in the personal experience of redemption. It is, at any rate, worthy of notice that it is the written word which in several passages in the New Testament is referred to as 'the Word of God'.[4]

The first advocates of the higher criticism implied in their manifold writings their satisfaction with the disassociation of the idea of the Word of God from the Scriptures. The concept of the Bible as that which 'contains' the Word of God, was, for example, argued for strongly by F. W. Farrar. Farrar, in fact, goes so far as to contend that it is the doctrine of the Church of England that 'Scripture *contains* the Word of God'.[5] And he maintains that 'To assert that the phrase "Scripture containeth" (*complectitur*) instead of "is" (*est*) the Word of God is only *an accident* of the formularies of the English Church is the reverse of the fact'.[6] Farrar says that 'The Bible as a whole may be spoken of as the word of God, because it *contains* words and passages of God to the human soul; but it is not in its whole

---

[1] Robert Preus, *The Inspiration of Scripture*, A Study in the Theology of the Seventeenth Century Lutheran Dogmaticians, 1955, Chapter 2.

[2] H. R. Hagenbach, *Compendium of the History of Doctrine*, 1880, Vol. 2, p. 406.

[3] J. K. S. Reid, *The Authority of Scripture*, 1957, p. 279.

[4] Cf. H. D. McDonald, *Ideas of Revelation*, 1959, pp. 277–8. Cf. W. M. Horton, *Christian Theology*, An Ecumenical Approach, 1955, pp. 65 ff.

[5] F. W. Farrar, *The Bible, Its Meaning and Supremacy*, 1897, p. 136.

[6] *Ibid.*, pp. 136, 137.

extent, and throughout, identical with the Word of God'.[1]
Farrar endeavours to destroy the proposition by which the
Puritan writer, Thomas Cartwright, in his *Treatise of the
Christian Religion* (1616) had sought to demonstrate the thesis
that the books of the Bible may be 'discerned to be the
word of God'.

A popular exposition of the idea that the Bible can at most be
said to *contain* the word of God only was given by R. F. Horton.
Horton tells in his *Autobiography* how he was compelled to reject
the idea of 'the verbal infallibility of the Bible',[2] and as a consequence set out on a 'quest to find the sure foundation'.[3] Of one
fact alone could he be sure, he acknowledges, namely, that faith
must be centred in Christ and the Christian experience. He had
hoped to clarify the position regarding the relation of the Bible
to revelation, but he boldly states that his book, *Revelation and
the Bible*, 'pretends to be nothing more than a series of tentative
suggestions'.[4] He, however, maintains, not merely as a
suggestion but as an assured fact, that to speak of some parts of
the Bible—his instance in this particular is the Book of
Ecclesiastes—'as the Word of God is an impiety'.[5] Earlier he
had contended that 'Nothing could be further from the truth to
describe Psalm LXXXIII, for example, as the Word of God; it
is by its very form the word of men, of men, too, who have not
entered very deeply into the counsels of God'.[6] Statements of

---

[1] F. W. Farrar, *The Bible, Its Meaning and Supremacy*, 1897, p. 131; note heading
of chapter 'The Bible contains the Word of God'.

[2] R. F. Horton, *Autobiography*, 1918, p. 144.   [3] *Ibid.*, p. 100.

[4] R. F. Horton, *Revelation and the Bible*, 1892, second edition, Preface, p. viii.

[5] *Ibid.*, p. 204.

[6] *Ibid.*, 1888, pp. 188–9. Even a more explicit statement will be found in his
Verbum Dei, 1893: 'The unthinking dogma of orthodoxy that the Bible as such is
the Word of God . . .' (p. 107) is a typical declaration. Cf. His *Inspiration and the
Bible*, 1888, Preface, p. 10. Yet note Horton's strange words in his *Verbum Dei*,
'The Bible itself is in so unique and peculiar a sense the Word of God . . .' (p. 155).
   In the volume *Inspiration, A Clerical Symposium*, 1884 (ed. F. W. Farrar), there
is an explanatory subtitle in the form of a question to which the eleven contributors
sought an answer: 'In what sense, and within what limits, is the Bible to be
regarded as the Word of God?' Three of those who wrote on the subject, S. Leathes,
John Cairns and G. W. Oliver, contended that the phrase 'the Word of God' is
applicable to the Bible as a whole, and they emphatically rejected the idea that the
Bible 'contains' the Word of God (see esp. pp. 23 ff.). Other writers who find a
place in the company of the historic orthodox Christian Churches (there are writers
in the volume who do not stand in this association; there is, e.g. a Jew, a Sweden-
borgian, and a Unitarian), contend for the idea that the Bible *contains* the Word of
God. Here E. White and F. W. Farrar are the two most important.

this nature, which could be paralleled from other sources, were, to say the least, disconcerting to those who had been taught to regard the Bible in itself as the Word of God. Horton's position was a popular rehash of Robertson Smith's doctrine,[1] although stated in a rough and crude manner. 'The Word of God authenticates itself' the slogan ran: and it does so through those parts of the book which the enlightened Christian consciousness can appreciate. Taking their cue from the Coleridgeans, these writers maintained that the Scriptures become the Word of God in the context of experience. It is not to be regarded in itself, in its totality, as the Word of God: it is the vehicle of the divine activity, the witness to revelation.[2]

C. H. Dodd gave refined exposition to the thesis. 'In the expression "the Word of God" ', he says, 'lurks an equivocation'.[3] It is a 'metaphorical expression'.[4] He sees the Bible as the 'seminal' word, but not the final word. It mediates the 'Word of God' and herein lies its authority.[5] Dodd's position appears to be, concerning the Bible, that those parts of it which 'find' me most, reveal God best. Whatever commends itself to the aroused moral consciousness within the seeking individual is to be designated the 'Word of God'. 'The criterion' contends Dodd, 'lies within ourselves, in the response of our own spirit

---

[1] Cf. T. M. Lindsay, 'Professor W. Robertson Smith's Doctrine of Scripture', *Expositor*, fourth series, Vol. X, 1894, pp. 241–64; see also Smith's own *Answer to the Form of Libel*, 1878, pp. 18–44.

[2] The importance of the new emphasis is reflected in the differences introduced into the Articles of Faith of the English Presbyterian Church about this time. In 1888, after three years of study the appointed committee proposed the draft form of the new creed which was recommended as an interpretation of the old Westminster Confession. The article on Scripture was put No. 18 instead of at the beginning as in the case of the Westminster symbol. In place of the term 'Word of God' that of 'Revelation' was proposed. More significant, instead of the emphatic declaration that the Bible 'is' the Word of God came the suggestion that it should read (as in the Shorter Catechism) 'is contained in'. The alterations were vigorously challenged and emendations suggested. After an extended period allowed for consideration and discussion a compromise was reached and was adopted by the Synod of 1890. In the adopted articles the one on Scripture comes as the nineteenth. The phrase 'is contained in', which was regarded as recent and inadequate by the conservative opposition was omitted. But they were unsuccessful in gaining the admission of the Westminster declaration that the Bible 'is' the Word of God. The article as it now stands, and subscription to which was required by the Synod of 1892, reads: 'This Revelation has been, so far as needful, committed to writing by men inspired of the Holy Spirit, in the Scriptures of the Old and New Testaments, which are to be devoutly studied by all as God's written Word or Message to mankind'.

[3] C. H. Dodd, *The Authority of the Bible*, 1928, p. 16.   [4] *Ibid.*   [5] *Ibid.*, p. 289.

to the Spirit that utters itself in the Scriptures.'[1] This means that
a subjective valuation of what is to be understood as the Word
of God is proclaimed. It is, indeed, emphatically declared that
'Nowhere is the truth given in such purely "objective" form
that we can find a self-subsistent external authority'.[2]

On the lips of the more radical critics any reference to the
Bible as the objective Word of God was specially abhorrent. The
more advanced became the critic, the more was the gospel
conceived to be a message *about* God, not a message of God, and
certainly not a message from God.

Dialectical theology, we have seen, has reserved the title the
Word of God for Christ alone. W. M. Horton in his essay in the
symposium *Revelation*, believes it to be one of the distinctive
results of the modern discussion of the subject that this antithesis should be maintained. He says, 'We are not likely again
to identify God's eternal Word with the Book which contains
the record of its revealing'.[3] Actually in the same volume
Sergius Bulgakoff does seek to give significance to the Scripture
as itself the Word of God; but he, of course, does not stand in
the same tradition as the other writers. The rest, in spite of their
deep differences (for the difference between Barth and Temple,
for example, is great) are at one in repudiating the idea that
the concept 'Word of God' can be properly applied to the Bible.

By its failure to give any significant meaning to the historic
description of the Scriptures as the written word of God, the
older liberalism stands condemned. It was, as T. H. Manson
observes, so 'vitiated by its dogmatic presuppositions' that it
could not deal adequately with 'the history of Biblical religion'.[4]
The romantic and evolutionary ideas which undergirded it were
insecure. Manson is perfectly right to speak of 'The failure of
Liberalism to interpret the Bible as the Word of God'.[5] The only

---

[1] C. H. Dodd, *The Authority of the Bible*, 1928, p. 296.   [2] *Ibid.*, p. 289.
[3] *Revelation* (ed. John Baillie and Hugh Martin), 1937, p. 264.
[4] *The Interpretation of the Bible* (ed. C. W. Dugdale), 1944, p. 102.
[5] Cf. Title of T. H. Manson's essay, *op, cit.* Cf. C. J. Cadoux, 'Dr T. W.
Manson's Attack on Liberalism', *Congregational Quarterly*, Vol. 24, 1926, pp. 25 ff.
Although not actually using the word Cadoux seems to regard Manson's attack as
a betrayal. Cf. The remarks of Nathanial Micklem: he tells that when earlier in his
experience he wrote his Liberal appreciation of Christ 'it brought no protest from
any responsible person in the Free Churches, while later writings, in which I have
appeared to be swinging towards orthodoxy, have been widely represented as a
kind of treason!' *What is the Faith?*, 1936, Preface, p. 12.

way open, he believes, is to retrace our steps to where Liberalism went off the track; and, having reached that point, we must go forward, not backward.[1] Courage, he adds, is needed to believe that God has spoken.[2]

Manson has the older Liberalism in view in his castigation. But many are beginning to think that perhaps the same thing could be said about neo-liberalism. Here, too, there is an inadequate understanding of the way the Scripture is related to the Word of God.

In the period of the high-tide of criticism there was evident disquiet and dissatisfaction with the growing tendency to refer to the Scripture as 'containing' the Word of God. In an earlier footnote, attention was called to the opposition within the Presbyterian Church of England to the proposed change in its Articles of Faith, from the emphatic declaration that the Bible 'is' the Word of God to that of the Word of God 'is contained in' the Scriptures. Scholars of the stature of James Orr and Robert Rainy saw no difficulty in speaking of the Bible in the terms of the Westminster Catechism. They were as clear as anyone else that there is a human element in the inspired record, but they could not, on that account, admit the distinction which was sought by the critics.[3]

As will be expected the preachers of the conservative evangelical school who had already rejected the critical method could not give their assent to the new slogan. History and tradition they knew were on their side. And they could not but feel that the present critical phase would pass. There did not seem to be sufficient reason to make concessions to what was considered an ephemeral mood. It was his uncompromising insistence that the Bible was to be regarded in its totality as the Word of God which was in part the cause of Spurgeon's involvement in what became known as the 'Downgrade' controversy.[4] Spurgeon, indeed, criticized Alfred Cave for compromising in a

[1] *The Interpretation of the Bible* (ed. C. W. Dugdale), 1944, p. 101.
[2] *Op. cit.*, p. 107.
[3] Cf. 'If we would speak in the language of Scripture faith, we must hold that it is better to say, "The Bible is true, because we have found it to be the Word of God", than to say, with Coleridge, "The Bible is the Word of God because we have found it to be true".' James Bannerman, *Inspiration*, The Infallible Truth and Divine Authority of the Holy Scriptures, 1865. Cf. S. T. Coleridge, *The Confessions of an Inquiring Spirit*, p. 73.
[4] Cf. esp. *The Sword and the Trowel* for the years 1887–90. W. Y. Fullerton, *C. H. Spurgeon, A Biography*, 1920, pp. 296–301. J. C. Carlyle, *C. H. Spurgeon, An*

measure the traditional view of the Bible in the latter's Congregational Union Lectures of 1888. Cave took as his subject *The Inspiration of the Old Testament Inductively Considered*, and courageously attacked the Graf-Wellhausen theory, and sought to restore the traditional view. The critics' verdict on Cave's attempt was naturally unfavourable and Cave himself was written off as an ignoramus. A reviewer in the *Spectator* maintained that he omitted from evidence items in his sources which seem to conflict with his view.[1] W. G. Elmslie contended that Cave's treatment would be ineffective in allaying suspicion about the Old Testament. Spurgeon, however, felt compelled to disassociate himself from Cave's defence because Cave had conceded that Genesis gave evidence of being a composite document. Such an admission Spurgeon considered unnecessary; at any rate, it compromised the genuine historicity and accuracy of the account. Cave had attempted to prop up faith in the Bible as the Word of God. Spurgeon retorted that no such props are needed by those whose judgement is not perverted by critical unbelief.[2]

As it fell to R. F. Horton to give a popular exposition of the view of the Bible as 'containing' the Word of God, so it was another eminent Congregationalist divine who sought to give popular statement to the view that the Bible 'is' the Word of God. Thus Joseph Parker of the City Temple opens his book, *None Like It*, with a chapter entitled 'The Word of God'. He refers to those who 'regard it as not *being* but as *containing* the Word of God'.[3] Such claim, he goes on to say, 'that humble and obedient souls may find "the Word of God" in the Bible'. Parker takes exception to the assertion that Jesus Christ alone is the Word of God. When did He make that claim? he asks.[4] Parker does, of course, believe that Jesus Christ is the Word of God; indeed, 'not only the Word of God, he is God the Word'.[5] He sees a parallel between Christ and the Scripture. 'I am disposed to think that the very process by which the Bible is

Interpretative Biography, 1933, p. 245. A. C. Underwood, *A History of the English Baptists*, 1947, pp. 229–32. Sir James Marchant, *Dr John Clifford*, 1924, pp. 27, 29, 81, 155 f.

[1] *Spectator*, Vol. LXI, 1888, p. 1330.
[2] *British and Foreign Evangelical Review*, Vol. XXXI, 1882, pp. 205–38. *The Sword and the Trowel*, 1891, p. 246.
[3] *None Like It*, 1893, p. 15.   [4] *Op. cit.*, p. 21.   [5] *Op. cit.*, p. 22.

turned from *being* the Word of God into *containing* the Word of God might for the self same reason and without loss of one degree of cogency be employed in an attack upon the deity of Jesus Christ.'[1] The book of Ecclesiastes with all its materialism, its sensuousness and its pessimism, can be described as the Word of God because it is part of the unified whole without which the Scripture would not be complete. Parker stresses that he has no scruples about speaking of the Bible as the Word of God.[2] 'If I may not say that the Bible is the Word of God because the infidel will at once draw my attention to a hard verse', he says, 'neither will I tell him prayer is answered, because he will at once tell me that many a prayer for safety has been followed by a shipwreck, and many a prayer for recovery has been followed by bereavement.'[3] Parker's book was written as he says 'from the standpoint of a preacher'.[4] He therefore appends a chapter addressed '*Ad Clerum*'. But this has not added anything very substantial to the rest. It must, indeed, be acknowledged in all honesty that Parker's efforts had little effect. The critic, if ever he bothered himself to read it, would not have been impressed. There are to be sure Parker's brilliant epigrams and powerful and pointed sentences. But in the main there was more assertion than argument. Yet, it is right, for anyone seeking to give an account of the conflict, to make reference to this popular defence of the orthodox position that the Bible *is* the Word of God, as we have alluded earlier to R. F. Horton's popular statement of the opposing view that the Bible *contains* the Word of God. Horton's attempt it should be added was no more weighty than that of Parker's.

In more recent years increasing evidence of a desire to give to the Bible the title 'the Word of God' is to be observed. Theologians who cannot be claimed as belonging to 'Fundamentalism' are expressing dissatisfaction with the antithesis between the record and the word of God in the record. A new emphasis, as we noted earlier, is being placed upon the unity of the Bible. And it is this fact which seems to hinder us from isolating some parts as more 'divine' than others. Thus J. W. C. Wand argues that 'the title, Word of God, if it is to be used at all, as we hold it must, applies to the whole Bible and not to mere

---

[1] *None Like It*, 1893; cf. Chapter IV.
[2] *Op. cit.*; cf. p. 44 f.   [3] *Op. cit.*, p. 148.   [4] *Op. cit.*, p. 197.

parts of it, however supreme their value may be'. It is impossible, he argues, to distinguish some short sentence out of the whole as having a divine character above the rest. 'The Word of God', he concludes, 'is heard both in the events themselves and in the record of them.'[1]

By reason of this prevailing unity in its variety, it is being felt, that the Bible must be accepted as a whole. Throughout it there is to be heard the notes of one Divine music. In this connection, J. K. Mozley writes his conviction about the Bible, 'its nature as the Word of God, as the book in which the deeper tone of the one divine voice is heard through the many changing tones of the human voices, is not open to demonstration, but, in the Christian view of the Bible, it is finally true that it is the word of God, just as it is finally true about Christ that He is the Word of God. In neither case would the substitution of the expression "contains" or some similar term be an adequate embodiment of Christian faith'.[2]

L. S. Thornton is voicing the conviction of a growing number, in spite of outspoken protests on the other side, that the Bible can be rightly assessed only as it receives the designation 'the word of God'. Thornton's own particular explanation of the position of the Bible in religious experience and the relation between the human and the divine element in it, appear to satsify neither side in the controversy. He has critics to the right of him and critics to the left. He does, however, compel the assent of an increasing number, we appear warranted in claiming, by his assertion that 'It is not enough to say that the Word of God is contained *in* the Scripture. We must insist once more that the Scripture *is* the Word of God'.[3]

Reflecting upon the literature over the last half century one becomes aware of a move from both sides to urge the legitimate use of each formula. Whether each side can be satisfied with the precise meaning involved by the other party is another matter. Our own observation is that those who would normally refer to the Bible as 'containing' the Word of God, seem ready to speak of it as being the Word of God on that account. On the other side, those whose faith is expressed in the dictum that the Bible 'is'

---

[1] J. W. C. Wand, *The Authority of the Scriptures*, 1949, p. 83.
[2] *The Christian Faith* (ed. W. R. Matthews), 1944, p. 55.
[3] L. S. Thornton, *Revelation and the Modern World*, 1950, p. 130.

the Word of God, because it is in all its parts accounted so, can maintain that it must 'become' the Word of God in experience.

At an early date A. S. Peake referred to the dispute between those who say that the Bible 'is' the Word of God and those who say it 'contains' it. He gives his own understanding of the reasons for the controversy. Those who plump for the first do so because of a belief, contends Peake, 'that from the beginning to the end the Bible was dictated by the Holy Spirit Himself to selected men who acted as His amanuensis. Nothing in it had a human origin, the book was wholly divine in all its parts'.[1] Under the impact of critical assessment this 'high-sounding theory' broke down. There was so much crude morality, low spirituality and defective theology discoverable in it that such an exalted view of its origin could no longer be entertained. A book so evidently human could not be called the Word of God. Thus the formula was coined, the Bible is not the Word of God but it can be said to *contain* it. Peake rather optimistically regarded this state in the discussion as passed. He maintains that the 'antithesis is unreal, the distinction concentrates on a false issue'.[2] In the old conception, the Bible was regarded mainly as a compendium of doctrines and ethics. No longer can it be so conceived, he states, in this fashion. Nor, indeed, do we think of it as a book in which a clear-cut dichotomy can be seen between the divine and the human in it. It is impossible to say at what point God is speaking and at what it is only man's voice that can be heard. There are in the Bible words of God to man, authenticating themselves as such by their own intrinsic quality. The ideas, which were at first part of the human consciousness, were later framed in speech and recorded. On the other hand there are in the Bible words of men to God, words prompted by the Holy Ghost. There is, then, in the Bible the intermingling of the human and the divine. But it must be stated, both from the immediate and the wider context of Peake's teaching, that the 'human' element appears to be very human indeed. At any rate, he seems to suggest that the Bible is entitled to the designation 'the Word of God' because it is the record of God's coming into human life in an intense and human way.[3]

---

[1] A. S. Peake, *The Bible, Its Origin, Its Significance, Its Abiding Worth*, 1913, pp. 398–9.   [2] *Ibid.*, p. 399.

[3] *Ibid.*; cf. p. 400. Cf. also his book, *The Nature of Scripture*, 1922.

Conservative writers could no doubt have retorted that Peake has given a very false account of their position. But be this as it may, one fact is certain, writers on the other side could not have been happy about the way he explained the Bible as that which *is* the Word of God. They will have seen here a rather compromising illustration of 'accommodation'. For them the Bible *is* the Word of God because here the Word of God is verbally expressed; and expressed in words given by the inspiration of God. Peake, on the other hand, can say, 'The inspiration we find in the Bible is that of supreme religious genius'.[1] On this showing those who were maintaining that the Bible *is* the Word of God could not but feel doubt about the rightness of Peake's designation of it as such in the light of his general approach. It is not, we think, unfair to say, that by the drift of all his teaching Peake's sympathies must be, in the long run, with those who think of the Bible as 'containing' the Word of God merely.

Cunliffe-Jones, to take an example from a living author, approaching the subject as one who accepts the critical conclusions, is strong in his insistence upon the idea that the Bible is the Word of God. In a chapter of his entitled 'The Bible as the Word of God',[2] he is willing to grant that the title should be applied to it in a primary as well as a derivative sense. It is the Word of God in the first sense because, he argues, it is from the Bible we gain our knowledge of Jesus Christ, the revelation of the prophets and the apostles and the content of preaching. The Bible is to be treated as the Word of God because it is the supreme witness we have to the Gospel of God. At the same time, he goes on to contend, the Bible 'becomes' the Word of God in experience. Both formulae are to be retained. The Bible *is* the Word of God because it is a standing witness to the gospel, and yet it must become the Word of God 'in a special way' as 'a living power in our hearts'.[3]

From the conservative side, in more recent years, acknowledgement will be found of the right to admit the formula that the Bible 'contains' the Word of God. But this concession is granted only, it must be immediately added, on the strength of the

[1] A. S. Peake, *The Bible, Its Origin, Its Significance, Its Abiding Worth*, 1913, p. 402.
[2] H. Cunliffe-Jones, *The Authority of the Biblical Revelation*, 1946, second impression, 1948, Chapter XII.   [3] *Ibid.*, p. 133.

conviction that the whole Bible *is* the Word of God. The position
is stated with commendable clarity by J. I. Packer. Packer
readily allows that there is a sense in which it is correct to refer
to the Bible as 'containing' the Word of God. He asserts the
identity of Scripture and the Word of God. 'The Bible' is then 'a
written document declaring a message'. It is 'the inspired
volume as a literary product, a verbal expression of thought'.[1]
In this sense 'the Bible' and 'Scripture' are synonymous: 'it will
thus be correct to call the Bible the Word of God, and to affirm
that what it says, God says'. If the Bible should be thought of
simply as a printed book, then according to Packer, 'it will not
be wrong to say that the Bible *contains* the Word of God, in the
same sense in which any other book *contains* the pronouncements of its author'.[2] Packer is, however, not too happy about
the admission of the concept 'contains'. It would, he thinks, be
better to avoid it 'since Liberal theologians have been in the
habit of using this formula to insinuate that part of what the
Bible contains is no part of the Word of God'.[3] He adds, therefore, the declaration: 'When we call the Bible the Word of God,
we mean, or should mean, that its message constitutes a single
utterance of which God is the author'.[4]

The hesitancy expressed by Packer concerning the formula
the Bible *contains* the Word of God is not shared by all who
accept his fundamental position. What Packer would have us
avoid, others of the same school of thought boldly assert.

In an article in the *Evangelical Quarterly* in 1949 there is an
interesting statement of the confusion which follows when

---

[1] J. I. Packer, *'Fundamentalism' and the Word of God*, 1958, p. 88.
[2] *Ibid.* Cf. The New Curriculum, Second and Third Articles on New Teaching
Material in Preparation for the Presbyterian Church, U.S. ii 'Revelation', *The
Presbyterian Journal*, Vol. XIX, No. 47, March 22, 1961. iii 'The Bible and Church
as Witnesses and Instruments of Revelation', *Ibid.*, Vol. XX, No. 48, March 29,
1961.   [3] *Ibid.*, pp. 88–9.
[4] *Ibid.*, p. 89. Packer's position is understandable as an answer to H. G. Hebert's
outspoken volume *Fundamentalism and the Church of God*, 1957. Hebert really
adopts the formula that the Bible 'contains' the Word of God. He speaks of 'the
study of the Word of God in the Bible'. He appears to limit the designation to
Christ. He then makes a slashing attack upon what he calls 'fundamentalism' which
has an 'evil sense' and as such 'is a grave menace to the Church of God'. Hebert
does little to allay suspicion about the use of the designation of the Word of God
as applied to the Bible by adherents of the liberal school. Packer's volume, *'Fundamentalism' and the Word of God*, 1958, is a vigorous reply and must be evaluated in
this context.

revelation is identified with inspiration. Although the writer of the article is a Frenchman he would have most of his readers, we believe, on his side. Underlying all the subjects of the Ecumenical agenda, its debates on the Sacraments, the Ministry, the Church, and so forth, is, the writer contends, the fundamental question of the exact rôle of the Holy Spirit. It is the place of the Holy Spirit in revelation and inspiration which needs clarification. The testimony of the Spirit in experience is not to be confused with the Quaker idea of the 'inner word', even when that experience is 'evangelical'. It is in the Scripture that the Holy Spirit speaks. It is maintained that 'Revelation and Inspiration constitute eternal acts of God. In other words, the Word of God is always actual in the two senses of the word. It is always an *act* of God, never a theory about God; and this act is always *present*, never bound to the age of the document which transmits it'.[1] Developing this proposition it is stated that the Bible is, for the reader, the Word of God, and also 'that He speaks *to me today* through Jeremiah, St John and St Paul, in vivifying their testimony by that of His Holy Spirit'.[2] It is then concluded: 'The whole Bible is *in itself* Word of God, but *for each of us* it only becomes Word of God in a living fashion where the Holy Spirit brings conviction of it'.[3] The Bible *is* the Word of God *for faith*, it is declared. Bucer's parallel between the Bible and the Word of God and the Church visible and the Body of Christ is then upheld. The Bible, like the visible Church, is the garment with which it is clothed in order to take a place in visible reality. The Church as the 'sign' of the invisible Church is holy but to faith only. So is it with the Bible; it *is* the Word of God but only to faith. In spite of its human defects, its faults of style, its errors in name, and so on, it is still to be believed in as divine. Yet all its words are God's words, even those texts which the Holy Spirit may not as yet have 'inspired' for us. It is impossible to sort out in the Bible the Word of God from the human word.

In an earlier part of this section we made reference to Farrar's contention that the formula, that the Bible *contains* the Word of God, is the specific teaching of the Church of England. It will,

---

[1] Jean de Saussure, *The Evangelical Quarterly*, Vol. XXI, No. 1, January 1949, p. 22.   [2] *Ibid.*, p. 23 (italics in original).
[3] *Ibid.*, p. 24 (italics in original).

therefore, be of interest to bring this assertion into contrast with the conviction of another writer of the same communion. W. H. Griffith Thomas, sometime Principal of Wycliffe Hall, Oxford, while openly acknowledging his readiness to accept the thesis that the Bible *contains* the Word of God, is none the less emphatic that it is the intended and consistent teaching of the Church of England that the Bible is the Word of God. The Anglican Church quite plainly urges that God Himself is the Source of Authority; but it states, according to number vi of the Thirty-nine Articles, that the seat of authority is to be found in the Word of God recorded in the Bible.[1] Griffith Thomas remarks upon 'the emphasis placed in recent years' on the 'human element' in the Scriptures. He has no scruples in admitting the 'traces of the idiosyncrasies of various writers'. Too much, however, he thinks, can be made of them. 'Inspiration', he then declares, 'means such a union of the Divine and human elements that the result is guaranteed to us as the thought of God for the life of man.'[2] But the two cannot really be separated and distinguished. It is not a case of the Divine *and* the human, but, more accurately 'the Divine *through* the human'.

Griffith Thomas has a comment to make upon Coleridge's dictum that it is that in the Bible which 'finds' us which is of the Holy Ghost. He grants that, in contrast with uncanonical literature, the Bible does reveal its inspiration by 'finding' us more thoroughly than any other book. He adds, however, that Coleridge's view is inadequate 'unless this effect is understood to arise out of the supernatural revelation objectively contained in the Scripture'.[3] The Bible, not only 'finds' us, but as James Denney, contends, by its truth it creates and transforms.[4] The two formulae, the Bible 'contains' the Word of God and the Bible 'is' the word of God are acceptable to Griffith Thomas. Both are true, he says, if held together. Either taken alone is liable to misunderstanding. To say the Bible 'is' the Word of God only is to lose sight of the fact that it contains words of men also. And some of the words of men it records are not true in themselves, though the record that they were spoken is true. On the other hand, to limit belief to the phrase that the Bible

---

[1] W. H. Griffith Thomas, *The Principles of Theology*, An Introduction to the Thirty-nine Articles, 1930, second edition, p. 117.

[2] *Ibid.*, p. 118.   [3] *Ibid.*, p. 119.   [4] *Ibid.*

'contains' the Word of God, leads us to the entirely impossible position of having to discriminate between what is God's word and what is man's. It is, therefore, concluded, that the 'Bible *is* the Word of God in the sense that it conveys to us an accurate record of everything God intended man to know in connection with His will. The Bible *contains* the Word of God in the sense that in it is enshrined the Word of God which is revealed to us for our redemption'.[1] Although Griffith Thomas stresses the fact of the union of the Divine and the human, he can still say that it is the presence of the Divine element 'that constitutes the Bible, the Word of God'.[2]

We have given our own conviction on this matter elsewhere. In any final statement of the meaning and the significance of the Bible, it was contended, there certainly must be an acceptable union of the two ideas. Perhaps, as yet, the antithesis has not been resolved in a manner with which both sides can agree. It may well be that this will be one of the permanent results which will emerge from the discussion. Our own view was declared. In spite of the problems which beset the declaration that the Bible *is* the Word of God, this, we believe, designates more clearly and truly than any other its precise nature. The assertion that the Bible merely *contains* the Word of God, or that it is a *witness* to a possible revelation when made, as it sometimes is, to repudiate the proclamation that it is in itself the Word of God, is not only misleading, but certainly false.[3] Allusion was made to the words of Bishop Martensen, whose *Christian Dogmatics* was translated into English in 1866, as being for the present and for ourselves, at any rate, a happy conclusion to the matter. Those who use the formula, the Bible *contains* the Word of God, as Martensen allows, are anxious to safeguard the human element, while those who say the Bible *is* the Word of God seek to maintain its divineness. Both ideas, as in the Person of our Lord, must be asserted: 'not only the union of the divine and human in Scripture, but at the same time the distinction between the two. The old proposition, *the Scripture is the Word of God*, expresses the union; the modern dictum, *the Scripture contains*

---

[1] James Denney, Article 'The Authority of Christ', *Dictionary of Christ and the Gospels* (ed. Hastings), *ad. loc.*
[2] W. H. Griffith Thomas, *The Principles of Theology*, p. 118.
[3] H. D. McDonald, *Ideas of Revelation*, 1959, p. 280 (note); cf. pp. 276–83.

G

the Word of God, expresses the distinction. The first proposition is clearly preferable to the second, which is vague and indistinct, and may be applied to many writings. The first, however, is untrue, if it be taken so to affirm the union, as to exclude all distinction of the divine and human elements in the Bible. . . . The opposite proposition, which does not venture to assert that Scripture *is* the word of God, but that it only *contains* the Word of God, considers only the distinction between the divine and human elements, and overlooks the all-pervading, obvious, and typical union of these in Scripture, the sacred, all-pervading apparent, and fundamental truth, which in unsullied clearness enwraps and even subdues the temporal and human narrowness'.[1]

All, we think, will wish to concur with the declaration of T. H. Robinson, on behalf of most, 'if not all' the contributors to the volume *The Old Testament and Modern Study*. Whatever be their individual explanation of the assertion, each writer, we are told 'would regard the Old Testament as the very word of God, ranking second only to the person of Christ Himself. It is, therefore, rational to assume that it is in some way or other valid for all generations of mankind and for all types of humanity . . . the Old Testament is a God-given book, produced by divine inspiration . . . according to the principle that God works always through human agents, and that without eclipsing their personality'.[2]

The Old Testament is a God-given book indeed; and, of course, the New Testament no less. For all men this Bible of both Testaments is objectively the Word of God whether they are awakened to it, found by it, or not. But to the faith-awakened it has *become* such; for to them the Scripture has spoken as the Word of God through the Spirit.[3]

---

[1] H. Martensen, *Christian Dogmatics*, 1866, p. 403. Cf. H. D. McDonald, *Ideas of Revelation*, pp. 281–2.

[2] *The Old Testament and Modern Study* (ed. H. H. Rowley), 1951, pp. 347–50.

[3] Reflecting upon the discussion of this section as it relates to the subject of the Scriptures and the Word of God, we find ourselves driven to the conclusion that much misunderstanding has been due to an extraordinary instance of the logical fallacy of 'false conversion' or of '*A dicto secundum quid ad dictum simpliciter*', for which both sides are in varying degree responsible. The declaration that the Bible is the Word of God has often been defended in such a way as to suggest that its simple converse is also to be regarded as true. On the other hand, those who oppose are often found contending against this very converse which they have tacitly

assumed, and which careful writers (of the opposition) would have repudiated. To say that the Bible is the Word of God is one thing, but to maintain that the Word of God is the Bible, is another matter, and is, indeed, altogether false. It is theologically correct to say that Jesus Christ is God, but it is obviously very theologically incorrect to convert the proposition simply and to declare that God is Jesus Christ. The failure to grasp this distinction is at the bottom of much of the inability to come to grips with the fundamental issue.

An interesting illustration of this confusion will be found in a provocative little volume by Albert Ervine, which carries a commendation by C. F. D'Arcy, Archbishop of Armagh and Primate of All Ireland. Ervine's argument, in which he strongly repudiates the designation the Word of God as applicable to the Scriptures, seems to us to proceed on the assumption that all who make the assertion would have to defend the converse; and judging from the favourable reviews given by acknowledged conservative leaders, for example G. Campbell Morgan among others, it is evident that they failed to see the implications of Ervine's position (Albert Ervine, *Bible Studies*, 1935, pp. 9–15). Ervine indeed falls back upon the idea that the Bible 'contains' the Word of God (p. 27 f.), but his last chapter seems to undermine his own thesis since in his presentation of Christ he simply draws together the biblical statements regarding Him and leaves us wondering as to what view of Christ these may be said to 'contain' (cf. also his pamphlet, *Divine Words and Human Symbols*, n.d., in which he gives a synopsis of his views and a repudiation of the idea of verbal inspiration which he assumes is inherent in the designation of the Bible as the Word of God).

There has been throughout the discussion a too-easy acceptance or rejection of the term. The manifoldness of the idea 'the Word of God' has not been given rightful assessment. While we would not concur in every statement of an article by David W. Hay (Professor of Systematic Theology, Knox College, Toronto), yet we do agree with him when he says that 'The habit of referring to the Bible as the Word of God has disguised the fact that the expression has a multiplicity of uses in Scripture' (David W. Hay, 'The Expression "Word of God" in Scripture', *The Canadian Journal of Theology*, Vol. II, No. 3, July 1956, p. 135). 'Men want to have', he says later in the same article, 'a simple notion of the Word and think they can achieve it by a simple identification of the Word with the Bible' (p. 141).

CHAPTER SIX

The Question of Biblical Inerrancy

The second half of the nineteenth century witnessed a change within the Church in its valuation of the Bible. Prior to the year 1860, the idea of an infallibly inerrant Scripture was the prevailing view. What has been stated as the characteristic estimation of the Bible throughout an earlier era could with equal exactness be referred to the years down to the middle of the nineteen hundreds. Apart from the Quakers, 'The doctrine of unerring literal inspiration was almost everywhere held in the strictest form'.[1] Such indeed was the view of the Bible before the change of Zeitgeist brought about by the appearance of Darwin's evolutionism. The orthodox apologists in their polemic against the Deists moved on the assumption of a Bible at once verbally infallible and inerrant. There may be truth in Leslie Stephen's contention that the downfall of the Deists was due to the inherent weakness of their theories rather than to the superior logical acumen of their opponents.[2] There was certainly a climate of opinion in favour of the orthodox apologists. The Bible was by general consent regarded as an inspired book, which, as such, must be inerrant and infallible.

And apart from the dogmatisms of the orthodox in this respect, had not this high estimate of the Bible been demonstrated by the preaching of Wesley as creatively effective in the experiences of thousands? It was Wesley who had vindicated the reality of the Bible's inspiration, and he, too, had maintained its inerrant infallibility. To say that the Bible is *not* inspired, he

[1] *The English Church in the Eighteenth Century*, Abbey and Overton, Vol. I, 1887, second edition, p. 243.

[2] Leslie Stephen, *History of English Thought in the Eighteenth Century*, 1881, Vol. I, p. 90; cf. pp. 169–72.

had contended, would be tantamount to admitting error in the
sacred volume. Thus he declared, 'if there be any mistakes in the
Bible, there may well be a thousand. If there be one falsehood in
that book, it did not come from the God of truth'.[1]

Such, then, was the position. It fell to the Deists, if they were
to gain their end, to demonstrate the falsity of such an estimation. The burden of proof lay with them. The Deists
endeavoured to secure their particular purpose by seeking to
reveal series of inconsistencies in the Bible itself. It was not too
difficult for their opponents to show the inconsistencies in their
allegation of inconsistencies; and, at the same time, to offer
some explanation of these supposed contradictions. As far as
Christians generally were concerned the issue was clear-cut.
Either the Bible is to be dismissed altogether as a tissue of
errors and deceits, or it is to be accepted *in toto* as a verbally
inspired and inerrant Book. There was no middle path. The
question really resolved itself into whether there is an authentic
special revelation of God or not. It was the purpose of the Deists
to disprove the general belief that there was such, and they
consequently set themselves to destroy faith in a trustworthy
Bible. Their attack was not directed specifically to the question
of whether there is a verbatim revelation, but to the larger issue
of the existence of a special revelation. It was, therefore,
consistent for their opponents not to focus their attention on the
existence of alleged minor discrepancies, but to take their stand
upon the general reality, certainty and trustworthiness of the
special revelation of the Bible as a whole.

The Deists really lost their case by overstating it. They
supposed that by indicating, what they jubilantly proclaimed as
'errors' in the record, the whole notion of a special revelation
had been shown to be false. Their opponents had merely to stake
their case upon the substantial truth of the Scripture. And having
demonstrated this fact, the general belief in its inerrancy
remained unshaken. Besides, even if difficulties could not all be
solved and inconsistencies all be reconciled, it did not follow that
the Bible was anything other than what Christian faith claimed
it to be. Had not Butler, after all, made it clear that there were
things in nature which could not be understood? And, by

[1] John Wesley, *Journal*, Wednesday, July 24, 1776. Cf. H. D. McDonald, *Ideas
of Revelation*, 1959, pp. 255-9.

analogy, was it not reasonable to suppose that there must be much in revelation beyond our comprehension?

In a period in which faith in the Bible as an inerrant Book was general such a reply had point. Inability to resolve all alleged contradictions was not to be taken as evidence that they were ultimately real. An answer would be forthcoming: the assurance was, someday we will understand. Meanwhile, patience, not panic, was the becoming attitude for the devout. The general trustworthiness of the Bible had been demonstrated against the Deists and the divinity of its truths had been convincingly sustained.

A. THE RENOUNCIATION OF INERRANCY

But this situation was to change after 1860. The *Origin of Species* became the 'bible' of the new age, and it seemed, to some at any rate, to be regarded as inerrant and infallible as the Scriptures it was held to replace. There was a conflict, everyone was made aware, between Genesis and Darwin, between the Bible and the *Origin of Species*. The general esteem of the Bible was undermined. It was Darwin that the common people were to hear gladly, since in doing so, they were assured, that they were no longer common people, but informed and modern and open-minded. And who really wanted to be other? No longer was it possible for scientifically instructed men to believe in an inerrant Bible. Darwin had brought such a notion to collapse. The recommendation to wait in faith for further light or to accept it that unresolved difficulties must be allowed in revelation, as well as in nature, was received with impatience.

It was for this reason that certain important works in defence of the Bible failed to satisfy. Perhaps the ablest in this regard was Henry Rogers's Congregational Union Lectures of 1873 entitled *The Superhuman Origin of the Bible Inferred from Itself*. In lecture ix, Rogers discoursed 'On Certain analogies between the Bible and "The Constitution of Nature" '. It was a formidable oration. In it Rogers declares that 'If the Bible be from the same source (i.e. as the constitution of nature), it is in analogy with this that he (i.e. man 'the minister and interpreter of nature', Bacon), is summoned to similar functions here. The Bible has its difficulties and mysteries, as nature has; and it requires, just as nature does, prolonged thought and effort to penetrate or decipher them'.[1] The 'errors' of which men are so often aware, are, like the *idola* of Bacon, within the mind, to be dispelled only by a determined effort. Useful as Rogers's book was it did not suit the new situation. This was clearly seen by Marcus Dods who pointed out that it was more of an apology for Christianity itself than for the Bible.[2] The *British Quarterly Review*, while giving the volume a favourable review, likewise observed that it did nothing to rehabilitate the plenary inspiration, scientific accuracy and eternal trustworthiness of the Scripture.[3] It was the contention of the *British and Foreign Evangelical Review* that Rogers's argument was merely a restatement of Butler's, which in the new context 'altogether fails to understand and meet in a scientific way the speculative (and critical) difficulties which are advanced against the thesis Mr Rogers defends'.[4]

A defence of the same kind was made by G. W. Olver. He, too, urged that it was not for the Christian believer to profess that he could iron out all the problems and harmonize all the statements in the Bible since neither he nor anyone else 'can solve all difficulties and harmonize all facts of Nature'.[5] But the contention was no more valid by being made by Olver than by Rogers.

The plain fact is that the idea of an inerrant Bible was being discarded. The view had prevailed that the Bible was one book, a unity which stood or fell as a whole. This situation seemed no longer possible. The unity of the Bible had to be disrupted to fit into an evolutionary context. The vigorous application of the historical method cast doubt upon the factuality of the record, as well as did the increasing uncertainty as to the genuineness of the miraculous element in the account. All this added up to an open acknowledgement, it was claimed, that the Bible was no longer to be regarded as an inerrant volume. As a result the way was prepared for the easier acceptance of the higher criticism. The regrettable delay, as it was referred to by some writers, in

[1] Henry Rogers, *The Superhuman Origin of the Bible inferred from Itself*, 1873, New York, 1875, p. 385.

[2] Marcus Dods, *The Expositor*, fourth series, Vol. VIII, 1893, p. 158.

[3] *The British Quarterly Review*, Vol. LIX, 1874, pp. 585–9, *ibid*.

[4] *The British and Foreign Evangelical Review*, Vol. XXIII, 1874, pp. 582–4, *ibid*.

[5] *Inspiration*, A Clerical Symposium (ed. F. W. Farrar), 1884, p. 134.

yielding to the claims of the new criticism was not a result of its contradicting the doctrine of inerrancy. This doctrine was being renounced on other grounds.[1] It had become the fashion to make reference to the 'errors' in the Bible and it was held to be an evidence of honest biblical scholarship to admit their existence. It might be argued that the progress of criticism was facilitated because of the prior weakening of belief in an inerrant Bible. It was the difficulties found by many in the acceptance of an unerring literal inspiration which in part accounts for the readiness with which the critical assumptions were accepted. Rigorous research into the origin of religion revealed, it was argued, the unauthentic nature of the biblical claim.[2]

The *Essays and Reviews* were influential in this direction. Its writers expressed openly their sympathy with the naturalistic approach to the Bible. Their attitude with regard to biblical criticism was on the whole conservative. But the loose views on the inspiration of the Bible presupposed in their contributions led to a denial, either openly or implicitly, of the central doctrines of the Church's faith. R. Williams expressed rather radical views concerning the atonement and resurrection,[3] while Baden Powell showed evident disregard for miracles.[4] B. Jowett virtually denied the doctrine of original sin and the personality of the Holy Spirit.[5]

It was thus observed by many that a lessening of the idea of verbal inspiration must necessarily weaken faith in an inerrant Bible. The *British and Foreign Evangelical Review* condemned the *Essays* on this score.[6] This periodical, it may be noted in passing, had already defended inerrancy against Samuel Davidson. In a review of his new edition of Horne's *Introduction* it asks, 'If the Biblical writers were liable to error in one

---

[1] But cf. 'Until criticism made it impossible for us any longer to identify infallibility with literal inerrancy, it was a delusive and non-existent infallibility that was ascribed to the Bible'. Marcus Dods, *The Bible, Its Origin and Nature*, 1905, pp. 138–9. Also Biblical Criticism destroyed 'the theory of the infallibility and inerrancy of Scripture'. A. S. Peake, *The Bible: Its Origin, Its Significance, Its Abiding Worth*, 1913, fifth edition, p. 310. Cf. B. J. Snell, *Gain or Loss?* 1896, p. 20.

[2] Cf. W. Robertson Nicholl, 'The Coming Battle', *British Weekly*, 11, 1887, p. 225.

[3] Cf. *Essays and Reviews*, pp. 80–1.

[4] *Op. cit.*, pp. 133–4.   [5] *Op. cit.*, pp. 358–9.

[6] *British and Foreign Evangelical Review*, 'The Oxford Essayists—Their Relation to Christianity and to Strauss and Baur', Vol. X, 1861, pp. 407–30.

particular, what guarantee have we that they were not equally fallible in another?'[1]

Such statements, however, did not stay the tide. General opinion was running against the idea of an inerrant Scripture. It may be acknowledged that the higher criticism would have made necessary modifications in the religious attitude to the Bible. But such modifications would have been, perhaps, less decisive, less acceptable and less conclusive had the doctrine of inerrancy not been previously so seriously questioned. The abandonment of the traditional view of inerrancy was, then, a cause of the acceptance of the higher criticism, not a result. The reason for the wholesale rejection of the historical idea of inerrancy is therefore to be found in the climate of opinion. The period which began with Darwin's *Origin of Species* was of a different spirit from that which had gone before.

Gore's famous essay in the *Lux Mundi* did much to induce Churchmen to settle for an errant Bible. Gore there made clear his repudiation of what he later gave as a title for his little volume *The Doctrine of an Infallible Book*. Even more cogent and captivating for its thesis was the contribution of A. B. Bruce who, in association with three American scholars, C. A. Briggs, L. J. Evans and H. P. Smith, produced the volume, *Inspiration and Inerrancy*. Bruce, writing in the Introduction, maintains that a true doctrine of Scripture does not involve such an idea as inerrancy. He declares openly and unequivocally against it.[2] So it was that inerrancy was boldly repudiated.

Something of the strength of the rejection of an inerrant Bible can be seen in statements made by acknowledged leaders of religious opinion. Alexander Raleigh, who at any rate as late as the year 1875 believed higher criticism to be merely a form of infidelity, could declare in 1868, when Chairman of the Congregational Union, that there were 'errors and mistakes' in the Bible.[3] R. W. Dale, too, in 1873 made the same

---

[1] *British and Foreign Evangelical Review*, 'The New Edition of Horne's Introduction', Vol. VI, 1857, p. 404; cf. 'The Book of Genesis', Vol. IX, 1860, p. 533, and 'Inspiration', Vol. XVI, 1867, pp. 537–56.

[2] A. B. Bruce and C. A. Briggs, *Inspiration and Inerrancy*, 1891, pp. 32 ff. Cf. 'Nothing could be more fitted to mislead us as to the nature of Inspiration than to lay emphasis on the supervision necessary to insure perfect harmony'. p. 32, A. B. Bruce in Introduction.

[3] Mary Raleigh, *Alexander Raleigh: Records of his Life*, 1881, pp. 143 f. and 283 f.

admission.[1] Nothing, indeed, is so extraordinary in this respect, as the reversal of the earlier estimation of the Bible. The earlier apologists had with fairly general consistency stood by an inerrant Scripture. Those who followed the year 1860 contended that such a notion was impossible to sustain and they believed the idea an unnecessary burden. Christian faith did not depend upon a verbally infallible Book. Thus John Clifford, for example, admonishes preachers to avoid such 'surface' questions as the 'apparent discrepancies of Scripture'.[2] He asks elsewhere, 'Are there errors in the Bible?' He has no hesitation with the answer. 'It is not God's way', he avers, 'to give us an absolutely inerrant Bible and He has not done it.'[3] 'It would be an unspeakable convenience if the theory of total Biblical inerrancy were according to the facts',[4] he says. But it is not so, Clifford maintains. He then seeks to answer what he regards as the three defences of an inerrant Bible.[5]

R. F. Horton was even more outspoken. As a writer Horton showed himself to possess few inhibitions. He was scathing in his repudiation of what he calls 'the cast-iron theory of inspiration'. Although Horton's book, to which reference is now being made, bears the title *Inspiration and the Bible*, the major portion of it is devoted to an elaborate statement of the ways the new criticism has contradicted the old view of the Bible and thus justifies the total rejection of inerrancy. The evidence of inconsistencies he finds everywhere; in Paul's interpretation of the Old Testament, in the Book of Acts and the Epistles, between the Gospels, in the accounts of the ascension. Commenting on Gal. iii. 20, he tells us that the verse has been given some 430 different interpretations and, according to his own belief, not one of them satisfactory. Here Paul has been guilty of the grossest obscurity. 'Such want of lucidity it may be less dangerous to charge upon St Paul than on the Spirit of God.'[6] As far as Horton is concerned, the Old Testament abounds in errors. The result of his treatment is to make the whole Bible appear little more than a fallible

---

[1] R. W. Dale, 'The Old Testament and the New', *Congregationalist*, ii, 1873, pp. 321–2.

[2] Sir James Marchant, *Dr John Clifford*, 1924, pp. 41–2.

[3] John Clifford, *The Inspiration and the Authority of the Bible*, 1889, third edition, 1899, p. 49.   [4] *Ibid.*, p. 42.   [5] Cf. Chapter V, *ibid.*

[6] R. F. Horton, *Inspiration and the Bible*, 1888, pp. 49–50; cf. pp. 36–78 and 144–75.

record in which evidences of human mistakes are everywhere revealed.

G. P. Mains attributes the false idea of inerrancy and infallibility of the Bible to the Reformers. 'There need be no misunderstanding of the fact,' he says, 'that, so far as the Bible is concerned, the Reformation left the Church as a part of its inheritance the conviction of an infallible Book.'[1] In the brief compass of seven pages, having quoted Marcus Dods for support, Mains dismisses the whole subject with the assurance 'that Christian scholarship has been forced to abandon the hypothesis of Scriptural inerrancy'.[2] In a conclusive manner W. L. Knox summarizes the general attitude to the Bible when he writes, 'The scientific development of the last century has rendered untenable the whole conception of the Bible as a verbally inspired book, to which we can appeal with absolute certainty for infallible guidance in all matters of faith and conduct'.[3]

B. THE ASSERTION OF INERRANCY

While Gore, Bruce, Clifford and Horton and many others were declaring themselves against the doctrine of an infallible and inerrant Bible, the traditionalists, as they came to be called, were insistent that it was only an infallible and inerrant Bible which could be used as God clearly intended the Bible to be used. Only such a Book, it was their contention, could give 'absolute certainty for infallible guidance in all matters of faith and conduct'. In maintaining this position they considered themselves to be remaining true to the historic Christian faith and to the more recent Confessions. Infallibility and inerrancy were terms used to indicate the Church's faith in the divine origin and the absolute truthfulness and trustworthiness of its Scriptures.

During the nineteenth century the description of the Holy Scriptures as 'the infallible truth' came into vogue to express repudiation of the growing proclamation of its errancy, although, it may be noted, the expression was already used in the Westminster Confession. The traditionalists, by adhering to

---

[1] G. P. Mains, *Divine Inspiration*, 1915, p. 81.   [2] *Ibid.*, p. 109.
[3] W. L. Knox, *Essays Catholic and Critical*, 1926, third edition, 1931, p. 99.

the words—infallible and inerrant—felt they were giving validity to the Scriptures as an objective authority. Christianity was, after all, an historical religion based on an historical revelation and it is in the Bible alone that that revelation is to be found. If no sure appeal could be made to the record, then the serious question arose, What ground is there for certain faith?

It was, of course, replied that the traditionalists were wrong in asserting that the Bible was authoritative in itself when what was actually authoritative was the revelation to which it was a witness or a record. But this was precisely the question at issue. As far as the traditionalists could see there was no existent or evident revelation apart from the Bible. No one could say, 'Lo, it is here', or, 'Lo, it is there'. The only revelation known is the Bible revelation; consequently, if that revelation is punctuated with errors, then there is no certainty left in divine things, since there is really no 'infallible truth'. The only alternatives to such an understanding of the Scriptures were for the adherents of inerrancy and infallibility impossible. There were those, it appears, quite ready to renounce the Protestant and Reformed faith and fall back upon the authority of the Church. Others, however, sought to emphasize the ultimacy of religious experience, only to find themselves bogged in the quagmire of subjectivism. As far as the traditionalists were concerned, they saw the traditional valuation of the Bible by the Church openly repudiated within the Church itself, wounded, indeed, as they declared, in the house of its friends. But most tragic of all, in their view, was the way the Bible, as God's direct message to men, was being snatched from the hands of the common man to be acclaimed as a book fit only for the researches of the scholar. No longer was it for the wayfaring man, who was unequipped with critical techniques to reconstruct it according to the new pattern and detect its manifold mistakes.

Joseph Parker had no hesitation in pointing out the tragic religious consequences of making the Bible 'a priest's book'. And he asks, 'Have we to await a communication from Tübingen, or a telegram from Oxford, before we can read the Bible?'[1] John Kennedy charged the critics with assuming for themselves the

---

[1] Joseph Parker, *None Like It*, 1893, pp. 73 ff. Cf. ' "Theology in Transition" and the Bible in "Suspense" ', *Wesleyan Methodist Magazine*, Vol. CXVI, 1893, pp. 714–15.

infallibility they deny to the Bible. They pronounced *ex cathedra* on the dates and the unreliability of the documents of Scripture with an assurance and certainty no whit less than their opponents whom they condemned for their dogmatism.[1]

It is because the traditionalists held firmly to the practical identity of the revelation with its record that the arguments of the 'errorists' had such little effect. It was not, of course, difficult to trap them by urging that they were ensnared in the net of the circular argument. The charge went like this: inerrancy is no self-evidencing truth. The traditionalists' doctrine of it is based on their 'cast-iron theory' of inspiration. Their logic then is; the Bible must be inerrant because it is verbally inspired, and it is verbally inspired because it is inerrant.[2]

To such a charge the great preachers, at any rate, were unconcerned to reply. But if they did not, and perhaps as some will think, could not, they were able to stress that belief in an infallible and inerrant Bible was productive of the greatest practical and theological good. They were deeply concerned with the possible ill results for the cause of the Evangelical faith that the idea of a Bible fraught with 'errors and mistakes' would have. Liddon, Parker, Spurgeon, Moule, Ryle were a few of those who maintained a firm belief in the inerrancy of the Bible and the infallibility of its truth. It was, indeed, Spurgeon's constant insistence that a Bible with mistakes is a Bible without a message. And it was the open descent from the position taken by Clifford on this point which was in part the cause of the controversy which finally led to his withdrawal from the Baptist Union.

J. C. Ryle, in a passage in which he is stating the view of the Bible held in an earlier period by such Christian leaders as Grimshaw, Venn, Berridge, Harvey and others of their company, is really giving expression to the position occupied by himself and those of like evangelical spirit. The 'spiritual reformers of the last century', he writes, 'taught constantly *the sufficiency and supremacy of the Holy Scriptures. The Bible, whole*

[1] Cf. John Kennedy, *Old Testament and the Rights of the Unlearned, Being a Plea for the Rights and Powers of Non-experts in the Study of Holy Scriptures*, 1897.

[2] Cf. How Paul Tillich for his own purpose contends for 'the circular character of systematic theology' and adds 'theologians should not be afraid to admit this circle. It is not a shortcoming'. Paul Tillich, *Systematic Theology*, Vol. I, 1950, p. 135.

and unmutilated, was their sole rule of faith and practice. They accepted all its statements without question and dispute. They knew nothing of any part of Scripture being uninspired. They never allowed that man has any "verifying faculty" within him by which Scripture statements may be weighed, rejected or received. They never flinched from asserting that there can be *no error* in the Word of God; and that when they cannot understand or reconcile some parts of its contents, the fault is in the interpreter and not in the text. In all their preaching they were eminently men of one book. To that book they were content to pin their faith, and by it to stand or fall.'[1] Like their Puritan forefathers, the Evangelicals of the following centuries continued strenuously to maintain that the words of the Bible, because given by the Holy Spirit, constitute the whole volume infallible and inerrant.

In a powerful chapter in his *Old Paths*, Ryle contends that as an inspired book the Bible reveals an 'extraordinary accuracy' in facts and statements.[2] He does not, apparently, actually use the term 'inerrant', but certainly the idea is maintained throughout. Among a fairly generous number of footnotes, all intended to sustain the accuracy of the Bible record, he quotes with approval from Bishop Wordsworth on *Inspiration*: 'We affirm that the Bible is the Word of God, and that it is not marred with human infirmities . . .'.[3] He faces the question that may be raised, 'Have the writers made no mistakes?' Ryle argues that talk about 'grave discrepancies' in the Biblical record is 'grossly exaggerated'. And he contends that 'in many cases they are only apparent, and disappear under the touch of common sense. Even in the hardest of them we should remember, in common fairness, that circumstances are very likely kept back from us which entirely reconcile everything, if only we knew them'.[4]

The thinking evangelical of the time, and they were not all as John Oman seemed to think, 'encased in the jointless armour of obscurantism hard enough to turn the edge of any fact',[5] saw that the liberal dilemma was a real one. The devout critics strove to maintain some sort of objectivity and givenness for the revelation in the Bible so as to escape the pitfalls of a complete

---

[1] J. C. Ryle, *The Christian Leader of the Last Century*, 1873, p. 26.

[2] J. C. Ryle, *Old Paths*, 1897, new and improved edition, p. 10.

[3] *Ibid.*, p. 20 (footnote). Cf. C. Wordsworth, *Inspiration of the Holy Scriptures*, 1861, p. 11.　　　　[4] *Ibid.*, p. 27.

[5] John Oman, *Grace and Personality*, 1919, second edition, revised, p. 9.

subjectivism. They sought on the one hand to retain the idea of an errant Bible, and, on the other hand, to neutralize the effects of such an idea by insisting that the same Bible was still the only authority for faith and doctrine. They did not succeed in showing how the Bible could be acclaimed as the judge of human errors, when, at the same time, man appointed himself as a judge of the 'errors' of the Bible. The Bible was commended as a true witness, while it was being condemned as containing falsehood. Spurgeon and Parker, and the others mentioned above, were keenly aware of the liberal difficulty. And it is this awareness which lies behind their clear-cut alternative: let us have either a Bible which we can keep as entirely trustworthy or let us admit it to be a book with 'errors and mistakes' and honestly discard it as not being of decisive authority for faith and doctrine.

If the protagonists of inerrancy were unable to match argument with argument, they could, at least, appeal to the results which the loss of faith in an infallible Bible had brought about. On all sides there was floundering, uncertainty and hesitancy. Horton's was no exceptional case. He was typical of numbers of clergy and ministers who, like him, could no longer base their faith 'on the foundation of Biblical infallibility', and as a result had to set out on the quest to find the sure foundation.[1] After a time of search, however, Horton could only report his discovery of 'a series of tentative suggestions'. Meanwhile, without a sure resting-place themselves, how, asked their opponents, were they supposed to bring certainty to others? With the great evangelical preachers of the day it was otherwise. They, as Spurgeon urged, had their authority. They were expounders of an infallible truth, propagators of the sure Word of God.

Further, those who stood for an infallible Bible were able to point to the religious and spiritual results that a Bible so understood and proclaimed secured. As a lion let loose, as Spurgeon contended, the Bible could maintain itself from all the assaults of its enemies. Parker appealed to the power of the Bible to convert, to comfort and sustain. He will not let the critics rob him of it until they have something more to offer than 'a series of tentative suggestions'.[2]

[1] R. F. Horton, *An Autobiography*, 1918, p. 100.
[2] Joseph Parker, *None Like It*, 1893, p. 244.

C. RENEWED CONFLICT OVER INERRANCY

For over a period of years now there seem to be evidences of a reawakening of faith. The cloud may be only the size of a man's hand, but those who know the spiritual weather-chart appear to be confident that there is a reviving interest in spiritual things throughout the land. Coming with this reviving interest is a new emphasis upon the Bible as infallible truth. It is not our business here to discuss whether this new emphasis is a cause or consequence of this reawakening. Of the fact there cannot be the slightest doubt. In opposition to this association comes evidence of a renewal of insistence that the doctrine of inerrancy and infallibility is no integral part of genuine Christian faith.

Throughout the years intervening between the time when inerrancy was generally renounced and the present period which is witnessing a new stress on what the concept is meant to convey, the position of both the liberal and the conservative evangelical Christian remained unaltered. There was on the whole, however, no serious conflict, because, not only were other interests uppermost, but evangelicals were in the back-wood as far as convincing Biblical scholarship was concerned. They had, of course, their preachers such as J. H. Jowett, F. B. Meyer, J. Stuart Holden, W. Campbell Morgan, and others of lesser breed, who were committed to faith in the Bible as absolutely and altogether trustworthy. None of these would have allowed that there are 'errors and mistakes' in the Bible.

But as far back as 1924 Charles Gore gave voice to his concern about the possibility of a return to the idea of an infallible Bible. None had fought so strenuously against such a view, but he seems to express doubts about the finality and decisiveness of the victory which was claimed. He certainly regretted the evidence of 'a revival today of the position that faith in Christianity, as really the divinely-given gospel for the world, is bound up with the old-fashioned belief in the Bible as the infallible book'.[1] During recent years the very thing Gore sought so much to restrain has come to pass. The phenomenal growth of the Inter-Varsity Fellowship groups in colleges and universities is some indication of the strength of the movement in which the idea of an infallible Bible is fundamental. The

[1] C. Gore, *The Doctrine of an Infallible Book*, 1924, p. 7.

campaigns throughout the country of the evangelist, Dr Billy Graham, with his assertion, 'the Bible says', has also been another factor creating the modern re-emphasis upon the Bible as an altogether trustworthy book. Of no less importance is the influence of the revived interest in Puritan studies which has become a characteristic of our times.

We may be saying too much in asserting that at the present time A. G. Hebert seems to have taken on the rôle which Gore had earlier assumed, namely, that of urging upon the Church that Christian faith is not to be tied to the idea of an inerrant and infallible Bible.[1] In his volume *The Authority of the Old Testament*, Hebert appears as the true successor of the author of *The Doctrine of an Infallible Book*.[2] And incidently Hebert gives his allegiance, as did Gore, to the High Church group in the Anglican communion. Hebert shows his concern, too, for the apparent revival of the 'old-fashioned belief' in a verbally infallible Bible. It is consequently his aim to divorce the growing interest in Christian faith from the idea of literal biblical inerrancy. He therefore makes an attack upon those whom he refers to as 'Fundamentalists',[3] who, in holding to 'verbal inspiration' are said to be guilty of a 'materialistic conception of inspiration'.[4] They declare that the Bible is consequently 'free from error' and therefore 'inerrant'. He adduces a number of 'duplicate' and 'inconsistent' accounts designed to show that the 'doctrine of the Inerrancy of the Bible must be then regarded as, at least in reference to material fact, extremely vulnerable'.[5] He charges the Fundamentalist 'with asserting something that no previous age has understood in anything like the modern sense' in proclaiming literal inerrancy.[6] He declares that the New

---

[1] Cf. C. H. Dodd, *The Authority of the Bible*, 1928, p. 353. William Temple, *Nature, Man and God*, 1949, pp. 351 ff. John Baillie, *The Idea of Revelation in Recent Thought*, 1956, pp. 111 ff.

[2] Cf. C. Gore, *Reconstruction of Belief*, 1921, etc., new edition in one volume, 1926, reprint, 1945, pp. 621 f. and 864 f. It is of interest to note how Gore, as does Hebert, makes use of the 'mystical' and 'allegorical' sense of Scripture. Cf. pp. 884 ff.

[3] Cf. A. G. Hebert, *Fundamentalism and the Church of God*, 1957, Chapter I. J. I. Packer, *'Fundamentalism' and the Word of God*, 1958, Chapter I. Douglas Johnson, *The Christian Graduate*, March 1955. Correspondence in *The Times* on 'Fundamentalism', August 1955; cf. esp. letter by J. R. W. Stott, 25 August 1955. See also Robert Abba, *The Nature and Authority of the Bible*, 1958, pp. 63–5. J. K. S. Reid, *The Authority of the Bible*, 1957, pp. 158–64.

[4] A. G. Hebert, *The Authority of the Old Testament*, 1947, p. 25; cf. pp. 93–100.

[5] *Ibid.*, p. 31.   [6] *Ibid.*, p. 98.

Testament writers inherited from the Jews the idea of inspiration as involving inerrancy, but while they did not criticize it, they did *not* accept it.[1] The apostolic writers assumed the inerrancy of the Old Testament 'but did not take over unadulterated the rabbinic notion of Inspiration'.[2] In truth, the doctrine of verbal inerrancy is not after all an 'old-fashioned belief' but something quite new to Fundamentalists' circles, something different from the idea of 'theological and religious inerrancy'. This materialistic inerrancy, Hebert asserts, 'has been a potent cause of modern unbelief'.[3]

Armed with these assurances, Hebert, in a later volume sets himself to make a more pointed attack upon the position regarding Scripture advocated by the Inter-Varsity Fellowship of Christian Unions in general[4] and by *The New Bible Commentary* in particular.[5] The Bible, according to Hebert, is the record of God's saving purpose in history and its 'truth' is therefore limited to this theological reality. This saving purpose has been consummated in the person of Christ; and it is through the 'words of men' that this 'Word of God' becomes known to us. 'It is', he then declares, 'in this larger context that we need to study the words Inerrancy and Infallibility'.[6] Because these words are 'negative' they are pronounced to be 'troublesome and unsatisfactory' 'like the word "sinless" applied to our Lord'.[7] Hebert is committed to the allegorical method of interpretation and he can consequently refer to the Bible as 'true history' in so far as it 'truly relates the working in history of God's Purpose of salvation'.[8] The 'rigid theory of factual inerrancy' is then stated to be 'too narrow'[9] because it 'seems to

---

[1] A. G. Hebert, *The Authority of the Old Testament*, 1947, p. 235. But cf. the following, 'The Church from the outset accepted the old Jewish Scriptures and regarded them, just as the Jewish Church had done, as the verbally inspired teaching of God'. W. L. Knox, *Essays Catholic and Critical* (ed. E. G. Selwyn), 1926, third edition, 1931, p. 98. Then C. Gore, 'Nothing, I think, is less justified on the whole than to represent our Lord as accepting current Jewish interpretations on the meaning of inspiration, however true it is that it returned in great measure upon the Church in later days'. *Reconstruction of Belief*, p. 877. It will be remembered that Gore who now cannot think of our Lord as accommodating himself to current ideas of inspiration, earlier argued that He did in connection with biblical dates and authorship.

[2] *Ibid.*, p. 236.   [3] *Ibid.*, p. 307.
[4] A. G. Hebert, *Fundamentalism and the Church of God*, 1957, p. 10.
[5] *Ibid.*, p. 84 f.   [6] *Ibid.*, p. 42.   [7] *Ibid.*
[8] *Ibid.*, p. 43.   [9] *Ibid.*, cf. pp. 55–6 and 148.

allow for a satisfactory account of the story of Adam and Eve'.[1]
Hebert can go so far with regard to the Old Testament, at any
rate, as to say that taken by itself it contains errors 'not in small
matters of literal fact, but in matters of faith and morals'.[2] He
admits it is a 'paradox' to assert 'the Book of God's Truth'
contains 'error'. But 'a deeper consideration of the word "truth"
and "error" will solve the problem, since', he assures us, 'the
"error" is not of the absolute sort'.[3]

Having made his case in this manner, Hebert seeks to apply
his results to *The New Bible Commentary*, which was published
by the Inter-Varsity Fellowship in 1953.[4] He endeavours to
show that the writers of the volume have not been able to
interpret the Bible in a manner consistent with their declared
faith. Packer, he observes, uses the 'rigid word "infallibility" ',
whereas Bromiley 'avoids it'. Hebert then accuses the Fundamentalists with upsetting the ecumenical cause. They demand
as the Ground of Unity, not merely the Gospel of God, but the
gospel *plus* the Inerrancy of the Bible and the necessity of a
particular kind of conversion.[5]

Such accusations have not been left unanswered by the
conservative evangelicals. J. I. Packer, for example, attacks
Hebert head on. Attention is here called to this reply because it
is certainly as scholarly as the work it opposes. He points out
that, historically, the Church had always taken the position that
the Bible, because inerrant, was there to correct tradition and
reason.[6] He denies that faith in it as 'the infallible word' is 'a
form of idolatry'.[7] He sees the understanding and evaluation of
the Bible as the 'crucial issue' of the present day. The opponents
of Fundamentalism, basing themselves on the presuppositions
and conclusions of nineteenth-century critical Bible study,
believe it to be necessary to assert that statements are definitely
erroneous. They 'cannot accept the axiom that whatever

---

[1] A. G. Hebert, *Fundamentalism and the Church of God*, 1957; p. 43.
[2] *Ibid.*, p. 46. Cf. 'We are led to question the traditional belief, because it seems
plain that the Bible contains inconsistencies and contradictions, not only on points
of historical fact but in matters of 'faith and morals', which can be reconciled with
belief in its inerrancy or infallibility only by doing violence to intellectual honesty.'
John Burnaby, *Is the Bible Inspired?* 1940, Vol. 9 in the Colet Series of Modern
Christian Thought and Teaching (ed. W. R. Matthews), pp. 112–13.
[3] *Ibid.*, p. 55.   [4] *Ibid.*, pp. 84 ff.   [5] *Ibid.*, p. 123; cf. p. 125.
[6] J. I. Packer, *'Fundamentalism' and the Word of God*, 1958, p. 48.
[7] *Ibid.*, p. 62.

Scripture is found to assert is part of the word of God; for untruths cannot be God's word. Hence they think it impossible to take seriously the "Jewish" conception of the nature of God-given Scripture which Christ and the Bible teach. Instead, they say, we must use our Christian wits to discern beneath the fallible words of fallible men the eternal truth of God'.[1] Packer boldly maintains that 'Evangelicals are accustomed to speak of the Word of God as *infallible* and *inerrant*'.[2] But this does not mean the infallibility and inerrancy of every interpretation put upon the Scripture, nor does it imply that the writers of the Bible did not use modes of speech about the natural order and human experience as were current in their day, and the language that was common to themselves and their contemporaries.[3] Hebert is in error, he insists, in crediting to the Evangelicals a rigid theory of factual inerrancy of the Bible which excludes any symbolic mode of interpretation.[4] It is simply not true, Packer contends, that the inerrancy of the Word of God commits its adherents to a literalistic type of exegesis.[5] Packer draws attention to the analogy used by Hebert between the divine and the human in Christ, and the divine and the human in the Bible.[6] And he replies that the analogy 'can be only a limited one'.[7] It is right enough to point to the union of the divine and the human in both, but if the analogy is pressed it is contrary to the conclusion Hebert desires. The human nature of our Lord was free from sin 'so Scripture, though a truly human product, is truly free from error. If the critics believe that Scripture, as a human book, errs, they ought, by the force of their own analogy, to believe also that Christ, as man, sinned'.[8]

The conflict concerning inerrancy and infallibility has thus become once again a live issue. Hebert, like Gore before him, does not appear to apprehend the ideas which the Church throughout the ages sought to convey by these words. Nor is he

[1] J. I. Packer, '*Fundamentalism*' and the Word of God, 1958, p. 72.

[2] *Ibid.*, p. 94. Cf. '. . . the idea of Biblical inspiration which defines it as the "dictation of the Holy Ghost" and makes it incompatible with any error in the writings so inspired . . . (is) the traditional belief of Christendom'. John Burnaby, *Is the Bible Inspired?* 1949, p. 111.

[3] *Ibid.*, p. 96.   [4] *Ibid.*, pp. 98–9.   [5] *Ibid.*, p. 99.

[6] Cf. '*Fundamentalism' and the Word of God*, pp. 82 ff. A. G. Hebert, *Fundamentalism and the Church of God*, pp. 73 ff., esp. pp. 77–8. H. D. McDonald, *Ideas of Revelation*, 1959, pp. 153 ff.

[7] J. I. Packer, '*Fundamentalism*' and the Word of God, p. 83.   [8] *Ibid.*

always consistent in his criticisms. He, for example, builds his case upon the 'materialistic view of inspiration' which he credits to his opponents and yet acknowledges that the 'dictation-theory' is repudiated by all conservative evangelical leaders.[1] But all along he is virtually crediting them with this notion. Packer, on the other hand, has on several occasions assumed the position he is out to prove.

It would be quite wrong, however, to regard the whole thing as a mere strife about words. The issue is a real and deep one. Yet there was a question about the use of the words inerrancy and infallibility. Hebert sought for what he calls the 'positives to describe the inspiration of Scripture'. Having made reference to the Biblical passage II Tim. iii, 16 and II Peter i. 21, he adds, 'The positives of Inerrancy and Infallibility might be "true and faithful witness to the Truth of God" '.[2] Packer, too, would not contend for the mere terms. They 'are not essential for stating the evangelical view'.[3] He goes on to expound his position like this: ' "Infallibility" denotes the quality of never deceiving or misleading, and so means "wholly trustworthy and reliable"; "inerrant" means "wholly true". Scripture is termed infallible and inerrant to express the conviction that all its teaching is the utterance of God "who cannot lie", whose word, once spoken, abides for ever, and that therefore it may be trusted implicitly'.[4]

It would, of course, be idle to pretend that in the end Hebert and Packer are saying the same thing. The simple fact is that

[1] A. G. Hebert, *Fundamentalism and the Church of God*, p. 56.
[2] *Ibid.*, p. 42.
[3] J. I. Packer, *'Fundamentalism' and the Word of God*, p. 95.
[4] *Ibid.*, p. 95. Cf. E. J. Young takes up a statement of C. A. Briggs who argued that the Bible's infallibility is limited to matters of faith and practice. (Cf. C. A. Briggs, *The Bible, The Church, The Reason*, 1892, pp. 93–4.) Young asks, Where does 'faith' end and historical details begin? What, in other words, are the precise limits of 'faith' in the first chapter of Genesis? What are the matters of 'faith' herein revealed concerning which we may say the Bible is infallible? And more than that, we may ask, who is to tell us what is and what is not a matter of faith? E. J. Young, *Thy Word is Truth*, 1957, pp. 101–2. Young contends that the word, 'infallibility' applied to the Bible means that the Scripture possesses an indefectible authority (p. 113). He rejects the *a priori* approach to the question of Inerrancy and Infallibility (p. 114). He contends, to take the example of the parallel passages in the gospels, that by 'Inerrancy' it is not meant that each account should be in exactly the same words, but that each writer told the truth, recorded matters accurately, has given us a true picture of what transpired (p. 136). The quotations from the Old Testament in the New reveal that there was 'no mechanical parrot-like repetition' (p. 161). The human writers acted as responsible agents. And, he

Hebert divorces the revelation of God's saving purpose from the Scripture and credits the 'positives of inspiration' to the former. His words quoted above do not mean exactly what they say. Hebert, we think, does not intend us to infer that the positives of Inerrancy and Infallibility apply to the Bible as a witness to revelation, but, as his whole thesis seeks to prove, to the revelation itself. Packer, on the other hand, wishes us to conclude that what the words signify belong to the Bible as the written Scripture.

The whole question needs the most careful rethinking. The wholesale repudiation of inerrancy in the days before and following the coming of the higher criticism may well be revealed as having been too hasty. In discarding the word something of real and permanent significance may have been lost which modern theologians are seeking if haply they might find.

Geoffrey W. Bromiley, well known as the editor of the translation of Karl Barth's *Church Dogmatics*, has drawn attention to an interesting fact. He has shown how the Lutheran and Reformed dogmaticians of the seventeenth century are in line with the main teaching of the Reformers themselves respecting their doctrine of Scripture. But he observes withal 'certain shifts of emphasis, slight in themselves but serious in their historical consequences'.[1] These dogmaticians tended to return to the patristic overwhelming of the human author by the divine thus giving rise to ambiguous words and phrases in relation to inspiration, as, for example, 'dicto' and 'assistants and amenuenses'. The result is 'a tendency to press to an unnecessary extreme the intrinsically true doctrine of verbal

contends, it is precisely here that 'we begin to understand the true nature of verbal inspiration and also inerrancy' (p. 161). Young is sure that the original autographs of Scripture are without error and it is the purpose of scholarship to restore them. If we assert that the autographs of Scripture contain error, we are saying that God is guilty of having told us something that is not true. It may be a matter which we ourselves would call minor, but in this case a minor error is no less an error than a major one. . . . If God has communicated wrong information even in so-called unimportant matters, He is not a trustworthy God. It is therefore the question of Biblical theism which is at stake. . . . If, as a matter of fact, the revelation of God is not free of error, the message of Christianity must ever remain in doubt' (pp. 165–6); cf. Chapters 5 and 6 on 'What is Inerrancy?' and Chapter 7 'Are there Errors in the Bible?'

[1] Geoffrey W. Bromiley, 'Church Doctrine of Inspiration', *Revelation and the Bible* (ed. Carl F. H. Henry), 1958, p. 213.

inspiration'. Bromiley then specifies the third shift of emphasis which brought about an important consequence as 'a tendency to give a false importance to the doctrine of inerrancy, as if the inspiration of Scripture were finally suspended upon the ability to prove it correct in every detail. To be sure, inspiration is itself the basis of inerrancy, and there is no obligation to prove the latter. But in face of attacks upon the inerrancy of the Bible, whether by those who do not regard it as essential to inspiration or by those who deny both, it is only too easy to reverse the true relationship and to come to think of inerrancy as the basis of inspiration'.[1] There are other developments due to the highlighting of certain aspects of the Reformers' doctrine noted by Bromiley which do not concern us here. But he goes on through the brilliant period of the eighteenth century rationalism to show how the Christian apologist took a false step in seeking to answer Lessing and Herder by trying 'to defend inspiration in terms of inerrancy' and thus 'to commit it to inevitable relativization'. It was Herder who initiated the intensive research of the modern period with its more or less sustained polemic against inerrancy and therefore upon the special revelation of the Bible. By reducing inspiration to the aesthetic level and uniting it with the idea of the inward testimony of the Spirit, he opened the way for that complete subjectivism of which Schleiermacher was the father and liberal Protestantism the offspring. And before the flood the orthodox seemed helpless. They could erect no staying barrier. The truth is that the 'attack on the historical reliability of the Bible was damaging just because orthodoxy no longer had a full confidence in the witness of the Spirit but must find for it rationalistic support by a reversal of the relationship between inspiration and inerrancy, suspending the former on the latter'.[2] As Bromiley sees it, the real need is to go back to the Reformers 'and through them to the Bible and its self-witness by which all our views of inspiration must be tested, corrected, strengthened, and empowered'. Such a method is not by any means to weaken inspiration, nor yet is it to compromise

---

[1] Geoffrey W. Bromiley, 'Church Doctrine of Inspiration', *Revelation and the Bible* (ed. Carl F. H. Henry), 1958. Cf. 'The Reformers not infrequently speak about the Bible in ways to suggest its literal inaccuracy. But this verbal inspiration is a *consequence* of their view that God is the author of Scripture, not the *basis* of it'. Paul L. Lehmann, 'The Reformers' Use of the Bible', *Theology Today*, Vol. 3, p. 339.   [2] *Ibid.*, p. 216.

with any distortions and dilutions of the truth. The prophetic and apostolic word comes as the word of divine wisdom not to exalt man's mind, but to summon all the rationalism of man to repentance and renewal. The Bible comes with God's saving message to man. 'The inspiration of Scripture is genuinely the work of the sovereign Spirit, whose operations cannot finally be subjected to human analysis, repudiation or control, but who remains the internal Master of that which he himself has given, guaranteeing its authenticity, and declaring its message with quickening and compelling power.'[1] With such a note we may conclude this section since it seems to us that to such a conclusion we are being driven by our reflection upon the subject of the Bible's significance and by our observation of the hesitancies and uncertainties which afflicted an earlier period in which the 'humanness' of the Bible, if the paradox be permitted, was virtually defied.

The immediate result of the breakdown of belief in 'literal inerrancy and infallibility', to take up the story again, was to open up for prolonged discussion the allied subjects of the inspiration and the authority of the Bible. 'Criticism compels us to revise our doctrine of the inspiration of Scripture', declared A. F. Kirkpatrick in October 1902 at Northampton, in a paper on 'Modern Criticism and its Influence on Theology', read at the Church Congress. 'We must not ascribe' he goes on to maintain, 'an equal value and authority to every part of the Old Testament. We must no longer talk of its infallibility and inerrancy. We must distinguish its temporal, imperfect elements. Our Lord Himself taught us to do so. While we hold fast to the belief that the Old Testament contains the record— the divinely-shaped record—of God's revelation of Himself to Israel, we seem forced to admit that the record was not given and has not been preserved in such forms as we might antecedently have expected as has generally been believed.'

In a reference to the cognate subject in an issue of the *Expository Times* for the year 1892, in a notice of Marshall Randles's book, *The Design and Use of Holy Scripture* comes the statement: It is 'the great controversy of today—The Authority of Scripture. We have barely entered upon it yet. So the signs

[1] Geoffrey W. Bromiley, 'Church Doctrine of Inspiration', *Revelation and the Bible* (ed. Carl F. H. Henry), 1958, p. 117.

demand to be read. And it threatens to assume proportions we never dreamt of. The Authority of Scripture—of how much Authority? and who have this Authority?'[1] The inspiration and the authority of the Scriptures, then, were the topics which became the centre of theological debate and which to this day continue to be issues of major importance. Volume after volume has appeared bearing such a title as The Inspiration and Authority of the Bible, or with the more restricted one of, The Authority of the Bible, and the like.

It is our purpose in the next two chapters to treat these two topics separately and to draw together something of what has been said respecting them.

[1] *Expository Times*, Vol. IV, 1892–3, p. 43.

CHAPTER SEVEN

The Discussion of Biblical Inspiration

The whole period following the general repudiation of inerrancy
and the introduction of the higher criticism has been marked by
an attack on the 'mechanical' theory of inspiration. It is just,
however, to point out that this was a view of inspiration credited
to the traditionalists generally rather than actually taught by
them. The traditionalists have been consistent in contending for
a doctrine of verbal inspiration but it was not the main view that
this necessarily involved a mechanical process.[1] The term
'mechanical' would denote a process, but it was agreed that little
could be stated in this respect. By the term 'verbal', on the other
hand, emphasis was placed, not on the process, but on the result.
The idea intended by the traditionalists in their use of the
concept was to insist that the words of the Bible are the direct

[1] Cf. 'It ought to be unnecessary to protest again against the habit of representing
the advocates of "verbal inspiration" as teaching that the mode of inspiration is
dictation.' B. Warfield, *The Inspiration and Authority of the Bible*, 1893, reprint,
1948, p. 173 (note). 'When for instance we find that anything partaking of the
character of Verbal Inspiration, is charged with turning the sacred penmen into
"human ventriloquists" and "automaton poets", the result being nothing less than
to "petrify the whole body of Holy Writ, with all its harmoniousness and sym-
metrical graduations"; all we need to say in reply is that whatever force such
objections may have against the theory of Inspiration which represents the writers
as mere *machines*, possessed of no power of choice in the selection and use of words
they used, they do not at all bear on the view of Inspiration which we have shown as
taught in Scripture, and which is in perfect harmony with the manifestation of
individual peculiarities'. D. Fraser, *The Inspiration of the Bible*, 1874, pp. 62–3.
The 'dictation theory' is 'repudiated by all the conservative evangelical leaders,
because it leaves no room for the individuality of the human writers'. A. G. Hebert,
Fundamentalism and the Church of God, 1957, p. 56.

'We do indeed believe . . . that the Holy Spirit spoke through the human authors
so directly that their words were in a real sense His words, but we do not imagine
that the process was a mechanical one'. J. R. W. Stott, Statement at Oxford
Conference of Evangelical Churchmen, 1960. Cf. Letter in the *Baptist Times*, by
V. Perry, November 10, 1960.

result of holy men of God being moved by the Holy Ghost. Inspiration relates to the words which have been given: it does not primarily describe what took place in the psychological nature or the spiritual experience of God's chosen men.

Opposition to the 'mechanical' theory, and because of its identification with verbal inspiration the consequent repudiation of the latter, became characteristic. Although his language may be more vehement than most, F. W. Farrar gives typical expression of this antagonism. He does not mince words. He allows that Paul shared in the Jewish ideas of inspiration as verbal and as demanding 'absolute infallibility'.[1] He then seeks to discredit the idea in which the apostle shared. Paul is made to set forth doctrines to be believed on a foundation which cannot be shared. 'To say that every word and sentence and letter of Scripture is divine and supernatural', says Farrar, 'is a mechanical and useless shibboleth, nay, more, a human idol, and (constructively, at least) a dreadful blasphemy'. It is a superstitious and fetish-worshipping dogma, 'not only unintelligible, but profoundly dangerous'. It 'has for many ages filled the world with misery and ruin' and 'has done more than any other dogma to corrupt the whole of exegesis with dishonest causistry, and to shake to its centre the religious faith of thousands, alike of the most ignorant and of the most cultivated in many centuries, and most of all in our own'.[2] This is certainly strong language indeed, but it is more eloquent than convincing. It is doubtful, to put it mildly, if any considerable fact could be adduced to support Farrar's contention. It seems besides to overstep the bounds of enthusiasm to credit the apostle Paul with being implicated in such a dreadful blasphemy which has filled the world with so much ruin!

The position being as it was, however, a reconsideration of the idea of inspiration became imperative. The general situation demanded it. And from a particular point of view, as Alan Richardson states, 'The rise of Biblical scholarship made necessary a new doctrine of the inspiration of Holy Scripture'.[3] This necessity arose, Richardson adds, because it was found

[1] F. W. Farrar, *The Life and Work of St Paul*, 1880, Vol. I, p. 49; cf. p. 341.

[2] F. W. Farrar, *Inspiration, A Clerical Symposium* (ed. F. W. Farrar), 1888, second edition, p. 219; cf. p. 241.

[3] Alan Richardson, *A Preface to Bible-Study*, 1943, second impression, 1944, p. 33.

'impossible to continue to hold to the "dictation" theory'.[1] We can perhaps say that it was Charles Gore's essay in the *Lux Mundi* which sparked off the conflicts.[2] The essay which he contributed to the volume under the title 'The Holy Spirit and Inspiration' was, at the time, described as 'broad'. Every race has its great interpreters who have had a 'divine inspiration' which was at the same time 'natural'. The Jews, however, had an inspiration which was 'supernatural', since they were a people specially chosen to teach the world of God's relation to men. This is the 'point of view' of the Bible. Here lies the inspiration of its prophets, psalmists and historians. The writers of the Bible were 'inspired' because they saw what God was about, but such 'inspiration' neither enabled them 'to dispense with the ordinary means' nor did it carry with it a guarantee of accuracy.

Driver sought to allay fears that criticism would banish all ideas of an inspired Bible and leave us with a book altogether human. 'Criticism in the hands of Christian scholars', he stated in the Preface to *The Introduction to the Literature of the Old Testament*, 'does not banish or destroy the inspiration of the Old Testament; it presupposes it; it seeks only to determine the conditions under which it operates and the literary form through which it manifests itself.'[3]

But withal the question was urgent and pressing. Where does inspiration lie? Is it to be found in the words which the Bible contains, or in the religious experience which the Bible attests, or in the creative message which the Bible conveys? The traditional answer, with which we are not concerned at the moment, of course, affirmed the first.

A. INSPIRATION—THE FOCUS WITHIN

Immediately following the upheaval brought about by criticism, there was a tendency to maintain the view that the locale of inspiration was particularly the experiences of religious geniuses. Contemporary thought, on the other hand, seems to regard inspiration as the redemptive message of the Bible as

---

[1] Alan Richardson, *A Preface to Bible-Study*, 1943, second impression, 1944, p. 33.
[2] Cf. *Expository Times*, Vols. I and II, 1889–91, i, p. 121.
[3] S. R. Driver, *Introduction to the Literature of the Old Testament*, 1891, Preface, p. xiii.

that message is realized within the responding individual. These two ways of stating inspiration are not exactly successive or clear-cut. They overlap at many points.

It was certainly a direct result of criticism to shift attention from the words of the Bible to the men to whom we owe its existence. A. E. Garvie set himself to 'correct' 'the prevalent error of viewing the Bible as primarily an inspired book', and to do so he emphasized the fact that revelation is historical. He then stresses the idea of Providence and appears to equate inspiration with the prophetic interpretation of Israel's history as the sphere of God's selective activity. Yet the 'personal' aspect of inspiration is to be noted in which 'God by His indwelling and inworking Spirit made the men fit and worthy to be His messengers'. 'How interesting', he adds, 'the Bible is because the Divine Author of the revelation disguises Himself in the dress of the human authors of the writings.'[1]

John Clifford expounds as well as any other the idea of inspiration which was to emerge in the context of the new Biblical criticism. It is his contention that the question of inspiration should not be made fundamental.[2] Experience, he urges, gives the key to the understanding of the idea of inspiration. We have known 'inspired men' whose presence quickened emotion, stirred the conscience and strengthened the will. And Biblical inspiration 'was of men' and the Bible is a *report* of the experiences of God-inspired men'.[3] Thus, as a man rightly uses the Bible so he will discover its inspiration. It is wrong to come to the Bible, with the mind made up regarding the method of inspiration.[4] One must accept what one finds. He however expresses the hope that 'the unhappy, inadequate, and misleading words "verbal inspiration"' should be got rid of. Inspiration appears to be in Clifford's treatment a matter of degree. He writes on 'Present Day Inspiration' and states that 'the last Word of God has not been spoken'.[5] He talks eloquently

---

[1] A. E. Garvie, 'The Value of the Old Testament', *Expository Times*, Vol. XLVIII, 1936–7, p. 376. Cf. 'The Synthesis of History, Experience and Reason, in the Knowledge of God', *op. cit.*, Vol. XLIII, 1931–2, pp. 103 ff.

[2] Cf. 'The question of the nature and effect of Inspiration is not fundamental to the Christian argument'. R. Rainy, *Critical Review*, Vol. I, p. 11.

[3] John Clifford, *The Inspiration and Authority of the Bible*, 1888, third edition, 1899, p. 18.

[4] *Ibid.*, pp. 34 ff.   [5] *Ibid.*, p. 232.

of the inspired life and adds, 'Inspired personalities inspire'. He therefore closes his book with the hope that all the Lord's people be, not readers or teachers, but 'prophets'.

Inspiration was then to find the focus within. Those who saw God's acts in history, who read the account from the religious point of view, were indeed inspired to see and to read in this way. 'It is not their *words* that are inspired—as one might say perhaps of "automatic writing"—it is the *men* who are inspired.'[1] And the men were inspired because they had what A. F. Kirkpatrick refers to as the 'religious eye'. Being in possession of this 'incomparable eye', to use a phrase preferred by Angus M. Mackay, the men of the Bible were able, as others were not, to see God active and to feel God present.

Religious genius and religious experience; such were the two operative words in the earlier statement of inspiration. R. Brook, for example, finds in the two words we have singled out the central truth about inspiration. Inspiration, he tells us, is the exercise of a profound religious instinct which some possess since there are those 'in whom this religious sense exists in a highly developed form, who have a special genius for religion, as others have for art of music'.[2] Marcus Dods likewise comes near to the same position. The fundamental problem is to rightly adjust the Divine and the human elements. The 'mechanical theory' is declared to be 'heathen' and 'Jewish'. But Paul did not accept it, nor can we, because it suggests that 'the Spirit of God inserts or puts into the mind of the inspired man a truth, as it were ready-made, and not in any necessary connection with the previous contents of the inspired mind or its moral action'.[3] Dods rejects also the 'essential dynamic theory' in which it is declared that accuracy is secured in all matters of conduct and doctrine, but need not be thought to extend to non-essential details and subsidiary particulars. In this case, the 'discrepancies' discovered in the science or the history cannot disturb. ('Perhaps they can be explained, perhaps they cannot, who cares a straw whether they can or no?' Coleridge.) Dods, however, rejects this on many accounts.[4] And having done so he leaves himself with less

[1] C. H. Dodd, *The Authority of the Bible*, 1928, p. 30 (italics in original).

[2] R. Brook, *Foundations*, A Statement of Christian Belief in Terms of Modern Thought, by Seven Oxford men (ed. B. H. Streeter), 1912, p. 52.

[3] Marcus Dods, *The Bible, Its Origin and Nature*, 1913, p. 117.

[4] *Ibid.*, pp. 122 ff.

than half a dozen pages to seek a 'positive' statement. This amounts to the assertion that inspiration has to do with the men, not with the words they have given. Its presence is seen in their perception of revelation. Those whom the Scriptures designate 'inspired' are so because they 'are distinguished above their fellow-Christians by a special readiness and capacity to perceive the meaning of Christ as the revelation of God and to make known what they see'.[1] Inspiration relates to character and godliness of life. 'The inspired man might not see the facts of history more clearly than the uninspired; but he saw God in history where the uninspired only saw human passions.'[2] In the last, inspiration is really the spiritual gift possessed by men of special godliness and character who could see what it is not given to others to behold.

A statement of the same import comes in Angus M. Mackay's *The Churchman's Introduction to the Old Testament* (1901). In the opening chapter on the subject of Inspiration he appears to regard it in the same general manner. 'Inspiration does not guarantee him who possesses it against all error', he writes, 'Here also an analogy may help us. When we say that Shakespeare surpassed all other men in *poetic* inspiration, what do we mean? Not that in dealing with disputed historical questions he was infallible, but that he had an incomparable eye for the *poetic* and *dramatic* elements in history. His genius did not make him an authority upon botany or astronomy, but only inspired him to turn flowers and stars to the very highest *poetic* uses conceivable. So the prophets were inspired in matters pertaining to God; they had a genius for religion.'

A. S. Peake hesitates to attribute inspiration to religious genius, but in the end he seems ready for the admission. 'What the inspiration of the Bible is,' he contends, 'we can assert only from the investigation of the Bible itself.'[3] It is reluctance to admit errors in the Bible which is responsible for the rigorous mechanical theory. But since these have been discovered by criticism, a 'more flexible theory' is demanded. 'The history (of Israel) as a whole', he maintains, 'is in truth inspired, when we look at it, that is to say, as an element in the development of our

[1] Marcus Dods, *The Bible, Its Origin and Nature*, 1913, p. 124.
[2] *Ibid.*, p. 125.
[3] A. S. Peake, *The Bible, Its Origin, Significance and Abiding Worth*, 1913, p. 29.

race.'[1] To supress the human in personality would be entirely
out of harmony with the Spirit of God.[2] In a chapter on 'The
Nature and Mechanism of Inspiration'[3] he claims that the 'old-
fashioned' doctrine of inspiration is now 'happily fast dis-
appearing'. Peake's whole endeavour is to show how the Holy
Spirit inspired the men. The inspired man is the 'possessed' man.
This leads him to discuss, in a manner followed later by J.
Burnaby,[4] the action of the Spirit in the lives of men in the Old
and New Testaments. It was Paul's merit, he declares, to stress
the activity of the Spirit in the lives of ordinary Christians;
'the Church was in danger of overrating the value of the
abnormal phenomena'.[5] The Spirit, however, does seek as
instruments those who have the qualifications. 'He desires the
religious genius rather than the physical subject.'[6] Yet this does
not reduce inspiration, he asserts, to a higher form of religious
genius, although a few pages later he writes, 'The inspiration
we find in the Bible is that of supreme religious genius, often
combined, it is true, with a superb gift of expression, but still
having its value rather in the fact that it is religious, than that
it is great literature'.[7]

Urging that 'the hearty recognition of the human element is
incompatible with a belief in verbal inspiration' Peake goes on
to refer inspiration to the men behind the Bible. It is they who
were inspired because they were religiously sensitive to the
movements of God in history. In them the divine and the human
so combined that the significance of what they were aware 'was
the joint product action of the Divine and human factors; that no
boundary line should be drawn between the two; that its primary
purpose is not to divulge doctrines or lay down moral principles
but to bring us into contact with God Himself and disclose His
action in revelation and redemption; that whatever errors be
recognized and uncertainties remain we have enough and far
more than enough for all our religious and moral needs'.[8]

Prior to the appearance of the *Lux Mundi* certain rather loose
views of inspiration can be noted. The idea of Samuel Davidson,
for example, gave particular offence. Strong objection was taken

[1] A. S. Peake, *The Bible, Its Origin, Significance and Abiding Worth*, 1913, p. 254
[2] *Ibid.*, p. 352.   [3] *Ibid.*, Chapter XIX.
[4] J. Burnaby, *Is the Bible Inspired?* 1949.
[5] A. S. Peake, *op. cit.*, p. 390.   [6] *Ibid.*, p. 395.
[7] *Ibid.*, pp. 402–3.   [8] *Ibid.*, p. 407.

to his stress upon 'degrees of inspiration'.[1] Colenso, too, it may be observed, although he nowhere expressed denial of the doctrine of inspiration, shows by some of his critical conclusions that he was opposed to any verbal theory.[2]

In 1884 there appeared the Symposium on *Inspiration* to which eleven writers contributed. F. W. Farrar, the originator and editor of the volume, himself contributed a chapter and gave a sort of summary of the views of the other writers. Farrar notes that S. Leathes, John Cairns and G. W. Olver 'appear to maintain the current view of the Bible as being throughout supernaturally infallible and inspired'.[3] The first of the trio, an Anglican, contended that the Bible as a whole is to be designated the Word of God and is therefore fully inspired. He does, however, stress that this does not necessitate any 'mechanical' theory.[4] At the same time he states, 'If the Bible is the Word of God at all, it must be so in such a sense as that we may trust its most important and crucial utterances to the very letter. Supposing the exact words to have been accurately ascertained, there seems to be no limit to which we may not trust and rely upon them to the very letter. If words are the vehicles of thought, then the more exact the thought the more accurate the words must be, unless they are to misrepresent and not do justice to it'.[5] To this view, the Presbyterian, Cairns, gives his fullest assent and in his own essay acknowledges his heavy debt to Leathes. Olver, too, writing as a Methodist, is in general agreement, although he declined to propound any specific theory of inspiration. He has none, he avers, except that which can be expressed in the words, 'Men spake from God, being moved by the Holy Spirit'. 'I accept the fact', he declares, 'and do not profess to explain the manner. The fact furnishes all the authority that the state of the case renders necessary. The result is a message from God. It is more. It is the one and only message so credited to the human race as "*the* Word of God".'[6]

Such a statement was too conservative for the other writers. An Independent, E. White and an Anglican, F. W. Farrar, took

---

[1] Cf. *The Wesleyan Magazine*, Vol. LXXIX, 1856, p. 116; Vol. LXXX, 1857, pp. 1118–20. See also J. Allanson Picton in *The Autobiography and Diary of William Davidson* (edited by his daughter), 1899, pp. 57–9.

[2] Cf. *British and Foreign Evangelical Review*, Vol. XII, 1863, p. 891.

[3] *Inspiration*, A Clerical Symposium (ed. F. W. Farrar), 1884, p. 207.

[4] *Ibid.*, p. 43.   [5] *Ibid.*, 44–5.   [6] *Ibid.*, p. 128.

H

a fairly extreme 'liberal' position. Edward White sees the Bible, not as a whole, but as a heterogeneous collection, and he argues that each separate contribution is a result of a 'divine personal instruction of men of old', to grasp as they were able the movements of the divine purpose. His view of inspiration he grants is 'exceedingly different from that of the ecclesiastical Canonists'.[1] He believes that a first step in coming to an understanding of inspiration sufficient to meet the modern situation is 'resolutely to fling aside the post-Nicene theory of the inspiration of "the Bible" as a whole; to resolve this Bible into its elements; and to regulate our view of each of these component parts by the writer's own testimony concerning the degree in which he was "moved by the Holy Ghost" '.[2]

F. W. Farrar states that his own views 'coincide in great measure with those of the Rev. E. White'.[3] The ideas which Farrar elaborated in more detail later are already expressed here. He strongly objects to the position taken up by Leathes and the other two and argues that it is wrong to say that the Bible *is* the Word of God: it only *contains* it. Verbal inspiration is repudiated and degress of inspiration according to the type of writing is maintained. As a book to inspire the value of the Bible is acknowledged, but it is a corrupting form of 'dishonest casuistry' to regard the Bible as a communication to men and for men of infallible divine truths.

In 1888, R. F. Horton, in line with his recent acceptance of the results of Biblical criticism, produced his *Inspiration of the Bible*. In 1884, Horton confesses he had never read a book on criticism. He had, indeed, heard Kuenen lecture at Oxford on 'Israel', and he had, he tells us, a vague awareness of the destructive criticism of the New Testament by the Tübingen school. It was, however, the publication of the Revised New Testament which stirred his interest and resulted in his wholehearted capitulation to literary and historical criticism.[4] In 1887 he began a series of lectures designed to introduce the new teaching to his congregation at Hampstead and the *Inspiration of the Bible* is the result.

Horton's conversion to criticism was, however, too recent for the task he undertook. He had not had time to reflect and he

---

[1] *Inspiration*, A Clerical Symposium (ed. F. W. Farrar), 1884, p. 148.
[2] *Ibid.*, p. 154. [3] *Ibid.*, p. 219.
[4] R. F. Horton, *An Autobiography*, 1918, p. 85.

failed to see the real issues. He had no constructive statement to give. Horton attacked with all the logic at his command and the light which he now supposed himself to have received, 'the cast-iron theory of inspiration'. His apparent purpose was to show that the Bible contained numerous errors and inconsistencies in order to make the 'mechanical' theory impossible to square with the alleged facts. But having done so Horton had nothing convincing to put in its place. In his later *Revelation and the Bible* (1892) he adds the note on 'Attempt at Reconstruction', but all that he could give was, as it was observed earlier, a 'series of tentative suggestions'. The earlier book, however, is characterized by the absence of any serious effort to offer even these. Horton rather naïvely remarks in his *Autobiography* that he had no thought of discrediting the Bible by his onslaught on the prevailing idea of inspiration. Indeed he imagined himself 'defending it from the assaults of Infidelity, which acquired all their force from an erroneous conception of what the inspiration of the Bible was'.[1]

It was the alleged errors in the Bible which led so many to declare against verbal inspiration. The *British Quarterly Review* of the year 1873, in an article on 'G. H. Augustus von Ewald' urged that what it referred to as the 'scribe theory' of inspiration, was no longer tenable in the light of the results gained by textual criticism. Ewald had maintained that the people of Israel, as God's selected nation, were 'inspired', and although he did not commit himself openly to the conclusion, he appeared to suggest that the Bible, as the record of the dealing of Israel with God, partook of inspiration in a derivative sense only.[2]

The focus on inner experience as the sphere of inspiration came specially to vogue after the appearance of Gore's *Lux Mundi* essay. So strong, indeed, did this insistence become that at a much later period, C. H. Dodd could use the emphasis to deny the possibility of verbal inspiration which he identified with the 'dictation' theory. 'Whatever such a process of "dictation" may be', he declares, 'it is naturally impossible to say, since *ex hypothesi* no living man has experience of it.'[3]

[1] R. F. Horton, *An Autobiography*, 1918, p. 85.
[2] *British Quarterly Review*, Vol. LVII, 1873, pp. 170–3. Cf. Heinrich Ewald's *Revelation and its Record* (E.T. 1884), where the same idea is elaborated, but there is actually no discussion of inspiration; but cf. pp. 270–99.
[3] C. H. Dodd, *The Authority of the Bible*, 1928, p. 35.

Gore did more than any other to revise the idea of inspiration. Elsewhere he reiterates in a more dogmatic manner the ideas of inspiration of his *Lux Mundi* essay. In one of the volumes which make up the trio published under the title *Reconstruction of Belief*, he acknowledges that belief in inspiration is the 'belief of the Christian Church' which 'has its ground in the inspiration of the Old Testament which they inherited from the Jews'.[1] But it was, he maintains, the prophets who were inspired, and the Bible comprises 'the books of inspired men'.[2] Gore argues against 'literal accuracy' and contends, as does Hebert later, that the notion of verbal inspiration has 'a very large place' among the 'root causes of present-day unsettlement in matters of religion'.[3]

Many were the efforts made to reconstruct the doctrine of inspiration in the new context. One of the most important of these was that made by W. T. Davidson, Classical Professor at the Richmond Methodist Theological College. In a paper read at the London Wesleyan Ministers' Meeting, March 16, 1891, and entitled 'Inspiration and Biblical Criticism', Davidson raised the question: 'How far is the doctrine of Inspiration and the Divine Authority of Holy Scripture affected by the modern Biblical Criticism?' He refers to the articles on the Bible in the ninth edition of the *Encyclopaedia Brittannica* and the fact that the *Lux Mundi* has reached its eleventh edition mainly because of Gore's essay on 'Inspiration' as evidence of the need to reconsider the question. He suggests that the 'ecclesiastical doctrine of Inspiration' which has become the common property of the orthodox, needs to be modified to meet the present situation. It is no longer possible to begin, as the earlier theologians did, with a statement of Inspiration and on that basis to assert the infallibility of the Scripture. 'The doctrine of Inspiration is the very last thing we come to in a time of searching inquiry and unsettlement of foundations.' There are other questions to be faced first; for example, the genuineness, the authenticity and so forth, of the several books. But if we do not begin with inspiration and infallibility where then rests the authority of the Bible? Neither on the authority of the Church

---

[1] C Gore, *Reconstruction of Belief*, 1921–4, new edition in one volume 1926, reprint, 1945, p. 875.

[2] *Ibid.*, p. 888.   [3] *Ibid.*, p. 874.

nor yet in the Coleridgean dictum that what *finds me* in the Bible is true. It is in the experience of Jesus Christ that its authority is revealed and its 'inspiration' ultimately discovered. In a later article Davidson defends his position, maintaining that no 'preconceived doctrine of "inspiration", or any theories concerning what "revelation" ought to contain, or how far the records of the Scriptures must agree in detail must be held *a priori*'.[1]

Under a similar title, J. J. Stewart Perowne discussed the doctrine of inspiration.[2] Making reference to the Revisers' translation of II Tim. iii. 15–17, he sees the Scriptures as 'being full of the breath of God'. Yet it is not possible to define exactly the nature of the inspiration any more than we can define life itself. Possessing divine life the Scripture reveals its presence in its power and effect. Perowne, however, goes into some detail concerning the process of inspiration. 'Now I think we cannot too clearly or too firmly grasp the principle laid down by St Paul', he says. 'By inspiration we are to understand that influence of the Spirit of God upon the writers of the Old Testament, by which they were empowered to teach such spiritual truths, and in such a measure as was necessary for the religious welfare of those whom they addressed. Inspiration does not imply that the writers were lifted altogether above the level of their contemporaries in matters of plainly secular import. They do not antedate the science of the nineteenth century. Marvellous as is their historical accuracy, it does not imply supernatural infusion of knowledge on subjects lying within their own observation. They were the faithful witnesses and recorders of the things they themselves had seen and heard.'[3]

We have made reference a few pages back to A. F. Kirkpatrick's statement concerning the 'religious eye' possessed by those who saw God in the events of Israel's national life. The idea comes in his volume, *The Divine Library of the Old Testament: Its Origin, Preservation, Inspiration and Permanent Value* (1891). Concerning our present subject his thesis is that the essential nature of inspiration is to be seen as the purification of

---

[1] W. T. Davidson, *London Quarterly Review*, Vol. XCIII, 1900, pp. 1–24; cf. p. 13 f.
[2] J. J. Stewart Perowne, *Expository Times*, Vols. I and II, 1889–91, ii, pp. 54 ff.
[3] *Ibid.*, p. 55.

the primitive traditions by the Biblical recorders and their adaptation to religious purposes. These inspired men were able to show that it was God in His actions of grace who ruled history and was in it. Inspiration did not guarantee immunity from errors in matters of fact, science, or history, and most certainly it did not exclude imperfection, relativity and accommodation.

Two series of Bampton Lectures in the early years of the eighteen-nineties gave attention to the topic of inspiration. The first of these by A. Barry in 1892 was not dealing specifically with the question, yet he does feel it necessary to say something regarding it. In one of the lectures on 'Criticism and the Holy Scriptures', he begins by maintaining the legitimacy of criticism. He believes that in the midst of the diversity of the Bible there is discoverable by 'faith' a 'subjective unity'. This may be denied by criticism but Christians have a sure faith 'in a Supreme Inspiration—whether of origination or selection it matters not —which has guided and overruled all these varieties of age and authorship to one Divine Purpose'.[1] Barry admits that criticism has given 'some shock to the old unquestioning faith, which holds it to be above all human judgement, and is content to listen to every sentence as a complete Word of God'.[2] He contends however that we have learned, as a result of the recent discussion, that 'in grace, as in nature, the Divine Inspiration expresses itself in methods different from what we should have *a priori* expected'.[3]

Barry raises the question of the distinctive and essential character of the Scripture which justifies the Christian claim to it as the supreme authority. The enquiry, he suggests, resolves itself into that concerning inspiration. He doubts the correctness of speaking about 'an inspired Book'. It is its authors who were inspired. 'For inspiration is the action of the Spirit of God upon the living spirits of men.'[4] He adds, however, that inspiration must be thought of as extending to a choice of words 'though not (in) its usual sense of dictation, in which we can speak of "verbal inspiration" '.[5]

Barry is clearly anxious, in spite of this last admission, to

---

[1] A. Barry, *Some Lights of Science on the Faith*, Bampton Lectures, 1892, p. 265.
[2] *Ibid.*, p. 268.　　　　　　　　[3] *Ibid.*, pp. 271–2.
[4] *Ibid.*, p. 282–3.　　　　　　　[5] *Ibid.*

insist that inspiration refers to the men who wrote, not to what and how they wrote. To speak of an inspired book is to obscure the important truth, that the writers of the Holy Scriptures were not mechanical instruments through whom the Holy Spirit wrought. He expresses unhappiness about 'The Inspiration of the Bible'. He would have us draw a distinction between revelation and inspiration and refer to the Scripture as itself a unique revelation of God, whereas inspiration is to be 'viewed as the power by which the writers of Scripture were quickened to understand and to declare' the revelation.[1] He illustrates his idea from the experience of teaching. 'Revelation to others is for us comparatively easy: inspiration of others infinitely difficult.' To present, illustrate and enforce the truth we know is within the experience of many, but to inspire the minds of learners, to stimulate intelligence, to give insight, even to awaken interest is far from being an easy thing. This means for Barry, as he boldly declares, that inspiration is subjective and as such must vary in form and degree.[2] So difficult is it for us to understand inspiration in respect of ourselves that it becomes obviously impossible to comprehend the process by which God has moved men's minds. Contrasting the theory of 'mechanical' inspiration with the 'dynamical' and the special inspiration of the writers of Scripture with the general inspiration of Christian believers, may, he says, be useful in its way. But they are ultimately a mere matter of speculation: 'The one all-important thing for us is to know whether we have in Holy Scripture a real Revelation of Truth; how it was given, through what forms or measure of Inspiration, is one of the secrets of God'.[3]

In the following year W. Sanday discussed the whole subject of Inspiration from an historical and reconstructionist point of view. The main ideas were already stated in his volume, *The Oracles of God*. He there bluntly maintained with reference to the Bible that 'its text is not infallible; its grammar is not infallible; its science is not infallible; and there is grave doubt whether its history is altogether infallible'.[4] In the last of his later Bampton Lectures, having traced in a manner which he

[1] A. Barry, *Some Lights of Science on the Faith*, Bampton Lectures, 1892, p. 284.
[2] *Ibid.*, p. 289.   [3] *Ibid.*, p. 290.
[4] W. Sanday, *The Oracles of God*, Nine Lectures on the Nature and Extent of Biblical Inspiration and the Special Significance of the Old Testament Scriptures at the Present Time, 1892, fourth edition, p. 36.

appears to regard as satisfactory the origin and early history of
the doctrine of Biblical inspiration, he turns to compare what he
calls the 'traditional' view with the 'inductive or critical'. He
allows that the 'Inspiration implied by both is real and no fiction,
a direct objective action of the Divine upon the human'.[1] The
danger in the 'traditional' doctrine, he thinks, is that it might
easily slide into a dead and mechanical notion. In contrast with
it, the 'deductive' method seeks to understand inspiration 'by
examining the consciousness of the Biblical writers', to learn
from them what they have to say of their own inspiration.[2] At
times these prophetic men arrived at the truth through the
inspiration of devout meditation and reflection, and at times
they were vividly aware of a special divine *afflatus*. They were
not men 'dictated' to, but men 'inspired'. The divine revelation
'came through human *media*; and from time to time we are
reminded that the *media* are human'.[3]

We have already noted Farrar's harsh condemnation of the
'mechanical' theory of inspiration. In his book, *The Bible, Its
Meaning and Supremacy*, he returns to his aversion. He associates
the two words 'verbal' and 'dictation' and contends that they
suggest 'an untrue and unscriptural hypothesis', and he later
remarks on the 'dangerous results of the "supernatural
dictation" theory'.[4] Farrar seems to take a very broad view of
inspiration. It is apparently not specifically limited to the
writers of Scripture; they are rather an instance of that influence
which the Spirit of God exercises upon all men. They were, to
be sure, more responsive and co-operative. As all great literature awakens a response in the sensitive soul, so the Bible
'speaks directly and unmistakably to our inmost hearts and
consciences. We shall hear it each according to our capacity and
our power to receive it, and we shall hear it all the more surely
in exact proportion to the measure in which we have arrived at
"truth in the inward parts" '.[5]

The lectures of T. George Rooke, the late President of
Rawdon Baptist College, on the subject of Inspiration were
published posthumously in 1893 'edited by two of his students'.

---

[1] W. Sanday, *Inspiration*, Bampton Lectures, 1893, third edition, 1908, p. 399.
[2] *Ibid.*, p. 402.   [3] *Ibid.*, p. 423.
[4] F. W. Farrar, *The Bible, Its Meaning and Supremacy*, 1897, Chapters VII and
XII.   [5] *Ibid.*, p. 132.

They are the work of a scholar who made a serious attempt to understand his subject. Rooke is convinced that we should cease to talk of the Bible as an 'inspired Book' and reject such phrases as the 'Inspiration of the Holy Scriptures'.[1] He makes a study of the Biblical passages in which the idea connoted by the word inspiration comes up. Concerning II Tim. iii. 16, he says that it 'is impossible to show that the passage means anything more than this: "Every writing which breathes a divine spirit is also profitable for teaching, for conviction, for correction, for training, which (begins and ends) in righteousness" '.[2] Other passages, however, make it clear that the prophets spoke as the result of a Divine 'afflatus'. Rooke regards the idea of inspiration as but another name for genius to be inadequate, although, he adds, that it 'does not so much lower our thoughts of a Divine origin and authority in Scripture, as it raises our conceptions of a Divine origin and authority in things which we have been, perhaps, accustomed to regard as triumphs of unaided human wisdom and strength'.[3]

Gathering together the results of his investigation of the Scripture passages, Rooke then gives his definition of inspiration as 'the preparation of a man's heart or mind, or both, by the Holy Spirit, in view of some task for which God would use that man'.[4] He states that the 'theological term Inspiration' ought to mean 'the inward spiritual preparation of a man to know and feel what God chooses to communicate of His Divine thought and will'.[5]

Rooke, however, believed that the term 'inspiration' should be banished from theological textbooks[6] since the terms inspiration and revelation are to be regarded as correlatives, and the latter term should be retained as less question-begging. Because inspiration means the special preparation of a heart and mind by the Holy Spirit then many kinds of inspiration can be supposed. Rooke classified the theories of inspiration. He allows that the 'mechanical' view to which he refers first, 'does explain

[1] T. George Rooke, *Inspiration and Other Lectures*, 1893, p. 131.
[2] *Ibid.*, p. 119.   [3] *Ibid.*, p. 125.
[4] *Ibid.*, p. 131.   [5] *Ibid.*
[6] *Ibid.*, p. 133. Cf. 'But the best of all courses for the student will be to settle with himself once and for all never to use the word, 'Inspiration' unless he means "the inward (or suggestive) preparation of the human heart or mind by the Holy Spirit" ' (p. 134).

better than any other the origin and character of certain parts of Scripture'.[1] But there are objections to it which reveal it as 'positively harmful'. The 'dynamical, or assistance or direction theory' is also found wanting; so, too, is the 'illumination or mystical' view. Rooke then comes to his own 'Comprehensive theory' or as he prefers to call it, the 'Theory of Sufficient Knowledge or Gracious Purpose'. Although no book has yet been written to expound the theory, it is held, he states, by Farrar and is substantially the idea propounded by Martensen and Dorner. The ideas can be properly referred to as 'plenary' because it is 'full' in the sense that God's revelation is progressive, and inspiration and revelation are to be identified. Because inspiration is the preparation of heart and mind of man by the Holy Spirit to receive His revelation then the term is applicable to every part. He grants that the view is not 'absolutely satisfactory', but it is 'more helpful' than other views and it solves problems for which they have no answer; for example, the moral difficulties in the Bible and the like difficulties. Rooke tests out each theory of inspiration with reference to the various types of literature in the Bible itself and finds the idea of 'Sufficient Knowledge' or 'Gracious Purpose' as answering best the difficulties involved. He raises certain problems which the concept of inspiration brings to the fore, such as the character of the inspired men and of their records.

Rooke makes a special point of the analogy between 'the Living and the Written Word'. He regards the letter of Scripture as corresponding to 'the fleshly and material aspect of our Lord's humanity' and its 'matter' as corresponding to 'the human soul and spirit of our Lord'. The parallel is truly a strange one, but Rooke carries it through in thorough fashion. The flesh of Christ cannot be forever pervaded by His Deity. It was an indispensable vehicle of His real humanity to which Divinity has been inseparably conjoined. Rooke draws the conclusion that 'the Divine character of Scripture dwells inseparably, not in its letter and outward form as above described, but in the matter and spirit; we can think away the letter and distinguish it from the spirit, and perceive how incomparatively unimportant the mere vehicle of Divine revelation is'.[2] Yet the Bible is to be

---

[1] T. George Rooke, *Inspiration and Other Lectures*, 1893, p. 149.
[2] *Ibid.*, pp. 178–9.

cherished as the disciples cherish their Master's material form
and 'this attitude of ours towards the book is not Bibliolatry'
nor is it inconsistent with whatever defects there may be in it.
Rooke maintains, indeed, the possible existence of 'physical
blemishes' in our Lord's earthly life. His members could well
have been defective, as some of the Christian Fathers seem to
have thought, without detracting from the reality and power of
His divinity. The presence of deformities in Christ, if they were
proved to exist, would not cancel out belief in His divinity.
'Why then', he asks, 'should anyone allege in regard to the
Bible that it cannot be Divine in its matter unless it is also
faultless in its literary form according to the ever-shifting
standards of human taste, human logic, or human conceptions of
perfection in science, in history, in philosophy, and even in
morality?'[1]

As the nineteenth century drew to its close, all that had been
said concerning the Bible's inspiration was summed up in an
article by J. E. M'Quot. The rise of textual criticism, M'Quot
contended, had made it impossible to maintain the infallibility
of any existing document and so the discovery of discrepancies
and inaccuracies in minor matters of fact, as well as characteristic
varieties of style, necessitated a modification of the old
mechanical theory of inspiration.[2] If inspiration can be regarded,
he argues, as consistent with varieties of form and style among
the sacred writers, then it is but an easy step to admit still freer
use by the Divine Spirit of the literary methods of the times.
M'Quot contended then for the mythological and legendary
nature of certain parts of the Old Testament, particularly the
early chapters of Genesis. The superior quality of the Old
Testament, however, 'the divine purity and loftiness' of its
prophecy and the 'infinite deeper and more spiritual' nature of
its poetry, in contrast with heathen oracles and other kinds of
literature, is what is meant by Inspiration. M'Quot notes that
although the new understanding of it means that 'the lines of
external evidence are weakened', yet we still can 'cling the more
closely to the self-evidencing realities of the spiritual life'.[3] In
this way religion will, as a result, become more experimental

---

[1] T. George Rooke, *Inspiration and Other Lectures*, 1893, p. 179.

[2] J. E. M'Quot, 'Divine Revelation in the Light of the Old Testament Criticism',
Expository Times, Vol. XII, 1900–1, pp. 488–9.   [3] *Ibid.*, p. 494.

and inductive; more an affair of the heart, and thus the Bible will remain 'our one supreme and unerring authority'.

In spite of all that had been said, by the turn of the century the whole idea of inspiration had become suspect, due in part to the unsatisfactory account given of it by the new apologists. The optimistic mood, which prevailed as the twentieth century opened, preferred to see inspiration, if the word must still be used, as a specific instance of the spirit which was making humanity great. Besides, the literature of the New Testament which was being brought under criticism and discussion was centred upon the various sources, either known or unknown, which its several writers employed. The New Testament was considered to be as much the result of a patchwork process as the Old had ever been. It was all very natural and very human, and, as a consequence, the idea of inspiration seemed to be eliminated, or, at least, it became something very remote and vague. Thus, when in 1910 James Orr wrote his commanding volume, *Revelation and Inspiration*, the comment was made in the *Expository Times* to the effect that it was 'a courageous thing—for all the popular writing on revelation and inspiration at the present seem to be in the way of denying the existence of both'.[1] During the optimistic years before the First World War there was little thought for the idea of inspiration, while throughout the pessimistic years of that upheaval there was little time for a discussion of such a subject. The few contributions there were seemed bent upon stating inspiration in as 'natural' a way as possible.

In 1909 the Cambridge University Press published a book by T. H. Sprott in which an effort was made to give meaning to the idea of inspiration in the light of the modern criticism and its results.[2] Sprott includes a 'Table of dates and authorship' taken from J. E. McFadyen's *Old Testament Criticism and the Christian Church* in which these aspects of the critical reconstruction are set forth. In the Table will be noted such conclusions, for example, as these: 'Traditions, war-ballads, and other songs, 1200–1000 BC'; 'Deuteronomy, 621 BC'; 'Deutero-Isaiah, 540 BC'; 'Priestly Code (Leviticus, etc.) 500–450 BC'; 'Pentateuch in practically its present form, before 400 BC'; 'Daniel, 167 BC'.

---

[1] *Expository Times*, Vol. XXI, 1909–10, p. 373.
[2] T. H. Sprott, *Modern Study of the Old Testament and Inspiration*, 1909, Chapters I and II.

Sprott having expressed the conviction that he has given a 'substantially accurate view of the modern critical position' then asks, 'Can the writers of that literature have been the subject of a Divine inspiration?'[1] He regards the notion of the Bible being 'verbally inspired' as totally unacceptable. The Scripture itself, he contends, does not make such a claim, 'Neither does the authoritative teaching of the Catholic Church involve this theory, or furnish any definition'.[1] Having quoted some remarks of F. D. Maurice concerning the prayers, hymns and confessions of the Psalms, Sprott remarks that 'The phenomena, then, of the Biblical literature, as disclosed to careful study, refute the *a priori* notion of Divine dictation'.[2] Sprott then goes on to elaborate his theory of inspiration as the energizing of the faculties of the contributors to the Scripture. Prophecy is to be regarded as 'inspired preaching'. The conclusion of the matter is this: 'By Inspiration I understand the quickening and heightening of man's apprehensive powers by the Spirit of God, whereby he is enabled to apprehend the Divine revelation and become an interpreter of it to his fellows. Inspiration is not the direct communication of knowledge to the human mind: it is power of insight, so that he perceives the Divine meaning in Nature or Conscience or History, which though always there and always appealing, had been before unperceived'.[3]

In his volume, *The Inspiration and Authority of Holy Scripture*, J. M. Gibson, as P. T. Forsyth states in the Introduction to the work, sought to mediate 'between the world of modern knowledge on the one hand and the world of traditional religion on the other'.[4] Gibson declares for the general view of inspiration which we have seen stated by one and another in the preceding pages. He seeks, however, to exercise caution and to avoid extremes. But he confesses that he received much help from 'the work of the more spiritual critics' and gained, as a result, 'a conviction of the inspiration and authority of the sacred Scriptures far stronger and more satisfying than I had in the old days'.[5]

Following the statement in the *Expository Times* noted above

---

[1] T. H. Sprott, *Modern Study of the Old Testament and Inspiration*, 1909, p. 36.
[2] *Ibid.*, p. 42.   [3] *Ibid.*, pp. 55–6.
[4] J. Munro Gibson, *The Inspiration and Authority of Holy Scripture*, 1908, p. x.
[5] *Ibid.*, pp. 8–9.

in reference to Orr's book, it is instructive to examine the teaching of inspiration which appeared now and again throughout the following years.

In his *Inspiration and Prophecy* (1910), G. C. Joyce, a contributor to the *Encyclopaedia of Religion and Ethics*, applied psychology for the first time in an effort to explain the phenomenon of prophetic inspiration. Joyce conceives of inspiration as the communication of new truths. 'Recognizing and accepting the reality and authority of the revelation enshrined in the Bible', he declares, 'I am convinced that the fullest and freest inquiry into the various modes of Inspiration, so far from weakening faith, cannot but serve to increase our reverence for the work of the Holy Spirit among men.' Joyce regards inspiration as an abnormal, indeed, as a supernormal, activity of the mind, consequently it cannot be accounted for by the laws of text-book psychology. It is to 'Psychical Research' we must turn since it has shown the 'existence in man of faculties extending beyond the limitation of normal consciousness'. Prophetic inspiration is then an abnormal psychical occurrence. This does not mean that its reality is in any way lessened because its method is so to be understood. As telepathy is the work of one man on another, so prophecy is the work of God. The modes of inspiration change according to man's growing experience but what is given in any mode tends to take the position of a dictum after the analogy of all human custom and experience. The phrase, 'Thus saith the Lord', is frequent in Amos, for example. It was begun for the prophet in some 'substratum of mystical hearing' but in the process of time, the phrase acquired 'in some measure a conventional use'. Succeeding prophets did not have the same experience of 'mystical hearing' as it would be too much to suppose that every time any one of the prophets took the words upon his lips he did so in virtue of some physical experience in the way of audition.

In *The Higher Criticism* of which Driver and Kirkpatrick were, the joint authors, there is reference to the subject of inspiration. Kirkpatrick insists upon his right to call the Old Testament inspired, but he will 'not venture to define' its 'nature and limits'.[1] Driver scorns the idea of verbal inspiration and contends that the process of inspiration did not assure freedom

[1] Driver and Kirkpatrick, *The Higher Criticism*, 1911, p. 12.

from 'imperfection, error, and mistake in matters of fact'. He, however, describes inspiration as 'a Divine *afflatus* which, without superseding or repressing the human faculties, but rather using them as its instruments, and so conferring upon Scripture its remarkable manifoldness and variety, enabling holy men of old to apprehend, and declare in different degrees, and in accordance with the needs and circumstances of particular ages or occasions, the mind and purpose of God'.[1] The prophets show their inspiration, it is declared, 'in the spirit with which they breath into the narrative and in their interpretation of history; they show how a providential purpose overrules it; and bring out the spiritual and moral lessons implicit in it'.[2] He speaks of the 'Divinely quickened intuition' of the 'thinkers and seers of Israel' which enabled them gradually to elevate and purify their conception of God and to discern Him more clearly as history moved on and their own spiritual perceptions were enlarged.

G. P. Mains in his *Divine Inspiration* (1915), sees the Bible as leading up to God in contrast with the old view which regarded the Bible as brought down from God. The Bible 'finds' us and in doing so reveals its inspiration. The reality of its inspiration lies in its spiritual appeal.

A title now familiar comes once again from the pen of G. D. Barry. In his work, *The Inspiration and Authority of Holy Scripture* (1918), he points out that the central word in which belief in the paramount authority of the Bible is expressed occurs once only in the New Testament. In the passage in II Tim. iii. he maintains that the Apostle is simply giving a definition which 'Inspired Scripture' may be rightly expected to fulfil. It is not stated which books, in his judgement, are to be designated 'inspired Scripture' and which are not. But he has another declaration in which he tells us the originating source, which gave birth to the books of Scripture. 'Men spake from God, being moved by the Holy Ghost.' Here is the key to the deeper meaning of inspiration. Barry is, however, careful to insist that when influenced and taught by the Spirit their human powers were not suspended. Each exercised his own freedom under authority, expressing himself in his own characteristic way. The inspired writer absorbs into himself what has been communicated to him from God and then gives it out in his own

[1] Driver and Kirkpatrick, *The Higher Criticism*, 1911, pp. 53–4.   [2] *Ibid.*, p. 56.

language. 'The supernatural fertilises and does not annihilate the natural'—the individuality of the author, saturated, we might say, by the revelation, is still there in fullest expression.

In the year 1921, a comment appeared in the *Expository Times* declaring that, 'Now the doctrine of the inspiration of the Bible has been so severely handled of late that we can scarcely be sure if there is a doctrine left, and for the most part we have lost interest in it'.[1]

Within a few years, however, as if by way of protest against this comment, statements on the subject began to appear anew. True enough, for some time there were no formal treatises on the subject, but rather chapter treatment of it in the wider context of the significance and authority of the Bible itself. But the stress seems to be shifted from the idea of the Bible as a record of the religious experience of inspired men to an emphasis upon the Bible as a medium through which God speaks. This is not to say that the idea of the Bible as evincing 'degrees of inspiration' according to its power to awaken in us a genuine religious experience of God was discarded. This is by no means the case. The pragmatic test of inspiration still remained and the apologists were still concerned to show the validity of the religious experience, which the inspirational message of the Bible evoked.

To be aware of the Bible as that through which God speaks is to be aware of its inspiration, such was the view gradually emerging. This idea did not come out clearly for some time but it is more than hinted at in some remarks on the subject by E. A. Knox in his last charge as Bishop of Manchester, written, as he says, for those who seek to honour God with their minds as well as heart and soul.[2] A chapter on Inspiration in their volume *The Old Testament and Today*, by J. A. Chapman and L. D. Weatherhead, indicates the same movement of ideas. While Chapman himself in one of *The Fellowship of the Kingdom* pamphlets continues to stress the idea of the inspiration of the Bible as the gripping message which it speaks.[3]

Thistleton Mark, whose book is dedicated to Charles Gore and carries a brief forward by Hewlett Johnson, Dean of

---

[1] *Expository Times*, Vol. XXXIII, 1921–2, p. 5.
[2] E. A. Knox, *On What Authority?* 1922, chapter on Inspiration.
[3] Cf. J. A. Chapman, *The Bible and Inspiration*, 1929.

Manchester, seems to look back rather than forward in his scattered remarks on the subject. 'It is a gain, not a loss,' he says, 'to give up the comparatively recent doctrine of the word-for-word infallibility of the Scriptures, in order to win back our hold upon the abiding reality of their Inspiration.'[1] It is men of 'spiritual insight', he then declares, who have it in them to read more deeply the meaning and tendency of events. He grants that inspiration, though 'real' is 'not easy to define'. An 'inspired man', however, 'sees more history, and writes profounder history, than an inspired man'.[2] Paul is, at the same time, both 'human and inspired'.[3]

In his *Approach to the Old Testament*, J. E. McFadyen in a spirit akin to his earlier *Introduction to the Old Testament*, and *The Use of the Old Testament in the Light of Modern Knowledge*, begins with an attack upon 'verbal inspiration' which is equated with a mechanical process and regarded as excluding all human activity on the part of the writers. McFadyen's attack amounts to a play with Hebrew letters. Having indicated the possibility of variant translations occasioned by unpointed Hebrew and noting the different line taken in some passages by the Greek Septuagint translators, he asks, 'Which of the Hebrew texts is inspired, ours or theirs?'[4] Following this, he asks the same question concerning the differing accounts of parallel events in the gospels. After referring to the 'moral difficulties' in the Old Testament, he says, 'vastly too much has been made of them',[5] although he has himself been making quite an issue of them. The main purpose of his book is to meet the 'Conservative defence' of the Bible's inspiration and infallibility. He attacks four books, Martin Kegel's *Away from Wellhausen*, Thomas Jollie Smith's *Studies in Criticism and Revelation*, H. D. Woolley's *The Modernist Bible and How it was Compiled*, and W. H. Fitchett's *Where the Higher Criticism Fails*. These last three are selected, he states in a footnote, 'not because of their importance, but because of their representative quality: they are thoroughly typical of the conservative position'.[6] This section of the book is entertaining enough and doubtlessly McFadyen makes his

---

[1] Thistleton Mark, *The Appeal of the Bible Today*, 1925, p. 7.
[2] *Ibid.*, pp. 59–60.   [3] *Ibid.*, p. 124.
[4] J. E. McFadyen, *The Approach to the Old Testament*, 1926, p. 25.
[5] *Ibid.*, p. 51.   [6] *Ibid.*, p. 104 (footnote).

points with effect, except that few would have thought of these names as the first ones in the conservative camp.

Referring to Deut. viii. with its solemn warnings he says, 'Whatever be its date, it "finds" us, and for the purposes of religion as distinct from historical and literary criticism, that is all that matters'.[1] What he has to say on this passage is, we suspect, what he could say about the whole. It is what 'finds me' that reveals its inspiration by being inspirational.

T. H. Binley, in his volume on *Inspiration*, sees the phenomenon of the Bible as a particular instance of inspiration in general. He traces the idea of its infallibility to the Reformers' attack upon the infallibility of the Church and their substitution instead of the infallibility of a book. Inspiration is defined as 'that quality which stirs the divinest thing in us, which touches those chords in our inmost self which thrills to the Divine Breath'. A much 'broader' view of inspiration was taken by Snell of the Church Missionary Society in his slender volume *Inspiration*. This small word was intended especially for Indian pastors and its appearance caused concern amongst conservative Churchmen. Snell was ready to admit a fairly generous number of 'errors' in the record while the 'idealistic' view of history is allowed. To 'conceive of Scriptural prophecy as anticipated history is an inadequate conception', he says. So bluntly stated were Snell's 'liberal views' that it was hard to recognize any significant doctrine of inspiration at all in what he had to say.

It was the purpose of W. M. Grant in his *The Bible of Jesus Christ* (1927), to prove that Jesus did not teach any mechanical theory of inspiration. He showed a certain freedom of attitude in regard to the Old Testament so that by attributing Psalm cx to David He is not 'throwing His shield over the Davidic authorship of the Psalm'. Grant insists that the 'all or nothing' view of inspiration must be repudiated, and he contends that our Lord adopted an attitude towards the Old Testament of 'authority, superiority, and reserve'.

R. H. Malden's Cathedral Lectures for 1935 were published under the title *The Inspiration of the Bible*. Malden thinks that agnostics and fundamentalists are hindered from a careful study of the sacred volume because they assume that its value, inspiration and truth are bound up with the idea of a 'literal

[1] J. E. McFadyen, *The Approach to the Old Testament*, 1926, p. 98.

verbal accuracy'. It is Malden's set purpose to disabuse them of such a false notion. He investigates the Biblical use of the word 'inspiration' and concludes that the inspiration which possessed the men of the Scripture is authenticated within present religious experience.

A 'little book of quite distinctive character and excellence';[1] such was the enthusiastic description given to Alan Richardson's *A Preface to Bible-Study*. Richardson sees the question, What is inspiration? forced upon the Church by the rise of biblical criticism. The reply given at first was that inspiration of the Bible does not differ in *kind* but merely in *degree* from that possessed by other religious literature. It is, however, in contrast with this other literature that the merit of the Bible shines forth clear and uneclipsed. 'The Bible thus comes to be looked upon as the record of progressive deepening of man's religious experience and of the evolution of man's knowledge of God.'[2] To assert that the Bible is inspired was to assert that it was the record of the religious experience of inspired men. The inspiration of the Bible was, then, a matter of degree to be measured by the level of truth which it contained and by its power to awaken in man a genuine religious experience of God.

This theory of inspiration, widely accepted as it was by scholars, Richardson declares, did not satisfy the ordinary Christian believer: 'It was instinctively felt to be too thin'.[3] It was, indeed, based upon presuppositions no longer unquestionable. To begin with, it placed too strong an emphasis upon religious experience, and however valid such may be it is no sufficient basis for vital faith: 'we want God, not the experience of God: we want truth, not a true theory which explains the universe or life, but truth to live by, to serve and to obey'.[4] The deep question which this earlier view did not answer was, Is there a word from God? Furthermore, the idea of evolution which undergirded the whole thesis has today lost its magic and its appeal. The Bible, therefore, is no longer valid for us if it be the mere purveyor to us of richer religious experiences than in any other book. 'The question which our generation asks is not

[1] *Expository Times*, Vol. LIV, 1942-3, p. 309.
[2] Alan Richardson, *A Preface to Bible-Study*, 1943, second impression, 1944, p. 34.
[3] *Expository Times*, Vol. LIV, 1942-3, p. 309.
[4] Alan Richardson, *A Preface to Bible-Study*, p. 36.

where the highest human wisdom about God can be found, but whether there is any place in which God Himself speaks to us.'[1] It is not even what religious geniuses have to say about God which is of interest to us, but what God has to say to us. And we have become aware that the Bible is a book through which God speaks. This means that inspiration is not a proposition to which we give assent, but it is the recognition that we have in the Bible a message 'sent into the world with my name and address on it'.[2] 'Unless' therefore 'I find in the Bible God's word for me, I may be convinced that the Bible is supreme among books as a work of religion or morality or anything else, but I shall not know that it is inspired in the way in which the Christian Church has always understood the doctrine of inspiration and the authority of Holy Scripture.'[3] It is in the context of the Christian doctrine of salvation that both the inspiration and the authority find their meaning. God reveals His purpose to save men through Christ, that is the message of which the Bible is 'our only first-hand record'. Here we have the source-book of saving knowledge, the only witness to what God has done for us men and our salvation. 'Its uniqueness lies not in any special miraculous method of dictation by which it was received, nor yet in any exalted state of religious experience to which its writers attained, but in its testimony to the great things that God had done.'[4] Richardson's position is, we believe, substantially the same as that elaborated in N. H. Snaith in his Peake Memorial Lecture for 1956. Snaith's title is the *Inspiration and Authority of the Bible*, and in it he gives it as his view that both are revealed by the fidelity of the Bible to the essential idea of God as Saviour: 'The work of God the Saviour runs through the whole', he declares, and 'the Bible is all concerned with what God has done'.

It was the purpose of H. Wheeler Robinson in several of his studies to investigate the psychology of inspiration. This is, indeed, the particular end he had in view in his *Inspiration and Revelation in the Old Testament*. The prophet is to be seen as the main vehicle of the divine revelation. Revelation has 'a transcendent source', but it is only as it comes into contact with

---

[1] Alan Richardson, *A Preface to Bible-Study*, p. 37.
[2] *Ibid.*, p. 38.   [3] *Ibid.*, p. 40.
[4] *Ibid.*, p. 41. Cf. his *Christian Apologetics*, 1947, Chapter IX.

experience that it becomes possible of scientific study. 'The primary question to be answered', he says, 'is, how did the prophet himself become convinced that Yahweh was speaking to him and through him?'[1] Robinson contends that it was a fundamental belief of the Hebrews that human personality was open to invasion by some external energy or spirit. This 'invasive energy', they supposed, could take possession of the organs of the body and use any one of them 'in quasi-independence of its owner'.[2] Some of the essentials of revelation are, he asserts, 'forcibly expressed through the Hebrew psychology of inspiration in spite of what seems to us its crudity and its obvious ignorance of the true facts of physiology'.[3] Revelation begins with God and accordingly the prophet had no difficulty in believing himself to be instrumental of the divine activity. Although the ancients believed in a 'quasi-magical power' the modern psychological parallel 'is seen in artistic creation and/or scientific discovery'.[4] An important difference between aesthetic and intellectual inspiration and that experienced by the prophets is, however, to be admitted. The latter recognized the presence of a divine Person and it is this which gives to prophecy 'a peculiar and intense note of authority'.[5]

Robinson refers to what he calls 'the intuitional character of prophecy'. The term although suspect to every student of psychology and ethics and philosophy, in no way weakens but really proves the validity of the phenomenon of prophecy. It serves 'to bring out the ultimate *immediacy* of personal judgement which we have found to belong to prophecy, from its first reception by the prophets down to our own response to the record of it. Intuition is not taken here to beg the question of validity, but simply to mark that subjective feature of prophecy, and indeed of all religion, which we have again and again found to be present'.[6] The 'value-judgement' of the prophet is the ultimate psychological reality and in making it 'the prophet feels himself divinely directed to exercise his own judgement on all the medley of thought and feeling which is his'.[7] In this 'value-judgement' the total personality is involved.

[1] H. Wheeler Robinson, *Inspiration and Revelation in the Old Testament*, 1946, p. 178.
[2] *Ibid.*, pp. 181–2.   [3] *Ibid.*, p. 191.   [4] *Ibid.*, p. 192.
[5] *Ibid.*, p. 194.   [6] *Ibid.*   [7] *Ibid.*, pp. 194–5.

In his earlier contribution to *Record and Revelation*, a more precise account even is given of the divine communication as caught up in the prophet's consciousness. The divine consciousness, he there argues, is always associated with the character and historical conditions of the recipient. There is no escape from this human condition and mediation. Whatever God reveals, he declares, is revealed as part of the prophet's own consciousness and outlook. However the prophet might draw an absolute line between the divine oracle and his own reaction to it, we most certainly cannot. The 'event' which he was led to interpret as divinely controlled might mean something else to other eyes, 'there was nothing inevitable in its interpretation'. But, he contends, if God takes up a man's thought, words and deeds into the orbit of revelation, the result is not a partnership capable of analysis, but a blended unity.[1]

Much use is made by Robinson of his concept of 'intuitional judgement'. By means of it the Jewish and the Christian canon were formed. Some words are quoted from Origen to show that 'the appeal to an intuitional value-judgement is no device of yesterday invented by Coleridge when he said, "Whatever *finds* me bears witness for itself that it proceeded from a Holy Spirit" '.[2] Great stress is laid on the authority of religious experience. He argues elsewhere against the notion of a closed canon on the score that such a formal list of books is based upon the attribution to the prophet of an abnormal psychology which is made the test of inspiration. Deeper criteria must be found in which account must be taken of 'the life of the people in and through whose experience God is revealed'.[3] The Protestant cannot be satisfied with the definiteness of the Roman Church, 'he must base his own recognition of that unique quality on the intrinsic work and ministry of the books themselves, as witnessed by his own experience to their message under the guidance of the Holy Spirit'.[4] It is emphasized that this idea does

[1] H. Wheeler Robinson, *Record and Revelation*, 1938, pp. 315–6.

[2] H. Wheeler Robinson, *Inspiration and Revelation in the Old Testament*, p. 196.

[3] H. Wheeler Robinson, 'Canonicity and Inspiration', *Expository Times*, Vol. XLVII, 1935–6, p. 119. Cf. 'The Theology of the Old Testament' in *Record and Revelation*; also 'The Bible as the Word of God' in *The Bible and its Ancient and English Versions*, 1940.

[4] Cf. 'Canonicity and Inspiration', *ibid.* In our Ideas of Revelation we have noted how Brunner, like the Quaker Barclay, sees no conclusive reason to accept the idea of a 'filled-canon'. The scripture is given a 'second place' and the emphasis is on the

not make revelation merely subjective nor yet does it destroy the idea of canonicity.

H. Cunliffe-Jones joins issue here, it may be observed, with Wheeler Robinson. He contends that there is something wrong with the interpretation which allows such uncertainty concerning the canon. The authority of the Biblical writings depends upon something more than their being the finest expression of religious experience interpenetrated with the divine. Cunliffe-Jones contends for a closed canon and for the Bible as still the standard and rule of our faith and not merely the manifestation of it.[1] He refers to the question whether inspiration is something to be taken for granted *before* we study the Bible in detail and therefore as governing that study or whether it is something whose nature is strictly dependent upon an inductive study of what the contents of the Bible actually are. He maintains that a belief in inspiration is something which the Christian theologian brings with him and in this connection the summary of the position at the close of James Orr's *Revelation and Inspiration* is pronounced as still satisfactory.[2]

A. G. Hebert refuses 'to identify Inspiration with the personal insight of each writer'.[3] He prefers to attribute it 'to the Canon as a whole' and in so doing acknowledges that he is 'laying a great weight on the Canon, and asserting a providential guidance in the formation' of it.[4] Such a conclusion follows, he argues, when right emphasis is put upon the idea of God's activity in history through which men become aware of His saving purpose. 'The apprehension by men of God's revelation has been partial and imperfect; yet through His imperfect human instruments His word has been spoken. The Scripture, too, is inspired, and is imperfect; inspired because it is divine, and imperfect because it is also human.'[5] Hebert indeed insists upon the correctness of the distinction made by 'Conservative' writers between revelation and inspiration, but he thinks that the 'literal theory of inspiration' in which an identity is made

subjective. Cf. H. D. McDonald, *Ideas of Revelation*, 1959, p. 72. R. Barclay, *Apology*, tenth edition, 1841, p. 86. E. Brunner, *Revelation and Reason* (E.T. 1946), p. 132.

[1] H. Cunliffe-Jones, *The Authority of the Biblical Revelation*, 1946, second impression, 1948, p. 78.　　　　[2] *Ibid.*, p. 115.

[3] A. G. Hebert, *The Authority of the Old Testament*, 1947, p. 106.

[4] *Ibid.*　　　　[5] *Ibid.*, p. 104.

between inerrancy and inspiration ends with the unacceptable doctrine of an infallible book. On the other hand, to treat inspiration psychologically as denoting the religious experience of inspired individuals is to admit 'degrees of inspiration', and this, for Hebert is inadmissible in view of the facts. 'Yet it is obvious that there are degrees of *something*, not indeed of Inspiration, if Inspiration is co-extensive with Canonicity; but degrees of revelation, or of prophecy.'[1]

Hebert, of course, repudiates the notion of 'mechanical' inspiration as deriving, he states in a later volume, from 'pagan sources'.[2] He readily admits however, that such a 'dictation-theory' is 'repudiated by all the conservative evangelical leaders, because it leaves no room for the individuality of the human writers'.[3] It is not very clear from Hebert's two books in what precise way inspiration is to be regarded. It refers to the Canon as a whole, that we learn. But does it belong to the guidance of God by which the Church collected the separate books which make up the Bible into a whole, or to the message which is unfolded through the whole of God's saving acts and in the totality of which He speaks?[4] The word 'Church' which figures in the title of the second of his books seems to indicate that Hebert would stress the Church's part in the formation of the Canon.

The 'old view' of inspiration in which the writers were regarded as more or less unconscious instruments in the hands of God is rejected by J. W. C. Wand. According to him the inspiration of the Bible is revealed in a particular and general way: in particular passages which 'arrest the attention and stick in the memory',[5] and in the whole anthology which creates the effect of being a communication from another world—'a breath from heaven'. Wand asks the question, Where does inspiration lie, in the words or the total thought? 'It would probably be true to say', he replies, 'that the traditional answer would affirm the first, while our contemporary answer would be more likely to affirm the second.'[6] Wand finds difficulties in each view. The

[1] A. G. Hebert, *The Authority of the Old Testament*, 1947, p. 101; cf. esp. pp. 71–2.
[2] A. G. Hebert, *Fundamentalism and the Church of God*, 1957, p. 57.
[3] *Ibid.*, p. 56.
[4] Cf. A. G. Hebert, *The Authority of the Old Testament*, pp. 70 ff.
[5] J. W. C. Wand, *The Authority of the Scriptures*, 1949, p. 54.
[6] *Ibid.*, p. 55; cf. p. 60.

traditional doctrine, he thinks, tends to make every word an organ of divine revelation and to conceive of inspiration as equally distributed in every word. The inspiration of the Bible, he then declares, is the substance of which the inspiration of Virgil and Shakespeare and Goethe is the shadow. It is the merit of the 'modern view' to have shifted the 'onus of inspiration' from the book to the writer. 'We do not call a writer inspired because he has written an inspired book, but we call a book inspired because it was written by an inspired writer.'[1] Factual accuracy is no guarantee of inspiration. Acknowledging that his view of inspiration may be disappointing to some, he asserts, 'The sacred writers enjoyed no gift of infallibility'.[2]

Is the Bible Inspired? is the title-question which J. Burnaby gives to his volume in which he considers the subject. At the beginning the familiar comment is made to the effect that the assured results of criticism have rendered the traditional doctrine of inspiration impossible, and this in spite of the acknowledgement that the 'old view' was grounded in the Church's faith from the first. Burnaby discusses the idea of inspiration in pagan literature and then goes on to seek the 'marks of prophetic inspiration'.[3] The subject of the Spirit's action in the Bible is then assessed and it is contended that the 'influence of the Holy Spirit upon the soul of man is therefore rightly to be understood by analogy with the influence of person on person'.[4] Inspiration presupposes election so that 'inspired men of God are thus necessarily an élite', although they are not to be regarded as a 'moral autocracy'.[5] Their authority is not absolute since they seek to persuade not to impose. From this 'general theory' of inspiration Burnaby comes to the question of his title.

Essentially inspiration consists in the power to *see* the things, which are of God. But the general theory of inspiration to which

[1] J. W. C. Wand, *The Authority of the Scriptures*, 1949, p. 60.   [2] *Ibid.*; cf. p. 102.

[3] John Burnaby, *Is the Bible Inspired?* 1949, The Colet Library of Modern Christian Thought and Teaching (gen. ed. W. R. Matthews), pp. 53 ff.

[4] *Ibid.*, p. 80.

[5] *Ibid.*, p. 88. Cf. 'This phenomenon (inspiration) is not confined to Biblical characters, nor is the controlling power always good; it may quite well be evil. Hence it is hardly possible to speak of the Bible as inspired in any literal sense of the word. . . . Its inspiration lies wholly in the extent to which the things it says compel the assent of our conscience and our minds'. S. H. Hooke, *What is the Bible?* 1948, p. 69.

the major part of his book is devoted, 'cannot provide us with any tenable doctrine of inspiration of the Bible, unless their inspiration be found predictable of the Bible as *a coherent whole*, an organic unity'.[1] The Bible is inspired, it then appears, because it demonstrates the principle of election carried to its highest pitch. The Bible is to be held as inspired 'since it begins with the stirring of men's hearts by the Holy Ghost'.[2] Its inspiration is revealed in its message of God's saving acts which runs right through it and of which it is the record. Inspiration does not lie in any part of either the Old or the New Testament, but in the whole.[3] Men are inspired because they saw and responded to certain events as God's acts. It has nothing to do with inerrancy and infallibility. The Bible is inspired in a unique way, because it contains the interpretation which 'inspired men' gave to certain events in which they had been enabled to, and in which they enable us, to see the story of God's salvation.

In 1951 the important volume entitled *Biblical Authority for Today*, appeared, edited by Alan Richardson and W. Schweitzer. The 'tentative character of the document' was indicated in the Introduction.[4] Writers representing the several Churches contributed, and, although the main purpose is to indicate the nature of biblical authority, there are to be found statements regarding the inspiration of the Bible. Georges Floroosky, for example, maintains that the Scriptures are 'inspired' and 'are the Word of God'. He is, however, unable to say what inspiration is. There 'is a mystery therein', he says. Holy men of God heard the word of the Lord, but how they could articulate it in words of their own dialect is beyond understanding? 'Yet, even in their human transmission it was the voice of God.' The mystery and the miracle of the Bible lies in the fact that here is the Word of God in human idiom. The Scripture transmits and preserves in human words the Word of God.[5] In the same volume, Vinjamuri E. Devadutt states, 'The Bible is an inspired record of revelation. When we say it is inspired we mean that the people who share

---

[1] John Burnaby, *Is the Bible Inspired?* 1949, The Colet Library of Modern Christian Thought and Teaching (gen. ed. W. R. Matthews), p. 94 (italics in original).   [2] *Ibid.*, p. 95.   [3] *Ibid.*, p. 109.

[4] *Biblical Authority for Today* (ed. A. Richardson and W. Schweitzer), 1951, A World Council of Churches Symposium on 'The Biblical Authority for the Churches' Social and Political Message', p. 8.

[5] *Op. cit.*, p. 172.

in its writing were under the guidance of the Spirit of God. Inspiration is not verbal communication, making of the writer merely a pen for the Divine Spirit. Inspiration is that which moves and guides. It is such an inspiration of the Divine Spirit which enables the writers of the Bible to see God's activity'.[1] Clarance Tucker Craig, in his essay, likewise repudiates verbal inspiration. It is not to be found in a communication of truths nor yet is it a mere supervision of the Holy Spirit for their right formation. The 'word in book-form' like the Word incarnate constitutes the union of the two elements, the divine and the human. The 'essence of the Bible is divine, and the form human', it is declared. Inspiration is chiefly related to the essence, yet it is a matter of degrees.[2] The subject is also touched upon by W. L. Knox, who contends that the gift of the Holy Spirit does not imply that the writers of Scripture 'wrote with explicit consciousness of anything but ordinary human motives, or that they were divinely delivered from the possibility of human error'.[3] He does, however, allow that the Bible possesses an inspiration different from that which is to be found in the greatest monuments of human literature.[4]

One of the most voluminous writers on the Bible, especially on the Old Testament, in recent years, is H. H. Rowley. He has made a massive contribution, in which, we believe, it would be true to say that there can be detected a growing appreciativeness of the permanent spiritual significance of the Scriptures as a whole. In several of his books he makes passing references to the subject of inspiration, and in a couple of them he has sought to deal with it in more detail.

It seems to us that his general position is somewhat akin to that of H. Wheeler Robinson to whom he readily acknowledges his debt. Thus, having made the comment to the effect that 'Revelation is fundamentally the divine-unfolding, while inspiration lies in the use of human personality for the declaration of the message', he refers his readers, in a footnote, to Robinson's *Inspiration and Revelation in the Old Testament*.[5] In the main, Rowley regards the Bible as a record of profound religious

[1] *Biblical Authority for Today* (ed. A. Richardson and W. Schweitzer), 1951, A World Council of Churches Symposium on 'The Biblical Authority for the Churches' Social and Political Message', p. 71. [2] *Op. cit.*, p. 23.
[3] *Op. cit.*, p. 102. [4] *Op. cit.*
[5] H. H. Rowley, *The Faith of Israel*, 1956, p. 21 and footnote references.

experiences. Like other writers in the same general context he is anxious to maintain the essential human element in the sacred records. 'Few today', he states, 'regard it (i.e. the Old Testament) as a purely superhuman book, whose words bear none of the marks of the spirit of its human authors, but perfectly and exactly reflect the *ipsissima verba* of the inspiring God.'[1] The point is reiterated in a later volume in which it is declared that 'The divine inspiration came through the organ of man's personality. Though they were men who were consecrated to God and sensitive to His Spirit, they were nevertheless imperfect men, with false presuppositions and with limited outlook'.[2]

Rowley allows, too, for degrees of inspiration. 'There have been some,' he writes, 'and alas! there are still some, who regard the whole Bible as on a flat level of inspiration and authority and who make no differentiation whatever in this respect between the Old and New Testaments.'[3] He argues convincingly elsewhere for what he calls the 'dynamic unity' of the Bible, but, he insists, nevertheless, that this admission does not permit the conclusion 'that the whole Bible is on a flat level in inspiration and authority'.[4]

These references come from volumes in which Rowley does not have it as his purpose to expound the idea of inspiration. In two other books, however, he does seek to give a fuller account of his view. We shall follow what he has to say in the earlier of these two since there is no important deviation from his main thesis to be observed in his later *The Authority of the Bible*.[5]

A characteristic note is struck when Rowley asks the question in a chapter entitled 'The Prophets of the Old Testament', 'From whence did the prophets get their inspiration?'[6] A little further on the answer is given, 'it was ever from their experience of God that they found their inspiration'.[7] In an earlier chapter Rowley writes specifically on 'The Inspiration of the Bible'. The 'older view', which maintained that the divine origin of the

---

[1] *The Recovery of the Old Testament*, 1945, p. 25.
[2] *The Unity of the Bible*, 1953, p. 15.
[3] *The Recovery of the Old Testament*, p. 13.   [4] *The Unity of the Bible*, p. 14.
[5] Cf. *The Authority of the Bible*, 1950, pp. 5 ff.
[6] *The Relevance of the Bible*, 1944, p. 73. Cf. H. H. Rowley, 'The Inspiration of the Old Testament', *Congregational Quarterly*, Vol. 18, April 1940, pp. 164–77.
[7] *Op. cit.*, p. 74.

Bible guaranteed it against all error, is naturally set aside. The difficulties in it are regarded as needing 'little demonstration'. Rowley, however, proceeds to indicate certain disagreements and discrepancies in the records. The writers of the Bible were, he declares, 'real men, responsible for their writings as we are for ours'.[1] This leads him to urge that, since revelation was mediated through human personalities, it must partake of the characteristics of these personalities. 'Were the writers of the Old Testament helpless instruments in the hand of God, completely controlled by Him, the revelation would be independent of their personality, but if they were imperfect and fallible, then their imperfections and infallibilities could not but affect the revelation.'[2]

Rowley, however, expresses dissatisfaction with the view that the inspiration of the Bible is due to the writers' 'own reflection and skill and penetrating insight' by which they saw the heart of God and recorded what they saw. Men of serious spirit and clear judgement they were undoubtedly, but the notion that it was even the insight of such men, which was the source of their inspiration and authority is pronounced 'inadequate'. The prophets, indeed, made no such claim that it was a result of their own wisdom and insight that they came with their 'Thus saith the Lord' message. What they saw of God's purposes was the result of God's grace. They were not themselves the originators, but the organs, of the divine word, human though they remained and enfolded in their imperfections as was the divine word. 'The errors and the imperfections we find in no sense challenge the foundation of our faith, for that rests, not on our view of inspiration, but on a living experience of the grace of God in Jesus Christ.'[3]

Rowley refers to 'the process of inspiration'. He reiterates that, 'It was not a case of the writer's hand being supernaturally controlled to write words that came to him wholly from without'.[4] He sees the Old Testament, not as giving exact records of history, inerrant in every detail, or as authoritative revelations of the future, or even as wholly trustworthy revelations of God. It is rather a record of the experiences and thoughts of men who

---

[1] *The Relevance of the Bible*, p. 25.
[2] *Op. cit.* Cf. *The Faith of Israel*, 1957, pp. 39 and 86.
[3] *Op. cit.*, p. 36. [4] *Op. cit.*, p. 42.

reached out after God, and responded to God's reaching after them.[1]

The question comes, Is the New Testament to be regarded in the same light? Rowley thinks that it is. The idea of inspiration is fundamentally the same in the New Testament as in the Old. There is no verbal infallibility: indeed, there are here, too, inaccuracies, and reflections of the ideas and expectations of the fallible authors. The case of the New Testament is as that of the Old; each of its writers was, as Paul, 'charged with a divinely given message, but that for the form in which it was delivered he was himself responsible. He was the ambassador, not the postman'.[2] In the last, however, it is Christ who is the test of the truth and the measure of the inspiration of the Old Testament, as He is of the New. Inspiration does not elevate the letter to a place of final and unchallenged authority. The Church itself is 'the vehicle of inspiration', and consequently has, Rowley contends, an authority beside the Bible. Yet neither is an ultimate authority since both go back to Christ and derive both their inspiration and authority from Him; 'For God is Spirit, and through Spirit He speaks His final Word to us'.[3]

Two books stating similar conclusions appeared in successive years. Reference has been already made to J. K. S. Reid's *The Authority of Scripture* (1957). Reid approaches the subject from the historical point of view and seeks to state the Reformers' understanding of the matter. His conclusion is in general agreement with that of Raymond Abba's. Abba has remarks to make on the subject of inspiration, which bring him into the context of ideas with which we have been concerned. He speaks of the 'dynamic' nature of the Bible's inspiration, and contends that it 'has to do with its content rather than with its evolution'.[4] He firmly rejects the doctrine of verbal inspiration and quotes from a review of Warfield's *Inspiration and Authority of the Bible* by McIntyre the statement that the notion of plenary inspiration is 'a patent *petitio principii*'.[5] Abba is particularly anxious to insist that inspiration in no way and in no sense

---

[1] *The Relevance of the Bible*, p. 43.
[2] *Op. cit.*, p. 47.   [3] *Op. cit.*, p. 51.
[4] Raymond Abba, *The Nature and Authority of the Bible*, 1958, p. 108; cf. p. 103.
[5] *Ibid.*, p. 108. Cf. Review of Warfield, *The Reformed Theological Review*, Vol. IX, No. 2, p. 20.

curtailed the human bearers of revelation,[1] and he quotes several writers to support him.[2] Abba contends that the inspiration of the Bible is something 'felt'. 'It is through an experience of the spiritual power of the Bible' that the term inspiration 'first comes to have real meaning'.[3] Coleridge's words about the Bible finding the soul are quoted and herein is indicated the position occupied by this writer. This dictum of Coleridge's we have in fact seen stated again and again by writer after writer with whom we have been concerned in this section. It is here we have the setting for and find the key to these views of inspiration which have their focus within.[4]

The main purpose of these reconstructionist views of inspiration, it was acknowledged, was to seek a theory which would allow for the 'errors and discrepancies' which, it was urged, must be allowed in the sacred volume since its writers, whatever the degree of their dedication, were still imperfect men. At first the emphasis was put upon the view of inspiration as the penetrating insights of religious geniuses, whose thoughts about God have been preserved in the pages of the Bible. The religious genius, even in his own realm, any more than any other genius in his, is not infallible. And when he comes to make observations which fall outside his particular sphere he must be less so. In the recording of these insights there was no special act of God keeping the writer from added mistakes.

[1] The idea of man as a 'deficient instrument' in the process of inspiration was a Scholastic, not a Reformed doctrine. It was the position taken up by Aquinas. Cf. 'In the case of Prophetic Revelation, the prophet's mind is moved by the Holy Ghost in the same way as a deficient instrument is used by the principal agent.' H. Pope, A.P., of the Collegio Angelico, Rome; 'Article on the Scholastic View of Inspiration', *The Irish Theological Quarterly*, July 1911. Produced by the Professors in the Faculty of Theology, Maynooth, St Patrick's College.

[2] Raymond Abba, *The Nature and Authority of the Bible*, p. 108. Cf. T. H. Robinson, *Prophecy and the Prophets*, 1923, p. 20; H. H. Rowley, *The Relevance of the Bible*, 1944, p. 47; J. W. C. Wand, *The Authority of the Scriptures*, 1949, p. 16; James Orr, *The Faith of a Modern Christian*, 1909, p. 16; H. B. Swete, *The Holy Spirit in the New Testament*, 1909, p. 339.

[3] *Ibid.*, p. 103. Cf. J. Strachan, 'Inspiration', *Encyclopaedia of Religion and Ethics*, Vol. VII, p. 347.

[4] Cf. 'This subjective theory of inspiration (of which Schleiermacher is the father) soon found its way into this country, and although not indigenous, may now be said almost to be naturalized. We are indebted to Coleridge, more than any other, for the importation of it first, and for the currency afterwards among ourselves, of forms of expression and thought in connection with inspiration unfamiliar to British theology, and deriving from Germany.' James Bannerman, *Inspiration*, etc., 1865, p. 144. Cf. H. D. McDonald, *Ideas of Revelation*, 1959, Chapter VII.

The idea, it was noted, did not continue to satisfy. It had the result of putting the Bible apart and remote from the experiences of ordinary persons, who felt that they had no gift of religious genius and no special spiritual faculty as such. It was in this way that the claim made by many that they were giving back the Bible to everyman in a fresh and fascinating light, and in a context they could understand, was nullified.

A change of emphasis is therefore to be observed. Inspiration came to be less and less identified with the insights of religious geniuses and began to be identified more and more with the inner illumination of the Spirit of God. The Bible was then conceived to be the record of these revelations which this divine illumination assured to chosen men. Often reference was made to the Biblical teaching concerning the believers' illumination by the Holy Spirit as being an illustration of this concept of inspiration. Such an action by the Spirit, it was stressed, did not involve infallibility. In the case of those to whom we owe the Bible the process was the same, only, of course, much more intense; but even here there was no guarantee of infallibility.

It is certainly true that there is an illumination of every man by the Spirit of God. But there is also a vast and vital difference between the illuminated Christian and the inspired prophet or apostle. In the former case the Holy Spirit works to give a vivid apprehension of truth already revealed: in the latter case there is a communication of truth altogether new. It is not a question of mere difference of degree, but a difference of kind. There is a subjectiveness in the view of inspiration reviewed above which makes uncertain any sure objective standard of truth and duty. Wescott warns against failure to appreciate this objective necessity: 'if we regard inspiration only subjectively', he observes, 'we lose all sense of a fresh and living connection of the prophet with God. He remains indeed a man, but he is nothing more. He appears only to develop naturally a germ of truth which lies within him, and to draw no new supplies of grace and wisdom from without. There is no reunion of the divine and human in the soul on which a Church may rest its faith'.[1] No canons were given by which varying degrees of reliability of the record could be adjudged. In the end, the Illumination theory of inspiration seems to regard as inspired

[1] B. F. Wescott, *Introduction to the Study of the Gospels*, 1882, p. 32.

that which inspires. That which commends itself to the individual reason or conscience or moral sense is of the Holy Spirit. In this way the single individual becomes the judge of truth, and man the measure of things. Such a doctrine of inspiration has its origin in Schleiermacherian and Coleridgean subjectivism and is based on a pragmatist epistemology.

Others sought to illustrate the relation between the divine and the human in the Bible by reference to the two natures in Christ.[1] By separating the human from the divine they felt themselves able to regard the Biblical history and *Wissenschaft* as subject to the defects of human imperfections. Those who emphasize the humanity of Christ in such starkness as do Barth and Brunner can easily view the Bible, on its human side, as a very imperfect vessel in which the divine treasure is carried. The crib in which the divine Christ lay, was set there by human hands and was crude and rough and inadequate in itself. From Him who was within it has gained its glory and got its significance.

But the parallel is not rightly drawn. It was, indeed, the error of the mechanical dictation view to adopt an Apollinarian attitude with regard to the agents of divine revelation. Its advocates saw the human element, as it were, 'reduced' and the deficiency made up by the presence of the Spirit: only in this way, it was believed, could the Bible be secured from all error. This Alexandrian approach, in which exclusive emphasis was placed upon God's activity, secured the divineness of the Bible, but at the sacrifice of the obvious fact of its humanness. 'The human side of the record of Scripture, certainly, cannot be ignored. There is not, nor could be, in Divine inspiration any suppression of human genius, faculty, or individuality. Limitations in the instrument condition receptivity for the message. The treasure is in earthen vessels (II Cor. iv. 7). But the Divine moulds the human to its ends, and in the result God's strength is perfected in human weakness (II Cor. xii. 9).'[2]

---

[1] This is not really a modern illustration. Compare the remark made by James Bannerman in his *Inspiration*, etc., 1865. 'There is a remarkable parallel often noticed in connection with this controversy, between the case of the union of the divine and the human natures in the one person of Christ, and the case of inspiration' (p. 465). Cf. J. I. Packer, *'Fundamentalism' and the Word of God*, 1958, pp. 82 ff.

[2] James Orr, *The Faith of a Modern Christian*, 1910, p. 16.

I

The opposing view, with which we have been concerned, like Nestorius, set the human and the divine in juxtaposition, and introduced an unwarranted cleavage between the two. But having done so, its protagonists did not consistently apply their thesis. The divine is severed from the human so that the 'errors and mistakes' in the Bible might be allowed for, but, Does this hold in the case of Christ with whom the Scripture is brought into this analogy? The fact is, a very opposite conclusion from that desired would follow if the parallel between the two natures in Christ and the divine and the human in the Bible is to stand.

B. INSPIRATION—THE FOCUS WITHOUT

It will have been noted how consistently, and at times vehemently, the idea of a verbally inspired Bible was repudiated. The focus was within. Believing that verbal inspiration was one and the same thing with a mechanical process it was not difficult to show the considerable strain such a doctrine put upon faith. Under the pressure of a sustained attack the idea of a mechanical process of inspiration was made to look raffish. Since verbal inspiration was consistently equated with it, that too, fell into disfavour throughout the last half of the nineteenth century. To continue to assert the doctrine of verbal inspiration was due, it was maintained, to inability to meet squarely the new situation in which the Church found itself and the altered view of the Bible which honest criticism necessitated. Conservative writers, it was thought, continued to serve up the dish as a sort of spiritual réchauffé, but to men aware of the new situation, it was no longer digestible or palatable; it had lost its flavour and relish. The new day demanded a new diet.

The charge persists. 'Nowadays we call this traditional view the theory of verbal inspiration, or fundamentalism', says Alan Richardson. 'It is still met with amongst those who have not had the opportunity of sympathetically understanding the achievements of modern Biblical scholarship, and amongst those few better-educated Christians who confuse the doctrine of the Spirit in our hearts with the theory of verbal inspiration. From the second to the eighteenth century the theory was generally accepted'.[1]

[1] Alan Richardson, *A Preface to Bible-Study*, 1943, p. 25. In the 1950 edition of

It was asserted early in our period that all competent writers had become convinced that inspiration could no longer be referred to the words of Scripture. British scholars to a man, it was declared, were unable to take up the gauntlet thrown down by the opponents of inerrancy and infallibility.[1] W. R. Nicholl in a letter to James Denney under date, August 7, 1894, declared that 'the only *respectable* defenders of verbal inspiration' are 'the Princeton school of Green and Warfield'.[2]

The situation, however, is not altogether as these statements seem to suggest. It is not a fact that there were no capable writers able to defend the traditional cause, and that the victory was complete for those who had renounced the notion of a verbally inspired Bible. By no means all had fallen in line behind Coleridge. There were those who persisted, in spite of the reiterated charge of obscurantist, to urge that any theory of revelation and inspiration which limited it to thoughts and ideas is inadequate to the facts and to the necessities of the case. Such writers were not satisfied with the thesis that God had no regard for the language in which the biblical writers clothed their thoughts and embodied their ideas. Inspiration, if such there be, must penetrate words as well as thoughts, it must find its living medium in language. Inspired thought there may be, but it has no permanent significance unless it is finalized in words capable of and adequate to its transmission. Wescott was quite sure that this must be so. 'The slightest consideration', he says, 'will show that words are as essential to intellectual processes as they are to mutual intercourse. . . . Thoughts are wedded to words as necessarily as soul is to body.'[3]

There were several writers, as we shall see, who could gain nothing from their allegiance to the traditional doctrine, who were thoroughly convinced of its truth. To talk of inspired men, they maintained, was less than half the truth. What was

Chambers's Encyclopaedia, Richardson defined 'Fundamentalism' as 'the theory of biblical inspiration which regards words of the Bible as divinely dictated'. *Ad. loc.*, cf. J. I. Packer, '*Fundamentalism*' *and the Word of God*, 1958, pp. 10 ff.

[1] Cf. 'The Pentateuch Controversy', *London Quarterly Review*, Vol. LXXIII, 1890, pp. 290–1.

[2] T. H. Darlow, *William Robertson Nicholl*, 1925, p. 341.

[3] B. F. Wescott, *Introduction to the Study of the Gospels*, 1882, p. 40. Cf. D. Fraser, 'Because the Mechanical Theory of Verbal Inspiration is manifestly incorrect, it does not, however, follow that no authority attaches to the *words* of Scripture'. *The Inspiration of the Bible*, 1874, p. 72.

required, they felt, was an inspired Bible. Their opponents
limited inspiration to the men who gave us the Bible, but in
order to understand what was meant by 'inspired' men, they
investigated the meaning of the term itself as it occurs in the
Bible. They attached a significance to the very word. They
quote the words of Scripture to sustain their view that inspiration does not spread to its words and in this way proclaim their
belief that the words were only the individual's own unaided
human statement of the position. Such an idea seemed to be, not
only the elimination of all certainty, but the destruction of the
very idea of inspiration which was being maintained.

The doctrine of verbal inspiration was, as we have seen,
criticized on the score that it was essentially mechanical. But
that identification, it has been shown, was not acceptable to or
accepted by traditional writers.[1] In fact, as James Orr points
out, 'The phrase "verbal inspiration" is one to which so great
ambiguity attaches that it is now very commonly avoided by
careful writers'.[2] Lee prefers the term 'plenary', and James
Bannerman 'dynamical', although he, too, refers frequently to
plenary inspiration.[3] Both Hodge and Warfield, although they
are not prepared to discard the term 'verbal', yet insist that
it must be carefully explained. 'There is more excuse'
they say, 'for this misrepresentation because of the extremely
mechanical conceptions of inspiration maintained by many
former advocates of the term "verbal". The view, however,
we repudiate as earnestly as any of those who object to the
language in question.'[4]

[1] B. F. Wescott, *Introduction to the Study of the Gospels*, 1882, p. 40.
[2] James Orr, *Revelation and Inspiration*, 1910, reprint, 1952, p. 209.
[3] James Bannerman, *Inspiration*, etc., 1865, pp. 312 ff.
[4] Cf. James Orr, *Revelation and Inspiration*, p. 209. Cf. A. A. Hodge and B. B.
Warfield, Article 'Inspiration', *Presbyterian Review*, April 1881, p. 233. Cf. also
B. B. Warfield, *The Inspiration and Authority of the Bible*, reprint, 1948, p. 105.
Cf. 'we would take exception to the principle . . . that there is nothing which can
claim the authority of Verbal Inspiration, save words immediately dictated by the
Spirit, and in regard to the uttering of which the inspired writers were mere
machines. . . . We have no sympathy with that theory of Verbal Inspiration'.
D. Fraser, *Inspiration*, 1874, pp. 70–1. Fraser is not too happy about the use of the
word 'plenary' used as a substitute for 'verbal'. 'Different degrees of importance in
the truths revealed must not be confounded with different degrees of Inspiration'.
he writes. 'From this it follows that the phrase "Plenary Inspiration" as employed
to some writers, is inaccurate, and calculated to mislead. The qualifying adjective
plenary tends to obscure, rather than to throw light upon the subject. It lends
countenance to the erroneous notion that there are *different degrees* of Inspiration.

By insisting upon the idea of verbal inspiration the purpose was to emphasize, against the Insight Theory, that inspiration is not a natural process: and, on the other hand, to insist against the Illumination Theory that inspiration is not a partial process. Not a part of the Bible, but the Bible in all its parts is to be regarded as the Word of God. By contending that the Bible was verbally inspired interest was centred, not on the method, but the result. The idea was that the Holy Spirit so bore along the writers of the Scriptures that their words are to be regarded as in a very real sense His words. Peake had stated that the new theory of Inspiration sought to give 'hearty recognition to the human element'. The traditional writers replied that they did not obscure the human element, but they were anxious to give hearty recognition to the divine element. It was, then, the specific purpose of the writers we are now to review to contend for the objectivity of inspiration. Here, in contrast with the Insight or Illumination view, the focus was without. The Bible itself is regarded as an inspired Book.

Before the date from which our investigation commenced, there appeared two important volumes in which it was closely argued that inspiration has only valid significance if it relates to the words of Scripture. In 1830 came Robert Haldane's *The Verbal Inspiration of the Scriptures Established*, and twenty-four years later William Lee's *Inspiration of the Holy Scripture*. Lee's work has remained as a classic, and within a few years after our period it had reached its fourth edition. 'The Bible presents to us,' he premises, 'in whatever light we regard it, two distinct elements: the Divine and the Human.'[1] There is, he argues, a divinely given revelation and there is a conveyance of that revelation in human language by the men specially chosen for

All Inspiration is plenary, that is, full and complete, or it is no inspiration at all. We are free to acknowledge great and striking diversities in the mode or process of Inspiration, and also different degrees of importance in the truths revealed; but as to their inspired authority, they are all on a level. All are true and their Inspiration by the Spirit is the guarantee of their truthfulness' (*op. cit.*, pp. 65–6).

Cf. '. . . unfortunately, the view of Verbal Inspiration has so often been associated with dictation, that as soon as it is mentioned, it is in many quarters at once branded "mechanical", and that hard word is made to do duty for argument—indeed, it is thought there is no need for arguing with us or considering our belief. We repudiate as strongly as any the idea of "mechanical" in this connection . . .'. A. McCaig, *The Grand Old Book*, Being Lectures on Inspiration and the Higher Criticism, 1894, second edition, p. 168.

[1] William Lee, *Inspiration of the Holy Scripture*, 1854, fourth edition, 1865, p. 18.

the purpose. There has been, he notes, a tendency to accentuate the divine element at the expense of the human and to end up in a 'docetic view' of inspiration, to quote the later words of Dorner. On the other hand, of recent years, the human side has been over-stressed. This has been done by those who have 'changed the formula "The Bible *is* the Word of God", into "The Bible *contains* the Word of God", and by all, who like Daniel Wilson,[1] argue for "degrees of inspiration", as well as by those who follow Schleiermacher in regarding the Bible "as having the sole power of conveying a Revelation to man by awakening and elevating his religious consciousness" '.[1]

Lee lays down two conditions which need to be satisfied in any true doctrine of inspiration. First of all due emphasis must be given to the human element in Scripture. The writers of Scripture did not resign both body and mind to God in a passive manner.[2] They were God's penmen, not His pens. A purely mechanical theory fails to do justice to the human element. Lee contends for a 'dynamical' view in which, he declares, 'the divine and human elements, mutually interpenetrating and combined, form one vital, organic whole: not mechanically, still less ideally, but as it has been termed, *dynamically* united'.[3] The second condition to be satisfied is the necessity of drawing a distinction between revelation and inspiration. Revelation is a direct communication from God to man of a knowledge, which is otherwise beyond man's natural sagacity or reason to acquire or discover. Inspiration is the 'actuating energy of the Holy Ghost, in whatever degree or manner it may have been exercised, guided by which the human agents chosen by God have *officially* proclaimed His will by word of mouth, or have committed to writing the several portions of the Bible'.[4]

Lee carries through the discussion of these two conditions. 'The human element', he insists, 'instead of being supressed, becomes an integral part of the agency employed: moulded, it is true, and guided, and brought into action, by the co-operation of the Spirit; but not the less really, on that account, participating in the result produced.'[5] He argues that the 'dynamical' theory,

[1] William Lee, *Inspiration of the Holy Scripture*, 1854, fourth edition, 1865, p. 20 Cf. Daniel Wilson, *Evidences of Christianity*, 1828.
[2] *Ibid.*, p. 21.   [3] *Ibid.*, p. 26
[4] *Ibid.*, pp. 27–8.   [5] *Ibid.*, p. 146.

however, is not sufficient to account for all the phenomena which the Bible presents. It satisfies the first condition mentioned. We must, therefore, he continues, seek for a second principle to meet the demands of the second condition. Here he returns to a discussion of the relation between revelation and inspiration, and suggests that there are instances of divine communications not having been committed to writing for some time after they were received, in some cases, indeed, only after the lapse of several years. In such instances, it must be granted, the Holy Spirit acted 'to bring the original communication before the mind of the sacred writer, in its primitive perfection, and to enable him to record it with infallible accuracy'.[1] By using the distinction between revelation and inspiration, Lee can argue further that what some regard as errors or imperfections in the Bible as God's revelation are nothing of the kind. They are indeed 'nothing more than historical details which have been inserted as simple matters of fact in the Scripture narrative, under the guidance of its Divine Author'.[2] Lee maintains that the impartation of the Holy Spirit to the Apostles was for the purpose of rendering them, in their official teaching, infallible organs of the Truth.[3] In their case the influence of the Spirit was 'absolute, unique, and *specifically* different from those preventing and assisting graces of the Holy Ghost which have been the gift of Christ to His Church'.[4] The Scripture, it is concluded, is the result of this absolute, unique, and specifically different movement of the Spirit in the experiences of God's chosen vehicles for the perpetuation of revelation in written form.

It is not possible in short compass to do justice to the massive volume of nigh on 600 pages in which James Bannerman, Professor of Theology at New College, Edinburgh, states and defends his high view of inspiration. There is evidence that this book profoundly influenced such giants in theology as James Orr and A. H. Strong. Bannerman maintained that the difference between an inspired and an uninspired Bible is the same as that between a divine and a human faith.[5] He sets down the proposition 'that inspiration in its results comprehends these two

---

[1] William Lee, *Inspiration of the Holy Scripture*, 1854, fourth edition, 1865, p. 149.   [2] *Ibid.*, p. 150.   [3] *Ibid.*, p. 242.
[4] *Ibid.*
[5] James Bannerman, *The Infallible Truth and Divine Inspiration of the Holy Scriptures*, 1865, pp. 96 ff.

ideas—namely, the *infallible truth* and the *divine authority* of everything which the inspired man asserts or sanctions as true'.[1] Having argued that an inspired Bible gives faith an objective basis and a sure ground, he goes on to insist that faith without such a foundation stands in the wisdom of men.

Bannerman refers to the two propositions which, when taken together, exhibit, he says 'the substance of the immemorial and all but universal doctrine of the Church of Christ in regard to the inspired Scriptures'.[2] In the first place, the Scriptures contain a communication of truth from God supernaturally given to man: and in the second place, they contain that truth supernaturally transferred to human language, and therefore free from all mixture or addition of error.[3] Revelation has reference to the first of these processes and inspiration to the second. The mode of revelation is, he contends, inexplicable. It is, however, essentially objective and is finally co-extensive with the Scripture. Inspiration he conceives of as a supernatural power of God, which enables the prophet unerringly and without failure to transfer the revelation given to him to permanent written form.[4] This means that inspiration is itself supernatural[5] and finally inexplicable as to its mode.[6] Bannerman joins issue with the subjective idea of revelation advocated by Coleridge, Maurice, Arnold, Hare, Morell, MacNaughton and others. They reject verbal inspiration and yet retain the term for that which is hardly anything more than a mere sharpened insight or an increased illumination. Bannerman, however, sees that the term verbal inspiration can be misunderstood, since it may be equated with the idea of a mechanical process and thus 'open to the objection of being inconsistent with the free exercise of the faculties of the writers according to their ordinary laws'.[7] It is for this reason he prefers the term 'dynamical', but he is still sure that the words of Scripture are really words which the Holy Spirit has given. Bannerman is convinced that the Scripture itself establishes that inspiration is supernatural and plenary. He therefore proceeds to an investigation of both Testaments. At the end of a long and thorough research, he concludes that the

[1] James Bannerman, *The Infallible Truth and Divine Inspiration of the Holy Scriptures*, 1865, p. 94 (italics in original).

[2] *Ibid.*, p. 149.   [3] *Ibid.*, pp. 149–50.

[4] *Ibid.*, p. 214.   [5] *Ibid.*; cf. pp. 218 ff.   [6] *Ibid.*; cf. pp. 243 ff.

[7] *Ibid.*, p. 246.

Bible is a product of a two-fold authorship—God's and man's. It is of God and it is by man. And in neither case is there a deficiency. Here all the human is divine and all the divine is human.[1] 'The supernatural and the natural, each in its peculiarity and entireness—the divine and human, both in their fulness and freedom—the objection from without, and the subjection from within—must be combined to make up a Bible such as we actually have it. The divine idea coming down from God, and true as it came from Him, must meet with the human idea fresh from the heart of man, and purified from its imperfections; and the two must become one in order to constitute the inspired Scripture.'[2]

Placed beside the substantial tome of Bannerman's, the work by Donald Fraser constitutes a slender volume, but it is, none the less, marked by deep thought and sincere conviction. The substance of what he has to say, had already been delivered as lectures to the students of Airdale College, of which Fraser was President and theological Tutor. Fraser boldly asserts verbal inspiration, but he is careful to distinguish what he means by this from any mechanical notion.[3] Inspiration is not to be confused with genius since the inspiration of Scripture belongs essentially to 'the economy of grace'.[4] Fraser maintains that the important issue in connection with inspiration is not to determine its mode or manner, but rather, 'With what authority does it invest the truth revealed, and what moral obligation does that truth, in consequence, lay upon us?' In other words, 'What has an inspired record that any other truthful record has not?'[5] He is, however, emphatic that, as regards the mode, the idiosyncrasies of each writer are manifest. The human is certainly there.[6] The question is then, Where is the evidence of the divine? In the direction of the minds of the writers of the choice of those words to convey the truth to subsequent generations. Fraser insists upon this. 'The *words*', he says, 'as they exist in the record, reveal to us the mind of the Spirit, and come with His seal as to their truthfulness.'[7] As he sees it, the words of Scripture are God's words, however mysterious the mode of their giving must

[1] James Bannerman, *The Infallible Truth and Divine Inspiration of the Holy Scriptures*, 1865, pp. 96 ff.; cf. pp. 418 ff.   [2] *Ibid.*, pp. 449–50.
[3] D. Fraser, *Inspiration of the Bible*, 1874; cf. pp. 54 f., 62 f. and 72 f.
[4] *Ibid.*, p. 37.   [5] *Ibid.*, p. 39.   [6] *Ibid.*, p. 53.
[7] *Ibid.*, p. 46.

remain. Fraser refers to what unsatisfactory conclusions a denial of this must inevitably lead. He then deals with objections to his position on the score that anything partaking of the character of verbal inspiration means the turning of the writers of the Bible into human ventriloquists and automaton poets. The objection holds only if the idea of verbal inspiration be identified with a mechanical process; and this Fraser denies. 'Because the Mechanical theory of Verbal Inspiration is manifestly incorrect, it does not, however, follow that no authority attaches to the *words* of Scripture.'[1] Fraser rejects the idea of degrees of inspiration and concluded that the Bible is inspired 'not in special portions merely, but in its entirety'.[2]

One of the strongest statements of the traditional view of inspiration comes in the Carey Lectures of 1884 by Robert Watts, Professor of Systematic Theology at the Assembly's College, Belfast. Watts, one of the contributors to the *Lex Mosaica*, among his several volumes had already written one on *The Newer Criticism and the Analogy of Faith* (1882), which is referred to in a subtitle as '*A Reply to the Lectures of W. Robertson Smith on the Old Testament and the Jewish Church*'. In the Carey Lectures, he first set about establishing the Bible to be the Protestant rule of faith. 'To serve us as a rule of faith and life', he then argues, 'the Scriptures must be infallible, and to be infallible they must be the Word of God, and to be the Word of God they must be Divinely Inspired'.[3] The question of inspiration is then discussed. The Bible is θεόπνευστος, 'God-breathed'. Watts contends that the inspiration extends to the language employed. He is not too happy about the adequacy of the epithet 'plenary'—'it is best to employ the term Verbal Inspiration', he avers, 'which properly understood expressed the doctrine of Scripture on this subject'.[4] Christ's support is claimed for this view. The apostles, it will be agreed, were inspired preachers, but, if inspired as preachers, 'how much more so as writers'.[5] New Testament passages, such as Matt. v. 17–18; John x. 33–36; II Tim. iii. 16, etc. are adduced as proof of the inspiration of the Old Testament Scriptures. Watts meets objections to the doctrine of verbal inspiration. It is not to be

[1] D. Fraser, *Inspiration of the Bible*, 1874, p. 72.   [2] *Ibid.*, p. 86.
[3] Robert Watts, *The Rule of Faith and the Doctrine of Inspiration*, 1885, p. 90.
[4] *Ibid.*, p. 97.   [5] *Ibid.*, p. 135.

equated with dictation, he asserts. Commenting on the term 'verbal inspiration' he observes, 'By the opponents of the theory, it is very commonly understood to teach that the Holy Spirit dictated to the inspired speaker or writer the words he was to employ. This is an idea entertained by no intelligent advocate of the doctrine in the present day.'[1] In this connection he pronounces Coleridge's statement in his *Confessions of an Inquiring Spirit* to the effect that the writers of Scripture in the view of the advocates of verbal inspiration were 'successively transformed into automaton compositors' as unjustified. The sacred writers, he adds, were not 'pens' but 'penmen'.[2] Watts pays special attention to the argument concerning the free quotation of the Old Testament by the New Testament writers. He sees this, not as a disproof of his conclusion, but as evidence of the sovereignty of the inspiring Spirit. In his last lecture he stresses, in defence of the 'Westminster Standards' against the criticism of William Lee that faith in Scripture as the Word of God must necessarily find its authentication by the inner witness of the Spirit. The Scripture is the instrument of the Spirit, Watts argues.[3] 'In substance and in form, then,' he concludes, 'the Bible is Divine. The Spirit of God has determined its matter and fashioned its mould.'[4] It is consequently the Word of God, 'a Divinely determined record, whose contents have been selected by the Holy Ghost, and recorded "not in the words which man's wisdom teacheth, but in words which the Holy Ghost teacheth" '.[5]

One of the most controversial books of the period dealing with the subject of inspiration was Alfred Cave's *The Inspiration of the Old Testament Inductively Considered*. This volume of just on 500 pages by the Principal of Hackney College constitutes the Seventh Congregational Union Lectures. Cave refers to the importance of the theme, as shown by a historical survey, in the Introductory Lecture. He points to the 'indefiniteness, if not disrepute, into which the Doctrine of Inspiration has fallen in many quarters'.[6] He notes how as a result of the heat and passion of Coleridge's attack upon the doctrine of mechanical

---

[1] Robert Watts, *The Rule of Faith and the Doctrine of Inspiration*, 1885, pp. 166-7.
[2] *Ibid.*, p. 172.   [3] *Ibid.*, p. 267.
[4] *Ibid.*, p. 270.   [5] *Ibid.*, p. 273.
[6] Alfred Cave, *The Inspiration of the Old Testament Inductively Considered*, 1888, second edition, p. 12.

inspiration, 'A great vagueness' 'has fallen of late upon all deliberate statements concerning inspiration. Men know what theory they disbelieve; they do not know how to express their belief in a theory.'[1]

Cave discusses his subject under two headings. He seeks first to gather the data for, and then, to elaborate a doctrine of, inspiration. His inquiry is to follow the inductive, as distinct from the dogmatic, method.[2] Three lectures are given to a consideration of the Book of Genesis. The subject of the Law, its authorship and divine origin, takes up two more, while the divine origin of prophecy is the burden of lecture seven. Throughout Cave shows himself a convinced and hearty believer in the supernatural. Revelation is no mere human discovery: there is a real divine self-disclosure. The Law and the Prophets alike, not only in the revelation which they give, but no less in the records of their revelation, reveal a supernatural origin. Inspiration, indeed, is involved in revelation. 'As the Inspiration of Moses is the pledge of the Inspiration of the Books of Moses, so the Inspiration of the prophets is the guarantee of the Inspiration of the Books of the Prophets.'[3] The prophets were inspired organs of divine revelation and when such inspired men committed their communication from heaven to writings 'the literary product was an inspired product'.

Having disposed of the Law and the Prophets with the assurance that they are inspired in regard to both the revelation and the record, Cave turns to deal with the third section of the Bible, the Graphia or Hagiographia. In contrast with the prophets who present us with a record of a progressive revelation, from Moses to Malachi, the Holy Writings *present us with a record*, not of revelation, but *of the assimulation of revelation*.[4] In the Graphia, we have a mirror of life in God. Here is portrayed religion, not revelation. Cave compares the Psalms with Isaiah. Both are exalted poetry: but whereas the Psalter is lyric, Isaiah is didactic. The Psalter depicts subjective experience: Isaiah describes objective revelation: 'If Isaiah details experience, it is in order to emphasize revelation; if the Psalter dwells upon revelation, it is to accentuate experience'.[5]

---

[1] Alfred Cave, *The Inspiration of the Old Testament Inductively Considered*, 1888, second edition, p. 12. [2] *Ibid.*; cf. pp. 17 ff.
[3] *Ibid.*, p. 439. [4] *Ibid.*, p. 455 (italics in original). [5] *Ibid.*

Reviewing what his study of the data has revealed, Cave emphasizes first of all that there can be no doubt about the human element in the Old Testament. This, indeed, has been taken for granted throughout his inquiry.[1] But 'the question of questions', as he puts it, 'which has engrossed us from the first has been, whether human causes suffice to explain the existence of the Old Testament'.[2] Cave contends that the inductive inquiry has made it abundantly clear that a supernatural cause is required for the Old Testament. It could never have been produced without divine assistance. Moses and the Prophets and the saints who wrote its several parts were 'fellow-workers with Deity'. This brings him to discuss the different kinds of inspiration. There is an inspiration, a co-operation of God with men which sustains life (cf. Gen. vi. 3). There is, also, an inspiration, as illustrated in the case of Bezaleel, which imparts excellence of intellect (cf. Ex. xxiv. 1–5). A special gift of ethnic prophecy was bestowed on Balaam (cf. Num. xxiv. 2). Believers, too, are subjects of divine inspiration, and there is, besides, an inspiration which blends masses of individuals who possess the Christian consciousness into one great organism.[3] He then asks is it possible to find the differentia which may distinguish the Inspiration which resulted in the Old Testament from other varieties of inspiration. Several kinds of inspiration are to be observed: first the Hagiographic type or the co-operation of the divine with man which issued in the assimulation of revelation.[4] This type of inspiration underlies every book in the Old Testament.[5] Prophetic inspiration enabled the prophets to be the media of revelation;[6] while, what he calls Transcriptive inspiration worked upon the authors so that, in co-operation with the Holy Spirit, they were led to preserve the communication they had received in written form. In this two processes can be observed: first, the inspired act of committal to writing, and second, the superintendence which imparted adequacy and faithfulness.[7] Cave adds a note on Canonical inspiration which is defined as 'that co-operation of the Holy Ghost which prompted the formation of the Canon'.[8] The sum

---

[1] Alfred Cave, *The Inspiration of the Old Testament Inductively Considered*, 1888, second edition, p. 12; cf. p. 457.   [2] *Ibid.*

[3] *Ibid.*; cf. pp. 460 ff.   [4] *Ibid.*, pp. 462 ff.   [5] *Ibid.*; cf. p. 477.

[6] *Ibid.*; cf. pp. 477 ff.   [7] *Ibid.*, p. 478.   [8] *Ibid.*, p. 495.

of the matter is this: 'Inspiration is a co-operation of the Holy
Ghost with the spirit of man, guaranteeing reliableness of the
record'.[1] Cave adds that inspiration assures the substantial truth
of the record: this is the result to which the inductive inquiry
leads. 'That the record is absolutely devoid of mistakes we do
not know; the record is a human record of the Divine; but that
the record is substantially true, is veracious, trustworthy, and
historical, our whole inquiry has shown. It has also shown the
need of the greatest caution before errors are attributed to the
Old Testament.'[2]

As was to be expected, Cave's book was vigorously attacked.
His hostility to the new criticism was well known. He had
already revealed his opposition to the Graf-Wellhausen hypothesis and had bravely sought to demolish the arguments by
which Robertson Smith sought to make it acceptable in Britain.[3]
In the changing and challenging situation in which Cave found
himself, he could not hope for mercy from his opponents. And he
certainly did not get it. In their estimation he was fighting a
losing battle, and in spite of his reputation for scholarship, was
defending an obscurantist position. His thesis was ridiculed and
riddled. A recent writer states bluntly and unsympathetically
that Cave's work 'is a travesty on scholarship'.[4]

Weaknesses in Cave's position cannot be denied. It was
charged against him by a writer in the *Spectator* that his treatment of the critics was unfair. There is no doubt about his
knowledge of them, but it was contended that he quoted only
such statements as suited his purpose.[5] It was naturally
declared that his effort merely revealed the inability of
traditionalists to come to grips with the real issues and to admit
the humanness of the record and cease to talk about an inspired
Bible.[6] There was, however, evident enthusiasm by others

[1] Alfred Cave, *The Inspiration of the Old Testament Inductively Considered*, 1888,
second edition, p. 12.   [2] *Ibid.*, p. 496.
[3] Cf. Alfred Cave, 'The latest Phase of the Pentateuch Question', *British and
Foreign Evangelical Review*, Vol. XXIX, 1880, pp. 248–67; 'Professor Robertson
Smith and the Pentateuch', *ibid.*, pp. 593–621.
[4] Willis B. Glover, *Evangelical Nonconformity and the Higher Criticism in the
Nineteenth Century*, 1954, p. 189; cf. p. 190, etc.
[5] Cf. 'The Inspiration of the Old Testament', *Spectator*, Vol. LXI, 1888, p. 1330.
[6] Cf. Review of Cave's *Inspiration of the Old Testament*, *Academy*, Vol.
XXXVI, 1889, p. 252; cf. *London Quarterly Review*, Vol. LXXIII, 1890,
pp. 270–1.

because of Cave's boldness, on the one hand, in admitting the legitimacy of criticism, and, on the other hand, because, acquainted though he was with the Graf-Wellhausen theory, he rejected its validity and sought to reconstruct a view of Scripture in the context of biblical criticism more akin to the traditionalist position.[1]

Only a passing reference needs to be made to Francis F. Sharr's Fernly Lectures delivered in Nottingham, July 31, 1891, on the subject *The Inspiration of the Holy Scriptures*. Although this lecture comes some months after the one by W. T. Davidson, to which reference has already been made, it is significant for the reason that Sharr maintained the traditional doctrine of Scripture. A review of Sharr's statement is given in an edition of the *London Quarterly Review* for 1892.[2] This periodical had become less conservative with the years and consequently Sharr's view, in which the inerrancy of the Bible was defended, was not too enthusiastically received.

He 'has the ability to make even that which we now consider the extreme of conservatism seem not only the most reasonable, but the only possible position';[3] such is the statement made concerning James Macgreggor's *Revelation and the Record*. Macgreggor, sometime Professor of Systematic Theology in New College, Edinburgh, was nothing if not an exact scholar.

It was Macgreggor's conviction that the supernaturalism of the Bible's inspiration and the divinity of its authorship are one and the same reality. 'We will avoid', he says, 'as ambiguous the expression "verbal inspiration", and will proceed simply on the view that inspiration of a scripture means authorship of the (written) *word*. About any other kind of "verbal" inspiration— e.g. of the printer's ink?—we will not inquire. Nor will we inquire whether there can be any "literal" inspiration which is not "verbal".'[4]

Revelation, Macgreggor makes quite clear, is a different thing from its record. And he admits the possibility that though the revelation be divine, the record might be merely human. Indeed,

---

[1] *Congregational Review*, 11, 1888, p. 1058; *ibid*. n.s.1, 1889, p. 89, etc.
[2] *London Quarterly Review*, Vol. LXXVII, 1892, pp. 358-9.
[3] *Expository Times*, Vol. V, 1893-4, p. 85.
[4] James Macgreggor, *The Revelation and the Record*, 1893, p. 79 (italics in original).

it might be conceivable as an 'ideal possibility' that there should have been no record at all. But it is not in fact so. Macgreggor then seeks to justify his thesis of the divineness of the Bible's authorship. This leads him to deal with the question of whether there are errors and mistakes in the Scriptures. There can be no evasion at this point, he declares. But he contends that to suppose that infallibility has reference only to mysterious doctrines, and not to plain facts, *is* a form of evasion. 'Nor is there escape in merely harping on misconstructions of the doctrine of inspiration, as if it had meant that the printer's ink is infallible, or that the inspiration is in the "letter" *as distinct* from the spirit, while in fact *it is the spirit in the letter*. These are not ways of real escape from the difficulty, but may be ways of concealing, from ourselves or others, *denial of the fact of divine* inspiration.'[1]

Macgreggor repudiates the assertion of Rothe that emphasis upon the divinity of Scripture means an undervaluation of its humanity. Analogy with the Person of Christ is made, but the analogy must be consistently applied. The doctrine of a mechanical inspiration is also anathema to Macgreggor. The notion that the human is overborne by or submerged in Deity is 'a heathenish conception'. The Christian view of inspiration is something other than this. The mechanical view must be 'not only repelled as false, but revolted from as profane'. 'The imputation of that conception', adds Macgreggor, 'to Christians by whom it is repudiated is a shameful calumny.'[2]

Phrases such as the human authors of the Scriptures being 'pens of God, flutes of the Holy Spirit' have been used. But such statements, Macgreggor contends, do not mean that inspiration makes men to be merely passive organs of divine utterances. They are employed simply to describe the 'complete possession and use of the producing human writer's faculties by the Deity inspiring the Scripture produced'.[3] Of course the exact process is a 'mystery' and we have to accept the mystery unless we reject the fact. Inspiration had the effect upon, for example, the writer's judgement and memory. And it issued in an inspired utterance. These are two facts which Macgreggor strives to maintain. 'The divine possession is not a supersession, but the contrary', he says. 'What it involves is, not effacement or suspension of a creature's

---

[1] James Macgreggor, *The Revelation and the Record*, 1893, pp. 89–90.
[2] *Ibid.*, p. 95.   [3] *Ibid.*, p. 96.

free individuality (II Cor. iii. 17), but a completed fulness of God-given freedom for the individual. A pen*man* cannot be *merely* a man. But a man whom God employs as penman may be a *man-pen* of God ("Rabbi" Duncan). His being *God's* pen ensures his being completely free in all the writing; for, "where the Spirit of the Lord is, there is liberty". He is in full exercise of his own distinctive human individualities; for it is *this individual* man that is employed. A human flute of the divine Spirit is a man whose whole distinctive individuality is, *because employed* divinely, therefore most vividly alive and free; as were the dry bones in Ezekiel's valley when the Spirit breathed upon them (cf. Gen. ii. 7) to make them a great *army* (of *machines?*).'[1]

Macgreggor goes out of his way to state his belief in verbal inspiration. There is, in fact, he thinks, no other which has significance and permanent reality. 'Those who imagine', he writes, 'that there can be an inspiration of a Scripture that is *not* a "verbal" inspiration may have some notion of divine "ideas" floating in the air, like "songs without words", when men are talking like Moses and Elias on the Mount of Transfiguration. The world's greatest master of wisdom in song has a stricter conception of the relation of ideas of a Scripture to its words. To his apprehension—as in Justin Martyr's experience—so long as the ideas are only in the air—while "the poet's eye, in a frenzy rolling, doth glance from heaven to earth, from earth to heaven" they are but "airy nothings", as of "imagination bodying forth the forms of things unknown". That which fixes them (*Americanism*) [*sic*] "turns them to shape", "gives them local habitation and a name", so that (cp. John xiv. 22–4) we may apprehend them and they abide with us, is "the poet's *pen*".'[2]

The title, *The Grand Old Book*, put by Archibald McCaig to his volume of lectures given to the students of Pastor's (now Spurgeon's) College, of which he was the Principal was, perhaps, unfortunate. It might be supposed by some, not aware of the facts, that the author was a ranter or obscurantist. But McCaig was by no means either of these. By qualifying the title with the epexegetical addition, 'Lectures on Inspiration and the

[1] James Macgreggor, *The Revelation and the Record*, 1893, p. 96 (italics in original). Cf. A footnote to this passage which states: 'It is the *Scripture* that is inspired: the human writer is *employed* in producing it' (p. 96, footnote).

[2] *Ibid.*, pp. 109–10 (italics in original).

Higher Criticism', McCaig gave a better statement of his purpose. 'I have specially considered the views of the Critics as set forth in the writings of the representatives of the school in this country', he writes in the Preface to the first edition. 'Dr W. Robertson Smith, Dr Driver, Dr Cheyne, and Dr Horton, for although the last-named has produced no work specifically on the Higher Criticism, yet just as the before-mentioned trio have popularized the critical theories among students, so Dr Horton has endeavoured to familiarize the "common people" with the results of these theories.'[1]

McCaig conceived authority and inspiration to be one and the same reality. In the first four chapters Christ's authority is asserted against the critics as establishing the 'plenary and verbal' inspiration of the Old Testament, and their consequent veracity and accuracy. Several chapters follow in which the use of the Old Testament by the apostolic writers is claimed to yield the same result. 'We do not wish to twist the Scriptures to agree with our doctrine, but we hold the doctrine because, from repeated examination, we believe the Scriptures teach it.'[2] The fact of inspiration is patent all through the Bible,[3] and, he maintains 'we have not only the fact of the Inspiration of the *men* thus declared, but also the fact of *the Inspiration of the Book* indicated'.[4] It is not that holy men *thought* as they were moved by the Spirit, but they *spake*: not only were the *ideas* Spirit-given, but the verbal expression was under the direction of the Spirit.[5]

McCaig argues that, not only is the fact of inspiration everywhere evident in the Bible, but that there is also a clear account given of its form. The forms were, indeed, many and varied; by vision and dream and so forth: 'but in all these varied forms it was God who spake; it was a Divine message that reached the heart of the inspired man'.[6] The essence throughout was the same, so that the whole Book is the voice of God to us. 'No theory of Inspiration', he then premises, 'can be complete which does not take account of all the facts.' McCaig enumerates certain theories which he considers inadequate precisely in this respect. There is the Naturalistic or Ordinary view in which

---

[1] A. McCaig, *The Grand Old Book, Being Lecturers on Inspiration and the Higher Criticism*, 1894, second edition, Preface, p. vi.

[2] *Ibid.*, p. 2. Cf. chapter on 'Inspiration' in his *Doctrinal Brevities*, 1923.

[3] *Ibid.*; cf. p. 139.   [4] *Ibid.*, p. 140 (italics in original).

[5] *Ibid.*, p. 158 (italics in original).   [6] *Ibid.*, p. 163.

inspiration of the sacred writers is thought to differ only in degree from the inspiration of genius. In the Intermittent, or, as Farrar prefers to call it, the Illumination theory, reference is made to degrees of inspiration with the result that the individual finds it difficult, if not impossible, to decide which portions were perfectly, and which imperfectly, inspired. The Partial or Essential theory is also set aside because it confines inspiration to matters of doctrine and morality, and above all, matters of faith. A distinction is drawn between the Bible and the Word of God 'contained' in it. McCaig argues that doctrine, morality and matters of faith are so embedded in the historical, biographical and descriptive parts of Scripture that one cannot consistently attribute inspiration to the one element and deny it to the other.

In more detail McCaig protests against the Mechanical or Organic, sometimes called the Dictation theory. It is certainly right in declaring that inspiration is verbal, but it does not sufficiently recognize the human element.[1] He calls his own view, the Dynamical, or, as it is often called, Plenary—the more exact term, he then declares, is Plenary and Verbal.[2] It is plenary because 'full', and 'if the Inspiration is really "full", it must extend to the *words*, and so be also *verbal*'.[3] Under the possession of the Divine *Afflatus*, the speaker and writer retain the full and free use of their faculties. The man is not a machine, but a God-controlled man.[4] But inspiration relates essentially to the final product. 'There is', he states, 'no doctrine of Scripture but what is built upon *words*.'[5]

In part two of his volume, McCaig seeks to defend his doctrine from criticism. He meets such objections as, for example, the 'Alleged Impossibility of a Book Revelation',[6] and the immorality of the Old Testament,[7] as well as the assertion of incorrect historical and scientific statements,[8] and discrepancies and contradictions.[9] A discussion of variations in the quotations from the Old Testament in the New, and Paul's 'so-called disclaimer of inspiration' comes in Chapter XV. McCaig urges

---

[1] A. McCaig, *The Grand Old Book, Being Lectures on Inspiration and the Higher Criticism*, 1894, second edition, p. 165. McCaig returns again and again to a denial that verbal inspiration is mechanical. Cf. pp. 167–8, 170, etc.

[2] *Ibid.*, p. 166.   [3] *Ibid.* (italics in original).

[4] *Ibid.*, p. 170.   [5] *Ibid.*, p. 184.   [6] *Ibid.*; cf. pp. 187 ff.

[7] *Ibid.*; cf. pp. 204 ff.   [8] *Ibid.*; cf. pp. 225 ff.   [9] *Ibid.*; cf. pp. 246 ff.

that 'The same Spirit which inspired the Old Testament inspired the writers of the New to quote the Old in the way they have quoted it'.[1] McCaig is sure that the admission of various readings in Manuscripts, and possible errors in transmission do not affect the position. He is not in the least 'opposed to legitimate criticism'. Indeed he welcomes it.[2] But he contends that 'while we speak of the inspiration of the original, we are not speaking of something which is hopelessly lost, and forever out of reach'.[3] God may well have permitted the loss of the original autographs lest, as in the case of the brazen serpent in Israel, idolatry might have resulted: 'if these manuscripts had been in existence, they would have been elevated into a kind of Christian Palladium; and as every supposed relic of the Saviour has been worshipped, so there would have been in reality what our opponents are fond of attributing to us—Bibliolatry'.[4] McCaig regards belief in verbal inspiration to have been the faith of the Church from the first, and he considers himself, and those who maintain the same position as himself, to be in the apostolic succession. The doctrine of the Plenary and Verbal inspiration of Scripture, he adds, in conclusion, is 'the doctrine upon which this College (of which he is the Principal) was founded and glories in proclaiming' and 'the doctrine fought for by our honoured Founder and President'.[5]

John Urquhart in his volume of 576 pages not only maintains, as was noted earlier, the inerrancy of Scripture, but contends that verbal inspiration has always been the presupposition and doctrine of the Church. 'Let men say what they will about "the absurdity" of Verbal Inspiration, no one can deny that every creed of Christendom had been hammered out upon that anvil.'[6] By its words is the Scripture really judged. It is the working hypothesis of all Christian teaching, that it is the words of the Bible which convey with intention and precision the mind of God. 'In other words,' he says, 'to use a well-known phrase, the common basis of study, teaching, and argument has been belief in the "Verbal Inspiration" of the Bible.'[7]

---

[1] A. McCaig, *The Grand Old Book*, Being Lectures on Inspiration and the Higher Criticism, 1894, second edition, p. 301.
  [2] *Ibid.*; cf. p. 304.   [3] *Ibid.*, p. 308.
  [4] *Ibid.*, p. 309.   [5] *Ibid.*, p. 322.
  [6] John Urquhart, *The Inspiration and Accuracy of the Holy Scriptures*, 1895, p. 18.
  [7] *Ibid.*, p. 19.

A view of inspiration in general agreement with this is stated by J. C. Ryle in the first chapter of his *Old Paths*. Ryle insists that inspiration to have any meaning must be verbal, and he, too, at the same time refuses to admit that this is the same as conceiving of it as mechanical.[1]

The name of Frederick Watson has already cropped up as one of the contributors to the *Lex Mosaica*. In his later years, Watson became interested in the subject of inspiration and his thoughts regarding it, found in manuscript form, were published after his death. There is evidence that Watson moved away from the strong conservative position he took up in his essay to the *Lex Mosaica*.[2] This may be, as has been suggested, because as theological lecturer in St John's College, Cambridge, he associated with such men as Jeremie, Selwyn, Swainson and Lightfoot, and their influence 'was congenial to Watson's temper and led him quietly towards the calm and cautious Churchmanship by which Cambridge has been privileged to influence a large number of English Churchmen'.[3]

In the book itself Watson does certainly show more sympathy with the higher criticism. Yet he contends 'that the Higher Criticism has nothing to say on matters of faith, and such the Inspiration of the Bible is'.[4] He bluntly asserts that 'Unbelief is the main element in a very large number of critical results'.[5] Watson is sure that the Bible is an inspired Book. He does not therefore limit inspiration to the writers. As an inspired book it is the Word of God.[6] And its inspiration is unique and distinctive. 'The Bible differs from all other books, in the character and degree of its Inspiration. It is the supreme manifestation of Divine inspiration embodied in human words.'[7] Watson finds proofs for this inspiration in the Bible itself, in, for example, its doctrine of sin, the harmony, purity and permanence of its teaching as well as the history of its chosen people and the reality of its prophecy. He makes a special point of the human

[1] J. C. Ryle, *Old Paths*, 1897, Ch. 1
[2] But note the following comment: 'This essay on Inspiration is not what could be called advanced, but it is in line with moderate criticism and the ripest scholarship of our day'. *Expository Times*, Vol. XVIII, 1906–7, p. 118.
[3] A. Caldecott in *Introduction to Inspiration*, p. v.
[4] Frederick Watson, *Inspiration*, 1906, p. 2.
[5] *Ibid.*   [6] *Ibid.*; cf. pp. 3 f., 16 f., etc.
[7] *Ibid.*, p. 17.

element in the Scripture.[1] It is in its nature like a sacrament. 'It has its outward and visible part, as well as its inward and spiritual grace.'[2]

The composition of the Books of the Bible is in very truth a work of man.[3] Concerning the psalms, for example, he remarks upon their expressions of human feelings, and their longings of the human spirit after God. 'But what an unreal and Docetic character', he adds, 'it gives these expressions of human desires and eagerness, if we regard them as "dictated" by the Holy Spirit.'[4] This means, as Watson insists, 'that the Bible though thoroughly Divine, is thoroughly human also'.[5]

On the human side imperfections are to be allowed. Mistakes in details may be permitted. Docetism, he remarks, destroys our holy faith, so we must beware of introducing it into the Bible. 'Those who believe that our Lord was true man, and therefore weak man, should not stagger at the Bible's true humanity or at the imperfections which its humanity involves.'[6]

Watson admits degrees of inspiration; and he is not prepared to apply the term infallibility to the Bible as such, since 'infallibility, does not allow of degrees. He contends for what he calls 'practical efficiency' rather than for 'actual perfection' as the best term to describe its authority.[7] Those who have faith in Christ will not, he thinks, stumble at this admission. It is, indeed, this belief which makes sure that the Bible is the Word of God. 'Believing in one Lord Jesus Christ, Word of God, Son of God, Son of Man', he concludes, 'it becomes not impossible for us to believe that God and man have co-operated in the making of the Bible. We feel ourselves in no way compelled to admit that it is not the Word of God, when it is proved to us by unmistakable signs that it is the word of man.'[8]

A brief reference may be made to William Kelly's *Inspiration of the Scriptures*. Well known as one of the leaders of the Brethren Movement, his position will be anticipated. He argues resolutely for the full inspiration and verbal accuracy of the Bible as a 'God-inspired' volume. 'It is not a question of *man's* spirit, but of God's, who is beyond doubt able to secure the

---

[1] Frederick Watson, *Inspiration*, 1906, p. 2; cf. pp. 148 ff.
[2] *Ibid.*, p. 149; cf. p. 189.   [3] *Ibid.*; cf. p. 152 f.
[4] *Ibid.*, p. 167; cf. p. 176.   [5] *Ibid.*, p. 189.
[6] *Ibid.*, pp. 190–1.   [7] *Ibid.*; cf. pp. 20 f., 189 f.
[8] *Ibid.*, p. 248.

truth absolutely, as the Lord and the apostles and prophets everywhere assume and assert.'[1] A true plenary doctrine of inspiration does not allow for degrees, and consequently the idea is excluded of man being left to himself to set forth the revelation he has received; otherwise it would be 'really to leave out God, and to blow hot and cold in the same breath'.[2] Every Scripture is inspired of God; it is God-breathed. It may be acknowledged that the precise way God brings about this result is beyond us. 'Speculation into the "how" of inspiration is a prying into what is not revealed, and therefore unwise and unbecoming.'[3] Kelly however has a long section—chapter four—in which he seeks to show that this high view of inspiration does not exclude the human element. 'Nobody doubts', he says, 'that Scripture without exception has a human element. In it God speaks and writes permanently to man, and therefore in human language.'[4] By this stress he contends 'the reproach "mechanical" is unfounded, no less than the setting up of "dynamical" is cold and insufficient'.[5] He elucidates by adding, 'The inspired are through His goodness far beyond being His pen or even His penmen, as it has been said. Their minds and affections He uses as well as their language'.[6] Kelly proceeds to an examination of every book in the Canon with a view to showing the evidences therein of its 'Divine design'. Having fulfilled this task he remarks about the result, 'As it already exceeds 600 pages, I think it better to let the positive truth produce its own impression, which difficulties of the kind have no real title to destroy seeing that the most certain truth, save in matter or in abstract forms, is necessarily open to such questions. It ought not to be where God has spoken or caused His word to be communicated to writing.'[7]

The position of James Orr as stated in what the *Expository Times* called his 'courageous' book[8] is well known. Orr was a careful scholar. Beginning with a chapter of 'Revelation and Inspiration in Current Thought', Orr seeks to show how a certain confusion has been introduced into the discussion by the failure to state exactly the precise significance of each term. He

[1] W. Kelly, *Inspiration of the Scriptures*, 1907, second edition, pp. 31–2.
[2] *Ibid.*, p. 34.   [3] *Ibid.*, p. 38.
[4] *Ibid.*, p. 47.   [5] *Ibid.*
[6] *Ibid.*   [7] *Ibid.*, p. 597.
[8] *Expository Times*, Vol. XXI, 1909–10, p. 373.

then makes a study of the subject of revelation and concludes this investigation with the assurance that a real revelation of God has been given. But this revelation is made permanent and available to every generation in its record. Thus for all practical purposes the revelation is to be identified with the record.

Inspiration is the distinctive characteristic of the record. The Scriptures are the result of God's working in and upon the writers. But it is not 'mechanical' since 'inspiration does not annul any power or faculty of the human soul, but raises all powers to their highest activity, and stimulates them to their freest exercise'.[1] He believes that the Bible in its Old and New Testaments claim, and make good their claim, to be inspired. He notes the ambiguity attaching to the phrase 'verbal inspiration' but he considers, however, that it 'expresses a true and important idea'.[2] It correctly, he maintains, opposes the theory which would limit revelation and inspiration to thoughts and ideas, leaving the language altogether to the unaided faculties of the sacred penmen. Such an idea Orr considers defective. 'Thought of necessity takes shape and is expressed in words', he remarks. 'If there is inspiration at all, it must penetrate words as well as thought, must mould the expression, and make the language employed the living medium of the idea to be conveyed.'[3]

The doctrine of inspiration which these books expound is the same as that which traditionalists, as some call them, or as conservative evangelicals, as they prefer to call themselves, continue to maintain. It is the view stated again by R. B. Girdlestone a few years after Orr wrote. 'Inspiration', declares Girdlestone, 'is thus to be regarded as the handmaid of revelation.'[4] It is the Spirit's work which results in an inspired Scripture. 'The conclusion we are brought to is that the Scriptures of the Old Testament are believed to be the inspired Word of God, not only because of their contents, which are so largely of the nature of revelation, but also because the writers, who so far as we are able to trace them were prophets, were Divinely commissioned either to speak or to write.'[5] So, too, is

---

[1] James Orr, *Revelation and Inspiration*, 1910, reprint, 1952, p. 169.
[2] *Ibid.*, p. 209.   [3] *Ibid.*
[4] R. B. Girdlestone, *The Building up of the Old Testament*, 1912, Excursus on Inspiration, p. 297.   [5] *Ibid.*, p. 302.

it with the New Testament. But Girdlestone would caution the student against certain assumptions. The book is inspired, but this does not mean that those who copied them were kept free from error; the same is true of translators. A book in the Bible, although surely inspired, does not on that account mean that all the opinions and the conduct it records are approved of. 'The candour of the Bible is pre-eminent.'[1] The theological and moral ideas of some books are not final or complete because they are inspired. Inspiration does not obliterate the national and personal characteristics of the writer nor yet does it necessarily imply originality. It is, however, Girdlestone's conclusion that 'The books of the New Testament are in the same position as those of the Old, and the whole Bible may be unhesitatingly described as "God's word written" '.[2] Girdlestone adds that the writers were not acted upon mechanically; there was room left for much that was natural and personal.[3]

W. E. Vine in like manner defends the Bible as an inspired Book. The contents of the Bible, he argues, have proved their inspiration, by their power to probe the conscience, to penetrate to the inmost depths of the soul, and to appeal from every page to the heart of men. Vine underlines the fact of the human element in the process and insists that in inspiration 'God raised His human agents into co-operation with Himself, not excluding the natural factor, but developing and expanding their faculties'.[4] The evidences that God in no way set aside the human in the activity of His inspiring are abundant. The writers of the Bible were clearly men of like passions with ourselves. At the same time, 'the Divine and human are combined in the Scripture records, that is to say, that they were neither mere machinists nor solely responsible for what they wrote'.[5] Vine is, of course, assured that the only valid inspiration is that which relates to the words. 'The Inspiration of Scripture is the Inspiration of its words, and the words themselves must be taken to express its real intention.'[6] He believes, too, that this assures accuracy.[7] Vine seeks authority for this understanding

[1] R. B. Girdlestone, *The Building up of the Old Testament*, 1912, Excursus on Inspiration, p. 306.

[2] *Ibid.*, p. 310. Cf. Article 20 of the Thirty-Nine Articles of the Church of England.   [3] *Ibid.*

[4] W. E. Vine, *The Divine Inspiration of the Bible*, 1923, p. 18.

[5] *Ibid.*, p. 19.   [6] *Ibid.*, p. 23.   [7] *Ibid.*; cf. pp. 30 and 69 f.

of inspiration in the testimony of Christ. He endorsed the Old Testament and gave testimony to the inspiration of its words.[1] Passage after passage from both Testaments are adduced to show the emphasis which is placed upon their words. The book concluded with a section in which 'Some Objections' are considered. Questions relating to moral, scientific, and historical problems are dealt with. Problems, as for example, 'How can wrong utterances be inspired?' have not been avoided. This particular query is answered by stating that such statements as the mistaken utterance of Job's friends, the falsehoods told by Peter in his denial of the Lord, the speech of the town clerk in Ephesus, the oration of Tertullus, and the like 'were certainly not inspired in the lips of those who made them, but the records of their words by the writers of Scripture are inspired, and that these records are faithful and accurate has not been disproved'.[2]

Conservative writers, then, are agreed that inspiration is not something done *on* man, nor yet is it merely something done *in* man. They wish to focus attention on the writings themselves: and thus they see the Scriptures as something done by man and for man: yet as something done so decisively by God that the result of their work is rightly to be designated the Word of God. They see little value in probing the psychical reactions of a prophet to whom the word of the Lord came. Their interest is in the word which has come. 'When we speak of the *Scriptures*', F. F. Bruce declares, 'we use a word which etymologically denotes the writing and not the material.'[3] Without writing, he adds, there would be no Bible at all 'for the Bible is God's Word *written*'. Basil F. C. Atkinson, too, insists upon the doctrine of an infallible and inspired book. The Bible is, he maintains, an inspired volume. It is the result of the Holy Ghost's action. 'His inspiring work had not only the negative side of preserving them from error as they directed their thoughts to their books and wrote them. Greater still was His positive work of bringing to bear through their varied minds, the message that God intended to deliver to men.'[4] Atkinson compares the union of the human in inspiration with the human in our Lord's nature and concludes

---

[1] W. E. Vine, *The Divine Inspiration of the Bible*, 1923, pp. 32 ff., esp. p. 38 f.
[2] *Ibid.*, p. 110.
[3] F. F. Bruce, *The Books and the Parchments*, 1950, p. 15 (italics in original).
[4] Basil F. C. Atkinson, *The Christian Use of the Old Testament*, 1952, p. 12.

that just as Christ was sinless so, too, must be the Bible.[1] The Old Testament, he urges, stakes a claim to be inspired and authoritative and this claim is vindicated by our Lord Himself and the writers of the New Testament. He would maintain 'the highest view of inspiration. because such only, he believes, is consistent with the facts.

We can reach a conclusion of this investigation with a reference to a slender but scholarly booklet by T. C. Hammond. In it Hammond rejects, equally with those whose works have concerned us in this section, the mechanical view of inspiration. Had God proposed to deliver to us a mechanical message, he suggests, he would most certainly have chosen mechanical means. 'If man can teach a parrot to talk, and produce the sounds of the human voice on a revolving disc, God, it is to be assumed, could deliver a message of mere words, without soul or mind behind them.'[2] But God did not choose to do this. He spoke through men. 'The Divine message was formulated under the guidance of God in those conditions which are incidental to the development of human thought.'[3] The Divine influence did not nullify human peculiarities. Hammond, however, insists that inspiration is essentially verbal. We have an inspired Scripture. Thoughts without words, ideas without language, have no significance for others. 'If all God's teachers had heard only unspeakable words, there would be no Bible.'[4] Therefore, concludes Hammond, it is not accurate to say, as is popularly said, that 'the men indeed were inspired but not their utterances'.[5] Hammond is in agreement with Orr and Girdlestone as to the general veracity of what has been preserved. 'The message of God has been preserved in verbal form with substantial accuracy.'[6] It is in this way that Hammond regards the various accounts of our Lord's words. The evangelists were directed to record the words as they heard them or as they had come to them. They were not 'newspaper verbatim reporters'.[7]

---

[1] Basil F. C. Atkinson, *The Christian Use of the Old Testament*, 1952, p. 11 f. Cf. 'How was this inspiration brought about? We cannot exactly tell, just as we cannot exactly tell how the Lord Jesus Christ became a man except that it was by the operation of the Holy Spirit'. Basil F. C. Atkinson, *Is the Bible True?* 1933, third edition, 1934, p. 20.

[2] T. C. Hammond, *Inspiration and Authority*, 1935, Inter-Varisity Papers, No. 3, p. 23.   [3] *Ibid.*   [4] *Ibid.*, p. 17.
[5] *Ibid.*   [6] *Ibid.*, p. 37.   [7] *Ibid.*, pp. 35–6.

An understanding of the position contended for by conservative writers has now been reviewed. It was emphasized thoughout that inspiration is not simply a subjective phenomenon, not merely the stirring of the inner life of a legislator, a preacher, a poet, a prophet or an apostle. The significance of inspiration lies in its result—in a Book which gives to men in human language the message of God. In a very real sense the claim is made that the words of the Bible are the words which the Holy Ghost taught men to speak from God.

It should be pointed out, however, that there were writers who tended to overstate their case and consequently gave some justification to those who credited the traditionalists with a mechanical theory of inspiration. This undue emphasis upon the action of God, which gave the impression of virtually obliterating the human agents of inspiration, can be seen in three important volumes of our period. C. Wordsworth, in his book on the subject, does at times make statements, which seem to border on the idea of a mechanical dictation, although he seeks to correct this conclusion by urging that the writers were spontaneous and free and that the human element had its genuine place in the process.[1]

L. Gaussen's book translated into English by David Scott in 1863 exercised a profound influence. Gaussen states boldly that 'the miraculous operation of the Holy Ghost had not the sacred writers themselves as the object . . . but that the objects were the holy books themselves'.[2] Taken by itself such an utterance could be, and indeed was, misunderstood. It was concluded by some that he regarded the writers as machines. Yet strongly as Gaussen expresses himself, it is but justice to observe that he does admit the interplay, in the process of inspiration, of the human personality.[3]

Constant reference is made to the famous sermon preached by J. W. Burgon at Oxford in 1860, which Alan Richardson wrongly quotes as a classical statement of 'Fundamentalism'. 'The Bible is none other than the *voice of Him that sitteth upon the Throne!* Every book of it, every chapter of it, every verse of it, every word of it, every syllable of it (where are we to stop?),

---

[1] C. Wordsworth, *The Inspiration of the Bible*, 1861, p. 5.
[2] L. Gaussen, *Theopneustia: The Plenary Inspiration of the Holy Scriptures* (trans. David Scott, 1863), p. 24; cf. p. 281.   [3] *Ibid.*; cf. pp. 38 ff.

every letter of it, is the direct utterance of the Most High! *Pasa graphe theopneustos.*'[1] Such a statement has been much used by those who see verbal inspiration to be one and the same with a mechanical process. Perhaps the passage has not been fairly used, since as J. I. Packer justly points out, 'This is nothing more than a rhetorical affirmation of the divine origin of all Scripture. Burgon is affirming the fact of inspiration; he is not discussing the mode of it, and the passage contains not a word to suggest that dictation was the method whereby Scripture was given'.[2] In actual fact, Burgon later explicitly repudiates the mechanical theory and admits quite frankly that the method of inspiration is one of the many things he cannot understand.[3]

We would ourselves want to insist that there must be in any acceptable and sufficient account of inspiration, adequate emphasis given to the double aspect: the Divine and the human; the outward and the inward; the Spirit and the letter. It is, indeed, in the combination of these that the very essence of the process consists. The relation between the Divine and the human is not easy to comprehend, but it is a fact to which all genuine Christian experience bears abundant witness. Of the possibility, indeed, of the reality of such a combination the believing man has his own certain awareness. And the combination of the Divine and the human in inspiration is a special instance of this interplay for a particular spiritual purpose.

Men of faith will not regard it as something impossible with God who is Lord of all life, for the fulfilment of His plan of grace, to deal thus with chosen men for the sake of humanity. 'To enlarge or inform any faculty is evidently a secondary operation of the same power by which it was first given and quickened.'[4] This does not mean that the human faculties of the selected messengers do not act according to their natural laws even though they are supernaturally strengthened. The man is not converted into a machine, even in the hand of God. It is in that required union of the Divine and the human that the message of God is given. But to be complete the message must find its fulfilment in language. Without it the mysteries unveiled

---

[1] J. W. Burgon, *Inspiration and Interpretation*, reprint, 1905, p. 86.
[2] J. I. Packer, *'Fundamentalism' and the Word of God*, 1958, p. 180.
[3] Cf. J. W. Burgon, *Inspiration and Interpretation*, 1905, reprint, pp. 122 ff.
[4] B. F. Wescott, *Introduction to the Study of the Gospels*, 1882, p. 36.

before the eyes of the seer would remain confused shadows, but with it they become permanent and authoritative for human life. When addressed to the man, the human element becomes a part of the Divine message, since the Divine message can be grasped only when defined and moulded according to the laws of his own nature. This means, quite emphatically, that the Book is rightly said to be inspired no less than the prophet. The Book will, of course, reflect and perpetuate the peculiar idiosyncrasies of each prophet but it does not create them. The prophet is not merely a man who sees, he is one who sees and speaks what he sees: he is in a profound sense a speaking man. He *is* his language: 'between being and the word there does exist an irrefragable unity', says Gabriel Marcel. Elsewhere we have drawn attention to a distinction which may be made between 'use-language' and 'being-language'. It is 'being-language' which is declarative and convictive. 'Ultimately we are what we say. The prophets were men who spake from God. And it was their speech which betrayed them, which showed them to be God's men. There is a very vital relationship between the person and the word. Nowhere is this unity seen so effectively and so significantly as in the One of Whom it is declared that He is the Word made flesh. In Him there is no disharmony between language and life. Here the language-of-being is the Divine Word in human form —truly Divine and truly human. In Him the "I am" and the "I utter" are one and the same. Here is *Homo Confessor* and *Deus Loquens*.'[1]

In the Scriptures we have not just what the prophets thought, but we have the declarative and the convictive language of what was given them from above. Unless this is so there is an end of all certainty. The writing does not introduce any limitation into the representation which does not belong to the first conception and expression of it. For man the purely spiritual and absolute is but a vague thing—a dream perchance. It is language which is the condition of our being, the determining factor and the essential medium of ideas which are divine in their origin. In the process of Biblical inspiration, then, there is combined harmoniously the two factors, the Divine ideas and the human language. 'Each element performs its perfect work. . . . The

[1] H. D. McDonald, 'Is Speech the Key to the Riddle of Man? Language as Tool and Mirror', *The Baptist Times*, October 6, 1960.

letter becomes as perfect as the spirit; and it may well seem that the image of the Incarnation is reflected in the Christian Scriptures, which, as I believe, exhibit the human and the divine in the highest form, and in the most perfect union.'[1]

[1] B. F. Wescott, *Introduction to the Study of the Gospels*, 1882, p. 41.

CHAPTER EIGHT

The Problem of Biblical Authority

The conflict over the Bible initiated by the higher criticism made inevitable a discussion of the precise nature of its authority. If the inerrancy of the record and the inspiration of the words are renounced, then what is to be made of its infallibility? The question must be faced, In what ways and in what words can its authority be expressed? Such was to become and to continue the central problem of the discussion of the subject of revelation. 'Nothing is more remarkable', it was stated in an article in an issue of the *Speaker* for the year 1891, 'than the ubiquity of the question as to criticism and the authority of the Scriptures.'[1]

For centuries the authority of the Bible had remained secure in the Church. There had been, indeed, attacks made on it from without, by sceptic and deist; but it had held its place of supremacy. Even from within there had been movements, such as those which can be classed under the general heading of Enthusiasm, which tended to undermine the objective authority of the Bible and enthrone in its place an individual subjectivism,[2] but even these movements did not greatly affect the general estimation of the Bible as fully and finally the external truth of God to man, and for man.

But the first and fundamental result of criticism was to shift the emphasis from the external to the internal and to set up the claim that the principle of authority was to be sought within, not without. It was maintained that this subjective emphasis was the outcome of the Reformers' position. This is, perhaps, too bold a claim. Luther to begin with certainly envisaged the problem of authority in terms of the supremacy of Scripture. Luther had

[1] 'The Churches and the Scriptures', *Speaker*, iii, 1891, pp. 724–5.
[2] H. D. McDonald, *Ideas of Revelation*, 1959, Chapter IV.

discovered the Bible through his own profound religious experience. But it soon became evident that it did not in all points tally with his experience. This led Luther to seek for the 'Bible within the Bible'. Concerning the New Testament, in particular, he asked, What is the Word of God? and gives for his answer that that is the Word of God which preaches Christ. It was statements such as this, which made Sabatier enter the claim that Luther 'moved the seat of authority from the Church to the Christian consciousness'. But R. E. Davies in his study of the matter has convincingly shown that this is not an accurate account of the case. He grants that it was the *tendency* of Luther's teaching, but it certainly was not his purpose. For Luther, the Word of God as religiously defined continued to be regarded as an external infallible authority.[1]

John Oman seems ready to admit another origin for the subjective emphasis. He refers to the parallel movement of the Reformation, the Renaissance, and contends that 'Its distinctive work was the conscious rejection of all external, authoritative infallibilities'.[2] It was the Aufklärung which renounced all objective authority and gave supremacy to the subjective. Revelation is not to be conceived as something *ab extra*, something standing, so to say, over against the individual. Revelation is the movement of God within, and such a revelation is its own sufficient authority. To seek an external infallibility is to seek what does not exist: indeed, declares Oman 'all infallibilities presuppose an idea of grace mechanically irresistible'.[3]

Without however pursuing this matter further it will have become evident that criticism did shift the locus of authority

---

[1] Cf. R. E. Davies, *The Problem of Authority in the Continental Reformers*, 1946, p. 39 f. Cf. G. H. Hospers, *The Reformed Principle of Authority*, 1924; P. L. Lehmann, 'The Reformers' Use of the Bible', *Theology Today*, Vol. 3, pp. 328–44, October 1946; A. M. Renwich, 'The Authority of the Bible, "The Attitude of the Reformers" ', *The Evangelical Quarterly*, Vol. 19, pp. 110–26.

Cf. the following quotation from Luther's Lectures on the Psalms, 1513–15. 'What pasture is to the beast, the nest for the birds, the stream for fish, the Scriptures are for believing souls. . . . They give everything the soul needs, and it is to tempt God, if anyone will not be satisfied with the Scriptures . . . God's will is completely contained therein; so nothing should be presented which is not confirmed of both Testaments and agrees with them. It cannot be otherwise, for the Scriptures are divine; and in them God speaks and they are His Word.'

[2] John Oman, *Grace and Personality*, 1925, second revision, pp. 3–4. Cf. A. Lecerf, *An Introduction to Reformed Dogmatics*, 1949, pp. 99 ff.

[3] *Ibid.*, p. 14.

K

from without to within. C. J. Cadoux notes the significance of what he calls the 'critical victory' in the areas of Christian morals, devotion, and especially theology. Although not always realized, he observes, its result was to give tacit recognition to the ultimate authority of the subjective powers conferred on man by God. Here is the sovereignty, by which all is to be tested. There is no need to hanker after objective authority. The claim of liberal theology, he says, rests upon 'the legitimacy of the inner light'. 'What ground is there for positing Revelation in any writing other than the fact that we find inspiration in it?' he asks.[1] The ultimate is the inward and here authority is to be discovered.

Cadoux may be stating the case in too extreme a way for the period in which he wrote, since there appears to be more readiness recently to give an external significance to the Bible than was the case in earlier days. The immediate reaction to criticism seems to have been to discard the objective authority of Scripture altogether. 'It is a sign of conservatism', was the verdict, 'not to believe in the authority of Scripture at all.'[2]

Criticism had forced some to accept the new estimate of the biblical records. And in this context our Lord's conception of the Bible was valuated. Was it possible any longer, it was seriously asked, to credit any authority to this patchwork volume? The Bible is a record of revelation, and authority really belongs to the revelation, not to the record. So it came about that the problem opened out into the wider question of where the seat and source of religious authority are to be found. If religion is to be allowed as an authentic experience, if it is to be seen as other than a paralyzing neurosis, a hollow illusion, or even a valuable emotion, then it must be asked, Wherein lies its authority? The problem of revelation is, indeed, the dominant one in contemporary religious thought. But with the wider

[1] C. J. Cadoux, 'Scripture and Theology', *The Congregational Quarterly*, Vol. 25, January 1947, p. 26. Cf. his *A Case for Evangelical Modernism*, A Study in the Relation between Christian Faith and Traditional Theology, 1938, in which the position is given a more elaborate statement.

[2] *Expository Times*, Vol. IX, 1897–8, p. 481. Cf. 'One of the most earnestly debated questions of our day is Authority. The feeling is that old authorities— especially of the Church and the Bible—are no longer authoritative. And there are those who assert that no authority whatever is left.' *Expository Times*, Vol. XXIV, 1912–13, p. 517 (comment on E. Y. Mullins's *Freedom and Authority in Religion*, 1913).

issues concerning its meaning and media goes the more fundamental, if narrower one, of authority. Indeed, as H. Wheeler
Robinson has said, the discussion of the principle of authority
is 'the nodal point, since authority must always be characteristic
of the Christian revelation'.[1]

At the present our concern is with the special subject of the
authority which is to be allowed to the Bible since it is agreed
by all that it has some connection with the Christian revelation.
To those who sought authority within, the Bible was conceived
to be, to begin with, a record of the insights of religious men. It
was their insights into, and experience of God's saving acts in
history, which are of ultimate significance for us. The Bible is the
self-authenticating record of such experiences; thus, it was
declared, its authority lies 'in the reality of the experiences of
men who stood in situations like our own'.[2] As time went on,
however, the individual's own personal experience was taken
into account as a vital factor, and the Bible was credited with
authority in so far as it authenticated itself in the inner spiritual
life of the one who makes the personal response of faith to God's
saving acts in history. But, in whichever way the position was
stated, there was virtually a rejection of the Bible as an outside
infallible standard: 'the authority with which the Bible comes to
us' says R. H. Lightfoot, 'can no longer be wholly or primarily
external'.[3]

Those who maintained that the Bible was an inspired Book,
it will be understood, insisted that it must, on that account, be
accepted as an infallible guide and an authoritative Scripture.
The position, then, on the question of the authority of the Bible
will be seen to follow the same pattern which we observed with
regard to inspiration. There is, on the other hand, the focus
within, and, on the other hand, the focus without. Some contend
that real authority is to be found in the experience of which the
Scriptures bear witness, and that whatever authority belongs to
the Bible derives from that experience. Others are just as
emphatic that the Bible holds its authority apart from
experience.

[1] H. Wheeler Robinson, 'The Principle of Authority in the Christian Religion'.
Ernest A. Payne, *Henry Wheeler Robinson*, 1946, p. 170.
[2] J. M. Graham, 'After Fifty Years', *Expository Times*, Vol. I, 1938–9, p. 539.
[3] *The Interpretation of the Bible* (ed. C. W. Dugmore), 1944, p. 90. Cf. A. Peel
in same, p. 52.

Something by way of detail concerning these two opposed views must now be given.

A. THE AUTHORITY OF THE BIBLE
BASED UPON EXPERIENCE

A beginning here may be made by noting how definitely some writers have maintained that spiritual experience is the sole and sufficient ground of religious authority. H. Hensley Henson, in his volume *The Value of the Bible*, sees this value as so founded. If we are Christians in fact as well as in name, he says, 'we, no less than the writers of the New Testament build the fabric of belief on the foundation of experience'. The new scholarship has brought us 'to understand that the Bible has been extensively misconceived by the Church, and we are not a little embarrassed by the fact that the place which the Bible holds in the system and custom of the Church was determined to no small extent, by that misconception'.[1] Henson refers to what he calls an 'inner certitude' which exempts us from 'fear from the most searching criticism of the historical memorials of our Master's life'. Authority is something within; indeed, he informs us, 'A faith which is based upon external authority, whether of miracles, or of the Church, or the senses, is in itself a poor thing'.[2] Although in this particular passage the Bible is not included, it is his position that external authority no more belongs to it than to the other items mentioned, since, as he quotes Coleridge to express his view, 'Faith is subjective'.[3]

The phrase, 'inner certitude' used by Henson, is a significant one and may be taken as the key to the whole position. R. H. Strachan boldly declared for the ultimacy of this 'inner certitude' in his book, *The Authority of Religious Experience*, being the Alexander Robinson Trust Lectures of the University of Glasgow for the year 1929. Strachan places authority squarely on the individual Christian conscience. He does however seek to safeguard his subjectivism from the vagaries and vagueness to

---

[1] H. Hensley Henson, *The Value of the Bible and other Sermons*, 1902–4, with a Letter to the Lord Bishop of London, 1904, p. 26.

[2] *Ibid.*, p. 196.

[3] *Ibid.*, p. 197. Note Henson's quotation of the passage from Coleridge, which refers to the Bible revealing its authority by the way its words 'find me at greater depths of my being' than any other book (pp. 33–4).

which unrestricted individualism is prone. He thus gives some respect to the religious community and to historical revelation. He is, however, sceptical about reliance upon any mere external authority, whether it be that of the Bible or the Church. A reading of the volume will show that when once the idea of the individual's religious consciousness is taken as the key to the problem of authority, it is difficult to keep out of the abyss of subjectivism. Strachan does indeed recognize that the historical side of Christianity is a datum preceding individual experience which the experience itself does not create, but has to accept and interpret. This fact, however, admitted on one page is actually contradicted on another.

In a similar way, Sidney Cave in his *Doctrine of the Christian Faith* (1931) stresses the experience of the gospel as the way to an understanding of Scripture. Religion is essentially a matter of experience, he argues. 'God has not willed', it is declared, 'to give to men a book of indubitable facts and clearly formulated teachings. A religion based upon an infallible handbook of religion and ethics would be a religion, static and legalistic. Christianity is not founded on a book, but on a personal revelation of the living God.' The Bible is to be regarded as the classic record of religious experience and authenticates itself as a 'true' witness, by the Spirit in believing hearts.

Two interesting statements of the inward nature of authority are worthy of mention. The one comes in a religious biography and the other in a paper delivered before a Church group. The first concerns the story of the life and experiences of Charles Hargrove by L. P. Jacks and is entitled *From Authority to Freedom* (1920). Hargrove had been, in his early life, a member of the Brethren and had accepted the authority of an infallible Bible. He later seceded to the Roman Church and submitted to its authority. But soon he became dissatisfied with this external authority. Thereupon he became a Unitarian and accepted the invitation to the pastorate of a congregation in Leeds. He found what authority he needed within his own 'enlightened' soul. Here is discovered the religion of the spirit in contrast with the religions of authority. Man is 'left to the guidance of his own conscience and the stars', he declared. It is noteworthy, however, that Hargrove in stating his position makes no reference to the Holy Spirit; and for that matter neither does his biographer.

In a paper on 'Authority in Religion' read at the Modern Churchmen's Congress, July 1949, W. R. Inge stated that Paul must be regarded as the founder of Christian mysticism. As he develops his thesis he virtually dismisses the Bible and the Church as unworthy of consideration. Reason likewise cannot be taken as the ground of authority. 'How can we pray to a mathematical God?' he asks. The centre of gravity has shifted, he urges, 'from external authority to inward experience' and he thinks rightly. 'My conviction is', he adds, 'that this inner authority is strong enough to take the place of those external authorities which, as perhaps most of you will agree with me, have lost most of their cogency.'[1]

This subjective approach to the problem of authority may be illustrated in the works of a number of writers over our period. John Clifford, having freely acknowledged 'errors and mistakes' in the Bible, raises the question, What and where, then, is its authority? His answer broadly is that the authority of the Bible lies in the elevation and universality of its religious ideas, and in the experience of Christ through which these ideas are vivified, applied and used. He makes reference to several kinds of authority and concludes that mere external and mechanical authority is less significant than that which operates between persons. The authority of the Bible is that of truth, wherein the witness is within ourselves.[2] But ultimately Christ is the Truth; consequently, 'the authority of the Bible is the authority of Jesus'. This means that 'the authority is personal rather than literary'.[3] Secondary authorities, such as Christian preachers and the Church, do exist, but these must not be elevated into the position of absolutes. Yet 'the crowning certainty is secured through these forces by the work of God in the spirit of man'.[4]

[1] W. R. Inge, 'Authority in Religion', Paper read at Modern Churchmen's Congress, July 1949. Cf. his earlier Authority and the Inner Light, Liverpool Diocesan Lecture, 1912. See also his Introduction to his Everyman's Bible, An Anthology. Here Inge asks, How is the will of God communicated? He suggests three possible ways: the Church, the Holy Scriptures and the Inner Light. He seems to desire a blend of the three but adds, that 'in the interpretation of the inspired books we have to depend on the inner light, on the wisdom which is from above'. W. R. Inge, Everyman's Bible, An Anthology—Arranged with an Introduction, 1931, p. xxv.
[2] John Clifford, The Inspiration and Authority of the Bible, third edition, 1899, pp. 83-4.   [3] Ibid., p. 85.
[4] Ibid., p. 89.

Robertson Smith had argued for this idea of biblical authority. 'The persuasion that in the Bible, God Himself speaks of love and life to the soul is the essence of the Christian conviction of the truth and authority of the Scripture', he had stated. It is the personal assurance of the Spirit bearing witness with our spirit, which is the source of individual certainty and which lifts faith out of the region of probable evidence and into the sphere of divine confidence. This statement of the case for the authority of the Bible was given more elaborate exposition by following writers.

H. Wheeler Robinson relates how in his own experience he came to a period when the idea of the Bible as a book of objective infallible truths failed to satisfy the needs of his soul.[1] In the title of his book *The Christian Experience of the Holy Spirit*, we have a succinct statement of his concept of religious authority. He sees in this 'neglected doctrine' the key to the understanding of the place of the Bible. He refers to what he calls a 'kenosis' of the Spirit in a passage in which he contends 'that we can have no properly theological doctrine of fellowship with Christ without full recognition of the doctrine of the Holy Spirit, involving Christian experience. Within that experience, our knowledge of Christ will be conditioned by our growth in grace; historical objectivity has to be partly surrendered to secure vitality, and there is a *kenosis* of the Spirit as well as of the Son'.[2]

In a series of articles under the general title *Things Most Surely Believed*, to which he with others contributed, he makes the point that the reality of moral authority, however mediated, lies in our being 'possessed'. 'The authority of the gospel always operates through the value-judgement of the individual believer. That authority rests on the intrinsic worth of the revelation of God in Christ.'[3] He returns again to the same idea in his article on 'Canonicity and Inspiration'. Having argued against the absoluteness of the *consensus ecclesiae* in reference to the formation of the Canon, he states that it 'cannot be objectivied and

[1] H. Wheeler Robinson, *The Christian Experience of the Holy Spirit*, 1928, p. 4. Cf. Ernest E. Payne, *Henry Wheeler Robinson*, 1946, pp. 56-7.
[2] H. Wheeler Robinson, *The Principle of Authority in the Christian Religion* Ernest E. Payne, *Henry Wheeler Robinson*, p. 177.
[3] H. Wheeler Robinson, *Things Most Surely Believed*, ii, *Expository Times*, Vol. XLVI, 1934-5, p. 55. See also H. R. Mackintosh under same title, vi, *op. cit.*, p. 246 f. Cf. F. R. Barry, *The Relevance of Christianity*, 1931, p. 142.

isolated in any external and material object'. Reference is made once again to the authentication within experience of the Books of the Bible as witnessed by the individual's own response to their message under the guidance of the Spirit. 'The authority of Scripture', it is then concluded, 'needs no testimony from man, because it rests on the testimony of the Holy Spirit Himself confirming His truth without by the creation of an echoing truth within.'[1]

The subject of authority was an important and recurring one for Wheeler Robinson. It could not be lightly dismissed, since he regarded it as the most urgent, as well as the final issue of the Church. He insisted that 'confusion on the question of authority means a partial paralysis of energy, a lack of conviction in utterance, even of doubt whether some other type of Church (he was in this instance addressing a company of Baptist Ministers) with a more plausible emphasis on apparently external and objective authority, might not be a better basis for preaching and worship and pastoral oversight'.[2]

There is no vital difference, he contends, among Christians about the source and the content of revelation. The real problem concerns its media. Robinson refers to three ways in which revelation may be said to be mediated. First, the historical—the tradition of events, which are interpreted as the mighty acts of God; and so interpreted, become Christian facts and the foundation of faith. Then the social or corporate organization of the Church, which, whatever else it is, is obviously a form of society made inevitable because of the inherent sociality of man. And, thirdly, of course, the individual, because every form of Christian faith must demand some kind of personal response. It is the reality of this personal experience, which can be revised and enlarged by contact with other experiences which delivers revelation, and consequently authority, from being merely subjective. In this way, 'The revelation, and therefore the authority, is both subjective and objective, and necessarily so'.[3] It is, he argues, only as the events of history are interpreted by faith that they become facts and factors for revelation. Like

[1] H. Wheeler Robinson, *Canonicity and Inspiration*, *Expository Times*, Vol. XLVII, 1935–6, p. 123.
[2] H. Wheeler Robinson, *The Principle of Authority in the Christian Religion*, Ernest A. Payne, *Henry Wheeler Robinson*, 1946, p. 125.
[3] Ernest A. Payne, *Henry Wheeler Robinson*, 1946, p. 178.

William Temple, Wheeler Robinson sees revelation as the product of event and interpretation, as an interfusion of history and meaning. Thus may the authority of Christian experience be regarded as, at the same time, both subjective and objective; and it is in this 'duality lies its continued vitality', he says.[1] Ultimately, however, the emphasis is put upon the subjective, since it is the Spirit within as 'the active partner and director' which is finally authoritative. In this context the Bible (and the Church) will be understood. They will be reverenced as 'subordinate authorities' by which the events of history become interpreted to us.[2] Both the Bible and the Church are 'secondary and delegated authorities in religion'. It is in 'the prophetic consciousness and its continuance in personal religion that there is found the ultimate sanctuary, in which the voice of God is still heard, the sanctuary in which the ancient Scriptures are still transformed into living oracles'.[3]

We have made particular reference to Wheeler Robinson's teaching at this point, because he was the dominant figure of the period on this side. He was, indeed, as Alexander McLaren is reported to have drily remarked, 'an able man And he knows it!'[4] There were, as we shall see, those before him who stated the same ideas, but they did not, and probably could not, do so with the same clarity of style and the same profundity of scholarship as were his. Others followed and took their cue from him, but in many cases they were mere echoes of the Oxford teacher. Wheeler Robinson was in fact the powerful spokesman of the thesis that the authority of the Bible gets its effect from the religious experience of the Spirit.

It remains, however, a fact that the uncertainty which was evident with regard to the authority of the Bible before Wheeler Robinson had written was not magically removed by what he had to say. While the question of inspiration was the immediate issue resulting from the controversy initiated by the higher criticism, it is the subject of authority which was destined to gather momentum, and to become, during the last three decades,

[1] H. Wheeler Robinson, *Inspiration and Revelation in the Old Testament*, 1938, p. 198. Cf. his 'The Bible and Protestantism', *Congregational Quarterly*, Vol. 16, January 1938, pp. 40–50, esp. p. 47.

[2] Ernest A. Payne, *Henry Wheeler Robinson*, 1946, p. 179.

[3] H. Wheeler Robinson, *Inspiration and Revelation in the Old Testament*, p. 198.

[4] Ernest A. Payne, *Henry Wheeler Robinson*, p. 56.

the most pressing, as well as the most perplexing, of theological problems. When, in the year 1951, Alan Richardson and W. Schweitzer edited the volume *Biblical Authority for Today*, the appropriate comment was made in the *Expository Times*: 'There is no more important subject at the present than the Nature of Biblical Authority'.[1] But while all those to whom we are making reference agreed that the 'old' doctrine of the Bible as an external authority could no longer commend itself, and that, therefore, the focus must be within, there was no real agreement as to the precise way the 'new' doctrine was to be stated.

This fact may be illustrated by drawing attention to two Church conferences which met within a couple of years of each other towards the end of the nineteen-twenties. In 1927 there was the Oxford Conference in which Congregationalists dealt with the subject 'The Christian Faith in the Light of Modern Science and Criticism'. An examination of the papers read at this conference will reveal that the urgent concern was with the problem of authority. R. F. Horton posed the question, 'What are we Congregationalists to present as our authority?' Certainly neither an infallible Church nor an infallible Bible, he replies. Yet to rest on the idea of the self-authenticating significance of truth is not satisfactory, since this involves the further question, What is truth and how are we to distinguish it from error? It is not enough, either, to state that our authority is Christ *qua* Christ. The answer must be Christ is the authority because He is the Truth. Christ must be; but why? and, how? To these inquiries there is no answer given. Nathaniel Micklem took the same line. 'In religion as a whole', he declares, 'there is no infallible authority except Christ Himself.' But still all is not clear. Micklem later states that 'Our authority is our personal consent to the faith of the Church as it comes to us through the Christian community and is for us corroborated in the Gospels'.[2]

The sheer fact appears to have been that there was a prevailing uncertainty as to what is the foundation upon which faith was

[1] *Expository Times*, Vol. LXIII, 1951–2, p. 97.

[2] Cf. *The Congregational Quarterly*, Vol. V, 1927. In 1928 the Congregationalists returned once again to a discussion of the subject 'Authority'. Note two papers read at a later Oxford Conference in 1934: R. S. Birch on 'The Holy Spirit and Individual Experience', and N. Micklem on 'The Holy Spirit and the New Creed'. *The Congregational Quarterly*, Vol. 12, 1934, pp. 510 f. and 545 f. Cf. also G. B. Storr, 'The Final Authority in Conduct', *The Congregational Quarterly*, Vol. 18, 1940, p. 283 f. The 'ultimate responsibility is with the individual' it is concluded (p. 289).

to take its stand. There was, indeed, evidence enough of a grim desire to stand on something if one could be sure what it was. But no one was quite sure.

About two years later the Sixteenth Annual Conference of Modern Churchmen was held at Cambridge and the subject discussed was 'Authority in Religion'.[1] These papers, too, show the same sort of hesitancy; the general tendency seems to be either to find authority in individual experience, or, with more assurance, in the community experience of the Church. Commenting on this Conference and on the fact that the Congregationalists had been 'twice already' concerned with the subject, the *Expository Times* remarked that 'on the showing of these papers (at Girton College, Cambridge) it may be hazarded that the modern Churchmen have not been much more successful'[2] in coming to a confident pronouncement respecting the seat of authority in religion.

As far back as 1891, W. T. Davidson, in his paper to the Wesleyan Ministers, had sought to establish the authority of the Bible upon faith in Christ and in doing so expressed dissatisfaction with the complete subjectivism contained in the famous dictum of Coleridge. 'In establishing its (i.e. the Bible's) authority', he says, 'we must go to the Lord Jesus Christ and make the doctrine of Scripture Christo-centric.' It is faith in Christ which gives authority to the Scriptures. 'For those who believe in Jesus Christ as the Son of God, there is an irremovable basis for the doctrine of Holy Scripture as a sufficient, complete, infallible guide in things pertaining to God, the sole authoritative rule of faith and practice.'[3]

In the same year V. H. Stanton wrote his book *The Place of Authority in Matters of Religious Belief*. He sought to escape from an excessive subjectivism by arguing that religious authority

---

[1] Cf. *The Modern Churchman*, October 1930.

[2] *Expository Times*, Vol. XLI, 1929–30, p. 97.

[3] T. W. Davidson, *Inspiration and Biblical Criticism, ad. loc.* In a chapter on 'Revelation and Authority' in *The Chief Corner-Stone, Essays Towards an Exposition of the Christian Faith for Today*—a symposium of which Davidson was the editor, says, 'Protestants should remember the rock whence they were hewn. The Bible is indeed "the religion of Protestants", but its authority is spiritually discerned, and the response to its appeal must be spiritual, given in the exercise of personal trust and personal activity of mind and conscience. No language can be too strong to describe the worth of the Bible as a spiritual guide' (p. 47).

arises out of a combination of the Church, the Bible and private judgement.

Actually a year earlier James Martineau's *magnum opus*, *The Seat of Authority in Religion* (1890), had appeared, but its critical position was so extreme that it was not received with general favour. Under the influence of Schleiermacher, Martineau maintained that authority belongs to the individual conscience. The Christian religion, he argued, has been false to its essential message by first crediting authority to the Church and after that to the Bible. Authority belongs to neither, but rather to the religious consciousness as that is stimulated and inspired by the challenge and example of Jesus.

To a book by a Frenchman may be attributed one of the most effective statements of authority as having its focus within. In 1900, Auguste Sabatier wrote his famous work, which was later translated into English under the revealing title, *The Religions of Authority and the Religion of the Spirit*. There is a profound difference to be noted between this volume of Sabatier's and that of the earlier Martineau, but there is agreement of emphasis with regard to the seat of authority within the quickened conscience. Sabatier rejected all external infallibilities although he is ready to grant that both the Bible and the Church may be regarded as possessing a relative and preparatory, as distinguished from an absolute and external authority. Sabatier did not feel it any stigma to be charged with opening the door to an 'unlimited subjectivity'. Indeed, in his Socratic dialogue with Adelphi, he brings the charge against himself and then seems to take special delight in his own condemnation. 'At last the great word is out, the scarecrow with which men think to reply to everything and ward off all dangers. We must avoid subjectivism, and for that reason we will not have a subjective criterion.' Then Sabatier asks, so as to call forth a negative reply, 'But can there be any other?'[1]

Almost immediately the idea of Sabatier was popularized by two influential scholars. We have already had occasion to refer to John Oman and to quote from his *Grace and Personality*. But it is in his *Vision and Authority* that this profound thinker sought to justify his thesis that authority is grounded on man's own

---

[1] Auguste Sabatier, *The Religions of Authority and the Religion of the Spirit*, 1900 (trans. L. E. Houghton), New York, 1904, p. 261.

conscience. All external authorities are of no use to the saving of man from the blight of fear and the burden of uncertainty. 'Every man's authority is within his own soul', he states.[1] An historical revelation there must be, but it is the inward vision and understanding of it which give it authority. Oman's book is a vigorous one and 'remains a spiritual and intellectual classic which cannot be neglected'.[2]

T. B. Strong in his *Authority in the Church* (1903) stresses the need for the subjective emphasis. All authorities must be personally accepted and individually appropriated. But Strong allows for the existence of a 'deposit of faith' which has normative value for the Church. It is, indeed, this deposit which provided an authoritative basis for the teaching ministry of the Church. Beyond this essential norm, there lies a wider area of inherited Church customs, some of which, like the two sacraments, are essentially binding, while others remain to us to be used or disused to suit need or taste.

In 1908, Edward Grubb published his *Authority and the Light Within*, in which, although he was critical of the Quaker position, yet comes out for an idea in general agreement with it. He sees authority as the opening of the inward eye to the light of Christ —the light which lighteth everyman coming into the world. He returns to the same emphasis in a pamphlet on *The Problem of Authority in Religion* (1911). In 1924 in his *Authority in Religion*, he omits his critical exposition of the Friends and goes on to assert in a positive way, 'Divine Authority is Inward Authority'. Grubb contends that when the word 'authority' is used it is generally taken to refer to something 'outward'.[3] He seeks instead an authority which 'compels us by its own inward force to acceptance of what presents itself to us as True, and Beautiful, and Good, is the Light Within of which the Mystics speak'.[4] Grubb seems in a closing chapter to equate the authority of the inner light with that of the *internum Spiritus sanctus*. He suggests that the Society of Friends shows the way to a real understanding of authority. 'That body' he observes, 'has tried to rest its whole Church polity on experience of Divine guidance,

[1] John Oman, *Vision and Authority*, 1902, p. 49.

[2] R. R. Williams, *Authority in the Apostolic Age*, 1950, Burrough Lectures at Leeds University, 1948, p. 118.

[3] Edward Grubb, *Authority in Religion*, 1924, p. 3.

[4] *Ibid.*, p. 4.

individual and collective, and, while maintaining this trust in the authority of the Spirit, it has kept together.'[1]

H. B. Swete, in his chapter in the *Cambridge Theological Essays*, stresses the religious significance of the Bible. He defines religion 'as the recognition on man's part of the bond which unites him to God'.[2] He then regards the Bible to be the witness to this assurance. It is his conviction that the value of the Bible is apprehended through its experiences of life and is 'proved by the experiences of the religious life'.[3]

In 1909, J. H. Leckie, in his *Authority in Religion*, strongly, urged that the question of authority is ultimately the question of conscience. Whatever is not of conscience is not of faith.

A. S. Peake made it clear that he regarded the older Protestant view of the Bible as an infallible authority as no longer tenable. The newer theory of Scripture, he contends, has not brought perplexity only but also the feeling of relief.[4] 'It is', he says, 'one of the infirmaities of human nature to desire an infallible authority.'[5] But with the rejection of the external infallibility of a Book, does this mean, he asks, that we are to seek God in our own soul. This leads him to discuss the significance of mysticism; but he finds it unsatisfactory since it gives exclusive emphasis to the emotions. Here 'feeling is private and dumb, and unable to give an account of itself, declines to justify them rationally, and on occasions is willing that they should pass for the paradoxical and absurd'.[6] Mysticism is open to the charge brought against it by William Temple of involving a 'scepticism of the instrument', denying, that is, the objectivity of value, thereby rendering 'all conviction impossible and all opinion temerarious'.[7] Mysticism, indeed, Peake sees 'weakens the rational and practical side of religion and inclines to substitute pantheistic absorption for spiritual communion'.[8]

[1] Edward Grubb, *Authority in Religion*, 1924, p. 112. Cf. G. K. Hibbert, *The Inner Light and Modern Thought*, The Swarthmore Lecture, 1924, in which sensitive appreciation of the authority of the 'inner light' is given in this tercentenary tribute to George Fox.

[2] H. B. Swete, Cambridge Theological Essays, *Essays on some Biblical Questions of the Day*, by members of the University of Cambridge (ed. H. B. Swete), 1909, p. 545.   [3] *Ibid.*, p. 556.

[4] A. S. Peake, *The Bible, Its Origin, Its Significance, Its Abiding Worth*, 1913, second edition, p. 447.   [5] *Ibid.*, p. 446.

[6] William James, *Varieties of Religious Experience*, 1902, sixteenth edition, 1909, p. 432.   [7] William Temple, *Nature, Man and God*, 1949, p. 255.

[8] George Galloway, *The Philosophy of Religion*, 1914, p. 161.

From a consideration of mysticism, Peake turns to investigate the claims of the Church to be an authoritative guide. It has, he argues, the merit of recognizing the collective consciousness and it must be welcomed as a corrective to the freelance spirit and self-assertive individualism in religion. 'Loyalty to the Church and enthusiasm for it are indispensable if we are to win for our religion the inward strength and outward victory for which we profess to be eager.'[1] But withal, the Church is not an infallible authority. The Bible belongs to the Church but this does not mean that it is to be conceived merely as the crystallized mind of the Church. Although the Church is responsible for the formation of the canon and its life is the presupposition of its writings, yet the collective consciousness is not expressed in them; it is guided by them. 'It was not the collective consciousness of Christians which guided Paul to pen his immortal expositions of fundamental Christian truth.'[2] Peake contends, however, that the Bible does become an objective standard because here we have stated the spiritual insight and experience of its writers. 'If the subjective illumination', he remarks, 'experienced by the saint is committed to writing or expressed in oral utterance, then the same kind of authority might be claimed for the outer expression as for the inward certainty.'[3] There may be a certain vagueness, he grants, in his thesis, but in the things which it most concerns us to know, the Bible carries 'its own witness within itself and is recognized by our inward faculty'.[4] Revelation must needs be verified within experience, limited though individual experience must be allowed to be. 'The individual', he argues, 'verifies the New Testament by the immediate response which it awakens within him.'[5] Herein indeed is the permanent value of the Scripture.[6] He then concludes with the remark: 'However high credentials may be they ought not to win assent unless they are ratified by experience. And this test also it satisfies. Not only did the theology take its rise in experience, but its truth is always being verified in new experience, and will, therefore, I believe, continue to be verified. Deep still calls to deep as his experience is answered in our own'.[7]

---

[1] A. S. Peake, *The Bible, Its Origin, Its Significance, Its Abiding Worth*, p. 457.
[2] *Ibid.*, p. 458.   [3] *Ibid.*, p. 459.   [4] *Ibid.*, p. 463.
[5] *Ibid.*, p. 476.   [6] *Ibid.*; cf. pp. 479 ff.   [7] *Ibid.*, p. 503.

It is almost an impertinence to put P. T. Forsyth's mighty
volume *The Principle of Authority*—of the same date as Peake's
—in the same context and to dismiss it in a few summary
sentences. What are supposed today to be new theological
'insights' were commonplaces in the thought of this gifted
writer. His book is the result of much reflection on the problem
of authority in matters of faith and ethics. A few years before its
appearance, Forsyth had given an indication of his views in two
powerful addresses delivered when he was Chairman of the
Congregational Union in 1905, under the suggestive titles 'A
Holy Church, the Moral Guide of Society' and 'The Moral
Authority of the Church'.

It would be altogether wrong to give the impression that
Forsyth's rightful place is among those who seek authority
within religious experience. He was, in fact, unhappy about
looking within the shifting soul of the individual for such. 'An
authority which has its source in ourselves', he says, 'is no
authority. In us authority can have but its sphere and its echo,
never its charter.'[1] Yet while Forsyth refuses to ground
authority within, he does seek in a way with which we would
ourselves agree, to emphasize the inward. It is, he contends,
within the sphere of experience only that authority has its
reality, however much he insists that the autonomy and finality
of mere experience is an end of all authority. 'A real authority'
he declares, 'is indeed *within* experience, but it is not the
authority *of* experience, it is an authority *for* experience, it is an
authority experienced.'[2] The ultimate authority is the grace of
God as revealed in the gospel.[3] It is therefore something
essentially redemptive and moral. The keynote of this ethical
salvation experienced in the gospel of the holy God is appropriation, not verification.[4] 'The faith we are born into must become
personal, and that is only done by its appropriation in a moral
act or process. We do not take it on the strength of external

[1] P. T. Forsyth, *The Principle of Authority*, 1913, second edition, 1952, p. 299.
[2] *Ibid.*, p. 75. Cf. 'We do not believe things *because* of an experience, but we do *in*
an experience. They are true not *by* experience, but *for* it. . . . Faith is a religious
experience, but religious experience is not faith' (p. 27).
[3] Cf. 'The Authority of the Cross', A Paper of 1906 by Dr Robert Mackintosh
with Annotations by P. T. Forsyth, *The Congregational Quarterly*, Vol. 21, 1943,
July 1943, pp. 209 ff.
[4] P. T. Forsyth, *op. cit.*; cf. pp. 334 ff.

authority; i.e. the belief of others is no sufficient ground for ours at last, though it is an essential school.'[1] But the Bible has its moral authority for life. It is not the mere classic of the faith of 'eminent Christians'. The New Testament especially is not to be thought of as mainly made up of ideas which grew upon the apostles out of their personal faith, their private and tentative interpretation of their religiosity. The question to be asked about the Bible is, 'Have we here men's thoughts or God's Word?'[2] Forsyth declares that at the very heart of the Bible, so to speak, there is the final revelation of the gospel of God. In the Scriptures is laid down once and for all and once for all, the meaning of the Christian fact and the sole principle of positive faith, which the true Christian experience could only ripen and explicate but never outgrow. Herein is to be found the finality and autonomy of the Bible for faith. 'The Christian experience is not something we bring rationally to the Bible to test scriptural truth; it is something miraculously created in us by the Bible in response to divine power acting as grace; and it can therefore be in no collision with the authority which makes the Bible what it is, the authority of the Gospel, of the Redeemer felt and owned as Redeemer.'[3] So it comes about that Christian experience is the experience of the authority of the gospel; it is not an experience which becomes the authority for the gospel.

In his book, *The Theology of Experience* (1916), H. Maldwyn Hughes puts great stress upon the creative significance of religious experience as the ground of an 'inner certitude'. Experience is the fundamental necessity, he argues; yet the preacher cannot make his own experience the test and limit of truth. His experience is not real and effective independently of the Bible and the facts of history.

In his contribution, K. Fullerton makes immense claims for the modern reconstruction of the Bible and its bearing on authority. The subtitle 'A Study in the History of the Doctrine of the Inspiration of Scripture' gives a more exact statement of its content. Fullerton regards the subject of prophecy as having decisive significance in testing the old and the new view of Scripture. The predictive element in prophecy, he thinks, on the old view, is to be interpreted as 'the result of a direct revelation

[1] P. T. Forsyth, *The Congregational Quarterly*, Vol. 21, 1943, July 1943, p. 335.
[2] *Ibid.*, p. 333.   [3] *Ibid.*, pp. 333–4.

from heaven which was *psychologically unmediated*'.[1] Thus the whole process must be regarded as mechanical and the writers as passive agents, each of which is a 'calamus', a penman, an amanuensis of the Holy Spirit. He objects to such a view because it is non-moral in character.

The modern reassessment of the Bible has changed all this. The prophet 'receives his revelations and as a man he gives them'.[2] Prophecy is, he contends, virtually unconcerned with the predictive element: it seeks to understand 'the relationship of the Prophet to the Spiritual and Moral needs of his own day'. A typical example is the Book of Daniel—'the modern scholar asks what possible meaning there is in Daniel's prediction to the Jews of deliverance from the persecutions of Antiochus Epiphanes at a time when all they desired was to be delivered from the tyranny of Babylon. To compare small things with great, it is as if a dentist should undertake to comfort a patient suffering with a violent toothache by telling him that he would eventually recover from a far worse attack five years later.'[3]

The modern view, Fullerton believes, emphasizes the moral element by connecting it with the spiritual experience of the prophet through whom it was delivered, thus giving a moralized view of inspiration, and with the needs of the people to whom it was originally given so stressing a moralized function of prophecy. Fullerton would eliminate an emphasis on the supernatural. But he seeks to answer the question concerning the authority of the Bible. Its authority is that of the spiritual insights of its prophets. They were the great discoverers of truth. They read the signs of their own day and called for justice, truth and righteousness. They announced that goodness was sovereign and must prevail.

The whole thesis is shot through with the optimism characteristic of the immediate post-First World War period which was supposed to witness the establishment on earth of the Kingdom of God, all bright and fair: 'not the reign of a thousand years, but the *City of God*, a broad and beautiful city which shall gradually enlarge its gracious borders till they are one with the confines of the habitable earth. In the building of this city man joyfully co-operates with God because he has faith in its ultimate

---

[1] K. Fullerton, *Prophecy and Authority*, 1919, p. 191 (italics in original).
[2] *Ibid.*, pp. 191–2.   [3] *Ibid.*, p. 193.

completion, a city purified of sin and all injustice, a city crowned
with the presence of the Lord, a city called into being not by the
magic rub of an Aladdin's lamp, but by the moral efforts of the
race, as they are guided and inspired by the Spirit of God'.[1]
Fullerton's picture was indeed a glowing one and breathes hope
and confidence in man. The only trouble is that man does not
seem to have co-operated in the great way that was expected.

An exposition of the 'new view' of the authority of the Bible,
which caused much controversy and concern comes in the article
with which E. Griffith-Jones opened Peake's *Commentary on the
Bible*. Our own observation would want to be, 'Alas master, for
it was borrowed!' There is no doubt that much of what is said is
drawn from Garvie and Peake. After the assurance that the
Bible 'brings man near to God' and, 'God home to man',
Griffith-Jones proceeds to the usual criticism of the 'old view' of
inspiration. Considered to be 'mechanical' or 'dictation', it makes
the author 'the "pen" of the Holy Spirit'.[2] Griffith-Jones writes
enchantingly about the 'baleful' and 'unfortunate and mis-
chievous results' of such an idea. He therefore suggests the
'dynamical' theory which in his understanding of it 'transfers the
problem from the form of the Bible as literature to the
personalities of the writers'.[3] It was really because these men
had sensitiveness and appreciation that they were inspired. They
were supremely men who *felt*. Above all they were spiritual
artists and seers; and 'The artist may not be a good historian;
the seer may be a poor logician'. With these ideas Griffith-
Jones sets out on his discussion of the 'authority of the Bible'.[4]
'There is', he says almost in the words of Peake, 'an instinctive
craving in the human soul for a standard of belief and conduct
which shall be accepted as infallible.'[5] But no such guide has been
given. Thus the mystic claim and the ecclesiastic boast are to be
dismissed. And the Bible long held by Protestants as an
infallible authority is no longer able to maintain this position.

Yet there is 'something' about the Bible which clothes it with
some sort of compelling atmosphere: it emits, we might say, a
virtue. From whence does this come? It is to be found in the

[1] K. Fullerton, *Prophecy and Authority*, 1919, p. 205.
[2] E. Griffith-Jones, 'The Bible: *Its Meaning and Aim*', Peake's *Commentary on
the Bible*, 1919, new edition with supplement, reprint, 1948, p. 3.
[3] *Ibid.*, p. 4.   [4] *Ibid.*; cf. pp. 7 ff.   [5] *Ibid.*, p. 8.

gospel which is enshrined therein. It is in the experience of that saving message that true authority lies. We are not bound perpetually by 'mere literalism; "My words", He said, "they are spirit and they are life" '.[1] It is not then in abstract terms but in living practice that the problem of authority is 'solved'.

The position occupied by Charles Gore on the authority of the Bible will be seen to follow from what he had to say with regard to its inerrancy and inspiration. A key, perhaps, to his view is provided by the fact that in the last of his three books which make up the composite volume, *The Reconstruction of Belief*, he gives a chapter to the subject of the authority of the Church before he comes to discuss the Bible. It would seem correct, therefore, to deduce from Gore's treatment that he attached a great importance to the Church and its established traditions. In matters of discipline, he asserts, the Church can act freely, and give injunctions of binding force, as circumstances require, on its own authority.[1] He rejects the Roman theory of infallibility and contends for the necessity of free thought. He refers to the 'doctrinal and sacramental authority' of the Church which is 'relative to its moral and social mission'.[2]

Coming to the discussion of the authority of the Holy Scriptures, he makes the revealing remark that he has sought 'to build up a constructive doctrine of God and Christ and the Holy Spirit in the Church without using the books of the Bible except as historical documents'.[3] But he has referred earlier to 'a curious question' which has to be faced. Was the ancient Church right in elevating the written books of the New Testament to a throne of solitary supremacy?[4] Certainly the Church came to believe that they were written under the inspiration of the Holy Ghost. It was 'this root conviction', which 'expressed itself in the doctrine that every book and every sentence of the Bible is infallibly true'.[5] Our Lord, however, did not fall a victim, as did the early Church, to the prevailing notion of 'a strict doctrine of the infallibility of the sacred books in all their details'.[6] He did not accept 'the current Jewish interpretation of the meaning of inspiration'.[7] Elsewhere, however, he has argued that Christ did

---

[1] C. Gore, *The Reconstruction of Belief*, 1921–4, new edition in one volume, 1926, reprint, 1945, p. 792.   [2] *Ibid.*, p. 781.
[3] *Ibid.*, p. 874.   [4] *Ibid.*, p. 872.   [5] *Ibid.*, p. 874.
[6] *Ibid.*, p. 877.   [7] *Ibid.*

accommodate Himself to the popular ideas of biblical authorship and the only reason for his refusal to allow that He did not fall in with the popular view of inspiration is that Gore wishes to use Christ's authority for his own theory of the Holy Scriptures. Like Hebert later, Gore favours the mystical sense of Scripture and he would limit the scope of its inspiration to 'the things of faith and morals'. He rejects what he calls 'the power of naked appeal to the infallible book',[1] and thus states that experience is the ultimate test whereby the word of God can be verified. The scholar may seek, by reason of his special vocation, to test the Bible in the field of critical history, but for most men the testing must be mainly practical. 'Put to account by faith, the claim verifies itself as divine in moral and spiritual experience.'[2]

The problem of religious authority had, over an extended period, special interest for A. E. J. Rawlinson. In 1923, he delivered his Paddock Lectures on the subject and there made explicit some of the ideas he had already expressed as far back as 1912 in his essay contributed to the volume *Foundations*.

In this earlier work, Rawlinson contended that there is no ultimate opposition between the religion of authority and the religion of the Spirit. The trouble has been the way the concept 'authority' has been 'popularly confused with infallibility'.[3] He considers the Infallibilist view of authority to have developed as a logical corollary of an over-mechanical idea of inspiration. 'The legal spirit reacted with transforming effect upon the conceptions alike of authority and inspiration.'[4] All infallible authorities are therefore due to a false emphasis. Papal infallibility is the result of the logical outcome of a one-sided development, while Protestantism reveals a position equally one-sided. 'Its intellectual basis, that is to say, was equally authoritarian with that of Rome, from which it differed merely in the substitution of the infallible Book for the infallible Church: a substitution which in itself was by no means an improvement.'[5] Both ideas, according to Rawlinson, have been finally discarded: 'the infallible Book has gone the way of the infallible Church'.[6] Some would, however, fall back on the 'witness of the Spirit', but this is considered

---

[1] C. Gore, *The Reconstruction of Belief*, 1921–4, new edition in one volume, 1926, reprint, 1945, p. 889.   [2] *Ibid.*, p. 894.

[3] A. E. J. Rawlinson, 'The Principle of Authority', *Foundations* (ed. N. H. Streeter), 1912, reprint, 1922, p. 365.   [4] *Ibid.*, p. 366.

[5] *Ibid.*, pp. 371–2.   [6] *Ibid.*, p. 372.

inadequate by Rawlinson. 'What is needed is rather a restatement of the principle of authority which shall avoid either confusing it with infallibility or legalizing it as despotism.'[1]

Rawlinson then examines the word 'auctoritas' in its classical meaning and contends that it would be best understood by such a phrase as 'corporate' or even 'inspired' witness. He points out that in actual religious psychology, a beginning is made by the acceptance of truth 'on authority'. This 'bondage to authority' period is, however, soon passed, when the right to criticize, or even to deny, is asserted. But there is the final stage which Rawlinson calls 'concrete freedom' to be gained; here comes voluntary assent 'on the ground of reason' to what was formerly believed 'on authority'. The critical stage, is, he thinks, the second. And it is just here that the authority of the Church, which is none other than 'the corporate witness of the saints to the validity of the spiritual experience on which their lives are based' is to be taken into account. It is thus concluded that 'the function of authority in religion (is) neither to compel assent nor to override reason, but to testify to spiritual experience'.[2]

In the Paddock Lectures, these views are given more precise statement, although meanwhile Rawlinson has reiterated something of what he has said in his essay on *Foundations* in his volume *Dogma, Fact and Experience*. The title given by Rawlinson to the Paddock Lectures, *Authority and Freedom*, would lead us to expect a clear statement of his position. He argues that real authority can exist only where there is complete freedom of thought. Authority lies in the truth of a self-evidencing revelation plus the accumulated experience of the ages. He thinks that the future belongs to what he calls 'Evangelical Catholicism', and that it is within this 'revived' New Testament 'Catholicism' that freedom and authority are reconciled.[3] He stresses the authoritative function of the sacraments in the life of the Church. In his article on 'Criticism and the Authority of the Bible' in *The Anglican Communion* (1929),

---

[1] A. E. J. Rawlinson, 'The Principle of Authority', *Foundations* (ed. N. H. Streeter), 1912, reprint, 1922, p. 373.   [2] *Ibid.*, p. 380.

[3] Cf. the later remark of R. B. Owen: 'Not all the philosophy in the world has yet succeeded in resolving the paradox (of freedom and authority). Yet in actual experience we know that freedom is born of an inner authority, a sense of compulsion within the soul of man himself.' *Expository Times*, Vol. LX, 1948-9, pp. 50-1.

Rawlinson gives emphasis to this idea in his apology for the self-evidencing reality of biblical doctrine as experienced within the 'Catholic tradition' of the Anglican communion.

Rawlinson deals with the subject of authority again in his contribution to *Essays Catholic and Critical*, a volume which is 'in its way, a new *Lux Mundi* which may be regarded as a manifesto of the Anglo-Catholic party'.[1] It seems that in this essay, which is entitled 'Authority as a Ground of Belief', Rawlinson puts greater emphasis than elsewhere on the authenticating significance of experience, although the importance of the Church is still much insisted upon.

Rawlinson begins by asserting that the Church is a divine institution, the Spirit-filled Body of Christ. It is, therefore, not irrational for a man to submit his judgements to its authority. Yet authority is never its own guarantee: its claims must be verified. The point is made by a quotation from F. Heiler's *Das Gebet* to the effect that the idea of authority is rooted in the revelational character of the prophetic type of religion.[2] Our Lord, it is observed, as a matter of actual historical fact, astonished the people by teaching independently of scribal tradition, with the unhesitating 'authority' of immediate inspiration.[3] The conclusion then to which he is lead is that 'final authority is not anything which is either mechanical or merely external, but is rather the intrinsic and self-evidencing authority of truth. It means that authority as such can never be ultimately its own assurance, that the claim of legitimate authority must always be in the last resort verifiable claims. The final appeal is to the spiritual, intellectual and historical content of divine revelation, as verifiable at the threefold bar of history, reason and spiritual experience'.[4]

In the same volume, it may be noted here, W. L. Knox writes on 'The Authority of the Church'. The idea of an infallible Bible is vigorously denied and set aside as the only source of authority. Yet it is allowed that 'all Christians would agree that in some sense the Bible possesses a permanent authority in matters of belief and conduct'.[5] The authority which the Bible has derives

---

[1] *Expository Times*, Vol. XXXVII, 1925–6, p. 532.

[2] A. E. J. Rawlinson, *Essays Catholic and Critical* (ed. E. G. Selwyn), 1926, third edition, 1931, p. 86.

[3] *Ibid.*   [4] *Ibid.*, p. 95.   [5] *Ibid.*, p. 101.

from its nature as it is realized and tested in Christian experience as found within the tradition of 'Catholic' Christianity. The Church is, indeed, the custodian of the Scripture and the organ of its permanent message.

This reference to W. L. Knox seems a good place to draw attention to another work to which he with A. R. Vidler contributed, namely, *The Gospel of God and the Authority of the Church* (1937). There is general agreement between what is to be found in this volume and the essay in *Essays Catholic and Critical*. The emphasis, however, of the book is strictly not on the question of the authority of the Church but rather on that of in what sense is the *teaching* of the Church authoritative. Authority is defined as 'title to be believed', and consequently to be distinguished from infallibility. The Church's understanding of the gospel is stated to be not a final or intellectually adequate statement of revelation, but rather 'the best available account of it'—a working hypothesis which is being constantly confirmed, a guide which is sufficient for the practical purposes of leading to the experience of the revelation of God in Christ. This does not leave the question of authority precarious, the authors affirm, by making experience the final confirmation of doctrine. It may be granted that in some instances errors are to be admitted, but 'as a developing whole Christian doctrine is entitled to be accepted as providing . . . adequate guidance to the practice of the Christian life'.

Authority in the Church (1928) by T. A. Lacey is a closely reasoned volume in which patterns of authority are noted, moving down from the ultimate authority of God Himself through the Bible and the Church. Thus while God is the source of authority, these other two are special media of it.

On the publication of C. H. Dodd's important book, *The Authority of the Bible*, a reviewer remarked 'one who is seeking in the Bible an external and infallible authority will get little comfort from Professor Dodd'.[1] Not only is this a correct observation, but it would, we think, be true to say that Dodd gives even greater emphasis to the subjective and the focus within than most. 'The criterion lies within ourselves', he remarks, 'in the response of our spirit to the Spirit that utters itself in the

---

[1] *Expository Times*, Vol. XL, 1928–9, p. 147.

Scriptures.'[1] And he contends that the 'inner witness of the Holy Spirit', of which the Reformers spoke, 'is in effect the "subjective" criterion of which we are speaking'.[2]

It is Dodd's purpose all through his book to establish the validity of the subjective principle by which to assess and attest Scripture. In the Preface, he states that 'the measure of any authority which the Bible may possess must lie in its direct religious value, open to discovery in experience'.[3] When he comes to the end he is able to look back and maintain, 'All through our study it has been clear that anything we can say about revelation is relative to the minds that receive it. Nowhere is the truth given in such purely "objective" form that we can find a self-subsistent external authority'.[4]

Dodd is convinced that the use of the Bible as a dogmatic authority has been undermined by criticism.[5] The whole notion of an external infallibility is beset with insuperable difficulties. The ultimate authority is truth itself as it reveals itself in experience and compels assent. The argument, that since the Bible is the Word of God, it must, therefore, be an infallible authority is no longer valid, since we have come to see that it merely 'mediates' the Word of God and that it is what finds us within it, is true.[6] In religion, it is asserted the attainment of truth imperatively calls for the sharing of a personal experience. It is, therefore, 'in this sense we find a religious authority in the Bible—the authority of experts in the knowledge of God, masters in the art of living; the authority of religious genius'.[7] Yet all the Bible is not the product of such genius. There are areas of the Bible, the greater part indeed, wherein the 'authentic marks of personal inspiration' do not appear. What authority belongs to such parts? Here Dodd calls for a widening of the understanding of what is implied in religious experience. It is never simply private and individual: it takes place in and is related to a much wider context of living.[8] And in this connection there is illustrated for us the effect of religion in the

---

[1] C. H. Dodd, *The Authority of the Bible*, 1928, p. 296.   [2] *Ibid.*, p. 297.
[3] *Ibid.*, Preface, p. ix.   [4] *Ibid.*, p. 289.
[5] *Ibid.*; cf. pp. 8 ff.   [6] *Ibid.*; cf. pp. 15 f. and 289 f.
[7] *Ibid.*, p. 24; cf. p. 133.
[8] *Ibid.* Cf. 'A religious man is not one who has "experiences" which he can describe with particularity, in class-meeting, or in reply to a psychological *questionnaire, as* the case may be, but one who takes all life in a religious way' (pp. 135–6).

larger areas of secular and common life. The value of the Bible
in this wider context of human affairs wherein truth reveals
itself will be obvious. Herein is indicated for us something more
than transient and individual 'religious experiences' as the basis
of faith.

Dodd has some observations to make about the authority of
the gospels which he regards as a product of the experiences of
the early Church and yet which enable us to go beyond that
experience to the events which created it. It is useless, he states,
to attempt to find in the words of Christ the last refuge of an
infallible external authority. Still there is eternal truth which
makes its impact upon the mind through its external expression.[1]
Right through Dodd again and again insists upon the subjective
necessity. 'Thus in every way', he adds once more, 'we are
brought back to the importance of the "subjective" factor.
Granted that religious authority somehow resides in the Bible,
how does it become authoritative *for me?*'[2] It is, then, finally,
according to Dodd, what authenticates itself within experience
is authoritative. There is strictly no objective infallibility, not
even the words of Jesus.

It may be saying too much to suggest that Dodd's subjectivism is less pronounced in his later studies. At any rate in
his 'course of "open lectures" given under the auspices of the
Divinity Faculty of the University of Cambridge' in 1945, there
seems to be a greater recognition given to the Bible as an
objective 'authority'. 'The Scriptures of the New Testament, or
in other words, the documents of the New Covenant', it is stated,
'are the authoritative record of that act of God by which He
established relations between Himself and the Church; and they
are the charter defining the status of the Church as the people of
God, the terms upon which that status is granted, and the
obligations it entails.'[3] He goes on to declare concerning the
Bible that the Church 'offers this book to us as "revelation" of
God'.[4] Dodd has not, of course, been forgetful of his earlier
insistence upon experience, he thus refers to the prophetic
experience of the Old Testament prophets and the New
Testament apostles as giving truth its authority.[5]

---

[1] C. H. Dodd, *The Authority of the Bible*, 1928, cf. pp. 231 ff.
[2] *Ibid.*, p. 290.   [3] C. H. Dodd, *The Bible Today*, 1946, p. 8.
[4] *Ibid.*, p. 12.   [5] *Ibid.*; cf. pp. 102 ff.

In 1930 Bertram Lee Woolf published his work on *The Authority of Jesus*. He had, however, given a fairly good indication of what could be expected in this volume by an article he had written earlier on 'The Authority of the Risen Lord' in an issue of the *Congregational Quarterly* for the year 1928. In this article Woolf argued that the resurrection of our Lord was decisively significant in the experiences of the disciples. They were caught up into a new relationship with the living Christ and here lay for them divine authority. It was through Pentecost that the resurrection was vitalized in their experiences. Thus the authority of Jesus was founded upon His immediate influence upon individuals and upon the believing society. Through the Spirit they became vividly and vitally conscious of a new life, power and personal communion with Christ as living Lord. So is it today: the authority of Jesus 'is only to be found in the inmost experience of the believing soul'. Jesus is indeed to be regarded as the ultimate spiritual authority, because He lives as everpresent in redeeming action as Lord of life.

These are the ideas which Woolf works out with fuller detail in his later thesis on *The Authority of Jesus*. The 'discovery of the ultimate freedom is the discovery of final freedom to live our lives', he urges.[1] And to live our lives in freedom is to know the redeeming inwardness of the living Christ. Writing in one section of 'Authority of the Christian Faith', he says, 'The Christian certainty of the supremacy of Christ is based upon the superior quality of the experience which believers enjoy'.[2] He expresses sympathy with Schleiermacher's emphasis upon religious feeling although he seeks to defend him from the charge of founding religion upon it. He allows that Schleiermacher does give to religious experience its own peculiar form of authority, and with that Woolf profoundly agrees.[3] He is able therefore to say: 'it is this constant and ever-renewed appeal to experience which constitutes the active authority of the Christian religion, where all authority is real in proportion to the vividness and the transforming power of the experience'.[4] He grants that personal experience 'to the one who is used to the important but secondary support of church, or tradition or

---

[1] B. L. Woolf, *The Authority of Jesus*, 1930, p. 39.
[2] *Ibid.*   [3] *Ibid.*; cf. pp. 21–2.
[4] *Ibid.*, p. 23.

scripture may feel this authority is too slender or delicate, and quite unable to bear the demands that will be made upon it'.[1] Woolf cannot grant that this is so. Experience is, he is certain, 'the only authority which has ultimate and effective ethical or religious power', so that as an individual becomes 'accustomed to its purity and its grace' so he 'becomes more aware of its strength'.[2] Jesus is, after all, the contemporary of every era. He is always modern. Thus the authority of Jesus is the authority of His active and living presence in every age. 'The authority of Jesus, in so far as it is felt to be modern, authenticates itself to be the authority of the Lord of Life.'[3]

The same focus upon the inward nature of religious authority comes in one of J. A. Chapman's *Fellowship of the Kingdom* pamphlets.[4]

C. J. Wright seeks to identify the self-witnessing nature of truth with the doctrine of the inner witness of the Spirit. In the past, he states, both the Roman and Protestant Churches, each in their own way, have sought to impose an external authority. He asks the question, 'Is Christianity concerned with "truths", or with "truth"? In other words, with doctrines which are held to be in accord with ultimate reality, or with an ethical attitude of heart and mind?'[5] He is prepared to admit that religious authority is concerned with both. With regard to the second, he argues, Christianity is certainly concerned with 'truth' in the sense of a personal ethical attitude and a personal spiritual insight. 'In the Gospels the test of real truth is never submission to external authority or ceremonial or precept.'

There is, however, the other aspect of the matter in which Christianity is not only bound up with the question of the 'authority' of one's personal attitude, but with the question of 'Authority' itself. Here arises the problem of 'absolute truth'. According to Wright, absolute truth is one and the same with the authority of the truth itself. He then asks, 'What precisely are these truths for which Christianity stands: and further, How can we know them to be true?'[6] The fundamental truth, which is the very essence of the gospel itself, is that of the grace of God.

---

[1] B. L. Woolf, *The Authority of Jesus*, 1930, p. 285.   [2] *Ibid.*   [3] *Ibid.*
[4] J. A. Chapman, *Authority*, 1930.
[5] C. J. Wright, *The Question of Authority in Religion, Expository Times*, Vol. XLIV, 1932–3, p. 440. Cf. *ibid.*, W. J. Sparrow-Simpson, *Modern Witnesses to the Value of Authority in Religion*, pp. 444 ff.   [6] C. J. Wright, *op. cit.*, p. 442.

This supreme truth which ultimately includes all others can be verified as true only in the actualities of experience. Here all things are proved. Divine truth wins its way into the heart and soul. Those who are persuaded and possessed will be ready to claim that the Divine Spirit has authenticated the Divine word within the depths of the human soul. 'What else', he asks as his conclusion, 'is the doctrine of the *Testimonum Spiritus Sancti* but the religious side of the philosophical doctrine of the self-evidencing nature of Truth?'[1]

A. E. Garvie seeks to rescue himself from the hopeless subjectivism to which all his theological writings shows him to be prone. Writing on 'The Value of the Old Testament for the Christian Church', he, too, gives a supreme place to the inner witness of the Spirit. 'Nor is this conviction solely *subjective*', he hastens to add, 'There are objective facts to sustain it'. These objective facts, however, turn out to be themselves subjective. We are to believe, it is told us, that the Holy Spirit 'moved' the 'prophetic consciousness' of the Bible prophets. But the reason for this belief is due to the fact that the Bible has become so assured within experience. The prophetic consciousness through the prophetic succession is the core of revelation, it is stated, and it is in the unfolding content of that prophetic consciousness that Garvie places the authority of the Bible.[2]

Two years after the appearance of his lectures on *Inspiration*, R. H. Malden added another book with the title, *The Authority of the New Testament* (1937). Critical scholarship, he assures his readers, has not impaired the New Testament as the final authority in the areas of faith and morals. Whatever truth there may be in the Bible, and whatever degree of probability is to be allowed to the evidences for its highest religious assurances, ultimately, it appears, for Malden, as for Hort, whose words we may quote here, the authority of the Bible 'is to be found in the light which it brings, far more than in any light which it reveals'.[3]

[1] C. J. Wright, 'The Question of Authority in Religion', *Expository Times*, Vol. XLIV, 1932–3, p. 443.

[2] A. E. Garvie, 'The Value of the Old Testament for the Christian Church', *Expository Times*, Vol. XLVIII, 1936–7, p. 375 f. Cf. 'The Synthesis of History, Experience and Reason in the "Knowledge of God".' *Ibid.*, Vol. XLIII, 1931–2, pp. 103 ff. Cf. also his *The Preachers of the Church*, 1926, and 'The Nature of Religious Authority and the Certainty of Christian Faith' in Mansfield College Essays Presented to A. M. Fairbairn, November 4, 1908, 1909, pp. 161 ff.

[3] F. J. A. Hort, *The Authority of the Bible*, n.d., p. 11.

In an article on 'The Authority of the Bible Today', H. Hodkin argued for, what he calls, the 'propaedeutic' authority of the Scripture. 'The Bible offers these twin truths to us', he writes, 'the truth about life and the truth about God. It does not call upon us to accept them merely because they stand written or because someone else has said that we ought to, but to verify and prove them for ourselves. If experience and testing bears out and establishes these truths, if the acceptance of them gives to the heart and mind that joy, power, and repose which only truth can give, then the authority of the Bible is vindicated. This authority is now seen to be essentially propaedeutic.'[1]

In his *Signposts to God* (1938), W. R. Matthews gives, we think, his clearest statement of religious authority. The title for another of his books, *God in Christian Thought and Experience*, will lead us to expect an emphasis upon the vindicating reality of experience. Matthew begins his less pretentious volume by specifying several kinds of 'signposts' to God, such as nature, history and conscience. Concerning conscience he remarks with the words of John Knox to Mary Queen of Scots, 'Conscience, Madam, requires knowledge'. The voice of authority is, Matthews declares, another and a most important 'signpost'. Some would argue that they listen to no authority. Whoever will not listen to authority, he replies, is 'bound to end up with a meagre and shallow creed'. The individual's own conscience is necessarily very limited. The pressing question is, Where does religious authority exist? There 'is a kind of authority in religion', he answers, 'which is rather like the authority of the people who appreciate art and music. . . . There seem to be persons who have a peculiar sensitiveness of the spiritual world. These are the creative individuals in the history of redemption'. The Bible is authoritative, he concludes, because it contains testimonies to the reality of man's religious experience of God to the Church which enshrines and interprets them.

A careful statement of the problem of authority is given by N. P. Williams. Williams sees the history of Israel as the '*praeparatio evangelica*' leading up to the 'temple of Christian faith'. He then adds, 'Of that temple, "other foundation can no man lay than that which is laid, which is Jesus Christ" '. He, therefore, and no other, is the primary authority for Christian

[1] *Expository Times*, Vol. XLIX, 1937–8, pp. 232–3.

faith, and the Old Testament is precious in our eyes because 'these are they which bear witness of me'.[1] We still have, however, to seek a 'secondary authority' to give us relative information and correct interpretation of Christ's teaching. In some sense the New Testament is to be regarded by all as providing these. But the question of how that teaching is to be derived from this source remains as the vital problem since 'the New Testament though unique as a historical authority' 'seems to refer us beyond itself for our ultimate doctrinal authority'.[2] What is this ultimate authority? Williams apparently regards it as continued Christian tradition which throughout the changing centuries has remained faithful to the primitive 'kerygma'. 'It is, surely, to the indivisible, yet real, weight and pressure of the central Christian tradition, rather than to an indefinite series of coincidences in the construction of inferences from the written page, that the unity of belief manifest at Lausanne and Edinburgh is due. And, whilst mere posteriority in time is in itself no guarantee that a particular phase of religious thought is more authoritative than the phase which preceded it, the conception of the corporate mind of the people of God, slowly growing through the centuries and clarifying the fundamental ideas of its revelation under the guidance of that Spirit who leads men into all truth, will provide us with the clue to the tangled history of Christian theology and with criteria whereby "false starts" and "blind-alley" developments in the interpretation of the deposit of faith may be distinguished from the true and Divinely-intended course of dogmatic evolution.'[3]

[1] N. P. Williams, 'Authority in Matters of Religious Belief', *Expository Times*, Vol. LI, 1939–40, p. 407.

A more 'High Church' statement of the same idea is found in G. W. Broomfield's book, *Revelation and Reunion* (1942). Broomfield contends that the 'authority behind the two creeds' (the Nicean and the Chalcedon) 'is essentially the same as that behind the formation of the New Testament canon'. That authority is, the Holy Spirit inspired Church. What is the real seat of authority, and What is the relation of the Holy Spirit to the Church? he asks. Authority, he urges, and all will agree with him here, is 'from above'. The crucial question is how does it come to us? Through what media is it channeled? Broomfield, and fewer will agree with him here, would restrict authority to the Church as ordered by its bishops; an authority, that is, which is derived by descent from the apostles.

A less forbidding account of the relation of authority to his own Church is given by E. C. Rich in his *Spiritual Authority and the Church of England* (1953). Rich is less inclined to grant to the Church the claim which Broomfield makes for it. His emphasis is upon the 'spiritual' aspect of authority.

[2] *Ibid.*, p. 408.   [3] *Ibid.*, p. 410.

Repeated references have been made in earlier pages of this work to the writings of A. G. Hebert which relate to our subject. Hebert, as we have seen, disavows the idea of an infallibly inspired Bible. The Bible is doubtlessly inspired, but so, too, are 'other books on religious and on "secular" subjects'.[1] They also are in some way born of the Spirit. Consequently if 'the Bible is authoritative because the Holy Ghost spoke through it, those other books should owe whatever authority they possess to the same cause'.[2] What marks a book as authoritative is the approximation to the knowledge of its subject and the wisdom it embodies. The 'difference between the Bible and other books should then be due to their respective subject-matter'.[3] According to Hebert, the main matter of the Bible concerns the Kingdom of God. The Bible is therefore the authority of the Kingdom. It has authority for us 'as the record of a divine Purpose worked out in history'.[4] The Kingdom of God can be considered under three aspects, represented by the Greek words $\dot{\alpha}\rho\lambda\dot{\eta}$ and $\lambda\acute{o}\mu os$ and $\tau\acute{e}\lambda os$. These words apply to the idea of the kingdom in its fundamental purpose, its outworking, and ultimate effect. As unfolding the developing Purpose of grace in all these phases, the Bible alone for the Old Israel and the New, is our 'authority'. Yet no infallibility can be claimed for the record. Imperfect though it may be, it does still contain 'a hard core' in which and through which the saving purpose of God can be traced. In the events of their history the prophets of the Old Testament saw something of the salvation of their God. In every phase of its disclosure of the Kingdom, the Bible bears an 'authoritative testimony'. Yet it is not the testimony of an infallible account, but the conviction of a sure faith. The stories of the Old Testament are 'designed for a specific purpose', they 'cannot be recognized'—he here quotes with approval Pythian-Adam's book *The Call of Israel*—as 'what *we* should call historical'.[5] It is only when we ourselves have penetrated behind the immediate purpose of the individual writer and the garb in which he has clothed it can we get an understanding of the facts 'which may not (the words are again Pythian-Adam's) be by any means recognizable in the *form* in which they are presented'.[6] But ultimately this penetrating activity is ours:

---

[1] *The Authority of the Old Testament*, 1947, p. 49.   [2-6] *Op. cit.*

apparently the Bible cannot be taken at its face value, there is a 'theological' and 'mystical' meaning which they of the Kingdom will appreciate, since, 'The Bible is the Book of the Faith, the Book of the divine Kingdom'.[1]

Following a section on 'The Inner Witness of the Holy Spirit', in his *Christian Apologetics*, in which he has maintained the fundamental necessity for this inner certitude, Alan Richardson then deals with the subject, 'The Divine Authority of the Bible'. The conclusions for which he has argued are substantially those for which he has contended in his *A Preface to Bible-Study*. He expresses the same dissatisfaction with the idea that the authority of the Bible is simply that of religious genius. 'To ascribe to the writers of the Biblical books an authority which is merely that of religious geniuses does not account for the undeniable fact that the Bible comes to Christians in the Church, not merely as possessing the highest human authority, but as the unconditional demand and gracious invitation of God Himself; nor does it in the least help us to understand why such a remarkable succession of "religious geniuses" should have "happened" in Israel and nowhere else.'[2] In the Bible we have not the record of man's search for God but God's search for man. It is from this point of view that its authority must be understood. The authority of the Bible is not to be 'looked upon as a "blind authority" which bludgeons the reason of men into unquestioning acquiescence or which asks of men a "blind faith" '.[3] It is the authority, we might say, of a gracious persuasion and of a divine winsomeness. Richardson stresses the need for the inner illumination of the Spirit since it is by the quickened intuition that the divine truth is apprehended.[4] The sum of the matter is, as his own words declare, 'It was the divine enlightenment of the eyes of the prophets and apostles which enabled them to understand and to interpret the events of the biblical history, and it is still this divine enlightenment which enables Christians today to believe and understand the message of the prophets and apostles, their testimony to Christ which the Bible contains'.[5]

H. Cunliffe-Jones takes a position on the authority of the

---

[1] *The Authority of the Old Testament*, 1947, p. 74.
[2] Alan Richardson, *Christian Apologetics*, 1947, p. 221.
[3] *Ibid.*, p. 222.   [4] *Ibid.*; cf. pp. 225–6.   [5] *Ibid.*, p. 220.

L

Bible somewhat akin to that of Hebert. He makes the point to begin with, with which all Christians will agree, that the ultimate authority must be God Himself. But the authority of God is not, however, that of God in the abstract, but that of God as clothed in His gospel.[1] 'The authority under which all men live which is acknowledged truly in the Christian faith is the authority of God in his revelation.'[2] To this authority of the gospel the Bible is 'the indispensable witness'. But it is God in His revelation in Jesus Christ who is the authority for the Christian. This means that 'What is ultimately authoritative for the Christian theologian is not the Bible as such, but the gospel of God to which it testifies'.[3] This declaration involves a discussion of the relation between 'The Gospel, the Church, and the Bible' which is Cunliffe-Jones's concern in chapter two of his book. It is the gospel as the revelation of the grace of God in Christ which is the final fact for Christian faith.

It is, however, the 'acknowledgement of the authority of God in his revelation which is life under the gospel is life in the Church'.[4] Indeed, life under the gospel involves churchmanship. It is in and through the Church that the individual believer is nourished. The question remains as to the place of the Scriptures; 'what is the function of the Bible, and what is the nature of its authority?'[5] Clearly the Bible is not a primary authority; its authority derives from the gospel to which it is a witness. A distinction is drawn between the theologians and churchly use of the Bible, and it is contended that in the case of the latter the Bible must be used as it stands. The historical approach has had the effect of destroying 'the old common believing use of the Bible, and has not yet enabled a common believing use, which takes for granted the general results of historical study, to govern the use of the Bible in the Church'.[6] It is in this way Cunliffe-Jones admits a sort of double standard of the authority of the Bible and accounts for the prevailing uncertainty concerning its position and place by the inability of the Church to accept the assured results of Biblical criticism in a believing way. Stress is given by Cunliffe-Jones to the witness of the Spirit[7] and it is asserted that 'The continued reappropriation of what the

[1] H. Cunliffe-Jones, *The Authority of the Biblical Revelation*, 1948, p. 7.
[2] *Ibid.*   [3] *Ibid.*, p. 13.   [4] *Ibid.*, p. 16.
[5] *Ibid.*, p. 18.   [6] *Ibid.*, p. 35.   [7] Cf. Chapter XI.

Bible says has very great relative authority for the Christian that he may truly submit himself to the absolute authority of God'.[1]

The year 1949 saw two important discussions of the subject of the authority of the Bible. J. W. C. Wand is insistent that the Bible possesses no 'infallible authority' in itself, and he acknowledges the sense of disappointment the declaration 'that there is no such infallible authority either in the Bible or elsewhere' will occasion. He, however, contends for its relative value and goes on to investigate what he regards as its sphere, source and nature. He finds the source of its authority in three particulars: first, in the writer's own spiritual genius and his humble recognition of the sources from which he draws. Its writers were good men, and 'Goodness is its own authority, and it is their goodness, as well as their ability to assess and present facts, which forms the first element in the authority of the writers and so of the Scriptures'.[2]

The second particular is the Church, in which, and for which, the Bible was produced. 'The Church authorized the Bible; and the Bible vindicates the Church.'[3] Finally, there is God Himself. Thus, remarks Wand, 'in the last resort a large part of the authority of the Scriptures must lie in the appeal that they make to our own conscience'.[4] They awaken a response, and in the response, the authority of the Bible is made effective. Ultimately the authority of the Bible lies in its persuasive appeal. It is not therefore an imperative authority like a military order which must be obeyed. Nor is it an exclusive authority. It does not extend to the whole range of thought but is limited to the necessities of man's salvation. It is not a universal authority, because there are other truths outside it which can be accepted:

[1] H. Cunliffe-Jones, *The Authority of the Biblical Revelation*, 1948, p. 21. A position something akin to this will be found in an article by E. C. Blackman, 'The Authority of the Old Testament: Is it Christian Scripture?' He, too, sees the authority of the Old Testament (that is his particular concern) focused in the 'gospel' which it enshrines. 'What we need from our teachers and guides is to be led through the details to this central truth' (p. 24). About the rough swaddling bands in which the Christ is laid we need not be ashamed or preoccupied. The 'dubious history and sub-Christian morality need cause no embarrassment' (p. 23). Cf. *The Congregational Quarterly*, Vol. 24, 1946, January 1946, pp. 13–24.

[2] J. W. C. Wand, *The Authority of the Scriptures*, 1949, p. 107.
[3] *Ibid.*, p. 108.   [4] *Ibid.*, p. 109.

and it is certainly not compulsive. We must therefore boldly acknowledge 'that the authority of the Scriptures cannot be quite so clear-cut as one might otherwise have thought'.[1]

It is H. H. Rowley's conviction in his Third Joseph Smith Memorial Lecture on *The Authority of the Bible* (1949), that the idea that authority is guaranteed by the inner witness of the Spirit in man comes near to 'the delusion of mere subjectivism', and he consequently pronounces it as 'unsatisfying'. Rowley quotes Millar Burrow's statement that 'what is ultimately authoritative for us is that which commends the assent of our own best judgement, accepted as the witness of the Spirit within us. The only ultimate basis of assurance is the witness of the Spirit with the believer's own spirit'. Such a view Rowley quite rightly observes would make the Bible authoritative for one individual and not for another. Equally to be rejected with this excessive subjectivism is the Roman Catholic view which rests the authority of the Bible on that of the Church. Such a theory, by making the Church primary and final, must justify its claims at the bar of reason. This does not make man a mere creature of reason, since he allows that there is a necessary non-rational element in religion. In man's belief in the authority of the Bible there may be indeed a non-rational element, but if it were wholly non-rational it could approve itself to reason. 'What is first of all in question', therefore, contends Rowley, 'is whether a belief in the authority of the Bible can approve itself to reason, when reason is free and unfettered.'

Rowley argues that there is an authority behind the Bible which remains valid independently of any individual's recognition of it. 'The supreme revelation of God was in the Person of Christ, and while the *story* of that revelation is given in the Bible, the revelation itself lay outside the Bible', he states. This means that the Bible is to be regarded as the record of the revelation. There is, however, something in the sacred history which stamps it as an authentic Divine revelation. There is, throughout, the account of God's grace in deliverance and salvation in which 'we have a complex of human and non-human factors, and neither could determine the other, and *the only possible common source of both is God*'. Throughout both the Old Testament and the New, this same complex pattern, in which the

---

[1] J. W. C. Wand, *The Authority of the Scriptures*, 1949, p. 115.

human and non-human interweave, can be observed. Rowley considers the story of the deliverance of Israel from Egypt by Moses the first significant illustration of this complex of history. 'The confidence', he says, 'of Moses that he was divinely moved to promise deliverance and the manner of his justification; the immense fruitfulness of his work in the religious development that emerged from it; the wide variety of hopes expressed by Old Testament prophets that converged to find their fulfilment in Christ and His Church; the confidence of Christ and the early Church that in them their fulfilment was to be found, in days when the world thought that confidence ludicrous, and the vindication of that confidence in objective fact—all this provides solid evidence that can deliver the Christian from any sense of intellectual shame in finding the hand of God in the Bible and in the history it records and in the persons concerned in it all.'

This view is certainly commendable for the reason that it refuses to base the authority of the Bible upon the idea of the sublimity of its teaching or the mere spiritual insights of its readers. It does seek to build it upon the conviction of God's activity in history. The weakness lies in the fact that this alleged action of God is justified only from the Bible itself. The question which still has to be pressed, But supposing the historical foundations are insecure, or the interpretation of its writers mistaken, What then? The revelation seen as God's acts in history is divorced from the Bible, and yet, it is obvious, we can know of such a revelation only from its pages. Rowley himself may be able to find the certain, solid, historical truth within the record, but then he may have the adequate equipment. What of the ordinary man? He has not the sight and the sense of the 'able historical critic'. Must he be left ultimately to the 'authority of the experts'?

To his Burroughs Lectures of 1948, R. R. Williams adds, for publication, two essays on the modern problem of authority. The lectures themselves are concerned with the concept of authority in the apostolic Church. And what he has to say in this respect is summarized in this way. He has argued that 'the authority recognized in the apostolic age was the authority of God, asserted in history by Christ, His vice-regent. This was conveyed to individual Christians and Christian groups in a variety of ways. There was the record of Christ's deeds and words, which could be personally known and increasingly appropriated by all. There was the existence of a ministry felt to be commissioned by Him. There was, too, the sense of His immediate presence, made real and vivid by His indwelling Spirit. Every man had to be fully persuaded in his own mind concerning his own actions, but actions which concerned larger groups and more far-reaching issues called for more formal decision, which was reached either by apostolic fiat or by conciliar discussion with prayer for the guidance of the Spirit. No one channel could be regarded as monopolizing the right to mediate Christ's authority. The right, if it lay anywhere, lay in the whole Church, and then only in so far as the whole Church was obedient and responsive to the Spirit. Life in the apostolic Church was life in a complex of relationships, through each and all of which Christ's authority was to work. No one aspect of it could have been easily isolated from the others'.[1]

In the first of his two supplementary essays, Williams seeks to give 'An Account of the Modern Discussion of Authority in Religion and in the Church'. He makes reference to about half a dozen books in which there is revealed in some of them a tendency to accentuate the religion of the spirit and in others of them to stress the religion of authority. Dealing then with 'The Contemporary Problem of Authority' he has some remarks to make on that of the Scriptures in particular. They have an authority because they are 'the classical, normative account of Christian origins'.[2] And although, according to Williams, they are not our only historical source (he specifies The Eucharist, as 'itself part of the historical tradition'), they are the written documents which give permanency and stability to the historical tradition. The Scriptures have an authority, besides, because they act as 'a salutary check on the Church's waywardness'.[3] Then, too, in harmony, as he maintains, with Augustine, Luther, Sabatier, Barth, the Bible is authoritative because through its pages God speaks to men and to His Church in every age. In the end, however, it is the saving action of God in Christ, recorded in the Scriptures, summarized in the Creeds, dramatized in the sacraments, where exists the locale of authority. 'It is the Holy

---

[1] R. R. Williams, *Authority in the Apostolic Church*, 1950, pp. 112–13.
[2] *Ibid.*, p. 132.　　　　[3] *Ibid.*

Spirit who brings home to Church and to Christian the authority of God in Christ. The Lord is the Spirit.'[1]

The very title of the symposium edited by Richardson and Schweitzer, *Biblical Authority for Today* marks it down for comment here. The reference in the Preface to 'the tentative character of the document' has been already noted.

Apart from one or two of the writers, the idea of an infallible Bible is denied. Regin Prenter giving the Lutheran view of the subject states that 'Fundamentalism' deriving from traditionalism, by making the Scriptures infallible 'actually turns Scripture itself into a tradition'.[2] As revelation is the *living* Word of God, the Bible and tradition witness to the fact, and it is the realization of this, which prohibits us from regarding the Bible 'as if it were a collection of supernaturally revealed truths'.[3] Stressing the testimony of the Holy Spirit, he declares that the 'Church must have the courage to preach the message of God's revelation without possessing an infallible Bible and an infallible interpretation of the Bible'.[4] Thus the authority of the Bible is not the authority of a book, nor indeed the authority of its authors, but the authority of the content of its message, the authority of the witness of the self-revealing action of the triune God, who is Himself the real authority for the validity of the Bible.

Barnabas Nagy, for the Reformed Church, maintains that the authority of the Bible is the living concrete authority of Jesus Christ who speaks by means of it. In this sense all other authorities are relative and limited. The unconditional authority of the Bible as God's words is above that of the Church and the inner witness of the Spirit. 'The position of these two authorities must never be reversed, nor may they be put on the same level.'[5] The Bible, in theory and practice, first and last, is exalted high above all human attempts to control it. But it is the Holy Spirit who 'makes the letters, the words, the texts of the Bible into a living witness, so that the living Lord Jesus Christ stands before us: God's Word in the human word'.[6]

[1] R. R. Williams, *Authority in the Apostolic Church*, 1950, p. 141.

[2] *Biblical Authority for Today* (ed. A. Richardson and W. Schweitzer), 1951. A World Council of Churches Symposium on 'The Biblical Authority for the Churches' Social and Political Message for Today', p. 110.

[3] *Op. cit.*, p. 111.   [4] *Op. cit.*   [5] *Op. cit.*, p. 89.

[6] *Op. cit.*, p. 91.

Clarance Tucker Craig, giving the Methodist contribution, shows a thorough dislike for the word 'authority'. He prefers to speak of the Bible as the primary 'source of guidance'.[1] Authority rests ultimately, he says, on the will of God and in the discovery of that will, authority is found. 'When faith responds to the testimony of the Bible that its witness is true, then the Bible has for that person a position for which the word "authority" is not too strong a word.'[2]

Panyotis I. Bratsiotis, speaking for the Orthodox communion, sees the Bible as 'the authoritative written expression of what God does and will do for the salvation of man, for the establishing and triumph of His own kingdom'.[3] The other writers, each with his own particular emphasis, reiterate the same general theme.

The article on 'The Bible: Its Significance and Authority', by H. H. Farmer in *The Speaker's Bible* is of some importance. The Bible is, he argues, certainly a standard and norm, but there are, he states, two types of such: an extrinsic or static, and an intrinsic or dynamic one. The Bible is of the latter sort. Yet while 'it is true that we cannot rightly apprehend the essentials of the Christian faith and life without using the Bible as an authoritative source and norm, it is equally true that we cannot apprehend the Bible as such a source and norm, still less rightly use it, apart from a living participation in the Church's faith and life'.[4] Having stressed that the essence of the faith is harmonious with the content and structure of the Bible, Farmer comes to discuss the question of the normative function of the Bible within the Church.

The creative and constructive principle of the Church is the living Christ Himself, who in all things rules and directs its faith and life through the Holy Spirit. But while Christ is the final and absolute authority the Bible is in some sense the supreme standard and norm. The crucial question concerns the relation of the authority of Christ to that of the Bible. The Bible, contends Farmer, 'indispensably participates in the authority of the living Christ'. Through it an encounter can be continually re-enacted with the historic Saviour.

---

[1] *Biblical Authority for Today* (ed. A. Richardson and W. Schweitzer), 1951. A World Council of Churches Symposium on 'The Biblical Authority for the Churches' Social and Political Message for Today', p. 35; cf. p. 41.

[2] *Op.cit.*, p. 32.   [3] *Op. cit.*, p. 20.

[4] H. H. Farmer, 'The Bible: Its Significance and Authority', *The Speaker's Bible*, 1952, p. 5.

The authority of the Bible is then not different from that of Christ.[1] Wherein then lies the authority of Christ? It is significant that Farmer quotes from John Oman's *Vision and Authority* in developing his answer.[2] Just here is the key to his position. The authority of Jesus, Oman teaches, was no external authority; it was the authority of an inward appeal. Thus, writes Farmer, 'it is a most grave disloyalty to Christ, and to the Scriptures which He uses to speak to men, to turn the latter into an over-riding authority of the extrinsic "yardstick" sort'.[3] Farmer seeks to answer objections to this account of the authority of the Bible which puts the focus within. He will not allow that to accept in the Scripture only that which compels our assent is to be exposed to the danger of an unchecked individualism. He retorts: 'It is to the insight of the individual Christian that Christ speaks, but to picture the individual Christian to whom Christ thus speaks as an isolated and self-contained unit shut up within the circle of his own mental processes is to deny in effect the two truths thus stated'.[4] These two truths which he has maintained are, first, that the new man in Christ has become incorporated in the new covenant community, and, secondly, that it is only as such he can understand and use the Scriptures. Farmer contends, too, that by throwing the Christian believer back on his own inward sense of truth, he does not overlook the fact of sin. In truth, he claims that the clamour for an authoritarian direction, which should dispel all our doubts and perplexities and exempt us from ever making mistakes, is itself a form of anxiety which betrays unbelief and lies somewhere at the very heart of sin. Closing with a section on 'The Bible the Authoritative Basis of Preaching' he returns once again to make the subjective emphasis.[5]

A reference is required concerning the paper prepared for a Joint Theological Commission in South India, under the chairmanship of L. Newbigin, by J. R. Macphail and others, with the title 'The Authority of the Bible'. The trite remark is made at the beginning that Jesus did not leave behind Him a single written word. The paper puts as the first regard a discussion of 'The Primacy of the Church'. It goes on to state that while the

---

[1] H. H. Farmer, 'The Bible: Its Significance and Authority', *The Speaker's Bible*, 1952, p. 24.   [2] Cf. *ibid.*   [3] *Ibid.*, p. 25.
[4] *Ibid.*   [5] *Ibid.*; cf. p. 31.

original witnesses of the saving acts of God in Jesus survived, there was no need for any other authority in the Church except the apostolic men and the Old Testament. But as 'the last living witnesses were taken one by one from among men, the Church set itself carefully and patiently to gather and to set apart a little library of books in which their testimony was preserved'.[1] This 'unique book', into which the collection was brought together, is so 'not because it is better than other books in the same way but because it is the original record of a unique story'.[2] Its contents derive their meaning from the fact that it is concerned with Christ. Unique, however, as it is, it is not a book without mistakes. And although its writers were indeed helped in their work by the Holy Spirit of Promise, they had still to use their own memory, imagination, knowledge, judgement and concentration of will. They were not 'mechanical instruments of supernatural power' rendered incapable of all error. Yet 'in spite of their mistakes, God's word is spoken and heard and done'.[3] Essentially, however, the reader of the Bible must be 'as truly inspired as the original writing of it was'.[4] But in the end the Bible has no authority but its own; the authority, that is, of the truth which it proclaims. Christ is the Truth and it is in the Bible's power to bring us face to face with Him 'that it becomes truth to us'.[5]

J. K. S. Reid's book *The Authority of Scripture*, lays stress upon Christ's authority as ultimate and final. And once again there is emphasis put upon the inner witness, which gives the Bible its validity and its relative authority. Raymond Abba is prepared to admit that the 'Fundamentalists' rendered 'valuable service to the Christian Church' in preserving 'the great supernatural facts of Biblical religion'.[6] No longer do they seem to be dismissed under the odious stigma of obscurantist. It is by reason of their continued insistence on inerrancy and verbal inspiration that they must be held outside the pale of the theologically respectable and the intellectually open. Abba, as we have seen earlier, castigates 'Fundamentalism' on these counts.

[1] J. R. Macphail and Others, 'The Authority of the Bible', *The Scottish Journal of Theology*, March 1956, p. 18.

[2] *Ibid.*   [3] *Ibid.*, p. 23.
[4] *Ibid.*   [5] *Ibid.*, p. 29.
[6] Raymond Abba, *The Nature and Authority of the Bible*, 1958, p. 65.

It is his view that the ultimate authority for the Christian is Christ Himself. And certainly no voice will be raised against such an assertion. It is to Him that both Church and Bible point. The question however remains as to the nature of Biblical authority. 'The nature of the authority of the Bible is determined by the nature of the Bible itself', he declares.[1] The Bible is not however a 'faultless and inerrant oracle'. It is such a notion, we are told, which is the reason for the Fundamentalist's dilemma. He begins with the 'unbiblical assumption' of the inerrancy of Scripture, and finds himself driven to sacrifice intellectual integrity in an attempt to vindicate every factual statement in the Bible, or he is compelled to abandon all belief in biblical accuracy.

The authority of the Bible, it is reiterated, is Christ in the Scriptures. This means that it is 'essentially a *religious* authority'.[2] It is the introduction of the divine–human encounter in which God confronts man in succour and demand. The authority of the Bible is, in fact, an 'accepted' authority, recognizable only within a faith-situation. 'The authority of the Bible, therefore, has to be experienced to be known.'[3] Abba, however, seems to place the Bible in the same category as the Church and the Inner Light. Authority, he says, is 'a cord with three strands' in which each of these has its place: 'the Bible needs to be read in the light of the living faith of the Church and authenticated in the heart of the believer by the inward testimony of the Holy Spirit'.[4]

The symposium, *On the Authority of the Bible* (1960), to which L. Hodgson, C. F. Evans, J. Burnaby, G. Ebling and D. E. Nineham contribute is in outlook and conclusion in general accord with the fundamental principles outlined in the main writings above.

Looking back over how one and another writer referred to in the previous section stated his understanding of the Bible, one is impressed by the strength and the weakness of the emphasis. It was a right and proper thing to give attention to the subjective necessity in validating the authority of the Scripture. The point had to be made in view of the tendency, which had earlier prevailed, to regard Christian faith as a sort of mental assent to a

---

[1] Raymond Abba, *The Nature and Authority of the Bible*, 1958, p. 304.
[2] *Ibid.*, p. 306.   [3] *Ibid.*, p. 308.   [4] *Ibid.*, p. 307.

body of 'Biblical doctrines'. Revelation, some had conceived to have been given in the form of a series of cold and calculated propositions. Against such there was a hearty reaction, In this Schleiermacher had earlier led the way, and those who followed him, appear, no more than did Sabatier, to be unduly perturbed by their subjectivism. They no doubt realized the necessity for, as well as the strength of, their position.

At the same time, it was not sufficiently grasped, that it was no adequate foundation for a robust faith, to build theology on changing experience, even if it be designated 'religious' or even 'Christian' experience. It is one thing to say that the knowledge of God is discovered by experience, but it is quite another to maintain that it arises out of experience. It should, of course, be allowed that authority has no final meaning unless it is experienced through surrender and obedience. It was, however, a rightful protest which Forsyth entered against the 'cult of experience', to insist that God alone speaks of God and that God is known through God alone. There must therefore be an authority for the redemptive experience, not merely psychological, but historical, at least in the sense of *Geschichte*, Forsyth contended; and 'it must be', he adds, 'the Christ of the historical and redeeming cross'.[1]

Objective authority in religion, it had been asserted, was essentially a false note. It was a transgression of man's fundamental freedom and corrupting of his rightful autonomy. A book religion would be a hurtful burden because it means the dictating of truth *a priori*. Thus special delight was taken by writer after writer in making the observation that Jesus never left any written authority. Had He given to us a dictated volume, it was bluntly stated by Percy Gardner, it would have become 'a crushing weight on the Church'.[2]

By stating the case in the way they did, so as to repudiate the Scripture as an essential standard, several writers overstepped the bounds of the required emphasis. By turning within for the grounds of religious authority they were left with no ultimate standard by which religious experience itself could be sifted and settled. The only test for a genuine religious experience seems to be its quality or its vividness or its clarity. But the strength of

[1] P. T. Forsyth, *The Principle of Authority*, 1913, second edition, 1952, p. 63.
[2] Percy Gardner, *Modernism in the English Church*, 1926, p. 105.

an experience is no guarantee of its authenticity. The fact is, that when revelation or authority is made conterminuous with religious experience the whole content of both is destroyed. To read authority in terms of experience is to leave no possible escape from an unhealthy subjectivism.

There must be a revelation having truth-content if there is to be valid authority in religion. Revelation or religious authority, for they are two sides of the one reality, is not something *made*; it is something *given*. If a real objective revelation is denied, then the reality of authority is destroyed.

Many writers did seek a way of escape from the morass of subjectivism to which their revelational theory had brought them. Reference was made, for example, to the check of social experience, to the voice of truth itself, and so forth. 'By some sort of dance-step', charges Bernard Ramm, 'the objective is brought into the subject of religious authority without waltzing to the orthodox tune.'[1] The ideas were urged that, seen from the philosophical point of view, religious experience is the only means by which the Object of religion is grasped; and that the subjective experience thus asserted reached its apex in the life of Jesus Christ and that consequently His life is, then, to be reckoned as the 'objective' test whereby all subjective experience can be tested.

But this only raises the further question, as Ramm was not slow to observe, How does the life of Christ become such a valid, objective revelation? It can only be as it is properly documented. This means that that which exercises authority over Christian experience can be objective only because it is historical. It is no longer, then, merely 'of the spirit': it is the authority of a documented life. It is only an objective revelation which is historical and vice versa. 'The inner piety of Jesus is private, and it is available to neither contemporary nor historian unless it is communicated. The inner life of Christ can be known only if it is documented. Even if one insists that the revelation *per se* was private to Christ, yet the recorded documentation of that life of ideal piety must stand authoritative for Christian experience.'[2]

The sheer fact is that we know nothing of Jesus except through His words. It is by His words He is known and understood. This means that if the words of Jesus are true then the

---

[1] Bernard Ramm, *The Pattern of Authority*, 1957, p. 81.   [2] *Ibid.*, p. 82.

Church does possess an authoritative truth, but if we cannot trust His words then we have no key to an understanding of His filial piety. It is indeed a surprising fact how much the radical subjectivists profess to know about the 'consciousness of Jesus'. But the only way to an understanding of that consciousness is by way of His words.[1] 'Religious liberalism was so careful to protect the human spirit from unhealthy authoritarianism, to defend its freedom, to emphasize the necessity of experimental appropriation of religion, that it lost the Object of religion and His freedom to speak to man as He pleased. . . . In so carefully setting forth how religious truth is to be appropriated, religious liberalism in practice confuses religious experience, religious authority, and the Object of religion.'[2]

Readers will no doubt be confused by the contradictory claims made to support the same general thesis. There are those who, in expounding the idea of Biblical authority as based on experience, contend that this was the view of the primitive Church: others, however, argue that it was not. Some, too, have maintained that it has its origin in the Reformation, while others take the opposite position. Thus, to take only one example, A. L. Lilley, in a reference to Luther, states: 'No Christian doctor of the first rank ever disparaged the revelational role of the Scripture more consistently than the great reformer'.[3] On the other side, F. R. Barry puts Luther and Calvin together and asserts that 'In their zeal for the newly discovered Scriptures . . . the Reformers allowed themselves to become intoxicated with a crude and fanatical bibliolatry'. Disastrous results, he contends, have followed from their Bible worship; 'the authority of an infallible Scripture has proved to be more sterilizing in morals than the autocracy of an infallible pope'.[4]

Here are two writers who are to be found attributing to the Reformers opposing doctrines. 'On the one hand there are those who believe that the Fathers of the Reformation', to quote what we have written on this strange inconsistency elsewhere, 'rejected all external authority in the rediscovery of the freedom of the Spirit. On the other hand, there are those who stigmatize

---

[1] Cf. James Orr, *The Christian View of God and the World*, 1893, third edition, 1897, pp. 405–8.

[2] Bernard Ramm, *The Pattern of Authority*, pp. 83–4.

[3] A. L. Lilley, *Religion and Revelation*, 1932, p. 79.

[4] F. R. Barry, *The Relevance of Christianity*, 1931, revised edition, 1932, p. 24.

them because they substituted a new authority—an infallible Bible for an infallible Pope. They are thus supposed to be, at the same time, the creators of a new subjectivism and a new scholasticism. They are commended by some because they were "liberal" in their attitude to the Bible; and they are condemned by others because they were "bibliolaters".'[1]

Sometimes, too, it will have been noted, the opposers of the subjectivist emphasis are spoken of as Traditionalists, as for example, by Gore and Hebert. On the other hand, they are believed to be innovators of a new theory. R. R. Williams, for instance, says 'After the Reformation (comes) a new orthodoxy, an almost Judaistic reverence for the letter of Scripture. This was something new, not paralleled in either Medieval or Reformation times. It is known today as Fundamentalism, through the name given to all anti-modernists in America'.[2]

It will be hard for the student who seeks an understanding of this subject to reconcile all these contradictions. He must be forgiven if he remains uncertain as to the precise facts if he limits himself to these writings. Or he may, perhaps, see for himself in such contradictions an illustration of the subjective principle of authority and the uncertain results to which it leads if taken as the only criterion of truth.[3]

B. THE AUTHORITY OF THE BIBLE AS EXISTING APART FROM EXPERIENCE

Under this heading we do not intend to refer again to the volumes already reviewed in which the idea of a verbal inspiration of Scripture is stated and defended, and in which revelation was identified, for all practical purposes, with the written word. It will be sufficient to point out that all who take this position are at one in maintaining that the Bible is the objective standard of all religious truth and trust. It possesses in itself an

---

[1] H. D. McDonald, *Ideas of Revelation*, 1959, p. 207.

[2] R. R. Williams, *Authority in the Apostolic Age*, 1950, p. 131.

[3] An interesting example of the same effort to have the argument both ways may be noted in the methods by which the Roman Catholic controversialists sought to dispose of the Reformers' doctrine and preaching of justification by faith. To begin with they were charged with introducing a 'novelty' into the traditional teaching of the Church. Then, in order to regain their hold, it was contended that it was the 'old doctrine' of the Church—thus, says Luther in indignant sarcasm, these 'Popish writers pretend that they have always taught what they now teach . . . thus the wolf

authority which is independent of experience. Its authority, to be sure, must become effective within experience but it is not credited with an authority on that account. There must be the witness of the Spirit, but apart from that witness, the Bible is declared to be, objectively, and in itself, the word of God. The Spirit, it is argued, can only bear testimony to that which is true. And He leads to Him who is the Truth, even Christ, but He does it through the Scriptures, and for this reason, it is maintained, the Bible is the Word of truth. The authority of the Bible, no more than its inspiration, it is contended, cannot be abstracted from the words. In a very real sense its language is the language of the Holy Spirit and consequently its authority is not 'made' in the context of human experience.

It does, however, seem to be required that those who contend for this understanding of the authority of the Bible should be permitted to give some account of themselves. And to meet this necessity we have thought it best to allude to a few statements of the case to which reference has not been hitherto made.

A 'generous and well-informed apology for Bible infallibility', so a contemporary issue of the *Expository Times* describes D. M. McIntyre's volume *The Divine Authority of the Scriptures of the Old Testament* (1906). McIntyre argues that Christ's authority is a sufficient assurance of the authority of the Bible. But lest it be concluded that he conceived of faith as a mere assent of the truth of a writing, he added another volume sometime later on *The Spirit in the Word* (1908). In this attention is given to the supplementary inward action of the Spirit who makes the Word a living reality.

An article appeared in a 1908 edition of *The Record* in which H. Wace, Dean of Canterbury, dealt with 'The Authority of Holy Scripture'. It is vigorously maintained that the whole Bible is a reliable external authority. The Old Testament was certainly so to our Lord, and must consequently be so for us. Christ indeed submitted Himself to its authority, he argues by

---

puts on the sheep's skin till he gains admission into the fold'. Upon which summersaulting James Bannerman commented, 'That their original charge against the Protestant doctrine as a "novelty" and their subsequent claim to it as the "old doctrine" of the Church, could not both be true, is evident, for they are manifestly contradictory; and it might seem incredible that they could have been adopted by the same parties in good faith'. James Bannerman, *Doctrine of Justification by Faith*, 1867, reprint, 1955, p. 135; cf. pp. 138–41.

reference to five separate passages in the New Testament. As regards the New Testament itself, although Christ's example and words cannot be appealed to, yet 'It is no less unquestionable, that the Scriptures of the New Testament were, from the first, treated by the Church as similarly authoritative'. His assurance is, then, that in the Jewish Church in the period of Christ, and the Christian Church for the first two centuries, as well as for the apostles and Christ Himself, the Scripture of both Testaments were conceived to be historically true and divinely authoritative. This 'uniform belief of the Church in early ages', he concludes, cannot be considered ill-founded. The books which have come into our hands 'have been preserved under the Divine control, and consequently carry Divine authority'.

In the popular one volume *New Bible Commentary*, published under the auspices of the Inter-Varsity Fellowship, there will be found a carefully written article by G. W. Bromiley on the subject, 'The Authority of Scripture'. Bromiley opens up his statement with an investigation of the Bible's witness to its own authority. He then faces the charge that to claim for the Bible a unique authority by an appeal to its own testimony is an outrageous form of question-begging. He vigorously repudiates the suggestion. 'If the Bible did not make that claim', he says, 'we should have no call to believe it. And we could have no general confidence in the teaching of Scripture. But if the Bible stands before us as an authoritative Word of God, a Word which itself claims authority, then it is as such that we must reckon with it, receiving that Word and the authority of that Word, or resisting it.'[1] Both Testaments, he contends, everywhere in an implicit way, and in many places in open and direct expression, claim themselves to be more than of human origin. A definite authority belongs to the written words of the Bible. 'When we come to the apostles we find that their testimony to the divine authority of the Bible is equally clear.'[2] Certain passages, for example, II Tim. iii. 15–16; II Peter i. 21 and iii. 16, are evidences that 'the written word was itself treated as the inspired and authoritative form in which the content of divine revelation had been expressed and handed down'.[3]

[1] G. W. Bromiley, 'The Authority of Scripture', *The New Bible Commentary* (ed. F. Davidson, A. M. Stibbs and E. F. Kevan), 1953, p. 15.
[2] *Ibid.*   [3] *Ibid.*, p. 16.

Having dealt with some implications of this witness, he concludes that, in spite of certain difficulties, 'the Bible does lay serious claim to a divine origin, status and authority'.[1] Through its human writings may be traced the authorship of the Holy Spirit. In both the prophetic utterance and the historical events the supernatural are accepted. No artificial distinction is made between the inward content of the Word of God and the outward form. It comes with challenge to belief or unbelief and thus authenticates itself as God's written Word.

This view of the authority of the Bible is, Bromiley believes, in substantial agreement with the Reformed position. The leaders of the Reformation considered the Bible to be inspired and authoritative and the 'sole-sufficient' in matters of faith and conduct.[2] 'They did not take any radical step when they propounded this view' he adds. Such had always been the understanding of the Church with regard to its Scriptures. The Reformers emphasized the importance of the very letter of Scripture,[3] yet they did not do so at the expense of a clear doctrine of the sovereignty of the Spirit. They did, indeed, make much of the inner witness of the Spirit, but not as operating apart from the written Word, but as the indispensable counterpart of God's outward revelation. By 'that emphasis upon the Lordship of the Holy Spirit the Reformers safeguarded themselves against dead literalism and scholastic rationalism in their understanding of Holy Scripture. They yielded to none their loyalty to the given form of the Bible. They had a high view both of the Bible itself and also of its inspiration. They believed the Bible itself is inspired truth. They believed that it is the Word written, a Word given and applied by the Holy Spirit. They taught that that Word must always be respected and received and obeyed. Yet they remembered always that God is the Lord of Scripture, and that it is His voice which must be heard if the

---

[1] G. W. Bromiley, 'The Authority of Scripture', *The New Bible Commentary* (ed. F. Davidson, A. M. Stibbs and E. F. Kevan), 1953, p. 17.

[2] It will be of interest in this connection to compare two recent books in which the theological standpoint of each writer is not the same. Cf. R. C. Johnson, *Authority in Protestant Theology*, 1959, and John Murray, *Calvin on Scripture and Divine Sovereignty*, 1960, Chapters I and II. Both would confirm Bromiley's contention.

[3] Cf. 'There is no hint anywhere in Calvin's writings that the original text contained any flaws at all'. E. A. Dowey, *The Knowledge of God in Calvin's Theology*, 1952, p. 100.

Bible is to do its work. The Bible is not an academic textbook of divine truth, the Euclid of the Christian faith. The text is indeed given by God, but it is always in the hands of God and always applied by God. The Bible must be respected and received and obeyed not because it is a fixed and static letter, but because under the Holy Spirit that letter is the living Word of the living God both to the individual and to the Church'.[1]

Bromiley deals with certain modern trends and sees inadequacies in the Roman Catholic, liberal Protestantism and Barthian views. Concerning the last, he says, 'Barth has performed a useful service by showing that the categories of a dead (as opposed to a living) orthodoxy simply will not do. An abstract objectivism, or a mechanical conception of revelation, is as far from the truth on the one side as is a pure subjectivism or naturalistic view of revelation on the other'.[2]

He considers that the Incarnation provides the key to the correct understanding of the Bible. The ultimate problem concerns the proper relation between the divine and the human. In the case of the Bible, he asks, 'Ought we to think that the Bible is trustworthy merely because we can demonstrate its historical accuracy? Ought we to think it authoritative merely because we have come to know the truth of its message through the Holy Spirit, and irrespective of the historical reliability or otherwise? Ought we not to see the authority of the Bible in the balanced relationship of a perfect form (the objective Word) and a perfect content (the Word applied subjectively by the Holy Ghost)—the form holding the content, and the content not applied except in and with the form?'[3]

It is Bromiley's conviction that the Bible should be seen in this light and for this reason he finds help in the relationship between the divine and the human in Christ. In Him, these two are distinct, yet one. So is it with the Word written, which is the witness to Him. 'It is not enough to deny the divine, to see only a man here, a book there. But it is also not enough to ignore the human, to see only a God here, an oracle there. It is a true paradox (i.e. it is not irrational) that the man Jesus is the Son of

[1] G. W. Bromiley, 'The Authority of Scripture', *The New Bible Commentary* (ed. F. Davidson, A. M. Stibbs and E. F. Kevan), 1953, p. 19.   [2] *Ibid.*, p. 22.
[3] *Ibid.* Cf. G. W. Bromiley, 'The Authority of the Bible: The Attitude of Modern Theologians', *The Evangelical Quarterly*, Vol. XIX, No. 2, April 1947, pp. 127–36, esp. p. 136.

God (and faith by the Holy Ghost knows Him to be so). So too is it a true paradox (i.e. it is not irrational) that the book, the Bible, can be and is the revelation of God (and faith by the Holy Ghost apprehends it as such).'[1] The parallel between Christ and the Bible, he agrees, must not be pressed too far, since the Bible, however highly regarded, is still 'a creature'. At the same time, taking the Incarnation as our guide, it will help us to a truer and fuller understanding of the authority and integrity of the Scripture, not only in reference to its content, but also as regards its historical form.

In the Introduction to his published series of addresses on *Authority* delivered at a Conference of the General Committee of the International Fellowship of Evangelical Students in 1957, D. Martin Lloyd-Jones remarks, 'If I understand the modern religious situation at all this whole question of authority is one of the most important problems confronting us'.[2] He is aware, on the one hand, of the success following the claim to possess such authority, and, on the other hand, of the need for an authentic authority if Evangelical faith is to press forward vigorously and victoriously.

The first of his three lectures argues for the final and supreme authority of the Lord Jesus Christ. 'Jesus Christ is not one in a series, He does not represent one authority among a number of authorities. He stands alone. In the New Testament He is the sole authority.'[3] He then turns to consider the authority of the Scriptures. He sees this bound up with the assertion of the finality of Christ. 'In any consideration of final authority of the Lord Jesus Christ Himself (with which we have already dealt) we are driven of necessity to a consideration of the authority of the Scriptures.'[4] Lloyd-Jones contends that it was the immediate effect of the Higher Criticism to instil doubt about the authority of the Bible. Since then the charge has been levelled against the Conservative Evangelical that he is a 'Bibliolater'. It is claimed by those who utter this condemnation that they have freed themselves from the crippling burden of an infallible book. For them, not the Bible, but Christ Himself is their authority, they say. But

---

[1] G. W. Bromiley, 'The Authority of Scripture', *The New Bible Commentary* (ed. F. Davidson, A. M. Stibbs and E. F. Kevan), 1953, pp. 22–3.

[2] D. Martin Lloyd-Jones, *Authority*, 1958, p. 7.

[3] *Ibid.*, pp. 26–7.   [4] *Ibid.*, pp. 32–3.

impressive as this may sound it does not meet the demands of the situation. Lloyd-Jones asks of them the question, 'How do you know the Lord? What do you know about the Lord, apart from the Scriptures? Where do you find Him? How do you know that what you seem to have experienced concerning Him is not a figment of your own imagination, or not the product of some abnormal psychological state, or not the work perchance of some occult power or evil spirit?'[1] It may sound impressive to say that you go directly to Him, but there is no going to Him without the practical possession of certainty respecting His authority.

Bromiley had maintained with regard to the unique authority of the Bible that 'in the last analysis we accept that authority by faith',[2] and this is a special point made by Lloyd-Jones.[3] Faith does not begin with supplying an answer to the question of the authority of the Bible, it springs out of belief in and submission to that authority, as it is made real by the *testimonium Spiritus internum*. The authority of the Bible is not a matter to be defended, so much as to be declared. It is the presupposition of true biblical teaching and preaching. It is the whole Bible which is the Word of God and it must be viewed as a whole. Lloyd-Jones refers to the 'great army of powerful and convincing arguments from the Scripture itself' used by the Protestant Fathers and the dogmaticians of the seventeenth century, to establish the authority of Scripture. Yet these arguments are not to be considered primary, they occupy a secondary position in order to strengthen faith. Although Lloyd-Jones gives a brief summary of these arguments, he sees greater weight attaching to the Scripture's own claim for itself.[4] Our Lord's teaching, the New Testament view of the Old, and the authority of the Apostles, unite to establish the unique authority of the Bible. The authority, therefore, for which Lloyd-Jones contends, as final for the Christian and the Church, is the authority of Christ as that is documented and expressed in what he refers to, without acknowledgement to Gladstone, as 'the impregnable Rock of Holy Scripture'.[5]

[1] D. Martin Lloyd-Jones, *Authority*, 1958, p. 36.

[2] G. W. Bromiley, 'The Authority of Scripture', *The New Bible Commentary*, p. 15.

[3] D. Martin Lloyd-Jones, *op. cit.*; cf. pp. 38 ff.

[4] *Ibid.*; cf. p. 50 f.   [5] *Ibid.*, p. 60.

In his final lecture, emphasis is placed upon the authority of the Holy Spirit. It is He who is authoritative to lead, to strengthen, to convert and so forth. History has witnessed, however, a fatal one-sidedness in the matter of the relation between the Scriptures and the Spirit. There have been those who have so stressed the inner witness, the inner light, the inner experience, to such an extent that they have displaced the Scripture. While, on the other side, there have been others who have neglected the influence and authority of the Spirit in an exclusive emphasis upon the finality of the Bible. This is, adds Lloyd-Jones, 'a thoroughly artificial and false emphasis'.[1]

It is an undoubted fact that in the last couple of centuries of Christian history there has been, at one time, an overstress on the outward aspect of revelation and authority at the expense of the inward, and, at another time, the virtual disregard of the outward in the interests of the inward. Sometimes there has been a feverish effort revealed to make the objective authoritative in religion, and then there has come a reaction, with an equally frantic attempt to state the subjective as ultimate and final. The tendency to one-sidedness has been throughout recent theological discussion all too evident.

The right relation between the objective and the subjective in religion is an issue of the most fundamental importance and an enquiry demanding the greatest urgency. Whenever the balance between these two becomes upset, then some element of the full truth is inevitably lost. This fact is true over the whole field of epistemology, and such theological realities as divine revelation and religious authority are no exception. 'Theology is certainly a human enquiry, whether or not it be more, whatever its assurances of a more than human reference and validity in the objects with which it deals or the methods by which it deals with them. It is to be expected, therefore, that theology, too, will share in such human error which is common to humanity, and that sometimes such error will be the result of a disproportion of the subjective and objective factors in its special kind of knowledge.'[2]

[1] D. Martin Lloyd-Jones, *ibid.*, p. 63. For the same understanding of authority see *Evangelicalism*, Essays by members of the Fellowship of Evangelical Churchmen (ed. J. Russell Howden), 1925, Chapters VI and VII; and also Douglas Johnson, *The Christian and His Bible*, 1953.

[2] James Brown, *Subject and Object in Modern Theology*, The Croall Lectures, University of Edinburgh, 1955, p. 12.

For our own part we are convinced that the fullest account must be given to both necessities in revelation and authority. There must be no divorce set up between the Spirit and the Scriptures. No ultimate antithesis between 'Spirit' and 'Truth' is possible.[1] A one-sided relationship and emphasis cannot meet the demands of the situation or the needs of the soul. A much more intimate connection would appear to be demanded between the Scripture and the Spirit than the protagonists of the opposing views seem to permit. We are not, of course, suggesting the application of the Greek maxim μηδὲν ἄγαν 'nothing too much'; rather we would suggest both, very much. It is not a case of the Spirit without the Scriptures, nor is it a case of the Scriptures without the Spirit. The Spirit cannot do His work without the Scriptures and the Scriptures cannot do theirs without the Spirit. Revelation is not a matter of Spirit only, but of Spirit and Truth. God's word is 'truth', God's work is by the 'Spirit'. The two go together. It is the Scriptures themselves on their side, which give witness to the reality and actuality of the Spirit; they give the assurance that the Holy Spirit has come. It is their assertion, further, that the Spirit will vivify and verify to our understanding the truth of that which the Scriptures themselves declare. On the other hand, the Spirit authenticates to us through the reality of the Scriptures the fact that the Christ has come. But it is through the record, and through it alone, that we have our confidence in Him. It is, then, the Spirit who gives witness to the truths already documented and declared in the Scriptures. It is when the Spirit breathes upon the Word that the truth comes to sight.

To deny the inner activity of the Spirit would be to reduce Christian faith to a mere intellectual assent to the letter of a written Book. 'It is a well-known fact', stated Philip Melanchthon long ago, 'that the herd of Sophists call faith the assent to those things set forth in Scripture. Hence then, that is faith even what the impious possess.'[2] But such is not the true 'fiduciary'

---

[1] Cf. H. D. McDonald, *Ideas of Revelation*, 1959, pp. 284–5.

[2] Philip Melanchthon, *The Loci Communes*, 1521, 'On Justification and Faith', Section 2. Cf. '. . . it is not enough, nor is it Christian, to preach the works, life, and words of Christ as historical facts, as if the knowledge of these would suffice for the conduct of life, although this is the fashion of those who must today be regarded as our best preachers. . . . Rather ought Christ to be preached to the end that faith in Him may be established, that He may not only be Christ, but be Christ

faith of the gospel. It is a mere rational affair against which the
Epistle of James so strongly protests. On the other side, there
are those who conceive of faith as a direct and immediate
inspiration of God and deny the need for Scripture. Such an idea
is to equate faith with a sort of mystic feeling and to
miss altogether its truth-content, and the basic 'propositional'
requirements out of which faith, created by the Spirit, takes its
rise. 'Happily, however, we are not confined to the two extreme
theories; the elements of truth on which they are respectively
based are opposite indeed, but not contrary. If we combine the
outward and the inward—God and man—the moving power and
the living instrument—we have a great and noble doctrine, to
which our inmost nature bears it witness. We have a Bible
competent to calm our doubts, and able to speak to our weakness.
It then becomes, not an utterance in strange tongues, but in the
words of wisdom and knowledge. It is authoritative, for it is the
voice of God; it is intelligible, for it is in the language of men.'[1]
Thus a Scripture without the Spirit makes for a fruitless faith,
while the Spirit without the Scriptures makes for an undiscip-
lined faith. The one makes for a dead orthodoxy, while the other
leads to an unrestrained enthusiasm. The first gives lifelessness
to the Church; and the second, licence to the individual.

The reality of the Spirit's activity through the Scriptures must
be taken with the utmost seriousness. His sovereignty must be
unquestionably recognized. But so, too, must the instrumental
adequacy of the Scriptures be accorded its absolute place in the
scheme of God's redemptive act. It is not the Church, we would
even dare to maintain, but the Scripture, which is 'the extension
of the Incarnation', if anything is to be rightly so designated.[2]
The authority of the Bible, as a real objective reality, must be
given definite and decisive significance. It is still a valid procedure for the Church and the Christian to say: 'To the Law and

for thee and for me, and that what is said of Him, and what His name denotes may
be effectual in us. And such faith is produced and preserved in us by the preaching
why Christ came, what He brought and bestowed, and what benefit it is to us to
accept Him'. Martin Luther, *A Treatise on Christian Liberty, ad. loc.*

[1] B. F. Wescott, *Introduction to the Study of the Gospels*, 1882, p. 33.

[2] In such statements as the following, the Church is accorded a place which, we
believe, does not belong to it. We would ourselves contend that if the Bible were
substituted for the Church in these passages, then they might stand as nearer to the
truth of the matter. 'We can say that Christ and His Church are inseparable entities.'
Anders Nygren, *Christ and His Church*, 1956, p. 90. 'Christ and the Church belong

to the Testimony if they speak not according to these is it because there is no life in them'. The simple fact is, as Luther declared, 'there is no other testimony on earth to Christian truth than the Holy Scriptures'. The Church and the Christian must, indeed, try the spirits to see which are of God. But both will find that He will be authenticated to them as the Holy Spirit, the Spirit which is of God, makes the letter of the Bible the Word of the living God. By authentication of Himself as such, in this way, there will be validated at the same time the authority of the Bible as one with the authority of God. Only so can we declare that our faith does not stand in the wisdom of man, but in the power of God. In this connection there is a profound truth in some words of the 'old Luther' which show that in this particular the position was the same as that of the 'young Luther'. 'Dear Lord God,' he wrote, 'if the Christian faith were to depend on men, and be grounded on words of men, what need do we have for the Holy Scriptures, or why has God given them?'[1]

It may well have been, as Martensen thinks, that the older Protestantism gave undue prominence to salvation as solely and exclusively the reference and design of Scripture and as a result tended to a too individualistic use of the Written Word. Certainly the Scripture does contain much more than the individual needs to know for his own salvation. There is, therefore, a correct emphasis to be put upon the place and purpose of the Bible within the Church. But even here, as Martensen rightly insists, the Holy Spirit acts by means of the Scripture.

'The necessity of Scripture', he then declares in words which sum up the view of the matter with which we wish to end this chapter, 'is not *principally* for the individual, but for the Church; and its full import and design is stated rather in the assertion, that it contains all truth necessary for the preservation of the Church, and for its progressive development towards its final consummation. This again is to say, that by means of the Holy Scripture, under the guidance of the Holy Spirit, the Church not

together. They cannot be separated from each other.' 'The Church is a revelation of the invisible Lord, a continued incarnation of Christ on earth.' Gustaf Aulén, *Church, Law and Society*, 1948, New York, pp. 15 and 16. 'The Church is Christ, by reason of the fact that since His resurrection He is present with us and meets us on earth.' *This is the Church* (ed. Anders Nygren), 1952, p. 10.

[1] Quoted by R. C. Johnson, *Authority in Protestant Theology*, 1959, p. 41.

only may be kept in purity of doctrine and true worship, but
that in the whole course of her development there can be no
new practice or law established, be it in relation to doctrine or
to life, which she cannot abolish by means of the eternal
principle of truth and life laid down in the Holy Scripture:
moreover, that on the one hand, all critical and cleansing
activity of the Church, and on the other hand, all building up,
edifying and strengthening activity (taking this expression in
the widest sense), must find its governing type for all times in
the Holy Scriptures. Maintaining as we do that the Holy Ghost
guides the Church into all truth by means of the Scripture, we
attribute to the Scripture perfect sufficiency and clearness
(*sufficientia et perspicuitas*); in so far, that is, as the Church is
given through the Scripture the revelation of the Spirit concerning what is advisable or useful for *any particular time*, while
Scripture itself must be looked upon for *all times*—much that it
contains not being perfectly accomplished until the latter days.
Experience, moreover, teaches that whenever a true reform has
been accomplished in the Church, the word, *It was not so in the
beginning*, has been spoken with telling power against a lifeless
ecclesiasticism, because it has spoken in the strength of the Holy
Scripture. This holds good not only of the great Reformation of
the sixteenth century, but of the many successive protests which
have been made in the Middle Ages and in modern times. For
as the Church has, in every age, triumphed over that false
gnosis, which resolves Christianity into merely human reason,
by the Word of Scripture, this same word has been a safeguard
against a barren orthodoxy, which has built up ecclesiasticism at
the expense of Christianity; and it has continually led back to an
illumination inseparable from edification, because the apostolic
illumination is in itself an enlightenment which leads to
salvation.'[1]

[1] H. Martensen, *Christian Dogmatics* (E.T. 1866), pp. 405-6.

CHAPTER NINE

Revelation and Authority

The ultimate issue which emerged from the long and lively discussions and controversies of the past century, which our previous chapter was intended to make clear, concerns the problem of authority. The question of revelation passed into that of authority, and to discover the locus of revelation is to find the seat of authority. In the words of F. W. Camfield, to which we may refer again, it was agreed that 'We must find authority in Revelation, for authority is its hall-mark'. It seems, therefore, a matter of indifference whether we talk of the understanding of revelation or of authority. In the context of religion and religious faith, to say, Here is Revelation, is the same as to say, Here is Authority.

A. THE REVELATION OF AUTHORITY

Under this heading we may summarize, in a very few words in view of all we have said, the dominant ideas of the century. R. E. Davies, in his study of *The Problem of Authority in the Continental Reformers*, concludes that they all, Luther no less than Calvin, failed to emancipate themselves from 'the mediaeval error that the source of authority is necessarily to be found in some place wholly outside the individual'. Without discussing here the historical and theological accuracy of this statement, it may be safely maintained that the present century has witnessed an all-out bid to free itself from this suggested 'mediaeval error'. In the earlier part of our era, any view which identified revelation with its record was strongly resisted. It was, in fact, characteristic of the times to draw a sharp line of distinction between the two. More recent days have seen an equally definite divorce made between the Word and the Words. The significant emphasis of the present is that 'Jesus Christ, the Word made flesh' is 'recognized and acclaimed as the sole Word of God', thus necessitating, as a speaker at the Amsterdam Assembly of 1948 declared, a 'new understanding of the Old and New Testaments'.[1] This 'new understanding' is boldly referred to by Edwin Lewis as 'The Emancipation of the Word of God'.[2]

Lewis remarks, with the statement made at Amsterdam in mind, that 'Christ as "the sole Word of God"; in consequence, "a new understanding of the Bible"—this fairly describes "the new Biblicism"; but the difference from the old Biblicism is nothing less than radical. The old Biblicism shackled the revelation; the new Biblicism would set it free. The old Biblicism was concerned to take the Bible "as is". The new Biblicism is critical, discriminating, unafraid. The old Biblicism yielded a static authoritarianism. The new Biblicism promises to issue in the creation of a dynamic spiritual freedom'.[3]

Freedom from external authority is then the great discovery of our century. But, as even Lewis's own chapter reveals, this freedom from authority resulted in a crop of new theological 'reconstructions' in which each man was his own master, and each believed that to be right which was good in his own eyes. The student of historical theology will be able to add considerably to the list of extraordinary and eccentric consequences following from these new approaches unhampered by historical considerations and no longer bound by the 'mediaeval error' of seeking the source of authority outside and especially in the 'old Biblicism' which 'shackled the revelation'.

But the idea of authority cannot be allowed to pass. It must be sought, then, in the revelation to which the Bible, for the Christian at all events, has some sort of relation. It will be better, therefore, not to speak of the authority of revelation for then the idea of revelation is made to be something external and static. It will be more appropriate to think of the revelation of authority.

Revelation, and consequently authority, was conceived in a radical manner by some to be located in the sensitive conscience.

---

[1] Cf. *Man's Disorder and God's Design*, Vol. 1, 1949, p. 101.
[2] Edwin Lewis, *The Biblical Faith and Christian Freedom*, 1953, Chapter III.
[3] *Ibid.*, p. 31.

Conscience makes Christians of us all, the new gospel announced. Whatever is not of conscience is not of faith. Conscience, God immanent within, is the guide of life; here is that inner light of the soul to which if a man gives heed, he shall do well. To be sure Herbert Spencer had sought to explain conscience in a naturalistic way as the deposit left in the human race by its age-long struggle for existence, as a sort of 'hindsight' which for the next stage in the development becomes 'foresight' by which the upward moving man learns to avoid what frustrates his happiness and impedes his progress. Such a view was rejected as being no sufficient explanation of man's sense of the divine 'ought'. Rufus Jones notes that although Jesus, according to the gospel records, never used the term 'conscience', yet 'that inner tribunal which we name by that word is nowhere more clearly in evidence than in the stages of the decision that carried Jesus to the cross, in dedication to the untried, but ultimately irresistible power of redeeming love'. By His emphasis 'on the nearness of the divine to the human in man', he goes on to urge, Jesus showed that 'the Kingdom of God is an interior spirit and not an external power'.[1] Jesus stressed specially the idea of the Brotherhood of Man, and it was this thought which enlightening the conscience of men has been the reason for the undermining and destroying of long established evils such as Slavery and Feudalism; and by its authority War itself will one day be made to cease.

Conscience, the voice of God in the soul, the light which lighteth every man that cometh into the world, is, therefore, the ultimate locus of revelation and the final seat of authority. By conscience all must be tested: at this bar the 'morality' of the Old Testament is to be judged and rejected. A more sensitive conscience had now been developed under the influence of education and enlightenment. Paul is even quoted by some as a witness to the view, it would be a contradiction in terms to say as an authority: 'By manifestation of the truth commending ourselves to every man's conscience in the sight of God'.[2] And the

---

[1] R. M. Jones, *The Nature and Authority of Conscience*, 1920, pp. 21–2.

[2] II Cor. iv. 2. The Greek term 'syneidesis' rendered 'conscience' is used in the New Testament for what Kant called the 'practical reason' (cf. Acts xxiii. 1; xxiv. 16; Rom. ii. 15; ix. 5; I Cor. viii. 7, 10–11; II Cor. i. 12; iv. 2; I Tim. i. 5, etc.). The word may be an instance of the influence of the Stoic ethic on the moral vocabulary of the civilized world at the time of the Christian era. But the 'conscience'

place of Jesus in the scheme we shall not, we think, be far wrong
in saying that He may be regarded as the greatest educator of
conscience.

Not all by a long way could concur in this way of stating the
case for the source of authority within the individual. There were
those who preferred to see revelation supremely as the insights
of religious geniuses. The great prophets of religion were not
just men of tender conscience in their day; they were essentially
men of vision. They were men who could see. For the thousand
people who can talk, observes John Ruskin somewhere, there
are only a hundred who can think; but for the hundred who can
think there is only one who can see and can tell what he sees in a
convincing and challenging way. Revelation is, then, a thing of
profound spiritual insight by men who had what Clutton-Brock
calls a 'scent for truth'. They were men with the gift of apprehension and the grace of appreciation. They saw the movements
of God in the dramas of human history; and what they saw they
sought to interpret to others. What to less penetrating eyes
were but happenings were to the prophets the acts of God. And
they sought to persuade their own day and ours that God is real
and living and by thus believing they are blessed.

It was, of course, stressed that faith here is not simply
believing the prophets' beliefs. It is not a blind submission to
any outward authority. It is rather an 'inward beholding', or, as
it has been put, 'a keen-eyed response to the *inward* authority
with which God speaks to man through Nature, through
Conscience, through History and most of all through Jesus
Christ'.

The prophet, it is explained by W. R. Inge, 'commends his
message to us by awakening a response in our hearts. This is in
reality the only way in which a revelation is or can be made to
us'. When these men of 'strong soul'[1] speak 'Our hearts leap
out to meet their words; we recognize that this is what we
wanted; that here is the truth which we could not find for ourselves, the good news which we should not have dared to
believe'.[2]

as the New Testament conceives it is not the clear-eye of the soul which some have
supposed. It may be purified by grace (cf. I Tim. iii, 9), but it can also be defiled
(cf. I Cor. viii. 7).

[1] V. H. Stanton, *The Place of Authority in Matters of Religious Belief*, 1891, p. 32.
[2] W. R. Inge, *Faith and its Psychology*, 1910, p. 81.

Such a conception many writers were not slow to identify with the inner witness of the Spirit. Inge himself had, indeed, maintained that 'it is the indwelling Christ who is the primary authority',[1] and this expression about sums up what a large number of influential writers maintained as the truth of the matter. We have seen how the idea appealed to H. Wheeler Robinson. He found revelation and the authority which goes with it in the inner actuality of the Spirit. The testimony of the Spirit was regarded by many as the final reality both for the Church and the individual Christian. The Church was founded as a community of inspired people, the declaration went. The individual believer had his own inner certitude. It was only as the Spirit of God moved within his soul that the words 'Let there be light' could have their own individual illuminating certainty.

The idea was given an almost 'pantheistic' stress by some teachers. John Caird, for example, in his Gifford Lectures argued that our belief in Christ does not stand or fall 'with the proof of the authenticity of ancient documents'.[2] It has 'a more impregnable foundation than historic tradition—even on the inward witness of a spiritual presence here and now . . . the inward witness of the presence of that redeeming, purifying, hallowing Spirit that was incarnate in Him, and that is still and for ever living not only *for* us, but *in* us, and in all who open their spirits to its life-giving power'.[3] There is no need, he maintains, to bring Christ down from above, or back from a dim and vanished age with painful research. The divine is around and about and those who open their lives to the 'redeeming, hallowing, saving spirit' have 'the irrefragable proof' in themselves.[4] 'The Divine Spirit that was embodied in the life of Christ, and which realizes itself in every soul that yields to its transforming power, wherever and whenever it takes possession of human spirits, is in essence one and the same in all.'[5]

Some sought escape from the pantheistic and subjectivist drift of such a teaching by contending, on the one hand, for the 'sacredness of the human personality' and, on the other hand, by putting emphasis upon the corrective restraints of the 'inspired

---

[1] W. R. Inge, *Faith and its Psychology*, 1910, p. 136.
[2] John Caird, *The Fundamental Ideas of Christianity*, 1899, Vol. II, p. 97.
[3] *Ibid.*   [4] *Ibid.*; cf. pp. 98–9.   [5] *Ibid.*, p. 252.

community'. It was, however, the bold contention that authority is 'not to be sought by any mechanical reference to the letter of His (i.e. Christ's) words on earth, but by seeking and following His Spirit in the heart'.[1] Revelation is an affair of the heart, the Spirit's internal witness within the soul. And here is authority, not mechanical, not external, not static, but spiritual, and inward and dynamic.

That there is truth here must not be denied: indeed, we may say one 'half' of the truth is here. Of the other 'half' there was no clear recognition. It was not made evident, in fact it was not well understood, that there are two that bear witness on the earth, the Spirit and the Scriptures and these two agree in one.

It was not enough to repudiate the intolerable abstract intellectualism of scholasticism by finding relief in a sort of pietism which dwelt much on the mystical union of the soul with Christ, and construe that in the terms of a spiritualizing imagination. The tendency always is to seek escape from a barren dogmatic system by finding satisfaction in a spiritual subjectivism. Christianity, whenever it becomes scholastic, lacks the inspiration of the Spirit; when it becomes mystical it lacks the reality and balance of historical truth. Thus it came about that from the beginning of the present century an effort was made to find the Jesus of History. Revelation must be somehow centred upon and authority grounded in Him. Few saw more clearly than did D. W. Forrest the need to have some historical foundation for the illuminating and enlightening experience of the Spirit which had been set forth as the locus of revelation and the seat of authority. 'It sounds very heroic to affirm', he states at a time when his own words may be considered 'heroic', 'that that faith does not hang upon records, upon the accident of the preservation of the Gospels; that if God's Son entered our humanity and revealed Himself to a few souls in His own generation, who after His death beheld Him as the risen Lord and experienced the outpouring of His Spirit, then that same Spirit could continually work through regenerated men to the spiritual conversion and quickening of human souls, even though the traditions of Christ's humanity had vanished. But, however heroic this proposition may be, it is in the last degree absurd,

---

[1] Edward Grubb, *Authority in Religion*, 1924, p. 88.

because it is impossible to conceive such a contingency.'[1] Forrest, indeed, goes on to suggest that not only is the idea absurd, it is also, 'dangerous'. It is pleaded that 'faith is founded on an inward experience of your own, corroborated by the similar experiences of other people'. The historical element may as well be dropped. But it is, Forrest argues, exactly this direct touch with the historical Jesus which the simplest believer knows to lie at the root of his confidence.[2] In another volume Forrest seeks to demonstrate in more precise fashion the meaning and measure of Christ's authority. In his book *The Authority of Christ* (1906), he seeks to elaborate the thesis that after all that can be questioned by criticism has been set aside there remains an adequate 'historical residue' sufficient to tie faith to a genuine reality of history. Forrest's was a commendable effort to provide for faith some factual foundation.

At the same time, one is not fully carried by his endeavours, convinced as we are of the absolute need for faith to be firmly grounded in history. Forrest's lot was cast in the period when it was an urgent thing to provide for the claims of Christian experience an historical basis, but it was a day, none the less, when that was virtually impossible to discover. The New Testament had been so torn to shreds in the recent past that there was little which could be confidently pronounced factual. This was not just because Jesus was, as Matthew Arnold says, 'above the heads of His reporters',[3] but because critical analysis had already flowed over into the New Testament and applied to it the same presuppositions which had already weakened faith in the Old. Forrest, in both of the books to which we have made reference, appeared to be acutely aware of the difficulty when he remarks, 'One of the greatest problems is to disentangle the everlasting truth it contains (i.e. the "historical" report) from its accidental embodiment'.[4] The dilemma is then a real one. It appears that it is only by the application of subjective criteria that it is possible to arrive at any acceptable data, to find 'the everlasting truth' embodied in 'its accidental forms', for an historical account. It is in this way that the wheel comes full circle.

---

[1] D. W. Forrest, *The Christ of History and of Experience*, 1906, fifth edition, p. 329.   [2] *Ibid.*; cf. p. 330.

[3] Matthew Arnold, *Literature and Dogma*, 1873, Chapter VI.

[4] D. W. Forrest, *The Christ of History and of Experience*, p. 334.

M

Rejecting the records as altogether historically factual, there had to be eliminated from them whatever the conscience could not verify, or the reason could not explain or the spiritual sensitivity could not authenticate. The actual result was that there was no possible agreement as to what was to be accepted, because conscience and reason and spiritual sensitivity varied from writer to writer. In the end the much acclaimed 'historical sense' turned out to be even more subjective than the subjectivism which it set out to correct. The authority of Jesus came to be nothing other than that of the individual critic's ingenuity, or imagination or intuition, as the case may have been. The many volumes each supposed to present us with the authority of the Jesus of history were but the outcome of each writer's own uncontrolled dream or unrestricted daring.

The real truth of the matter is that the Authority of Jesus was lost because there was hardly any data left for a picture of a Jesus who could be authoritative. It was allowed as a sort of grudging apologetic that He saw more deeply into the truth of things than other men and therefore that it was proper to speak of His authority as greater in degree than that of other men. The idea is put by one writer with admirable frankness: 'the authority with which Jesus of Nazareth speaks of God, of sin, of forgiveness and of righteousness, is the outcome of that wondrous clearness of spiritual vision which shines everywhere on the Gospel pages, and which can only have been possible for One who lived ever in perfect communion with God. His authority covers the matters concerning which He had special knowledge, not those of which He had not. To quote His words in support of traditional theories about the Old Testament is to miss His true significance, to go back from the light and freedom of the Gospel to the darkness and bondage of the Scribes and Pharisees. He is our highest outward Authority in Religion; but no outward Authority can ever be final and absolute.'[1]

Was it as a revolt from such a conclusion that the Dialectical-Crisis theologians renounced all attempts to find revelation and authority in any measure in the historic Jesus? Harnack and company wanted an historical Jesus but could not find one: Barth and company are in a better position to have such but do not want one. The Barthians, it is well known, and we have

[1] Edward Grubb, *Authority in Religion*, 1924, pp. 80-1.

referred to the fact on a number of occasions, constantly repudiate what one writer refers to as a 'blind credulity of unimaginative verbalism'. The revelation of which the Bible speaks, it is asserted, is not to be 'mechanically equated with the total Biblical language'. The Word, the only Word, is the living Christ; and here is God's final redemptive Act. The gospels are not properly spoken of as the Word of God: the Word is He who became flesh.[1] Brunner especially insists that it is the Word of God that is the Revelation of God, and it is in the reality of the 'Divine–Human Encounter' that revelation becomes effective and authority dynamic. Thus has the Word of God been emancipated in the 'new biblicism'. The Word is to be sharply distinguished from the words. The Word is 'of God'; the words are 'of men'. Revelation and authority are not 'of men', but 'of God'. They are discovered in the 'encounter' with the living Word. The truth in this Barthian thesis must be acknowledged and appreciated. But it fails, we think, to give right significance to the words in its exclusive emphasis on the Theology of the Word. It will be sufficient, at the present, to re-echo a statement made above. Here we would state it like this: there are two that bear witness in heaven, the Word and the words, and these two agree in one.

Authority, then, we have seen, varies according to the understanding of revelation. Indeed, as revelation is, so is authority: there is the authority of conscience, of religious genius, of the experience of the Spirit, of the historic Jesus, or of the encountered Christ. We may perhaps appreciate anew the famous witticism of the thirteenth century of Alanus of Lille when he said, *'Auctoritas cereum habet nasum id est, in diversum potest flecti sensum'*: 'Authority has a wax nose; it can be twisted in different directions'.

B. THE AUTHORITY OF REVELATION

In a reference to the subject of revelation Karl Barth remarks that 'It is possible to speak in an original manner on every subject in the whole wide world except this one. Of this subject it is possible only to speak faithfully, i.e. exegetically'.[2] Conse-

---

[1] Cf. Edwin Lewis, *The Biblical Faith and Christian Freedom*, 1953, p. 45.
[2] Karl Barth, *God in Action*, 1936, p. 7. The cynic might be forgiven if he were

quently, while no claim to originality is made in what follows, it is our desire to give as faithfully, if not quite exegetically, as we can some positive statement of our own understanding of the topic of our heading.

It is frequently declared in present-day discussions of the subject that the ultimate seat of authority in religion is God Himself. And this is a most necessary truth upon which constantly to insist. It is, indeed, a fundamental fact that there can be nothing finally binding upon human beings, whose chief end is to glorify God, but God's holy will. Only that which is clearly and convincingly of Him can be decisive for religious faith. It is in the reality of and the response to the authority of God that man finds his freedom and fulfils his destiny. Man is essentially a responsible being before God. In the presence of God he discovers that his rightful attitude is that of a suppliant not a sovereign. Here he becomes aware that he does not exercise authority, he merely recognizes it. Before God the human understanding can find no reasons for owning God's authority. Here the will knows its own Master and the heart its Lord. 'God is His own authority for the religious, and therefore the last for the race; and He is the only Authority we have in the end.'[1] God remains for ever the Object of Man's authority, not the Subject for man's contemplation. God is holy imperative. Man, on the other hand, has a receptivity for authority. Herein is his distinctiveness, his essential greatness. He has power to *own* authority. This is the *a priori* in man, not itself an authority, but the capacity for authority. It cannot, therefore, be too emphatically declared that God is His own Authority for the religious. But this unqualified declaration, true and vital as it is, does not get us very far. The questions which immediately arise are, Where is this authority to be found? and, How does it come to us?

To answer such questions we will first of all venture the proposition that authority is located in the revealed will of God. In an age past Augustine wrestled with the problem of authority and urged on by the momentum of his own profound religious experience he came to realize that revelation and authority are correlatives. It is in His self-disclosure that God's authority is to

to urge that Barth in his *Church Dogmatics* has used much space about that which it is impossible to speak of in an original manner!

[1] P. T. Forsyth, *The Principle of Authority*, 1913, second edition, 1952, p. 146.

be found: God's authority is expressed in His revelation. This means that 'Revelation is the key to religious authority'.[1] There can be no authority of God unless there is revelation; for in the locus of revelation is the seat of authority. Revelation is the Object of religion disclosed as authority. God is known only in revelation. And in revelation God is disclosed not as an Object of leisurely, theoretic investigation. God is known in revelation as urgent, demanding and authoritative.

In revelation the main thing is not that God gives Himself to us to be *known* but He gives Himself to be *owned*. Herein is the contrast between religious knowledge and science. 'In religion the fundamental movement of the knowledge is in the reverse direction from that of science. In science we move to the object of knowledge; in religion it moves to us.'[2] Essentially then religion is only possible by revelation. And in revelation God as Ultimate Authority speaks to man who has a receptivity for authority. It is important, therefore, to insist that 'authority can only be found in the revealed will of God'.[3]

Yet even this statement of Griffith-Jones leaves the issue too vague. Something more definite and precise is called for. Authority is located in the revealed will of God, but where is that will revealed?

Revelation has, of course, a specific meaning. The word itself means 'a drawing back of a veil'. And this is exactly what God does in His revelation. In a general way, from Nature, from the movements of history, from the spiritual constitution of man, we may gain an idea that there is, so to speak, Something, perhaps Someone, behind the curtain. But revelation is God drawing back the curtain and showing Himself. In revelation God is not just giving us information about Himself; He gives Himself. He, actually, dramatically and savingly comes forth, disclosing His own being and character as the Triune God of all grace.

Christians believe that there was a preparatory revelation, a preparation of the stage, an announcement, so to say, of God's real forthcoming. There was a disclosure made to selected

[1] Bernard Ramm, *The Pattern of Authority*, 1957, p. 20.
[2] P. T. Forsyth, *The Principle of Authority*, 1913, second edition, 1952, p. 150.
[3] E. Griffith-Jones, 'The Bible: Its Meaning and Aim', Peake's *Commentary on the Bible*, 1919, new edition with supplement, reprint, 1948, p. 7.

persons before there was the Self-disclosure in a special Person. Revelation by proclamation preceded revelation by incarnation. In this preparatory revelation, however, there was a Word of God given. There were chosen spokesmen of a divine unveiling. And it was the revelation which gave them their authority. Their authority was not in their own person, but in the word uttered. No subjective experience, no inner light, no illuminated imagination gave them their authority. The word was their authority, the word which in coming to them reconciled them and recreated them and made them God's ambassadors. The word they heard was not for themselves alone or indeed for themselves supremely. It was a word which could not be hidden in their hearts; it had to be uttered forth. The word was the revelation and consequently the authority for those to whom it came, for here was the revealed will of God. For the Old Testament believers, their authority was the Word of God which came to them through the spokesmen of the divine disclosure. Thus it was that to disbelieve the utterance of the messenger of God was to disbelieve God and to disobey him was to disobey God. Their authority was not what appealed to them but what was declared to them. For no moral being is his own ultimate authority: in truth, that only can be our authority which has no authority beyond itself, which is its own authority. 'An authority which has its source in ourselves is no authority. In us authority can have but its echo, never its charter.'[1]

But for the Christian it is his assertion and assurance that God's revelation is to be found fully in Christ. Here has been embodied and expressed God's will in His purposes of pardon and grace. Christ stands as the final Exegete of God. True it is that 'We cannot make any mistake about God after we have known Jesus'.[2] For the Christian, then, the ultimate seat of authority is God's will revealed in Christ.

In an article on 'The Authority of Christ', James Denney has drawn attention to the fact that the first recorded comment on the teaching of Jesus is that, 'They were astonished at his doctrine for he taught them as one having authority and not as the scribes'. The scribes appealed to tradition, but He made no such appeal. It was evident that He was Himself the authority.

---

[1] P. T. Forsyth, *The Principle of Authority*, p. 299.
[2] Otto Borchert, *The Original Jesus* (E.T. 1953), p. 460.

All His teaching bears the character of this divine authority and the absoluteness of His authority in the sphere of ultimate knowledge of God is asserted in Matt. xi. 27: 'in the work of revelation and especially in the revelation of Himself as Father, God has no organ but Christ, and in Christ, He has an adequate organ'.[1]

The essential purpose of the divine revelation is redemptive; it is to give that knowledge of God in which consists eternal life. The 'chief end of revelation' is not philosophy, though it has a philosophy profound and worthy. It is not doctrine, though it has a doctrine satisfying and inspiring. It is not enjoyment, though it has its experience precious and lasting; it is not even morality, though it has its ethic unique and powerful. Christianity *has* all these, but *is* far more than them all. It is the religion of redemption, including salvation from sin, equipment for holiness, and provision for life to be lived in fellowship with God and for His glory.[2] God's revelation His of grace and truth; this means, as Warfield says, that 'God's authoritative revelation is His gracious revelation; God's redemptive revelation is His supernatural revelation'.[3] And echoing the words of Ramm, we would contend that the saving action of God in the world and in experience is an action of divine grace. God's imperial authority is most graciously expressed. When God binds His authority on men it is an act of grace. In God's supreme revelation in His Son, there is the epitome of revelation as grace and truth.[4] It is perfectly in accord with the requirements of the case then for Gore to assert that 'Jesus Christ is the summary of authority in religion. He is this because He reveals God, as being His image'.[5] It is central in the Christian Gospel and vital for Christian experience to give unhesitating stress to our Lord's finality and authority. But it is just here the real issue comes. 'To say vaguely that the revelation is Christ, or that Christ is its centre, is the source of all our confusion.'[6] The question may be immediately pressed, What Christ is this who is authoritative?

[1] James Denney, *Hasting's Dictionary of Christ and the Gospels, ad. loc.*

[2] Cf. W. H. Griffith Thomas, *Hastings Dictionary of the Bible*, one volume, p. 797.

[3] B. B. Warfield, *The Inspiration and Authority of the Bible*, reprint, 1948, p. 100.

[4] Cf. Bernard Ramm, *The Pattern of Authority*, 1957, p. 21.

[5] Charles Gore, *Incarnation*, Bampton Lectures, 1891, p. 172.

[6] P. T. Forsyth, *The Person and Place of Jesus Christ*, 1909, fifth edition, 1946, p. 151.

In answer to this we would enter our second proposition to the effect that the authority which is located in Christ as revealing the will of God is interpreted for us through chosen media. There is only one Christ who is authoritative. It is not the mere Figure of the gospel narratives. The fact is, of course, that there is no understanding of the historic Jesus apart from faith's affirmations, and at the same time, lest we fall a victim to the opposite error, we would stress that faith's affirmations are of a Figure who is genuinely historical. 'It is the whole Biblical Christ that is truly and deeply historical Christ.'[1]

It is often pointed out that Jesus never wrote a book even though we acknowledge Him as having for us the authority of the revealed will of God. But the fact is that this interpretation of the fact of Christ has come to us through His chosen apostles. Their business was to interpret Him. The apostles were men with a unique vocation; they were God's 'elect and providential personalities'. They were not corruptors of the self-disclosure of God in Christ: they were its conveyors. Their words were not an intrusion upon the revelation but part of the scheme of revelation. This means for us that the Christ who is authoritative is the Christ who is interpreted.

Gore has argued that 'the first Christians looked to two kinds of authority—the authority of the Old Testament and the authority of apostolic teaching or tradition'.[2] This is but another way of stating that the Christ who is authoritative is the whole biblical Christ: in the Old Testament prefigured, and in the New presented. It is impossible to speak of an authoritative Christ apart from the Bible in which He is set forth. The historical preparation and the apostolic interpretation are essential to a full estimate of the Saviour who alone is absolute. The Old Testament preparation for the revelation in Christ is not a mere ornamental prefix to it, nor is the apostolic understanding of God's revealed will in Christ a mere addition to it. They are part of it. In the one revelation is figured, in the other it is finalized. When, therefore, it is said that Christ is authoritative it must be understood that this is the Christ who is so.

The apostolic interpretation was not the result of human musings upon the fact of Christ. It was a part of the revealing act.

[1] P. T. Forsyth, *The Person and Place of Jesus Christ*, 1909, fifth edition, 1946, p. 169.　　[2] Charles Gore, *The Doctrine of an Infallible Book*, 1924, p. 33.

The apostolic men stood in close contact with Christ and for this reason they held a position historically unique; yet it was not merely their proximity to Jesus which gave them their interpretation. Neither was it the outcome of unusual insight nor religious genius. They were men instructed by the Spirit, men who received the gift of interpreting knowledge from the ascended Lord. Their interpretation was His instruction. 'The compilation of the New Testament out of the "Gospels", with their Apostles, and the "Apostolus", is clearly the expression of two convictions: (A) that in a certain sense the apostles are equal to Christ in that they, being chosen not only to be witnesses, but also dispensers of His power, are His continuation; and (B) that the *attestation* of a revelation is not less important than its *content*.'[1]

It will be observed how the ethical injunction of the apostles become authoritative because the New Testament knows no ethics save that of Christ redeemed lives. Paul, for example, charges his readers to bear one another's burdens. We have no precept of Christ's to this effect and yet he says to obey this word is to fulfil the law of Christ.[2] 'I am not obliged to obey Paul', remarks Kierkegaard, 'because he is clever, or exceptionally clever, but I must submit to Paul because he has divine authority.' It must then be insisted that 'the word of the apostles itself forms part of the revelation of God through Jesus Christ. The act of the historical divine revelation is completed only where, in the spoken word of the apostles, it becomes the knowledge of faith, the confession of faith, and the witness which creates faith. Only after Jesus Christ has revealed Himself to an Apostle has the divine revelation reached its goal; the circuit is now complete'.[3]

Geldenhuys has convincingly shown that a unique authority is involved in the very title 'apostle'. The Apostle was one set forth and sent out for a definite purpose. Commenting on several passages in his epistles, Geldenhuys concludes that 'Paul thus unequivocally declares that the preaching of the Gospel by him and by the other apostles has an ἐφάπαξ, once-for-all character, because Jesus Himself gave them the authority and the equipment

---

[1] Adolf Harnack, *The Origin of the New Testament*, 1914 (E.T. 1925), p. 44.
[2] Gal. vi. 2.
[3] Emil Brunner, *Revelation and Reason* (E.T. 1946), p. 122.

to act and teach as His שְׁלוּחָ׳ם '.[1] It was, then, through God's chosen media that the Church was given a normative gospel and a formative word.

Gore is therefore bound to give some qualifications to the bald assertion that 'The Christian authority is simply Jesus Christ'. He adds significantly that 'for the external knowledge of our Lord, the knowledge of what He taught and was, we are dependent, by His deliberate intention, upon the witness of His apostles'. Believers in Christ, he contends, will regard the apostles as something more than mere witnesses, they were, indeed, witnesses qualified for a unique function by a special inspiration. It was their call and prerogative to take of the things of Christ and declare them unto us. Wescott marks the position of the apostles as unique and so also by implication the office of the apostolic writings as a record of their teaching. 'Christians', states Gore, 'believe then that the apostles were specially enlightened to present to us without distortion the person and teaching of our Lord, and familiarity with their writings through nineteen centuries has confirmed that belief. We cannot as a matter of historical enquiry go behind the apostles, for our Lord wrote nothing Himself; as a matter of fact we do not need to go behind it. In the apostolic teaching, then, we find the ultimate court of appeal in respect of "the faith once delivered to the saints". He that heareth them, heareth Him.'[2]

The authority for religion rests in God but it has become a genuine reality for us because located in the divine revelation: and for the Christian that is Jesus Christ, the Word made flesh. But the Christ who is thus authoritative is the Biblical Christ, the Christ, that is, indicated and interpreted by divinely chosen and commissioned representatives. A further stage in presenting the position must now be taken. The proposition must consequently be advanced that the authority of revelation is perpetuated by the Written Word.

---

[1] N. Geldenhuys, *Supreme Authority*, 1953, p. 77. Cf. 'it is clear on what the apostles based their claim that they, and they alone, are the שְׁלוּחֵ׳ם of the Lord; namely, they saw the risen Jesus and He Himself chose, commissioned and equipped them to be His "apostles". . . . Never again could or can there be persons who possess all these qualifications to be שְׁלוּחָ׳ם of Jesus. Just as the revelation of God in Christ is ἐφάπαξ, "einmalig" (once for all), the action of the risen Lord in and through His apostles in laying the foundations of His Church for all time is once and for all'. *Op. cit.*, pp. 73–4.

[2] Charles Gore, *Incarnation*, 1891, pp. 188–9.

It has been observed that Christ wrote no book: this fact has been taken by some to argue that it was never His purpose to give to His Church authoritative records. But the simple fact is, of course, that our Lord could not have expanded and expounded the redemptive significance of His coming until the crowning event itself had been accomplished. It is, however, our conviction that He has fulfilled this necessity in the words of the apostles. True, He wrote no book, except through them: they were in a very definite sense His posthumous penmen. What He was unable to teach them in the days of His flesh He as the ascended Lord, by the power of His Spirit, spoke to them.

It was not possible that His whole enterprise of grace could be allowed to pass. Unless some adequate provision for its preservation were made His work would have been tragically still-born. But an open-minded reading of the New Testament makes it certain that He did make provision, not only for the elucidation and finalization of His revelation to the people for the first days, but also for its perpetuation for all days.

Calvin puts this conviction with telling cogency when he observed that 'since no daily responses are given from heaven, and the Scriptures are the only records in which God has been pleased to consign His truth to perpetual remembrance, the full authority which they ought to possess with the faithful is not recognized, unless they are believed to have come from heaven, as directly as if God had been heard giving utterance to them'.[1]

The Scriptures give us God's word written. Here is the embodied account of the revelatory fact. And the authority of God belongs as much to the interpretation and application of God's self-disclosure in grace as it does to the actuality of the event itself. 'The apostles were recognized in the Church', says Leitzmann without hesitation, 'as the only unconditional legitimate vehicles of the Spirit. Everything which claimed to be the working of the Spirit was tested by their messages. In this way their writings were regarded as inspired by the Spirit, and therefore of final divine authority. They came to be regarded as equal in origin to the documents of the Old Testament, or, to speak more accurately, as a necessary complement at its side and bringing it to a completion; they also were "Holy Scriptures". A New Testament came to stand along with the Old and it

---

[1] John Calvin, *Institutes of the Christian Religion*. Berridge's Trans., Vol. I, p. 68.

became customary to appeal to it by using the solemn words "It is written", in a way similar to that which at an earlier date had been applied only to the Old Testament.'[1]

The early Church had no doubt but that the ascended Lord fulfilled Himself in the words of the apostles, and consequently they regarded their words as His. These were the men who spoke in His Spirit and by His Spirit. In them the promise to lead into all the truth was made good. So certain was this to the first Christians that Harnack can say, 'the Holy Spirit and the Apostles became correlative conceptions, with the consequence that the Scriptures of the New Testament were indifferently regarded as composed by the Holy Spirit or the Apostles'.[2]

Revelation is then incomplete apart from the apostolic interpretation. In fact, in the apostolic interpretation we see the Christ explaining Himself. He as living and unsilenced unfolds the fulness of the conquest He has achieved. Having the Apostles' Word we do not lose God's Word: we gain it, we receive it. It is for this reason, and only for this reason could the apostles claim 'for their words, especially on eternal truth, a like permanent authority with Christ's. They even ignore His precepts, which they seldom or ever quote to their Churches; they make their own, and they expect from them the obedience due to Christ'.[3] This fact must be taken quite seriously. The apostles regarded their words on a level with Christ's because they believed that He spoke through them. Without this certainty it would have been nothing short of blasphemy from them to enter the claim they did; it would be tantamount to putting the redeemed above the Redeemer, and the servant above his Lord. Those to whom the word came were not bibliolaters when they received the apostolic proclamation, not as the mere desires of respected religious advisers, but as the authoritative statements of the divine will, as much His words as if He Himself had spoken or written.

The indicators and interpreters of God's revelation were not just a religious élite group. They knew themselves to be men

[1] H. Leitzmann, *The Foundation of the Church Universal*, 1938, p. 127. Cf. his *Beginning of the Christian Church*, 1937, p. 92.

[2] A. Harnack, *The Origin of the New Testament*, 1914 (E.T. 1925), p. 49 (footnote).

[3] P. T. Forsyth, *The Person and Place of Jesus Christ*, 1909, fifth edition, 1946, p. 165.

inspired of God. Their inspiration did not just give them religious ideas. An inspiration which is limited to thoughts may be a thrilling private luxury, but it has no significance, no relevancy and no permanency, unless it is embodied in language as the living medium of communication. In inspiration God's concern was not to excite the souls of the few but to transmit His thoughts to the many. An inspiration which is not conveyable and not conveyed is of no use. An inspiration which has no reference to its vehicle of communication would seem to be precarious. Floating notions, like 'songs without words', have no stability. It is when they take shape that they become significant. It is a serious question for faith whether we have inspired ideas in the past or an embodied inspiration in the present. It is not simply that holy men thought as they were moved by the Holy Spirit, but that they spake. It must be confidently asserted that not only were their ideas Spirit-given but that their verbal expression was under the guidance of the same Spirit. Under the superintendency of the divine Spirit the language which faithfully reproduced the thoughts was secured. There is no suggestion here, it must be urged, of a process. Our Lord Himself stated that the words which He spoke were not His own but those given to Him by the Father who sent Him. There is no idea of the method which brought about this result in His declaration. The fact is asserted but the process is not described. It would not be sufficient to say that Jesus had God-given thoughts. The truth is rather that the words He spoke matched His thoughts in a divinely adequate way. The disciples were not called upon to read His thoughts but to hear His words; and the words He spake they are spirit and they are life. No less is it the case with the words spoken by His apostolic men. It is in the union of the divine and the human that the essence of inspiration lies. It is not possible to comprehend this interplay, but all genuine Christian experience is a witness to its reality and actuality. In the process the man is not turned into a machine. But the whole process is completed only in the result, in its fulfilment in language. Without that the mysteries unveiled before the eyes of the seers and the ideas brought to the minds of the prophet and apostle, would remain confused shadows and vague notions. When they are expressed in an adequate language they become clarified, permanent and authoritative.

When addressed to man the human element becomes part of the Divine message, since the Divine message can be grasped only when defined and moulded according to the laws of man's being. This means quite emphatically that the Bible is rightly said to be inspired no less than its prophets and apostles. It is not simply that they had holy thoughts, but that they uttered divine words. Of course the Bible will reflect and perpetuate the peculiar idiosyncrasies of each prophet and apostle, of his time and his environment, but they do nevertheless give forth a divine word which is for all time and for all circumstances. Not only did the creators of the Bible see and hear, but they set forth what they saw and heard. They are in a profound sense God's spokesmen —God's penmen.

To remain Christians we must reproduce the Christianity of the apostolic gospel and the apostolic Church, but 'it is only through the apostles that we have received Christianity and that Christianity *only* is genuine, which can show itself to be *Apostolic*'.[1] But to reproduce this apostolic Christianity we are shut up to the written word as the only guarantee of that Christianity: 'For the Christian Church is the company of all those who, on the basis of the Biblical testimony, recognize and believe that Jesus is the Christ, i.e. the Messiah of Israel, the Son of the living God, the Saviour of the world.'[2] Being shut up to the written word, we are, *ipso facto*, bound by its pages as our authority. We have no real authority apart from the Biblical Christ, the Christ who reveals the will of God.

It was only when the conception of the Church changed from a fellowship of redeemed people into an institution in which the rule was vested in the few that the Bible was dethroned from its proper place. The first Church regarded the written Scriptures, not as the first word in an evolutionary process, but as the final word in the revelatory fact. To the redeemed community it was the word of God in which and through which it found its life, its authority and its nourishment. When the Church built up its sacerdotal system, it found itself unable to justify its accretions from the Scripture, consequently it adopted tradition as a sufficient warrant. The authority of the Bible was lost in the

---

[1] H. Martensen, *Christian Dogmatics* (E.T. 1866), p. 25.
[2] Wilhelm Vischer, *The Witness of the Old Testament to Christ* (E.T. 1949), Vol. I, p. 7.

Church when the Church had ceased to be that of the New Testament. Without the security of a written Scripture the mediaeval Church virtually lost Christ: saints and relics took the place of the Saviour and the Redeemer. 'The specific appeal to the Scriptures of the New Testament to verify or correct current tendencies is gone . . . the safeguard has vanished.'[1] The tie, as H. R. Mackintosh remarks, between the Scriptures and the Saviour is an absolutely vital tie. Only when Christ is seen and heard can He be worshipped and obeyed, and it is in and through the Scriptures that He is seen and heard.

This puts the relation between the Bible and the Church in right perspective. The Bible is, to be sure, in the custody of the Church but it is not in its control. The contention that since the Bible is a product of the Church, then the Church is to be regarded as the supreme authority does injustice to the facts. To acknowledge the historic fact that the Church was prior to the records is not to admit that the Church is pre-eminent to the records. To be first does not mean to be final. To be anterior does not prove an event to be superior. The truth is, of course, that the Church was itself the product of the apostolic word. It was the oral message which created the saved communities in which the apostolic word was regarded as authoritative. 'As long as the Apostles' teaching was available nothing was required, but as time went on it was necessary to embody the Apostolic message in permanent form. Thenceforth to all eyes its written Word became equivalent to the spoken Word as the seat of authority. The fact is the same throughout; the form alone has changed. Thus, the Apostles were the seat of authority at the first, and they have continued so to this day, the only difference being between their spoken and the written Word. The Word created the Church, not the Church the Word'.[2] Christ's work in its revelatory significance is transmitted and communicated by the written word. If salvation comes to men apart from the Word, if it is indeed found in the Church, then the necessity for the Bible has gone. 'If, in fact, the Church be

[1] Charles Gore, *The Body of Christ*, 1901, p. 33.
[2] W. H. Griffith-Thomas, *The Principles of Theology*, 1930, pp. 125–6. Cf. 'The Books of the Bible were given *to* the Church more than *by* it, and they descended on it rather than rose from it. The Canon of the Bible rose from the Church, but not its contents.' P. T. Forsyth, *The Person and Place of Jesus Christ*, 1909, fifth edition, 1946, p. 140. Cf. *The Principle of Authority*, pp. 96, 142, 146–55.

infallible, it is impossible to understand why the Bible was given.'[1]

The position adopted here can now be given a summary statement. God in His revelation is authoritative for religious faith. But that revelation which has been finalized in Christ has been interpreted by the apostles to become available for all following generations in the Scriptures. The Scriptural word, then, becomes the authority for the faith, life and guidance of the Church and for the individual believer. The Scriptures are the divinely inspired statement of God's revealed will and especially as that is demonstrated in the Person of Christ, His Son, our Lord. As the Old Testament prepared the way, so the New Testament proclaims the reality, gives the interpretation and assures the continuity of God's redemption. This action of God comes new to every age in the words of Scripture as it is read or heard, understood, received, believed and lived. Here God actually speaks forth His will which is authoritative for every generation. The authority of revelation is not however the characters of the alphabet printed upon a page but the authority of the Lord God Himself who has spoken, and speaks again, in, with and by the Holy Scriptures. The Apostles, therefore, 'were not panes of bad glass, but crystal cups the Master filled. They were not mere mediums even, but sacraments. They were not mere channels but agents, not vehicles of Christ but members of Him. They did not merely take their departure from Jesus, they had their life, and function, and truth in Him always. We have no testimony but theirs, in which also the fact itself touches us. The fact works upon us only in their interpretation'.[2]

A further proposition must be added here since it must be insisted that authority is mediated by the Holy Spirit. The Scriptures are authoritative for the Christian and in the Church, because it is part of the organism of revelation. But its authority is an authority which finds meaning and possibility only through the Spirit. Here is one of the important emphases made by the Reformers. It was neither the Bible alone as something to be

---

[1] G. Salmon, *The Infallibility of the Church*, 1888, reprint, cheap edition, 1933, p. 117. Cf. '. . . the Scripture as the product of the Spirit's interpretation gives testimony to the believer and lends authority to the Church instead of receiving from the Church its authority'. John Macpherson, *The Westminster Confession of Faith* with Notes and Introduction, second edition, 1882, p. 36.

[2] P. T. Forsyth, *The Principle of Authority*, 1913, second edition, 1952, pp. 134–5.

mechanically followed nor the Spirit alone as an inner impulse to be acted upon, that they stressed. A religion of the fixed word without the free Spirit is notional and a religion of the free Spirit without the fixed word is nebulous. The Spirit and the Word go together. This 'duality' of Spirit and Word, as it has been called, must never be lost. It is rightly declared that the Scriptures function in the ministry of the Spirit and the Spirit functions in the Word 'The *duality* of the Word and the Spirit must always be maintained, for it is in this *duality* that the Protestant and Christian principle of authority exists.'[1] The fullest insistence must be given to this union of Scripture and Spirit: it is not, indeed, a case of one above or prior to the other; but both together. 'These two principles must always be held together, so that it may be said either that: (1) our authority is the Holy Spirit speaking in the Scriptures, or, (2) our authority is the Scriptures sealed to us by the Holy Spirit.'[2] The Voice that said to the Apostle, 'Write', was the Voice of the Spirit, and what is written is then the Spirit's Voice; and he who hears the Voice has understood the living authority of the Scriptures.

It will conclude our conception of the stages of authority if a few remarks are added on the final proposition: authority is appropriated within Christian experience. This works out in three spheres, in the individual experience of the believer, in the community experience of the Church, and in the crystallized experience of the creeds.

Without expanding these ideas here, each one of which demands a volume on its own, the general drift of our point of view can be put in short compass. Real authority it must be clearly understood always exists independently of any personal appropriation of it, yet it must be recognized and received if it is to become a decisive reality within experience. In Christian experience God's redemptive will becomes our spiritual authority by faith. Indeed faith might be defined, in line with the duality of the Spirit and Scripture, as the illumination of divine authority by the Spirit and the recognition of divine authority in the Word. Faith is the mode by which authority is appropriated. The two, the existing authority and the personal appropriation, must not be confused. 'If the living God has spoken, His word of

---

[1] Bernard Ramm, *The Pattern of Authority*, 1957, p. 30.
[2] *Ibid.*, p. 29.

revelation is the authority in religion. If this word is made permanent through writing, then the written revelation is our authority in religion. A man accepts this written revelation as his authority in religion by personal appropriation. But whatever the subjective ground for receiving this revelation might be, it neither constitutes nor compromises the authority of the divine revelation.'[1]

Freedom in religion is the wisdom of obedience: it is the realization of authority and its appropriation in personal dedication. Absolute obedience, as Forsyth remarks, is the condition of entire freedom. The appropriation of God's redemptive revelation is at once the end and the limit of personal freedom.

It must be stressed that the mode of appropriation, or, indeed, the individual's own act of appropriation, does not itself make authority. The ground for the personal reception of authority is not in its turn another authority. To make the individual his own authority is to be guilty of confusing the appropriation with the actuality. Herein is the error of all who seek authority in the religious experience itself, or in spiritual insight or in inner vision and so forth. Every believing man must see his authority in the revealed will of God as that is centralized in the life and work of Christ and finalized and perpetuated in the Holy Scriptures. It is certainly true that this authority must be personally appropriated. God's revelation is a revelation of grace and truth and the one who has been apprehended by divine grace and truth has the witness in himself. Such can say, 'I know whom I have believed'. For such the authority of God has become an appropriated reality, an authority experienced. So has the authority for experience become the authority within experience. 'Christian obedience means actual obedience to an authority we have found, and found only because it first finds us.'[2]

The Church rightly understood is the company of those, each one of whom has appropriated the authority of God's revelation within experience. And the richness of the experience of the many is greater and fuller than that of the one. There is therefore a vital sense in which this wider community appropriation

---

[1] Bernard Ramm, *The Pattern of Authority*, 1957, p. 41.

[2] P. T. Forsyth, *The Principle of Authority*, 1913, second edition, 1952, p. 272.

of authority must affect the individual. To turn towards the One, says Berdyaev, is not to turn away from the Many. The devil alone is the Great Neutral. Wesley in one of his sermons makes the revealing remark that there are no friendships in hell. Thus arises the paradox: religion to be vital must be personal, but a purely individualistic religion is false to the essential nature of faith. 'The knowledge of God creates community, and indeed community is the aim of the divine revelation.'[1] The Reformation made religion personal, but it never made it individualistic. In the Church, however, the individual will find support for his faith. The believer will here realize that his is not a lone figure, an isolated unit, but that others share with him in his communion with the same Lord. In a very special sense, too, the Church can be said to be a reservoir of faith. In the religious community, as de Wette says, 'ideas and feelings which emerge in the individual are passed on, become common property, create a community in which these ideas are stored up, bequeathed to posterity and continually increase. And thus is formed an association, in which religion can develop historically, can assume shape, in which there is now also scope and sphere of action for the emergence of individuals of supreme distinction.'[2]

At the same time the Church must act as a corrective of faith. 'The necessary price paid for social worship is that spontaneity must accept the fetters of regularity, but that is itself a necessary part of religious education.'[3] Thus must be avoided a mere individualism which is the perpetual fallacy of mysticism, as it is the constant danger of Protestantism, and, on the other hand, a mechanical institutionalism which would suppress individual initiative. The extremes, 'all authority belongs to the Church', and 'no authority belongs to the Church', are ultimately false to the essential nature and experience of religion.

The great creeds of the Church arose out of the living experience of God's revelation in Christ. They were an attempt to put into a form of sound words what had been discovered by the appropriation of the Divine grace and truth of God's Self-disclosure. The creeds are in a sense the Church confessing its experience of Christ's authority. It is on this account that they

[1] E. Brunner, *Revelation and Reason* (E.T. 1946), p. 27.
[2] Rudolf Otto, *The Philosophy of Religion* (E.T. 1931), p. 199.
[3] H. Wheeler Robinson, *Redemption and Revelation*, 1942, p. 100.

have and must have our interest and a certain significance for the individual. Credal indifference in the backbone of the Church is a fatal disease. No Church and no believer can afford to repudiate the historic expression of the faith in the form of the creeds. It may be true that the Church does not merely preach dogma, yet it cannot really preach without it.

It is, of course, understood that to repeat the creeds in perfection is not saving faith. The creeds are signs not steamrollers. Calvin was certainly right at the Council of Lausanne to oppose Caroli who had contended that whoever could not express his faith in the exact words of the three ancient creeds could not be saved. Calvin challenged Caroli to repeat the Athanasian symbol and in doing so he broke down at the fourth clause. Calvin retorted, 'you yourself do not hold that faith; you do not express it in the exact words of the creed. Should you die suddenly the Devil must demand your eternal damnation for your inability to repeat the exact formulae'. Calvin was true to the great Reformation rediscovery of the Biblical understanding of faith as 'fiduciary' in repudiating the idea that the object of faith is always *articuli fidei*. The Reformed Churches, as Brunner has observed, refer to its formulated doctrine, not as dogma, but as Confession. It is the expression of the faith. Thus, he argues, the Confession is a 'Banner'; it is not a sign for the world but a flag to which it rallies. The Church has a confession because it believes, not in order to believe. The Roman Church has a 'password'. A banner rallies, but a password separates. The creed is a 'sign'. It is a 'norm' by which every individual member of the Church ought to examine himself to find out whether 'he belongs to it'. The creeds contain what the Church has understood of its appropriation of the revelation in Christ. They are not themselves a final authority any more than the community experience of the Church or the individual experience of the believer. They possess, like these, a derived authority, an authority which is only real in so far as it derives from God and has its authentication in the Scriptures known and understood through the Spirit.

'The final authority is a gracious God in salvation—miraculous, because if we would explain this act He would cease to be an authority, and the authority would then be the explanatory principle.

'All other authorities for the soul stand ranged into a hierarchy as they are near to this God, necessary for His purpose or full of His action. The authority of the first degree is therefore religious. It is God as actually and historically experienced, God in Christ, Christ in the Holy Spirit, through a Church. The authority of the second degree is theological. It is the witness, not of our soul's instincts or our heart's voice, but of the experienced nature and action of the prime authority. And it is given us first in the Apostles, and second in their prolongation in the shifted and select experients of the Church. Apostolic authority rests on the fact that in the Apostles we have something beyond ideas which grew out of their faith, ideas making them, at the lowest, tentative interpreters of their subjective faith, or at the highest, classics and no more. It rests on the fact that we have in them interpreters of God's revelation, who had this for their unique vocation, and were equipped by God accordingly, to open up Christ's wealth of significance once for all time. And the authority in the third degree is ecclesiastical, though not officially so. It is the Church of the experients as the social creation of the Gospel, the Church of worshippers, of the hymns and liturgies, the graces and virtues, the saints, martyrs, and blessed ministrants, rather than the creeds. It is not the Church as an institution prescribing faith, but as a community confessing and giving effect to every kind of faith. It wields an ample and intimate experience, and not prescriptive knowledge or impressive thought. Its power is felt in our heart and conscience, and owned in love, service and patience.'[1]

THE END

[1] P. T. Forsyth, *The Principle of Authority*, 1912, second edition, 1952, p. 30.

INDEX OF NAMES

INDEX OF SUBJECTS